DATE DUE

Modern European History
France

A Garland Series of
Outstanding Studies
and Dissertations

David H. Pinkney, Editor
University of Washington

Paul de Cassagnac, by Decam
Lithograph, 1878

Paul de Cassagnac and the Authoritarian Tradition in Nineteenth-Century France

Karen Offen

Garland Publishing, Inc.
New York & London 1991

Library of Congress Cataloging-in-Publication Data

Offen, Karen M.
Paul de Cassagnac and the authoritarian tradition in nineteenth-century France / Karen Offen.
p. cm.——[Modern European history. France]
Revision of thesis [Ph.D.]——Stanford University.
Includes bibliographical references and index.
ISBN 0-8153-0479-X [alk. paper]
1. Cassagnac, Paul de, 1843–1904. 2. France——Politics and government——19th century.
3. Conservatism——France——History——19th century. 4. Royalists——France——Biography.
5. Legislators——France——Biography. 6. Journalists——France——Biography.
I. Title. II. Series.
DC342.8.C37034   1991
944.08′092——dc20   91-23151
[B]

Designed by Marisel Tavárez

Printed on acid-free, 250-year-life paper.
Manufactured in the United States of America

CONTENTS

PREFACE AND ACKNOWLEDGEMENTS

This study of the political career of Paul de Cassagnac was undertaken at the suggestion of Gordon Wright, now William H. Bonsall Professor of History Emeritus at Stanford University, and, in its original incarnation as a doctoral dissertation, was completed under his supervision. I am particularly grateful for his encouragement and astute editorial comments. Research in France during 1966-67 was made possible by fellowships from the French government and Stanford University, with return expeditions financed by the Raymundo Foundation.

Among all those who contributed to the progress of this work, I want especially to thank the following for their generosity and varied forms of assistance: Norman and Ella Mae Stedtfeld, my parents; Pierre Albert, of the Institut Français de Presse; Guy-P. Palmade, of the Ecole Normale Supérieure; Alfred Grosser, of the Institut d'Études Politiques; Jacques Godechot, of the University of Toulouse-Le Mirail; the late Henri Polge and members of his staff at the Archives Départementales du Gers, Auch; the staff at the Archives de la Préfecture de Police, Paris; staff members at the Bibliothèque Nationale, Paris, and the Stanford University Libraries; Bernard and Micheline Sinsheimer, Paris; and Cynthia and Albert Schwabacher, Woodside, California.

Helpful suggestions and encouragement at critical times were gratefully received from my second readers at Stanford, Philip Dawson and G. Wesley Johnson, and from George V. Taylor, F. Keith Underbrink, Eugen Weber, John Woodall, and Theodore Zeldin. I must also thank five colleagues, Benjamin F. Martin, the late Robert Hoffman, Steven Englund, William Irvine, and Nancy Fitch for their repeated insistence that I resurrect, revise, and publish. Don English contributed two essential photographs from his research on the political uses of photography. Gordon Wright and David H. Pinkney gave me the extra push I needed to deliver this revised version to the Garland European History series. I am deeply grateful to George R. Offen, Michael Weiss, and Malcolm Brown for their advice and assistance in computerizing the original typed manuscript, and to Edith B. Gelles and Steven C. Hause for their critical readings of the final manuscript. Need I remark that mine is the final responsibility for what appears here -- and that all translations are my own, unless otherwise indicated.

Those who have read the original dissertation will note that the bibliography and notes have been updated, but that my earlier conclusions have been, if anything, reinforced by new sources and subsequent scholarship.

The sources for this work are wide and various; a few have taken years of sleuthing to locate. No biographical study, even of one man's political career, will emerge from one archival series, one press run, or even from one book. There are inevitably questions that remain unanswered, or that may never be answered, for lack of evidence; having since turned to women's history, I would particularly like to learn more about Paul de Cassagnac's mother, his wife, and his mysterious daughter, for which sources seem to be in short supply. There will always be new leads to follow up and new paradigms within which to reassess what one has already learned. But gestation has been unusually long and the delivery date for this book, despite its remaining imperfections, has come due.

There are some sources, however, without which there would be no book. I am greatly indebted to the Comtesse de Bonneval for permission to consult the voluminous papers of her grandfather, Baron Armand de Mackau, at the Archives Nationales in Paris. I owe special thanks to M. et Mme Jean de Cassagnac, for their counsel, and to M. Xavier de Cassagnac and his late wife Ghislaine, for their kindness in making accessible the Cassagnac family papers, which had formerly been at the chateau de Couloumé, and for taking me into their family in Graulhet while I classified and sorted through the files. A special touch was added to my research in 1966-1967 by young Paul de Cassagnac (then four years old), who with profound and not altogether unjustified suspicion circled my desk on his tricycle while I explored the career of his ancestor and namesake. He is now a grown man and I hope he will someday see this book.

Most of all, I want to thank my husband, George R. Offen, for sharing me with Paul de Cassagnac for so many years. This book could not have been completed without his cheerful support, sustenance, and sympathetic ear.

To him, on our twenty-fifth anniversary, this book is dedicated.

K.O.
Woodside, California
December 1990

LIST OF ILLUSTRATIONS

10. Caricatures from the "Parallel March," 1889
    a. "La Reprise de la Bastille," by Blass
    b. "Dévisseurs de Parlementaires," by Blass
    c. "Pour Faire la Trouée," by Blass
    d. "Il Baisse! Il Baisse!" by Pépin

11. Cassagnac and *L'Autorité*, 1890s

12. Portrait of Paul de Cassagnac
    Photograph, 1890s

13. Cassagnac as seen by *L'Assiette au Beurre*,
    1900s

Photo Credits

1. Bibliothèque Nationale, Paris
2. Reproduced from A. Dayot, *Le Second Empire*
3. *L'Eclipse*, 8 March and 12 September 1868
   From the author's personal collection
4. *Le Procès de Sedan*, Paris, 1875
   From the author's personal collection
5. Bibliothèque Nationale, Paris
   Courtesy of Donald E. English
6. Bibliothèque Nationale, Paris
7. *Les Hommes d'Aujourd'hui*, 13 December 1878
   Archives de la Prefecture de Police, Paris
   Photographed by the author
8. Archives de la Prefecture de Police, Paris
   Photographed by the author
9. Cassagnac Family Papers
   Photographed by the author
10. a. b. c., from *Le Pilori*, 1889, copies in Cassagnac Family Papers
    Photographed by the author
    d. Reproduced from Guilleminault, *La Jeunesse de Marianne*
11. Cassagnac Family Papers
    Photographed by the author
12. Reproduced from Boussel, *L'Affaire Dreyfus et la Presse*
13. Reproduced from Guilleminault, *La Jeunesse de Marianne*

Photo laboratory work by the Stanford University Publications Service.

LIST OF ABBREVIATIONS

The following abbreviations have been employed throughout in the citation of manuscript sources, parliamentary speeches and debates, and frequently-cited journals and periodicals:

A.N.	Archives Nationales, Paris
A.P.P.	Archives de la Préfecture de Police, Paris
A.D. Gers	Archives Départementales du Gers, Auch

Annales, C.L.	*Annales du Sénat et du Corps Législatif,* 1860-1870
Annales, A.N.	*Annales de l'Assemblée Nationale,* 1871-1875
Annales, Sénat et Ch.D.	*Annales du Sénat et de la Chambre des Députés,* 1876-1880
Annales, Ch.D.	*Annales de la Chambre des Députés. Débats parlementaires,* 1881-1893
J.O., Ch.D., Débats.	*Journal Officiel de la République Française. Débats parlementaires. Chambre des Députés,* 1876-1893

AHR	*American Historical Review*
BSAG	*Bulletin de la Société archéologique, historique, littéraire et scientifique du Gers*
FHS	*French Historical Studies*
RDM	*Revue des Deux Mondes*

All articles cited from *Le Pays* and *L'Autorité* are by Paul de Cassagnac, unless otherwise indicated.

INTRODUCTION

Paul-Adolphe-Marie-Prosper Granier de Cassagnac (1842-1904), known simply as Paul de Cassagnac, was a nineteenth-century French journalist and deputy, a contemporary and political opponent of Léon Gambetta and Georges Clemenceau, and one of the most colorful figures of his era.[1] As a defender of the authoritarian Second Empire, Cassagnac declared himself the enemy of the parliamentary form of government. He then became undoubtedly the most adamant opponent of the parliamentary Third Republic during the first two decades of its existence. His political career as a Catholic monarchist[2], an authoritarian democrat, and a declared counter-revolutionary thus spanned two regimes, presenting a remarkable instance of ideological constancy across half a century of French history.

Both as a Parisian journalist and as a deputy from the department of Gers (the Cassagnac family's political fiefdom in southwestern France), Cassagnac placed himself in the public eye. As a journalist, he acquired a reputation for vehement polemic that has overshadowed other less flamboyant but ultimately more significant facets of his career in the press. As a deputy, he achieved notoriety not for his prowess as a legislator but for his inflammatory oratorical skills and the interruptions from the floor which he used with such calculated precision to enrage his republican opponents and to spread dissension among them. Indeed, Cassagnac's provocative remarks earned him repeated censures and expulsions from the Chamber for violation of its rules during his five terms as a deputy.[3] Allusive though often misleading references to his "violence" continue to dot the pages of historical accounts on the early Third Republic. There is something fascinating, something compelling about Paul de Cassagnac's exceptionally combative and independent temper and role in political life that has guaranteed his presence, if only a shadowy, persistent, and misrepresented presence, in current historical writing on nineteenth-century France.

An aristocrat and a gentleman -- a man of honor to his fingertips -- Cassagnac viewed politics as war and democracy as a means of legitimating monarchical authority. He represented himself as a soldier in a crusade against the heresy and social danger represented by the notion of a republic, which he considered to be the spawn of revolution. He took it upon himself to exorcise the demons who spread notions of revolt against established hierarchical authority, yet -- and this is the great paradox of his long political career -- it was his lot to find himself opposed in this crusade first by his prince and, then, by his Church. Cassagnac aroused strong feelings among those with whom he dealt politically. His colleagues either despised him or adored him; none could ignore him. The Comte de Paris wrote privately to the newly-elected deputy-priest from Brest, Monseigneur d'Hulst, in 1892: "I will not speak here of your future colleagues on the Right. . . , with one exception, because it is most important not to have him against you, and a mere trifle can swing his decision for or against. He is Paul de Cassagnac."[4]

* * *

This work is not, strictly speaking, a "life and times" of Paul de Cassagnac. Indeed, the significance of Cassagnac's political contribution must be measured in terms of what it tells us about the character of political life in the late nineteenth century. The immediate context in which it is placed is that of a complex and confusing oppositional monarchist politics.

Paul de Cassagnac entered French political life as an arch-defender of the authoritarian Second Empire, attempting to block its *parlementarisation* by those who wished to increase the power of the legislature at the expense of Napoleon III. He combatted the granting of several liberties, freedom of the periodical press and political assembly, deemed essential by the liberals of that time, but which Cassagnac perceived (not wholly without reason) as potentially explosive. After the fall of the Second Empire, he declared himself the foremost enemy of the republicans and the champion of "Imperialism," his name for an integral Bonapartism enshrined in a system of plebiscitary, authoritarian monarchy. He consistently advocated a political alliance of all the monarchist parties, a "conservative alliance" in the interest of "social defense," the common denominators of which were the Catholic faith and a belief in a hierarchical society in which authority must necessarily be exercised from above, though it required ratification from below. Cassagnac's notion of democracy had little to do with what we understand today as self-government.

Cassagnac's political activities do provide a unique insight into the complexities of monarchist politics during the 1870s and 1880s. Although he is commonly identified as a Bonapartist, he was in fact no orthodox dynastic Bonapartist. Indeed, he often found himself in serious disagreement with the titular leaders of the Bonapartist party.

On many issues, Cassagnac was far more closely identified with the royalists -- not the legitimist *zelanti*, but those who composed the Moderate Right and Center Right groups in the National Assembly of 1871-75. These were the men (and he did mean males) he had in mind as allies in a "conservative alliance."[5] Consequently, he occupied a pivotal position within the framework of monarchist politics, the very existence of which is generally ignored by historians. By accepting uncritically the terminology and arguments of the dynastic parties -- Legitimist, Orleanist, and Bonapartist -- they spare themselves the trouble of confronting the overlap existing among these groups as well as the disagreements existing within each. Napoleon III remarked on this complexity in 1871, (while explaining French politics to a German journalist):

> You in Germany can never comprehend what an antidynastic opposition is like. You know only one political ladder, which goes from ultra-liberal to ultra-conservative by various nuances. It is easy to govern with that. But I had four of these ladders to deal with -- the Bonapartists, the Legitimists, the Orleanists, and the Republicans -- and each of these containing all these nuances.[6]

Under the Third Republic, the differences among the republicans themselves increased as they confronted the experience of wielding political power. Conversely, as the men of the dynastic parties met in opposition and their former quarrels over the proper political organization of monarchy subsided, those of similar nuances within each party were drawn together in new formations by similarities in basic outlook. By 1878 Paul de Cassagnac could write of an easing of competition among dynastic parties. He depicted a trend away from intransigence by the "reasonable men" of each party, especially the younger men, "those who were not personally involved in the struggles that made the past difficult" and who could speak in terms of "principles, doctrines, and preferences, without obscuring them by hate, rancor, or passion."[7]

By 1885 this group had effectively embraced the logic of plebiscitary democracy and had successfully mounted an electoral campaign based on "conservative union." Its leaders had reason to believe, given the level of overt discontent, that in 1889 they might even win a majority in the Chamber. Cassagnac, who was a central figure in forming this alliance and in publicizing it, began to speak in terms of "*n'importequisme*" and "*solutionnisme*," terms that suggest the evacuation of corporeality from the notion of kingship, the ultimate disembodiment of political authority. This coming together of the conservative alliance, along with its achievements and disappointments, including the much-misunderstood adventure of the "parallel march" with General Georges Boulanger, and the fate of its adherents in the *ralliement*, has been much misunderstood -- and, indeed, often maligned -- in subsequent historiographical writing. It has never been adequately assessed in terms of its own logic, accomplishments, and shortcomings.

$$* * *$$

The historiographical context is not without interest. The victorious have always tempted the chroniclers more than the vanquished. Moreover, the victorious have always had a stake in making their victory seem inevitable in retrospect. Consequently, the historiography of the Third Republic, like that of the French Revolution, has long been an *histoire engagé* -- both, as it turns out, on the Right and on the Left. The preoccupation with the constitutional evolution of the parliamentary regime effectively excluded any focus in the early historiography of the Third Republic on the nuances of antiparliamentary opposition to the republic. The major historians of the pre-1914 Third Republic, following in the magisterial footsteps of Charles Seignobos in the Lavisse series,[8] treated the regime in its parliamentary form as the inevitable culmination of the revolutionary processes begun over one hundred years before, a sort of pilgrim's progress, and in consequence, concentrated on describing the steps in that evolution. They presented the parliamentary republicans as heroes and, borrowing their heroes' phraseology and prejudices, spoke of the opposition after 1881 as "reactionaries," thereby dismissing them as a negligible force in French political life. This interpretation, which provided the norm for so many subsequent general histories, not to mention schoolbook histories, erased half the story.

Political history is above all else about the contestation of power, as well as about its uses. There can be no accounting for the curious development of the Third Republic without considering the determined efforts of its opponents to re-establish the preceding system of government -- the Second Empire. Even the most cursory excursion into the sources of the time make clear that the Third Republic was established *against* the empire, and the constitutional laws of 1875 were designed as a defensive monument, a fortress closed to prospective imitators of Louis-Napoleon Bonaparte, making impossible presidential *coups d'état* on the model of 1851 by rendering the president a creature of the legislature. Yet, with the exception of certain colorful incidents, such as the abortive attempt to restore the Comte de Chambord to the throne in 1873, neither the politics nor the political philosophies of the monarchist parties have received adequate attention from professional historians. The sensitive though critical studies by Daniel Halévy, written in the 1930's, and John Rothney's study of *Bonapartism after Sedan* from the liberal perspective, remained for many years the exceptions to the rule.[9]

In public statements the republicans of the later nineteenth century constantly minimized the importance of the monarchist parties. In private, however, they were virtually obsessed by the potential threat posed to the republic and its partisans by the princely pretenders and their supporters. The level of their concern is indicated by the enormous dossiers on monarchist activities and personnel in the files of the Paris Prefecture of Police. Although by 1879 the republicans had ousted their monarchist opponents from control of the three principal branches of government -- the Chamber of Deputies, the Senate, and the Presidency -- and had thus reduced the immediacy of direct threats to the newly-established regime, they were not yet able to eliminate them from control of other important sectors of French society. The monarchists retained immense social prestige, considerable wealth, important ties with the Church, the army, and the judicial establishment, as well as a great deal of power at the local level. Moreover, the most fervent among them were unwilling to capitulate without giving battle for their convictions; in the course of their battles, their earlier assumptions of their right to rule were displaced by an active quest for political power through the electoral process. Even though, with the establishment of the republic, the monarchists lost a great deal of the electoral support that they had taken for granted only a decade before, the respective parties and the views each represented with such tenacity retained the allegiance of many honorable and highly intelligent men.

Little of this was reflected in the historiography that treated the monarchist Right; history's losers are rarely granted much respect. The reasons for this are not hard to find. Historiography on the Right came from three main sources: apologists for the several dynastic parties; apologists for the Vatican-driven monarchist *ralliement* to the republic of the 1890s; and the theoreticians and historians of the *Action française* in the twentieth century.[10] For all three, for differing reasons, the kind of politics promoted by Paul de Cassagnac and the conservative alliance of the 1870s and 1880s were anathema. A return to the sources of the period, however, has permitted a reconstruction of this politics and provides the evidence to argue that both for the internal history of the Bonapartist party, for its relations with the Legitimist and Orleanist parties, and for the move to transcend both through electoral politics, Paul de Cassagnac is a key figure.

There is, however, a further dimension to the historiographical context within which this study of Cassagnac is set -- the context of the post-World War II debate over the origins and character of European fascism and about the problem of "totalitarianism".[11] In France, this debate prompted a certain urgency in reassessing Third Republic historiography, and a quarrel emerged among historians and political scientists over the question of fascism in France. Although the Nazi occupation and the "national revolution" of Vichy had ended in 1945, the search for fascists, proto-fascists, and crypto-fascists in French history had just begun.

At the same time the denials that France had somehow contributed fundamentally to the birth and maturity of fascism in Europe began to proliferate.[12] The term "fascist" was used systematically by the Left to castigate the Right. The history of the Third Republic -- and of Bonapartism as well -- was heavily implicated in this quadrille of blame, denial, of guilt and innocence. The political stakes were high. With the coming to power of Charles de Gaulle and the constitutional reforms of the Fifth Republic, which increased the power of the presidency to the detriment of the legislature, and reinstituted a type of plebiscite, the discussion only became more charged. In this context, in 1962 Jacques Néré could rightly claim that "the history of the Third Republic has not yet been written, even in part," and Eugen Weber could criticize the lack of attention given by historians to the political movements and ideologies of the Right.[13]

In 1954 René Rémond had published the first edition of his influential *La Droite en France*, which attempted to explain the twentieth-century Right as an amalgam of the three nineteenth-century dynastic traditions, inviting a generation of graduate students, myself included, to test his hypotheses.[14] When Gordon Wright first suggested working on a political biography of Paul de Cassagnac, I was intrigued. I soon found that Cassagnac had left an impressive paper trail, one that wound through the Parisian and departmental press, leading me through the corridors of the Chamber of Deputies, into the national archives, the Paris police archives, and finally, to family papers in southern France. There was evidence enough to smother under -- the man published a long editorial in the press virtually every day for thirty years!

What was more, Cassagnac offered a subject for research in which I had no absolutely political or personal investment, being neither French, nor a Catholic monarchist, nor a male authoritarian democrat. I was, instead, a young, curious female graduate student from the Snake

River plains of Idaho, of a liberal bent and with a commitment to fair play and accuracy. Having no immediate history within which to situate myself, I found myself fascinated by the sweep and grandeur of French history and culture, of 1960s Gaullism, the politics of nationalism, and, as it later became apparent, by the politics of historiography itself. But at the time I was quite simply interested in mastering the craft of researching and writing plausible history, history with human faces in it. Paul de Cassagnac seemed to offer an ideal vehicle.

Other issues arose, however, as I encountered the French historiographical tradition. Even an intrinsically compelling biographical subject seemed to require further justification. "Acts and facts" and doing justice to one's subject were not enough: the opportunity to assemble, digest, and analyze the abundant mass of evidence left over the course of one man's thirty-odd year political career did not offset the "politically incorrect" nature of the choice I had made in 1965 to study an individual subject, much less one who was identified as "right wing." As I discovered in 1960s France (and by extension in French historical studies more generally), biographical studies were not considered proper history. According to some, biography had no place in the canon of scholarly historical studies. Moreover, the tidal wave of social history, of "history from below" or "classes and masses" that had become such a defining characteristic of French historiographical fashion in the last half-century had, even at the time I began my research, virtually swept biographally-focused studies from the field.[15]

Today, however, a new and more positive attitude toward biography is emerging in French historical studies, although one can certainly find examples of a continuing tendency to disparage the study of individuals, or, in the poststructuralist mode, to speak of individuals not as persons but as "sites for analysis." In the late 1980s massive new biographies have been published in Paris by academic historians on such major Third Republic figures such as Adolphe Thiers, Georges Clemenceau, Jules Ferry, and Maurice Barrès, with the promise of others to come. Political history itself is experiencing a resurgence, indeed, a "resurrection" in the words of René Rémond.[16] Social history and a reinvigorated political history are reaching an accommodation and new arguments are being put forward for the writing of biographical studies of intriguing and historically significant (or not-so-significant) individuals.[17] The time was clearly ripe to publish this work.

My findings concerning Paul de Cassagnac and the French tradition of authoritarian democracy attest to the problematic results of focusing as intently as Rémond did on the Right's dynastic parties, and in particular of glossing over (indeed, omitting from consideration) the period from 1879 to 1899. More recently, the works of the French scholars Jean-Marie Mayeur and Philippe Levillain have restored the history of the political Right during this period to a degree of consideration in French academic scholarship.[18] The fact remains, however, that during the two decades since 1962 the bulk of research published on the pre-1900 French Right during the Third Republic has been the work of foreign scholars, especially Americans, not of French scholars in the French universities.[19] The legacy of Vichy, coupled by contestation of DeGaulle's presidential regime made it difficult for many French scholars, especially those who identified themselves with the Left, to consider such subjects dispassionately. The history of the Left itself, of the workers' movement, and the burgeoning of research in the new social history provided French scholars with a number of more acceptable routes to academic advancement and acclaim.

Thus, even after three decades of scholarly attention to the Right, the activities of the republic's opponents on the monarchist Right during the early Third Republic remain subject to misunderstanding and distortion. I believe this to be a consequence of the fact that conceptual and political difficulties continue to exist in French politics and historiography , making it difficult for scholars to come to grips with the ongoing reality of what I now call the French authoritarian tradition. Perhaps the perspective of an outsider from the Snake River plains, transplanted to California, can, after all, shed some light on this set of problems.

* * *

It seems to me that this study of Paul de Cassagnac and his political career illuminates the nature, content, and adaptability of French authoritarianism itself during the second half of the nineteenth century, and clarifies its relation to democratic theory and practice, and to a later nationalism. Paul de Cassagnac personified and elaborated at great length in the popular press a way of thinking about government that had deep roots in the mentality of the French. This authoritarian tradition was a product of France's many centuries as a strong, centralized, and powerful Catholic monarchy. Since the Revolution of 1789, the tradition -- haunted by the spectre of societal upheaval fomented by the revolutionary years -- had manifested itself in a counter-revolutionary form, calling for a strong leader, monarch or quasi-monarch, to govern the nation and provide an alternative to instability and disorder. The instability itself had resulted from uprooting an old, highly centralized, governmental system in a nation whose citizens had no long-practiced pattern or widely-accepted habit of self-government, and its effects had been magnified by the disruption of traditional social hierarchies and habits due to an accelerating and multi-faceted social change.

Following the revolution of 1848, and the institution of universal manhood suffrage, the call for an authority figure had been answered by Louis-Napoleon Bonaparte. But within a generation even his regime was on the defensive before the onslaught of an aggressive and highly vocal liberalism, with English affinities, which had been making headway throughout European intellectual and political circles.

It was at this point that Paul de Cassagnac made his political debut. During the next thirty years, it is argued here, Cassagnac interpreted the authoritarian tradition to a generation of citizens who had emerged from the rural and semi-rural environment of provincial France and who had been introduced to the practice of democratic government under the tutelage of the Second Empire. Cassagnac's audience was composed of country lawyers and magistrates, civil servants, soldiers, clergymen, small tradesmen, petty aristocrats, and the peasants who were only then (as Eugen Weber has since put it) being transformed into Frenchmen.[20] His audience did not include the enlightened urban bourgeoisie and liberal aristocracy, although he certainly had a following among the more socially conservative elements in the urban upper classes.

This was the milieu to which Cassagnac's Imperialism, and later his more impersonal authoritarian and antiparliamentary *"Solutionisme"* or *"n'importequisme"* appealed.[21] This was the milieu that supported the call for a political messiah, soldier or citizen, who could incarnate political authority and unite France behind himself, who could preserve civil and social order from attacks by the *voyous* above the competitive arena of factional struggles. Far from offering an appeal to the masses, this milieu was very suspicious of them, and concerned about the kinds of societal change that were producing them. Cassagnac, like the German chancellor, Otto von Bismarck, believed the electorate to be fundamentally conservative; law and order was the name of their game.

The authoritarian democratic perspective represented in the later nineteenth century by Paul de Cassagnac subsequently outgrew monarchism as its sole form of expression. Nevertheless, it remains to this day an enduring current in French political life: we saw it again with the rise to power of Charles de Gaulle and his reconfiguring of the French Republic. Could it be said to encompass François Mitterrand as well? Cassagnac was its most emphatic spokesman during a transitional period when it was passing into the very patrimony of the French republic; his "Solutionism," as Edouard Drumont pointed out at the time of Cassagnac's death in 1904, had prefigured Boulangism, certain aspects of *ralliement* politics, and nationalism:

> By preaching "solutionism" Cassagnac expressed in concrete form the idea that has bothered many honorable and patriotic Frenchmen as they have attested that the Republic is unfaithful to all its promises. . . . Anything but that which now exists; *n'importe qui et n'importe quoi*, as long as we can finally escape from the miserable and shameful situation in which we find ourselves before France is totally destroyed by it![22]

It is my view that we can learn something important by recapturing the perspective of history's ostensible losers. I contend in this book, then, that no apology need be made for studying the political thought and action of a historically significant actor who represented and transmitted to succeeding generations a particular mode of thinking about governmental authority and democracy in France during such an important period of political and socioeconomic transition. Further, I suggest that Paul de Cassagnac's political career offers us a window on the dynamics of political conflict during the early Third Republic. It provides us, first, with a new angle on the history of the Bonapartist party in particular and, more generally, on the history of monarchist politics prior to the *ralliement*. Second, it allows us to study in depth the political interchanges, both ideological and tactical, between the republicans and the monarchist opposition during two critical decades in French history. A reevaluation of the nature of the republicans' interchanges with their monarchist opponents is vital to an understanding of the republicans' tenuous yet ultimate victory -- and to the way in which the republic ultimately absorbed the authoritarian tradition. It is likewise vital to our appreciation of the way in which the historiographical record of the republican victory was subsequently constructed.

Finally, I argue that Paul de Cassagnac's political career, encompassing that of his associates, provides us with an unusual opportunity to confront and to reassess the development of the French authoritarian tradition during a critical century of democratization in political life. It may even provide some new insight on the problem of what Bonapartism is and is not, what nationalism is and is not, what fascism is, and is not, in French -- and European -- history.

CHAPTER I

THE MAKING OF A POLEMICIST

*Moi, j'ai fait du journalisme parce que je voulais
me mêler aux affaires de mon pays, et, n'ayant pas
encore une tribune à ma disposition, je saisis une
plume.*

Paul de Cassagnac
Le Pays, 1 March 1872

In contrast to many other prominent nineteenth century political figures, Paul de Cassagnac entered public life with considerable baggage, as the disputatious son of an already notoriously controversial father. As Cassagnac once remarked to his good friend Jules Claretie, who had congratulated him on having "arrived" in the world of Parisian journalism: "Yes, but you too have 'arrived,' and besides you have the good fortune not to be dragging a father like mine behind you."[1] The political career of Granier de Cassagnac, as Paul's father was known, had a marked impact on that of his son. Therefore it is quite appropriate to begin the study of the son's political career with a sketch of his father.

Bernard-Adolphe Granier de Cassagnac was born in 1806 in the department of Gers, near Avéron in the canton of Aignan. He was the eldest of seven sons of Pierre-Paul Granier de Cassagnac and his second wife, Ursule Lissagaray, daughter of a local physician.[2] His father was the last of a long line of ennobled glassmakers or *gentilshommes verriers* in the forest of Montpellier who traced their practice of the privileged glassmaking craft back to the Middle Ages.[3] The Cassagnac family affirms that its ancestor, sieur Eustache de Granier, obtained the privilege from Louis IX (Saint Louis) after accompanying that king on his first crusade (1248-1254). In subsequent centuries the Granier family split into a number of branches, each of which became known by an auxiliary surname designating the location of that branch. The branch known as Granier de Cassagnac claims direct descent from one such gentleman glassmaker, Peyre de Granier, of Fabas (Ariège), whose descendants added the designation *sieur de Cassagnac* following his death in 1549. Members of this family subsequently received patents of nobility under the full name of Granier de Cassagnac in 1668, 1676, and 1710, at which time they were established in the canton of Aurignac (Haute-Garonne). Due to a marriage alliance with another family of *gentilshommes verriers* in 1706, the Granier de Cassagnacs became masters of the glassworks in the forest of Montpellier (Gers).[4]

During the Revolution, in 1791, all titles and privileges of nobility were abolished. Thus, when Bernard-Adolphe Granier de Cassagnac was born in 1806, he was registered simply as Granier. His political enemies in later years took advantage of this quirk of fate to contest both his claim to be of noble origin, of which he was very proud, and his right to carry the double name. In 1877 the Cassagnac family went to court in an effort to end the controversy over name and rank, and their claims were upheld by several court rulings.[5]

Granier de Cassagnac was destined never to become a *maître verrier*. The glassmaker's craft had succumbed to technological and societal changes that had taken place during the later eighteenth century.[6] As one of ten children in a family whose traditional occupation had become extinct, Granier de Cassagnac had to carve out his own future. Consequently, he sought an education. He completed his secondary studies in Toulouse, where he lived after 1818 with his mother's brother, Laurent-Prosper Lissagaray.[7] There he acquired a precocious literary reputation and, just after receiving his baccalaureate, he became editor of the *Journal politique et littéraire de Toulouse*. Within a few years (1828-1830), he became a triple laureate of the *Académie des Jeux floraux* of Toulouse, twice for declamation and once for verse.[8] Throughout his years in that city, he read voraciously and studied law, with the ambition of lecturing on legal history.

With the revolution of 1830, Louis-Philippe, heir of the house of Orleans, replaced the reactionary Bourbon king, Charles X, on the French throne, an event that opened new opportunities for young men with ambition and the right connections. Thus it was that in 1832, Granier de Cassagnac set out for Paris in the company of two school friends, with a letter of introduction to the deputy for Haute-Garonne, Charles de Rémusat. As a protégé of Rémusat he soon met François Guizot, then Minister of Public Instruction, and made the acquaintance of Victor Hugo, who became his literary patron.[9] He could also make use of his kinship with Nicholas Soult, Marshal of France under Napoleon I, who was to serve Louis-Philippe as Minister of War and of Foreign Affairs.

Thanks to these fortunate connections, Granier de Cassagnac began his career in the Parisian press. He made his debut as a literary critic for the prestigious *Journal des Débats* and also contributed articles to the *Revue de Paris*. In 1836 he joined Émile de Girardin and his wife Delphine Gay at *La Presse*. He forged a reputation as a militant conservative and became an aggressive and even provocative supporter of the July Monarchy's party of order, as first incarnated by the Comte de Molé and then by Guizot. As his reputation for polemic grew, so did the ranks of his enemies. But their attacks did not seem to trouble him. "I am a pebble from the Adour, and nothing can dissolve me," he would remark to his friends.[10] "His was a pen of war," wrote a contemporary who was not an admirer, "one of those talents who are always embarrassing for the party they support and who compromise the best of causes by their excessive zeal and the ardors of their intolerance."[11]

To complement his journalistic endeavors, Granier de Cassagnac published novels (*La Reine des prairies*, *Danaë*, and *Le Secret du chevalier de Médrane*) as well as historical studies which we would now characterize as early attempts at social history. He first produced a history of the working and bourgeois classes, which he dedicated to Guizot, and then a history of the noble and ennobled classes, dedicated to his patron Hugo.[12] In these works he proposed a highly unorthodox theory of the origin of social classes, based on his studies of classical antiquity. There were two historic classes, he argued -- the nobles and the slaves. Both originated in the family unit of the earliest times. The working classes and the bourgeoisie were originally emancipated slaves, as were beggars, prostitutes and thieves. Granier de Cassagnac subsequently applied his social theories during his press campaigns against freeing the Negro slaves in the French colonies, which won him the lasting animosity of the anti-slavery liberals of the July Monarchy.[13]

Discouraged by the advent of Adolphe Thiers' ministry in 1840, Granier de Cassagnac rejected Thiers' efforts to win his support, and in October of that year he set sail for the French West Indies and America to visit friends and inspect colonial conditions at first hand.[14] During his stay in Guadeloupe, the planters of the island elected him to present their grievances on the slavery issue to the French government.[15]

At that time he also concluded a marriage with the eighteen-year-old Marie-Magdelaine-Rosa Beaupin-Beauvallon, a recent graduate of the Maison de la Légion d'Honneur at Saint Denis, near Paris. Rosa Beauvallon, born in 1822, was one of six children of a former imperial military officer, Jean-Jacques Monrose Beaupin-Beauvallon, who had established himself in Guadeloupe as a landowner and officer in the militia, and his wife Marie-Magdelaine Lesueur.[16] Rosa's older brother Rosamond de Beauvallon, like Granier de Cassagnac, was an aspiring Parisian journalist, and may well have sponsored their introduction.[17] The marriage arrangements, concluded in January 1841, occasioned a bout of political sniping by Granier de Cassagnac's enemies.[18] The Parisian satirical publication, Le Charivari, maliciously insinuated that his fiancée was a mulatto, whereupon her father sailed for France to avenge his daughter's honor. If there was one insult such French colons did not take lightly, it was that of racial intermixture.[19] The young couple was married in Paris in August 1841, following Granier de Cassagnac's return; the renowned novelist and playright Victor Hugo, recently elected to the Académie Française, stood as witness for the bridegroom. On 2 December 1842, Paul-Adolphe-Marie-Prosper, the first of the couple's five children, was born in Paris.[20]

From 1845 to early 1847 Granier de Cassagnac edited the Parisian newspaper, L'Époque. The paper's owners intended it to rival the highly successful La Presse of Girardin, and to become the Times of France as well. L'Époque devoted itself to the defense of Guizot's policies in a time when they were becoming increasingly unpopular. During this period, therefore, Granier de Cassagnac shared in the criticism directed against Guizot. In addition, Granier de Cassagnac's enemies attempted to implicate him in the several scandals of the time. One such scandal grew out of a duelling incident. In March 1845 Granier de Cassagnac's young brother-in-law, Rosemond de Beauvallon, killed Dujarier, Girardin's partner at La Presse, in a duel. He had used a set of pistols borrowed from Granier de Cassagnac. Those critical of the fiery journalist assumed that the death had been deliberate and prearranged, and their opinion was reinforced when the courts discovered that Beauvallon had lied when he denied having tested the pistols in advance. Granier de Cassagnac's role in the affair was never clear, and his enemies used the incident to cast discredit on him and, later, on his son as well.[21]

That same year a frustrated young poet published an account of corruption in the Parisian press in which he accused Granier de Cassagnac of having reviewed his poems favorably in exchange for expensive gifts. Granier de Cassagnac took the author to court and won his case. But the allegations made by the poet were never definitively refuted.[22] Yet another scandal concerned the establishment of L'Époque itself. In February 1847 the newspaper was purchased and merged with its rival, La Presse. That summer, Girardin accused Guizot's favorite minister Duchâtel of allowing Granier de Cassagnac to use his influence with the minister in order to obtain authorization for a new theatre; in return for the journalist's assistance, the proprietor of the new theatre allegedly put up much of the capital required to establish the pro-ministerial newspaper.[23] This series of affairs damaged Granier de Cassagnac's public credit and so, following the Austrian occupation of

Ferrara in August 1847, Guizot sent the controversial journalist to Rome, charged with founding a newspaper there to expound France's policy of non-intervention in the affairs of the Italian states.[24]

Granier de Cassagnac returned to Paris in January 1848 and was present during the February revolution that toppled the Orleanist regime.[25] He remained in the capital for two months, testing the political winds, but in April he sought retreat at his chateau of Couloumé in Gers, which he had acquired in the late 1830s.[26] There he devoted himself to writing a three-volume history of the causes of the Revolution of 1789, the first of several political histories he would write dealing with the earlier revolutionary period.[27] From Gers he kept a close watch on the events of 1848-1849 and supported the candidacy of Louis-Napoleon Bonaparte for president of the new republic.

Granier de Cassagnac became convinced by his study of history (so he subsequently claimed) that only the alliance of a strong leader with the people could hold back the floodtide of revolution. In his own words:

> The need for order and security which is apparent everywhere makes me believe that if universal suffrage were to ally itself with the principle of authority and heredity, and if it took under its patronage a superior power, free and directing -- an order of things similar to that under Louis XIV and Napoleon but controlled and contained by the will of the people -- this alliance of tradition and progress would be more capable than any other force of mastering the agitation imprinted on modern society by the upheaval of 1789. The desire to see the principle of authority adopted by the principle of liberty and a new dynasty raised by the free choice of a people makes me the convinced auxiliary of Louis-Napoleon.[28]

Perhaps the Emperor's heir could succeed where Louis-Philippe had failed. As Granier de Cassagnac's colleague in the press, Jules Barbey d'Aurevilly later wrote, in explanation of his friend's support of the Bonapartes: "The Napoleonic dynasty seemed to him to be the last monarchy possible; after it he could foresee no other."[29]

President Bonaparte, told of Granier de Cassagnac's articles supporting him in the provincial press, summoned the journalist to Paris. After some delay he arrived in April 1850 and quickly established himself as a defender of the social order, a champion of authoritarian democracy and an advocate of reestablishing the empire.

Within a month of his arrival, Granier de Cassagnac contributed a much-discussed series of articles to *Le Constitutionnel*, arguing for a ten-year extension of the president's powers.[30] Only then did he meet the prince-president in person and enter into a collaborative effort which began with a press campaign for revision of the constitution. Well before November 1851, when Granier de Cassagnac published his memorable article, "Les Deux Dictatures," he was considered the authorized interpreter of Louis-Napoleon's policies. Following the prince-president's long-anticipated *coup d'état* on 2 December 1851, Granier de Cassagnac became its principal apologist.[31] The proclamation of the empire the following year pleased him even more.

During the years that followed the establishment of the Second Empire, as young Paul de Cassagnac was growing up, the elder Cassagnac carved out an enviable position as counselor to the new emperor. He also consolidated a strong local position in the department of Gers and in 1852 was elected to the Corps Législatif. From 1861 to 1866 he edited the Corps' annual address to the emperor. In addition to his political responsibilities, Granier de Cassagnac continued his literary career, both as a man of the press (editing various newspapers including the short-lived *Le Reveil*, which he founded in 1858 in collaboration with Barbey d'Aurevilly to defend religion, morals and "decent" literature), and as a historian, with works on the Directory and the Girondins, and particularly with his account of the events of 1848-1852, which he published in 1857 under the title, *Histoire de la chute du roi Louis-Philippe, de la république de 1848 et du rétablissement de l'Empire.*

* * *

Young Paul de Cassagnac celebrated his ninth birthday on the day of the *coup d'état*. At that time he was a student at the Lycée Bonaparte in Paris. Shortly thereafter his family sent him to southern France to study at a Catholic *collège* in Perpignan, directed by his uncle, the abbé Louis de Cassagnac. The religiously-inspired secondary education made available by recent legislation was deemed more appropriate for a young man of his background. In 1860, Paul de Cassagnac obtained his baccalaureate in the Academy of Toulouse. He then began to study law at the Toulouse law faculty, but in 1862, he transferred to the faculty in Paris, where he was enrolled through the autumn term of 1863 and successfully completed several examinations.[32]

It is difficult to single out any one thinker or writer who contributed more directly than Granier de Cassagnac himself to the formation of

Paul de Cassagnac's sociopolitical ideas. There is little overt echo in his arguments, for instance, of the major ideas of the most articulate and influential philosophers of early nineteenth-century Continental conservatism -- Joseph de Maistre, Louis de Bonald, or Juan Donoso-Cortés.[33] His arguments remind one rather more of the pragmatic realism of two counter-revolutionary apologists, the Austrian chancellor Metternich and Friedrich von Gentz. They contain clear echoes of those Enlightenment writers whose systems anticipated "enlightened despotism" quite as much as any sort of democratic revolution. Intriguingly, they bear the concrete imprint of Jean-Jacques Rousseau.[34] Cassagnac himself complicated the historian's task by leaving no record of his intellectual development that might provide more specific clues. It seems evident, however, that many of his notions were reinforced by his study of the classics along with Roman and French law, and by the general climate of mid-nineteenth-century Catholicism, as well as by his father's histories.[35] He doubtless added to these in eclectic fashion by drawing on the ideas of influential persons in his immediate environment.

Cassagnac was fascinated by the world of the Parisian press and ardently desired to become a journalist like his father. In 1862, while still a law student, he tried his hand in the press, founding an ephemeral paper called L'Indépendance Parisienne.[36] Then he wrote book reviews for La Nation under a pseudonym and, for a brief period, edited another small satirical publication, Diogène, with his friend Claretie.[37] But his father had mapped out a safe and reputable career for him in the magistracy. Consequently, the next few years were tense with the contest between a stubborn, strong-willed son and an equally determined father. When Granier de Cassagnac attempted to curb his eldest son's journalistic flirtation by cutting off his financial support, young Cassagnac fled to the suburb of Bougival. There, according to one account, he lived for over a year, fishing, poaching small game, and swimming nude in the river to the great scandal of the peasant girls in the vicinity. Finally, "a bit calmed by the multitude of baths he had taken and brought back to wisdom by the utter void in his wallet,"[38] the prodigal son returned home, only to be presented by his father to the Minister of the Interior, the Marquis de La Valette, as a candidate for employment. In late 1865, Paul de Cassagnac was a lowly employee "5th class" in the newly-created Fifth Bureau of the Direction Générale du Personnel et du Cabinet, where he was one of six persons responsible for administration and correspondence. But his section chief gave him little to do, so that he might continue to indulge his propensity for journalism.[39] Finally Granier de Cassagnac relented.

When he was reappointed editor-in-chief of *Le Pays* in August 1866, he allowed his son to join him.

Like his father, therefore, Paul de Cassagnac would make his reputation as a polemicist. He thus conformed to a traditional pattern in the French daily press which, during most of the nineteenth century, was characterized by the highly literary, politically argumentative *journal d'opinion*, in which the assessment of events from a distinct point of view by a talented writer took precedence over the dissemination of news as the twentieth century knows it. As a group the polemicists were a hardy lot. They manifested firm convictions and most were capable of defending their convictions with the sword as well as with the pen. As one recent French writer has aptly noted, "Polemic is a combat and the pamphlet is a weapon. That is why the polemicist, like the soldier, is detested by sensitive souls."[40]

The appearance of polemic in the flourishing French daily press was the result of adoption by a new medium of communication of an old literary form, a form that had originated in the pamphlet literature of previous centuries. Despite the constantly increasing pressures exerted on the polemicist by the requirements of more frequent publication and commercialization of the press, he nevertheless considered his work a literary art, a composition that would outlast the immediate circumstances for which it had been composed.[41] As a later commentator remarked somewhat acidly, "The insults which the defenders and the adversaries of equally bad regimes address to one another do not count unless they contain a bit of literature, of art. This is the sole means of distinguishing a real writer mislaid in journalism from the valets of the pen, the sole means of making a writer live, long after the polemics are forgotten."[42]

Cassagnac's apprenticeship in the press was thorough, thanks to his father, who was acknowledged (even by his enemies) to be a consummate writer.[43] In later life, as Cassagnac reminisced about his debut in the press, he described his "school of journalism": every day his father required him to write several articles on a variety of subjects, which the former then read, corrected, and frequently jettisoned. In addition, his father put him to work reading documents from the revolutionary period -- the minutes of the Constituent Assembly, the Legislative Assembly, and the *Bulletin* of the Convention. "There's not one of these sessions that I haven't read and summarized," Cassagnac later explained. "By this crushing work," he claimed, "I learned to see clearly into the sophisms of politics and to be clear in my articles. 'Clarity,' my father told me, 'is the greatest asset of a journalist.'"[44]

As a polemicist, Paul de Cassagnac acquired a reputation before his style had ripened. At first, one biographer wrote in retrospect, Cassagnac seemed to compose exclusively with a cudgel: "No one could say he had no talent, but his talent lacked charm, finesse, and distinction." In that writer's opinion, Cassagnac only came into his own as a writer after 1872. "He needed to be vanquished as a party man in order to shine and triumph as a journalist. As is true of every good polemicist, he needed to be in the opposition."[45] Both in and out of opposition, Cassagnac's shotgun-style prose frequently betrayed a lack of precision in his use of words, an imprecision that bears witness to the extent to which he composed under fire but which complicates the task of the historian.

It was not youthful zest and intemperance alone, however, that fired Cassagnac's verbal excesses. In later years when there could be no question that youth had fled, his rhetoric still occcasionally tested the limits of genteel acceptability, particularly in his attacks on political opponents. Some of his contemporaries explained it as a function of his personality: "M. de Cassagnac lacks unction. . . . Moderation is neither a part of his character nor of his temperament, nor perhaps, of his views. . . . He reminds one of those good giants who, wishing to shake your hand, knocks you to the floor instead."[46] Yet others testified to the contrast that existed between the genial reserve of Cassagnac in person and the extreme aggressiveness of his verbal attacks, a contrast which exonerated the man but left his polemical stance open to the charge of being cultivated and artificial.[47] Cassagnac himself provided the key to this contrast in an 1877 statement, in which he commented on the excessive and intransigent stance taken in his articles:

> Ever since politics left the serene regions of the
> salons, ever since it descended into the street, there
> has been no choice but to follow it. You cannot
> ignore, gentlemen [he was addressing a group of
> deputies], that the language one speaks to the people
> must be a ruder, more emphatic language than that one
> speaks to worldly men like yourselves.[48]

Indeed, when Cassagnac was not pressing for political effect, he produced articles that were straightforward and candid and that contained much humor, subtle irony, and good sense. He wrote briskly and swiftly. He had that happy gift of conceiving his daily article "like a mathematical demonstration" in his head and quickly transposing it onto paper. In his later years, he boasted of writing his articles in twenty-five minutes once he had chosen his theme.[49] He was known to disdain proofreading and his articles were full of repetition in the form of frequent variations on a central theme; these, however, served the positive function of driving home his point. A fellow journalist wrote at the time of Cassagnac's death that "of the three men who, only yesterday, were considered the masters of the press, Rochefort was perhaps the wittiest, Drumont the most philosophic, but Cassagnac was, I believe, the simplest, the most accessible, the most luminous, the one whose articles should have made the most profitable reading for the popular masses."[50]

A career in journalism had become a springboard for entering political life. Given the relative weakness of political parties in nineteenth-century France, the journalist and his newspaper provided the principal means of forming public opinion on matters of political interest.[51] Because of his position in the public eye, the journalist could aspire beyond his position as a spokesman for or against reform to that of delegate of a given constituency in effecting or opposing it. This was particularly true on the right side of the political spectrum, where the importance of the press has recently been assessed in these terms by a leading historian:

> In the absence of organized parties, the newspapers of
> the Right determined an orientation, rallied opinion
> and formed its judgment. The authority of the
> journalists grew to such an extent that the party
> leaders couldn't compete with it. Throughout the 19th
> and 20th centuries, the teams formed around a certain
> number of newspapers and reviews constituted a sort
> of second force, whose initiatives and interventions
> fully belong to the history of the Right.[52]

Cassagnac was well aware of the close connection between the press and active politics and he unhesitatingly asserted an equality between pen and tribune. He regarded these two functions -- the political writer and the people's representative -- as dual aspects of a single role: the guidance of the public in its affairs. "They concern themselves with the same questions in different places," he wrote, "but, tribune or newspaper, these are two channels which flow into the same stream, that of universal suffrage."[53]

Paul de Cassagnac regarded journalism as "a kind of ministry" (as one of his colleagues in the press described it) "charged with spreading the truth, enlightening opinion, refuting the errors and lies of adversaries, and chastising those, whoever they were, who seemed to fail in the accomplishment of their duty."[54] He believed that the journalist should be ready to stand up for what he professed. For him, words and actions were two expressions of a single conscious position and should responsibly reflect that position. As he himself once wrote:

What a singular responsibility indeed, and what an intolerable situation is that of these journalists who by their stimulation have aroused the national élan and have then restricted themselves to talk without action.

For me, journalism which is merely theoretical has never had an estimable role and in no way surpasses the value of the trade of solicitor, such as certain people practice it. Words, phrases, and nobody behind them.

The journalist ought to practice what he preaches and conduct himself according to what he says.

Otherwise he is nothing but a virtuoso, who sings in court to earn some pocket money and who deserves the retort once made by Allem-Rousseau to a court clerk who interrupted his pleading: "Shut up! You are nothing but an inkstand!"[55]

Such was the high-minded conviction of the twenty-three year old writer who would soon be known as the *enfant terrible* of the Parisian press. It was not long before he had the chance to act in accordance with his opinions, by defending with the sword what he had written with the pen.

* * *

"Every man sees nature through the prism of a temperament," André Maurois has written.[56] And indeed, more than one commentator has accurately suggested that Paul de Cassagnac was, by his very nature, militant and intransigent. In the press he assumed the pose of knight-errant in pursuit of a chivalrous mission, thereby exhibiting many of the traits of the *ultra*, the extreme idealist, the romantic hero par excellence. In *Le Pays*, Cassagnac continually rode forth to do battle with the colors of his cause unfurled, ready to flay any protagonist who might present himself. His exalted pose seemed oddly anachronistic in an age that was increasingly attuning itself to the politics of expediency. Ultimately, Cassagnac was a militant by temperament, not a politician. This was true from the earliest days of his public career, when his opponents treated him as the Don Quixote of authoritarianism,[57] until the time of his death. His stance of bravado and derring-do was undoubtedly more appropriate to the front-line soldier or the king's musketeer (for he was a latter-day d'Artagnan) than to the smoke-filled room. "His warrior virtues, indispensable in the field, become dangerous in the councils of the general staff," wrote one attentive observer.[58] But Cassagnac was a Gascon, a southerner -- and to that observer this fact alone provided sufficient explanation of his character.

Both Cassagnac's physical appearance and certain aspects of his behavior lent support to this assessment of his character. Indeed, he had the stature of a fighter. He was tall (well over six feet, a height rarely attained in France in his time) and solidly built, with the look and the tastes of a real outdoorsman. "Chiseled like a sixteenth century soldier, his mustache large and turned up *en panache*, his skin lightly tanned, his step slow and haughty, Paul de Cassagnac could have been the idol of the masses by virtue of his physique alone," wrote Jules Richard, Cassagnac's colleague in the Bonapartist press.[59] Both popular crowds and women attested to his physical charisma.[60]

By all accounts, Paul de Cassagnac's public image as a swashbuckling chevalier and polemicist made him, by all accounts, enormously attractive to women. And he was attracted to them, to the point that he developed quite a reputation as a rake during his bachelor days. Whether his reputation was deserved or not remains unclear. It is unquestionably true, however, that he enjoyed significant and well-documented relationships with high-ranking women, some of a chivalric, platonic nature and some that were anything but platonic. He was considered something of a "matinee idol" figure by women in Parisian high society and as an eligible bachelor was much sought after by hostesses and prospective mothers-in-law.

In his early days in the press, Cassagnac took up the defense of Empress Eugenie, and by extension, that of Marie-Antoinette, whose cult the empress assiduously cultivated.[61] When he was awarded the *Légion d'Honneur* in 1868, Eugenie sent her personal chamberlain to congratulate the young journalist on her behalf. The well-known lady travel writer and feminist, Olympe Audouard, later attributed Cassagnac's ultra-imperialism to a youthful crush on the empress.[62] He was also closely associated with Isabelle de Bourbon, the exiled queen of Spain, who lived in Paris from 1868 until 1876, and who stood as godmother to Cassagnac's first-born son in 1880.[63]

During the early 1870s Cassagnac carried on a prolonged affair with the celebrated Italian beauty, the comtesse de Castiglione, who had figured prominently in the diplomatic intrigues of the early 1860s when she had been sent by Cavour to convince (through whatever means) Napoleon III to cement a Franco-Italian alliance. Castiglione considered Cassagnac to be the one great love of her life.[64]

A subsequent relationship with the exotic young Russian painter, Marie Bashkirtseff, was of an entirely different character. The two entertained a serious platonic flirtation, of which Bashkirtseff left an extraordinarily poignant record in her posthumously published journals and diary.[65] With his sudden arranged marriage to the wealthy and very Catholic Julia Acard during the summer of 1878, however, the curtain dropped on Cassagnac's amorous involvements.[66]

Paul de Cassagnac's image of derring-do and militance was reinforced by his prowess as a duellist. Cassagnac, like his father before him and his brother, was a swordsman of considerable repute.[67] He rarely hesitated to come forward when he considered that there was a legitimate point of honor at stake. Indeed, Cassagnac was a serious swordsman in an age when duelling was said to have had deteriorated to the status of a diversionary pastime for writers who had never before held sword or pistol in hand. "Among the amusements of Paris," mused Louis Veuillot (who had given up duelling when he returned to the Catholic Church years before), "must be counted duels between journalists."[68] Ever since 1836, when Girardin had killed the journalist Armand Carrel in a celebrated pistol duel, civilian duelling had become a general practice and was at least tolerated, if not heartily accepted. The justification usually offered for the *duel d'honneur* by civilians was that French law gave inadequate protection to individual rights, a situation that left personal confrontation as the sole recourse for satisfying honor in case of personal insult or other affront.[69]

In the course of his public life, Paul de Cassagnac fought twenty-five duels and participated as a second in countless others, most of which had their origin in political controversy. His first encounter in late 1863, in which he wounded Aurélien Scholl, the lion of literary polemic whose skill with a sword was reputed equal to his skill with words, brought him public notoriety.[70] Most of the others took place during the first ten years of his political career. His adversaries included such reputable swordsmen as Gustave Flourens, Arthur Ranc, and Adrien Lannes de Montebello, as well as many men of lesser skill. In 1882 an American student of duelling unreservedly praised Paul de Cassagnac as "today the most distinguished and most dangerous living duellist."[71]

It would be a mistake, however, to conclude that Cassagnac's militant stance impelled him to observe a corresponding political discipline. He held party discipline in utmost contempt. He could be doggedly loyal, but only to a cause of his own choosing and in the way he saw fit. His political career demonstrates this characteristic time and time again. Even during his early years in public life, Paul de Cassagnac jealously maintained his independence as a critic against both the imperial court and the radical opposition. A typical statement of his attitude is given in the following response to a reprimand, in a letter addressed to the emperor's personal secretary in 1869:

> I leave to others the agreeable and profitable role
> of approving what is happening and pushing even
> further ahead. I reserve for myself, Sir, the trying
> and ungrateful role of warning, of pointing out the
> danger.
>
> The Emperor . . . will render me justice
> someday . . . . He will remember that I dared stand
> against his adversaries, alone among them all, upright
> in the midst of enemy camps, in order to vanquish
> them, and against His Majesty himself, in order to
> serve him.[72]

He preferred the post of volunteer, of guerilla fighter and regimental maverick to that of the courtisan. His utter individualism in this respect was particularly infuriating to partisans who wished to keep him in check, whether by moderating his opposition to the liberalization of the empire prior to 1870 or later on by damping his utter dedication to the politics of conservative alliance against the republic. "Devotion and fidelity flourish in free air, not in antechambers," Cassagnac asserted.[73]

The only discipline Cassagnac acknowledged was that he imposed upon himself in the service of his own political ideal. He devoted himself to the cause of authoritarian monarchy, not to the service of men or of parties insofar as he perceived them to be capable of representing that idea. "I consider a man's political beliefs as a woven fabric," he wrote in 1873, "which serves as his bedsheet during his lifetime and as his shroud following his death, and in which he remains perpetually wrapped. . . . I cannot admit that a man may change his political opinion."[74] Numerous commentators have since acknowledged that Paul de Cassagnac did succeed in remaining consistent in his convictions throughout his lifetime.[75] Indeed, as he grew older, Cassagnac exhibited a perverse pride in the invariability of his political opinions, and viewed the lack of such principles in others as a symptom of decadence. "We have arrived at such a point of moral degradation," he wrote in 1883, "that he who by some chance has not changed his [political] opinion and has remained firm in his ideas is to be congratulated. Not to have varied becomes an exception; not to be an apostate constitutes a merit, and not to have betrayed one's party takes on the proportions of a signal virtue."[76] In contrast, he himself had tried to follow the counsel given him as a youth by Barbey d'Aurevilly: "My child, belong to the clan of those who do not alter their ideas."[77]

* * *

When Cassagnac and his father joined *Le Pays* in 1866, the newspaper had just become a government organ, which is to say that it received a subsidy from the Ministry of Interior and was used as an outlet for the presentation of official views. As editor-in-chief, Granier de Cassagnac was under contract to the *Société des Journaux Réunis*, which owned both *Le Pays* and its sister publication, *Le Constitutionnel.*[78] The Société, a joint-stock company, was originally founded in 1852 by the notorious financier Jules Mirès.[79] From the mid-1860s until 1885 it was controlled by another capitalist, Eugène Gibiat, whose other financial interests included railroads and mines. Gibiat was primarily interested in a return on his investment and, from time to time, he threatened to sell *Le Pays* out from under the Cassagnacs, alleging poor financial return. He did not seem to be particular about the means by which the newspaper made its way as long as he suffered no losses; a subsidy from the imperial treasury was as acceptable a means of support as any other.[80]

During his first few months at *Le Pays*, Paul de Cassagnac acquired a "precocious notoriety" with articles that precipitated both defamation suits and duels.[81] "He was not one of those who were most listened to," noted one biographer, "but one of those who made himself most heard."[82]

Cassagnac's first foray into political controversy took place in late 1866 when he attached both the editor and the publisher of the only authorized opposition newspaper, *L'Opinion Nationale.* In Prussia, Bismarck was concluding the annexation of Schleswig and Holstein to the Prussian domain, and *L'Opinion* had long since adopted the Bismarckian argument that so far as French interests were concerned, it would be preferable for Germany to be unified under Prussian leadership than under that of Austria.[83] Other Parisian journalists were highly critical of this attitude, which they considered an apology for Prussian expansionism. Auguste Vermorel, of *Le Courrier Français*, went so far as to accuse the publisher of *L'Opinion*, Adolphe Guéroult, of betraying the interests of his country.[84] In *Le Pays*, Paul de Cassagnac echoed Vermorel's charge in even more impertinent and insulting language.[85] Guéroult promptly took both journalists to court, suing them (along with their respective publishers, who were legally responsible under the press laws of that time) for defamation. When the case was heard in late December 1866, both defendants were convicted; Vermorel was sentenced to one month of imprisonment and Cassagnac to two months, while their publishers were each fined a token 100 francs.[86]

In the same issue of *Le Pays* (9 December 1866) that published the attack on Guéroult, Cassagnac had accused A. Malespine, the editor of *L'Opinion Nationale*, of plagiarism, charging that he had passed off as his own certain articles purloined from another newspaper. Malespine also took Cassagnac to court, and he was once again convicted.[87] But in each case, Cassagnac was pardoned by the emperor.

Yet a third incident took place during this brief period. On a snowy New Year's Day 1867, Paul de Cassagnac took part in a celebrated pistol duel with Henri Rochefort. The latter, though he had not achieved immortality with his *Lanterne*, was nonetheless a well-known journalist, writing at that time for *Le Soleil*. Cassagnac had issued the challenge, alleging that Rochefort, who was known for his opposition to clergymen and monarchists, had insulted the memory of Marie-Antoinette (some accounts claim it was Joan of Arc). "For the gentlemen of the 'literary democracy,'" charged Cassagnac, "all that is legend in France, all that is decent and noble, all that is venerated must be spat on and besmirched."[88] This duel gave rise to a comic anecdote that Cassagnac enjoyed recounting in later years. According to Cassagnac, he had hit his opponent in a seemingly vital spot, but Rochefort showed no sign of dying. When the latter's friends examined him, they found that something had blocked the bullet. Upon looking more closely, they found a medal of the Virgin Mary sewn into Rochefort's clothing, right at the strategic spot. It had evidently been placed there by Rochefort's mistress, who was known to be very pious.[89] The thought of the impious, anticlerical Rochefort being "saved" by the Virgin Mary delighted Paul de Cassagnac, who was himself a staunch defender of the traditional faith.

As a result of this series of affairs, the hot-headed young Cassagnac lost his position at the Ministry of Interior.[90] From that time forth he could and did devote all his energies to his press career. The timing was fortuitous, for only a few weeks later Napoleon III announced a program of liberal reforms in his regime. Therewith Paul de Cassagnac turned from the defense of Marie-Antoinette to the defense of the authoritarian empire. As of January 1867 the controversy-seeking journalist would have his hands full of affairs generated by his aggressive opposition to the "liberal" empire.

CHAPTER II

DEFENSE OF THE AUTHORITARIAN EMPIRE
1867-1870

Lorsque les loups et les renards sortent du bois et menacent la ferme, c'est aux dogues à faire leur devoir. Nous sommes les dogues, et sans chaînes, sans muselières, nous rodons autour de l'Empire, empêchant les demagogues d'assassiner et les communistes de voler.

Paul de Cassagnac
Le Pays, 15 January 1869

On 19 January 1867, Napoleon III announced his intention to proceed with several major internal political reforms. These reforms had been demanded for years by deputies of the liberal opposition. To the citizenry at large, the emperor offered to liberalize the legislation that confined the periodical press and restricted the right of assembly. To the Corps Législatif, he granted the right of interpellation; henceforth his ministers would defend their programs in person.

The Cassagnacs sounded the dissonant note in the chorus of approval voiced by many Parisian newspapers, declaring their firm opposition to the projected reforms. It appeared to Granier de Cassagnac that the Paris liberal bourgeoisie

had succeeded in persuading the emperor that the current of public opinion ran to political reforms, even though that current came only from the salon of M. Thiers, the offices of the *Journal des Débats*, and the corridors of the *Académie Française*. The rest of the nation, that is, the immense majority of proprietors both small and large, devoted to agricultural and industrial work and to the liberal professions, and satisfied with the success of the empire and confident in the emperor, viewed these maneuvers of the *ambitieux* of Paris with an indifferent eye.[1]

Consequently the Cassagnacs rose to the defense of the authoritarian status quo, insisting that the bulk of the population did not desire the proposed measures. In so doing, they drew down on their heads the wrath not only of the liberal establishment itself, but also of its republican allies, the irreconcilable opponents of the Second Empire, who stood to profit most from the liberalization of the existing legislation. By midsummer 1867 the two Cassagnacs, father and son, were openly at war with both groups in the pages of *Le Pays*.[2]

Paul de Cassagnac echoed his father's ideas when he objected that the prospective liberties were desired by and would benefit only a small number of Frenchmen. Such liberties were "de luxe," not "necessary," he remarked, alluding to the characterization given them by Adolphe Thiers a few years previously.[3] The cart was being put before the horse. The majority of citizens, those who lived in the provinces, he suggested, had other concerns that should take precedence over the measures proposed by the emperor. He cast the conflict as one between town and country, in which the political ambitions of urban dwellers were being preferred to the more immediate and pressing needs of people in the countryside. The desires expressed by the town dwellers were those of a vocal minority, a minority that was not merely unrepresentative but also,in his estimation, in such a state of permanent opposition that the granting of all its demands would not reconcile it.

> What a curious spectacle it is when we see all the demands being made by the enemies and all the reservations by the devoted friends [of the regime]. . . .
>
> In vain do you wish to give liberty to the opposition, which will never be satisfied. For it [the opposition], liberty will exist only on the day that the Empire no longer exists. . . .
>
> Grant liberty to the soil, to property, to the countryside, and you will see riches and well-being develop. . . . Grant liberty to the towns, and political commotions will incessantly repeat themselves, troubling all of France.[4]

When Paul de Cassagnac referred to town dwellers, he most frequently meant those of Paris. He reserved a special scorn for the capital city, particularly for the political aspirations and doctrinaire concerns of its literary elite: "The politics of Paris is the politics of a certain class of mandarins . . . which never leaves the domain of fantasy and theory."[5] In Cassagnac's eyes the demands of the Paris *literati* for liberalization of the regime were merely another step in a continual quest for privileges by a new aristocracy; such privileges were "the prerogatives of a lettered class, aristocratic, hardly numerous, which constantly tries to snatch power and . . . shows no reluctance to place its grudges and ambitions ahead of the interests of the greatest number."[6] Worse yet, this literary minority, writing in such papers as the *Journal des Débats*, chose to mock the country people who constituted the majority under universal manhood suffrage and made fun of the backwardness of the provincial mentality.[7] The Cassagnacs, on the other hand, championed the country people. They depicted themselves as "rural" and prided themselves on the fact.[8] They claimed to represent a sort of "provincial atavism"[9] that contrasted vividly, in their eyes, with the mentality of the Parisian bourgeoisie. Indeed, the Cassagnacs' conception of the rural character as essentially apolitical furnished the base upon which authoritarian democracy could be constructed; when they spoke of *le peuple*, the majority under universal suffrage, they meant the peasants, the *petits proprietaires* who put their immediate interests before abstract political concerns.[10] It is no coincidence that both Cassagnacs were lifelong defenders of agricultural interests, from the concerns of the winegrowers and *bouilleurs de cru* to those of the graingrowers whose markets were later threatened by the importation of grain from abroad.[11]

In 1867 Paul de Cassagnac had specific suggestions of measures that should take precedence over de luxe liberties. Many of his suggestions were for economic reform and were drawn from the emperor's Agricultural Inquiry of 1866, in which Cassagnac had participated as secretary to his father.[12] These reforms were the "necessary" liberties -- "the liberties that give the country its material and hygienic well-being .... Their object is the general provisioning of France, her commerce, her industry, and the development of her public instruction."[13] Such reforms would include the reduction of taxes on land, as well as the *octrois*, tariffs, and inheritance and sales taxes; they also included measures to improve the means of communication and establish more railroads in the departments.[14] These were the kinds of "liberties" which, in Paul de Cassagnac's opinion, would serve to consolidate the empire. When in July 1867 the emperor urged the construction of new railroad lines and local roads as well as the improvement of canals and river navigation, Cassagnac seized on this offering as justification of his own position, just as a week later he would point to petitions from the *conseils-généraux* as evidence of the nation's real desires.[15]

Cassagnac and his father never declared hostility to the notion of liberty in the abstract. Indeed, both paid homage to the principle of civil liberty through order that underlay the Napoleonic idea.[16] But they were indeed hostile, and this was certainly in keeping with their proclaimed position as authoritarian monarchists, to the particular conception of political liberty fashionable among the men who contested the totality of political authority vested in the emperor.[17] In retrospect, the Cassagnac's authoritarianism can be seen as a restatement of the *thèse royale* of the eighteenth century. Their position is defined by their propensity to grant precedence to the maintenance of monarchical authority and societal order over and against the claims of any individuals or groups who asserted that certain political privileges were theirs as basic rights. Like earlier proponents of the *thèse royale*, the Cassagnacs virtually (although never explicitly) rejected the thesis that men had a "natural right" to political liberty, that is, to share in the political power vested in the monarch. They thus found themselves in direct opposition both to the proponents of the *thèse nobiliaire* and to their liberal contemporaries, who used the arguments of natural law to assert the *a priori* nature of "Liberty" in order to establish their "right" to wield political control.[18] This partly explains why the Cassagnacs considered those who preached such abstract liberties as suspect of being mere *ambitieux* using seductive theories to camouflage a baser appetite for power.

The Cassagnacs acknowledged that such liberty might be possible in theory, but they thought that in practice it must be severely restricted. The maintenance of social order was their utmost concern and they believed that such maintenance could only be achieved by concentrating political power in one authority and preventing its dilution. This was, in their view, the lesson of history most recently repeated in 1848, a lesson that seemed to them futile to repeat yet again. It was even easier for them to deny claims for political participation when the demands were made not only by conditional friends of the imperial regime but also by overtly hostile minority elements in a nation that had such a long history of violent upheaval.

These were the considerations governing the two Cassagnacs' views on freedom of the periodical press and of political assembly, controllable political liberties which, in their eyes, posed direct threats to currently established authority. But unlike such extreme Catholic spokesmen as Louis Veuillot, who opposed "Liberty" on philosophic grounds,[19] the Cassagnacs couched their arguments against the projected liberties of 1867 in practical terms. They preferred to emphasize the unseasonableness and unsuitability of the emperor's proposals rather than to oppose them outright. Indeed their arguments sometimes sound astonishingly like Burke's earlier arguments against the French Revolution, and never more so than when they argued that liberties must evolve within the context of a nation's own political culture and could not be transplanted by fiat.[20] Moreover, they envisioned the potential for future mischief, which might well result from the granting of the political liberties in question by a monarch in the twilight of his reign, as outweighing any positive advantages the regime might obtain from them. In their view, one ought not fortify the enemies of the regime by increasing their ability to do harm on the eve of a transfer of power that might prove delicate at best. Nothing less than the reign of Napoleon IV was at stake.

Both Cassagnacs were emphatic in opposing unrestricted freedom of the periodical press. Indeed, Granier de Cassagnac had opposed it for many years. His speech on the subject in the Corps Législatif in January 1864, during debate on the address to the throne, is definitive. On that occasion he refuted the position of liberals like Jules Simon who claimed freedom of the press as a natural right. The press, argued Granier de Cassagnac, quoting from the Abbé Sieyès, is the most fearsome of powers. Taking his examples from French history since 1789, Granier de Cassagnac demonstrated that each regime which had established freedom of the periodical press subject only to common law (a move that implicitly meant accepting freedom of the press as a natural right) had either been forced to suppress it at a later time or had been overthrown by the efforts of the very press it had unleashed. "Of what value is it to institutionalize abstract principles when these principles succumb in practice?" he asked.[21] Every government, including that of England (so frequently invoked by the liberals and even by Napoleon III as the example to be followed) acknowledged a right superior to any other, he pointed out: the right of maintaining and defending itself. In practice, this had meant government regulation of the periodical press.

So long as the theories of 1789 concerning the press regime had not undergone the necessary and decisive test of experience through the years, one was authorized to believe in their truth and practicality. But when fifty years of practice have shown that these theories lead the press fatally to overturn society without even managing to preserve itself, it would be both criminal and foolish not to look for, not to give a new basis to legislation on the press.

The legislation of 17 February 1852 was born of that necessity, demonstrated all too frequently by numerous revolutions . . . . The existing legislation on the press is necessary -- this is its primary justification.[22]

Not only should the legislation of 1852 be maintained, he argued, but it should be more stringently enforced as well.

In the opinion of Granier de Cassagnac, the government's 1867 proposal to eliminate the system of administrative prior licencing of the press by substituting for it a system of post-publication judicial control appeared particularly inopportune. The proposal, slow to materialize, reached the Corps Législatif only in January 1868, at which time Granier de Cassagnac made an eloquent and telling speech against it.[23] The ministry wavered and even considered withdrawing the bill, but the emperor insisted on going through with it. Consequently, Granier de Cassagnac and six other deputies whom he referred to as the "seven sages of Greece" found themselves alone in voting against the principal article of the bill. When it was enacted the following March, however, there was only one dissenting vote.[24]

Despite the severe criticism levelled against his press law by the two Cassagnacs, Napoleon III nevertheless chose to honor Paul de Cassagnac in August of that year by designating him a chevalier of the *Légion d'honneur.* Symbolically, the arch-defender of the authoritarian empire was named simultaneously with his friend and colleague Robert Mitchell, who had been campaigning simultaneously for the liberalization of the empire in the pages of *Le Constitutionnel,* the sister publication of *Le Pays.*[25] Such a move was quite in character for the emperor, who did not wish to disavow any of his supporters, even when they found themselves in diametric disagreement.

* * *

The effects of the liberal reforms of 1867-1868, particularly of the press law, were most pronounced in provincial France. There, those harboring grievances or political ambitions acquired sudden access to effective means for pursuing them. The importance of the new press law lay in the sudden abolition of what had been a rigorous system of government supervision and controls over the press. The first article of the new law, considered to be its most important provision, did away with the requirement of government authorization as an essential preliminary to the founding of a newspaper.[26] Not surprisingly, the republican opposition to the empire was the first to take advantage of the change and, following enactment of the law, its partisans began founding newspapers as fast as they could.[27] These "liberated" journalists at once "repaid the government for this liberty by unbridled and virulent abuse."[28] Indeed, an excellent case study of the use made of the revised laws on the press and assembly by the republican opposition is furnished by the department of Gers, the Cassagnacs' own rural stronghold, where both laws were to have a pronounced impact on local politics. The department of Gers was (and still remains) predominantly agricultural. The region covered by the department, lying west of Toulouse on the northern slope of the Pyrenees, where the foothills flow down to meet the riverbed of the Garonne, is characterized by a traditional polyculture (grain, grapes, domestic animals and poultry). In the nineteenth century, Gers was not a region composed exclusively of small property holdings. The cultivated areas were nevertheless small, since many of the large properties were divided up and farmed by *métayers* or tenant farmers. The inhabitants of the department were widely dispersed except for small concentrations in the towns; Auch, the largest town in the department and an administrative and ecclesiastical seat, had a population of less than 15,000 in the 1860s and 1870s. Most of the farms were self-sufficient, with each family growing what its members and its animals could consume, selling any excesses at market for a small profit. Such commercial profits as were realized were generally from the exploitation of small vineyards.[29]

Throughout the nineteenth century, Gers had virtually no industry. There were no mineral sources of energy, no exploitable primary resources, no capital, and no commercial horizons.[30] Such artisanal activities as existed were directed toward supplying the needs of the peasant cultivator (cloth, shoes, hardware, containers, for instance).[31] The single product for which Gers was noted in the outside world was its brandy -- the renowned *eau-de-vie* of the Armagnac -- which was produced chiefly in the three most westerly cantons of the department, Eauze, Nogaro, and Cazaubon.

Since the establishment of the Second Empire, political life in Gers had been dominated by Granier de Cassagnac, who, in the late 1860s was "at the height of his influence and renown."[32] Following the *coup d'état* and Granier de Cassagnac's election to the Corps Législatif from the district of Mirande, he had obtained a number of important developmental concessions for his department, particularly railroad lines and canals.[33] In 1864 and 1866 he had hosted Napoleon III and Eugénie at his chateau of Couloumé, thus underscoring in the eyes of his countrymen his influence at court. But over the years, Granier de Cassagnac had also acquired numerous enemies and aroused deep-seated jealousies. Political opinion in the department was polarized into pro- and anti-Cassagnac factions. The notables of a liberal inclination came to identify themselves increasingly with opposition to the Cassagnacs, although as the decade of the 1860s drew to a close, they were not yet disposed to make common cause with the long-suppressed republican opposition.

With the passage of the press law, the republican opposition (which was small in numbers but long on memories of 1851-1852) found a voice. In August 1868, a new newspaper, L'Avenir, journal démocratique du Gers, published its first issue. The paper had been founded with the express idea of rallying the adversaries of Granier de Cassagnac and thereby undermining his position as local potentate. Its inspiration and principal backing came from a local notable, Jean David, scion of a long-established "liberal" family of Auch, who as head of the local republican forces would be found constantly contesting the predominance of the Cassagnac family well into the 1880s.[34]

David chose as the paper's first editor a young man named Hippolyte-Prosper-Olivier Lissagaray, who had established a reputation for himself in Paris as an intransigent democrat, a militant and remorseless enemy of the Second Empire.[35] Lissagaray was a thoroughgoing Jacobin in the old style. What made him most interesting to the Gersois republicans, however, was that he was the first cousin and sworn enemy of Granier de Cassagnac. His campaign against his cousin bore all the earmarks of a blood feud.

In the first issue of L'Avenir, which appeared on 15 August (the Emperor's official birthday), Lissagaray detailed its program, a resumé of every complaint against the imperial regime that had accumulated during the eighteen years of its existence, coupled with a call for individual liberties, decentralization, and responsibility of bureaucrats, separation of church and state, suppression of standing armies, and various economic reforms. "We have just received the first number of L'Avenir," noted the liberal daily Le Temps in Paris:

> Its sale on the street was prohibited even before its publication, and since no printer could be found, a special printing shop had to be organized. By these two signs, the public divines a liberal and useful newspaper which one is disposed to support before reading it and even more so after having read it.[36]

The same issue also published the first morsel of defamatory innuendo aimed squarely at the person of Granier de Cassagnac. But Lissagaray's campaign of personal insults had only just begun. The following week L'Avenir published a strongly-worded account of the 1845 Dujarier-Beauvallon duel, an account clearly intended to discredit the writer's objectionable cousin on his home soil in anticipation of the legislative elections scheduled for the following year.[37] A reply soon came from Le Pays in Paris, since at the time the Cassagnacs had no local newspaper at their disposal in Gers.[38] "We learn from *Le Siècle*," remarked *Le Pays*, "that the sale of *L'Avenir*, a paper of the most beauteous crimson, has just been prohibited."

> An idea of the paper's principles is indicated by noting that it considers governments "a necessary ulcer". . . . *Le Siècle* assures us that the campaign begun by *L'Avenir* against the candidacy of the deputy from Mirande will excite much interest and success. We shall see, later on. But we can guarantee *Le Siècle* that if M. de Cassagnac had had to choose an enemy in Gers, he would have chosen no other than he who, in disdain of the closest family ties, has constituted himself the insulter.[39]

Lissagaray rebounded in characteristic fashion:

> Today the Cassagnac sewer, *Le Pays*, gushes mud on *L'Avenir*. Our readers, honorable people, do not have to wait for our response. One doesn't put such types as the Cassagnacs at the end of one's pen -- nor at the end of one's sword. But since they have attempted to soil *L'Avenir* by revealing the relationship of its editor-in-chief to the *roi des drôles*, we owe the public an explanation.
>
> It is indeed true that we have the misfortune to be a close relative of Granier . . . . But today, at the age of twenty-eight . . . we give no one the right to reproach us for this original stain . . . . Can one who has never committed a low act, who has never shown himself to be servile, be a relative of Cassagnac?
>
> Can one be a relative of Cassagnac who can call to his defense such friends as Eugène Pelletan, Jules Simon, Jules Favre, Ernest Picard, Carnot, Glais-Bizoin, Garnier-Pagès?
>
> Ask them whether or not I have done enough to expiate this involuntary crime of relationship, and whether or not it renders me unworthy to defend the cause of democracy in this region.
>
> Let honorable men be the judge. . . .[40]

Paul de Cassagnac replied in a calculatedly arrogant tone, insinuating that Lissagaray the republican was a coward and a wastrel. He served notice that, despite such disqualifying attributes, he was nevertheless ready to take on this impertinent cousin in defense of his father's honor.[41] Lissagaray replied to the provocation with an "insulting, brutal, bitterly hateful" article entitled *"Le Triumgueusat"* in which he took aim not only at Granier de Cassagnac but at his sons Paul and Georges as well.[42] Lissagaray announced his intention to depart for Paris to challenge Paul de Cassagnac: "Don't bother to move, you braggart of *Le Pays.* Although you told me, 'Give a sign and I will come,' it is I who will arrive in Paris Saturday morning -- at your place, M. Paul Granier de Cassagnac."[43] As the official excuse for his challenge, Lissagaray cited certain insults made by Cassagnac to the Republic of 1848. He made it clear, however, that the real motive was far more personal:

> Let's have no misunderstanding. Whatever happens, if I am lucky enough to come back here, I will again take up my task at *L'Avenir.* Your father belongs to me, do you understand? And I hope to hang him so high that I defy all the thieves in the region to come and cut him down.

> Till Saturday morning then, M. Paul de Cassagnac. You have three days left to polish the pistols of Beauvallon.[44]

This exchange created a sensation, and *L'Avenir*'s small readership awaited the outcome of the promised duel.[45] On 30 August the cousins met in a suburban garden not far from Paris. Although Lissagaray was no mean swordsman, he tired following a slight hand wound and suffered a far more serious wound in the chest from the weapon of Paul de Cassagnac. After the encounter, Lissagaray refused to shake hands with his cousin, then lost consciousness.[46] He reissued the challenge from his bed. But Paul de Cassagnac refused, remarking, "Sir, I left you as full of holes as a strainer. I could consent to be your adversary, but it repels me to become your butcher."[47] Lissagaray did not return to Auch until mid-September, but when he arrived, it was as the hero of the republican opposition of Paris.

In an effort to curtail Lissagaray's campaign of insults, Granier de Cassagnac filed suit against him in Auch, charging him with personal injury and defamation. A hearing was scheduled for mid-September, but postponed until November; in the meantime Lissagaray continued his verbal assault by publishing "the file of Granier, called de Cassagnac." He cast discredit upon Granier de Cassagnac's claims of nobility and denounced him for allegedly using his influential situation for personal gain.[48] *L'Avenir* thus recapitulated the insinuations made during the 1840s. In addition to his attacks on the Cassagnacs, Lissagaray published his "citizens' catechism," portraying the sad fate of the peasantry, liberated by the Revolution but re-enslaved under the various monarchies of the nineteenth century -- including, of course, the Second Empire. Only in a republic could the peasant at last be free, he intimated. Lissagaray added substance to his catechism (which has been called "a most adroit work of polemic and propaganda"[49]) by attacking the parts of the tax regime that most directly affected the peasants.

In November, when Granier de Cassagnac's suit finally came to trial in Auch, the republicans were ready. One of the most distinguished Paris republicans, Ernest Picard, came to Auch to defend Lissagaray and thereby associate the cause of republicanism in Paris with the opposition in Gers. The courtroom was overflowing with spectators who had come to enjoy the family feud at least as much as the collision between republic and empire. The tribunal, however, was unmoved by this calculated display of republican solidarity, and found Lissagaray and his publisher guilty, fining them 2500 francs.[50]

The imperial government was next to prosecute L'Avenir for its unceasing provocation. Already in September the prefect of Gers had characterized the new publication as "one of the most violent and most hostile organs of the democrats."[51] Its character did not alter during subsequent months and in December Lissagaray and his publisher were convicted by default on a variety of charges. They demanded a new trial. Their request was granted and on 15 January 1869 they came before the tribunal again, this time with another illustrious republican from Paris, Jules Favre, as their attorney. Once again their hearing attracted a crowd and once again they were convicted. This time the sentence included a prison term for both.[52] These convictions were the first in a series of ten, for press and related offences, which Lissagaray was to harvest before he fled to Brussels in May 1870.[53]   Meanwhile, to complement the press campaign, David and his republican allies in Gers began to organize so-called "private meetings" in accordance with the latest jurisprudence relative to the new laws on public meetings. They carefully noted that such political gatherings could escape prosecution if certain practical rules were observed concerning the place of the meeting and the manner in which participants were invited to attend.[54]   The first meetings coincided with Lissagaray's trial in November; Picard presided over the meeting in Auch during which Jean David announced his candidacy for the Corps Législatif on behalf of the republican opposition. The government promptly ordered prosecution of the organizers of these meetings, which it regarded, accurately, as clear instances of electoral reunions. But as in the case of the suit against Lissagaray, hearing of the cases was postponed, and during the interim more meetings took place. The organizers were finally convicted in February 1869 and lost their appeals to the higher courts.[55]

The imperial government had hoped that court convictions would end the matter. Instead they only marked the beginning. For the republican opponents of the Second Empire had recognized that sensational journalism, trials, fines, and prison sentences provided excellent publicity for their cause. Following the sentencing of Lissagaray in November 1868, for instance, L'Avenir published a special edition (17 November) in which the mandatory publication of the verdict was subversively flanked by numerous congratulatory letters and articles contributed by friends of the opposition -- Favre, Victor Hugo, Louis Blanc, and Jules Simon, to mention only a few of the political celebrities.[56]

The republicans began to harvest the fruits of their labors in late November, when the Cassagnacs returned to Gers for a visit. During that visit, a number of local mayors felt sufficiently brave to boycott a gathering to which one of Cassagnac's supporters in Masseube had invited them. Moreover, thirty citizens of that same town petitioned the imperial prosecutor to prosecute Granier de Cassagnac for giving an unauthorized speech from the steps of the town hall.[57] Such occurences as these signalled the beginning of a concerted campaign against Cassagnac political hegemony in Gers. The republicans had succeeded in reviving political life and, in particular, in contesting the official candidates of the Second Empire, of whom the most important by far in Gers was Granier de Cassagnac. David, Lissagaray, and L'Avenir had accomplished their immediate goal.

By the time of the legislative elections in May 1869, it looked as though Granier de Cassagnac might even face trouble in his district of Mirande. But the notables of the arrondissement, dissatisfied with the situation of agriculture and annoyed (according to the district attorney in Agen) with Granier de Cassagnac's underlings,[58] chose as their candidate an independent liberal, Louis Lacave-Laplagne, and did not unite their efforts with those of their republican counterparts, who sponsored the Parisian Jules Favre. Together, however, the two challengers polled 41 per cent of the registered vote (35 per cent and 6 per cent respectively). Although Granier de Cassagnac was re-elected by a clear majority (53 per cent of the total vote cast; 47 per cent of the registered vote), his support had declined sharply from that in earlier elections.[59]

This public manifestion of dissatisfaction with Granier de Cassagnac was bound to affect the political future of his son Paul. Shortly after the May legislative elections, the member of the conseil-général for the canton of Plaisance died. Paul de Cassagnac immediately announced his candidacy for the vacant seat. The sub-prefect of Mirande assessed Cassagnac's chances as "serious" in view of "the support he will find among his father's friends," and advocated that he be given official support; the prefectoral administration preferred, however, to observe a prudent attitude of sympathetic neutrality, reserving official candidacy for cases in which support of the regime became an issue.[60] Paul de Cassagnac won the election without official backing by a clear margin (1293 to 1078), but his campaign was also marked by controversy, like that of his father before him.[61] Cassagnac's first election to public office had subjected him to the heat of bitter political cross-fire, which would continue unabated during his long career in local and national politics.

* * *

The elections of 1869 changed the balance of power in the Corps Législatif by returning both a considerable number of declared enemies of the regime and a large group of "official candidates" who favored its liberalization. When the new legislature convened in July, 116 deputies joined together to interpellate the ministry on the subject of further political reforms. In an effort to construct a new majority, therefore, Napoleon III proposed additional reforms, this time in the Constitution of 1852, which defined the character of the regime itself. His proposals, changing the attributes of the legislative bodies, were designed to increase legislative control and responsibility. The first of his constitutional reforms, embodied in the Senatus-Consultum of 6 September 1869, greatly increased the powers of the Corps Législatif by instituting a greater measure of legislative initiative and by giving the body a substantial degree of control over the ministers. The second proposed reform, finally embodied in the Senatus-Consultum of 20 April 1870, was more radical. This measure redistributed the functions of the Senate, whose principal business up to that time had been to examine laws with an eye to their constitutionality and to revise the constitution itself. The new reform would empower the Senate as a more general legislative body, and give the Corps Législatif a voice in constitutional questions. These measures were interpreted by many, enthusiasts and opponents alike, as steps in the direction of a parliamentary monarchy.[62]

Once again, as in 1867, the Cassagnacs opposed the envisioned reforms for pragmatic reasons. Both the extension of liberties and the initiation of parliamentary control, argued Paul de Cassagnac, amounted to a profession of weakness by the emperor that would adversely affect the future of the throne. The principal beneficiaries of these reforms would be the intransigent opponents of the regime, not its current or prospective adherents. "Concession is akin to fear," wrote Cassagnac in May 1869, "and all men of good sense are asking themselves whether this is the moment for the emperor to abdicate his power, . . . to appear hesitant and irresolute when it is a question of consolidating the empire and enabling his son to reign."[63] The time for enacting such reforms, Cassagnac suggested, would have been in 1859 when the emperor had been at the peak of his power; in 1869, given the bad state of his health, it seemed doubtful that he would have adequate time to establish his reforms firmly before they would be put to a severe test.[64]

For Cassagnac, it seemed essential to ensure the survival of the imperial institutions beyond the life of their founder. As he was to observe subsequently, in 1876, in his first speech in the Chamber of Deputies:

> There are but two ways to govern a people: by institutions and by men. The institutions are laws long practiced that have become customary. In countries where traditions exist, in America, in Germany, in England, the chief of state can die, but the institutions remain, the law is eternal. It is planted on a pikestaff like Gessler's hat . . . and the succeeding generations salute and bow down.
>
> But what happens in our country? What happens is that . . . all the institutions have been successively overthrown, all the laws have been violated at least once every ten years . . . . We are condemned to resort to the so-called "necessary" men, whether their names be Bonaparte, Thiers, or Mac-Mahon . . . . For my country, I dream a dream we all share: to achieve a legal situation such that these men count for little and the law counts for everything.[65]

In 1869 he predicted disaster for the regime if the emperor continued to capitulate to the demands of the minority, and he voiced his fears that the emperor might have to resort to force in order to reestablish his authority.[66]

When the Senate convened in August 1869 to act on the emperor's first constitutional proposal, Paul de Cassagnac declared himself chief spokesman against the innovations, the self-appointed voice of those on the Right who opposed the constitutional reforms. This opposition, he asserted, was "quite as radical and irreconcilable [concerning the constitutional reforms] as the opposition of the Left [concerning the regime]." As before,

Our opposition has its basis in the unrecognized interests of the countryside, the over-large participation of the towns in the governmental reforms. Forthrightly, loudly, in the name of the conservatives, in the name of those who desire peace, security and tranquility, we have attempted to check the government in its perilous march, to prevent it from falling into the abyss that awaits it.[67]

The focal point of the Cassagnacs' attack was what they perceived as the drift toward parliamentary government. Although Napoleon III had himself decried France's tendency to "copy and adopt the institutions of foreign countries,"[68] he was nevertheless a sincere partisan of the increased use of legislative power; both he and his new minister Émile Ollivier were partisans of a parliament that could serve a representative, although not a governing role.[69] Even though the emperor did not wish to go as far in the direction of parliamentary government as did the old Orleanists like Thiers, he was still less of an "imperialist" than his authoritarian supporters -- Rouher, the Cassagnacs, and the other deputies who did not wish the emperor to dilute his powers and, it must be added, who felt themselves being shunted to the sidelines, making way for Thiers and his friends, the liberals of the *tiers-parti*.

The authoritarians were obsessed by these latter, many of whom like themselves had gained their formative political experience (and a taste for the exercise of power) in parliamentary life.[70] They feared a renewal of the inadequacies that parliamentary government had demonstrated during the July Monarchy -- inadequacies dimmed by the nostalgia of twenty years' forgetfulness. They could not forgive the liberals, these Orleanists who, in spite of all its demonstrated shortcomings, continued in their Anglomania to invest with a supreme virtue the notion of parliamentary government, the very synonym for constitutional monarchy. They could not fathom a mentality that axiomatically identified liberal political reform with an English-style governmental structure in which the king reigns but does not rule, an identification so reflexive as to dismiss out of hand any other possible options for reform.[71]

Thus, to the authoritarian opponents of the proposed constitutional reforms, Napoleon III's plans smacked suspiciously of *parlementarisme* on the British model. The Cassagnacs vociferously denounced the reforms as a seemingly blind return to a past which, in France, had been a total failure. As far as these authoritarians were concerned, the parliamentary experience had irrevocably bankrupted itself as a model for any future governmental reform in France. "We are the implacable adversaries of parliamentarism," Paul de Cassagnac declared. "We believe sincerely that, like the rock of Sisyphus, in persisting in its desire to roll, it will crush you just as it crushed Charles X, Louis-Philippe, Cavaignac . . . ."[72]

In the opinion of authoritarians like the Cassagnacs, parliamentary government ran counter to the French tradition of a strong and independent monarchy, which for centuries had initiated reform from the top and thereby had become the pride of France. Parliamentarism was simply an unnatural import from across the Channel, "a flower of exile plucked in England by Louis XVIII," as one of Cassagnac's radical counterparts once remarked.[73] Paul de Cassagnac continually questioned the wisdom of transplanting foreign political customs without acknowledging the differences among national cultures. France, it seemed to him, had an unhealthy propensity to yearn longingly after the products peculiar to other nations: "Each country has its politics, just as it has flora and fauna of its own. It is as silly to introduce a constitution of foreign origin in France as to plant palm trees on the Champs-Élysées and pineapples on the plain of Grenelle. All you will get are stunted, unhealthy and absurd products."[74] Indeed, Cassagnac's distaste for English political exports in particular fuelled an anti-English bias that was conspicuously evident throughout his political career.[75]

In Cassagnac's eyes the swing toward parliamentary government constituted a fundamental violation of the basic principle of the empire, which combined both the authority and responsibility of governing in the person of the monarch-executive. Cassagnac did not oppose increasing the consultative role of the legislature within this framework -- as long as it did not alter the basic relationship. But he denied to the emperor the right to abandon (or even share) his responsibility and authority to such a body.[76] To do so would be to submerge the distinctive difference between the tradition of the Orleans dynasty and that of the Bonapartes. It would mean (to borrow Cassagnac's colorful figure of speech) that the Napoleonic eagle had descended from the skies to join the Orleanist *coq gaulois* who, earthbound, flirted with the hens in the coop.[77] The emperor's initiative was, in sum, unconstitutional, unless ratified by the electorate.[78]

Although the first Senatus-Consultum was enacted without ratification by the electorate, the second one, initiated by the Ollivier cabinet of 1870, was considered to be so drastic that the Senate itself made plebiscitary ratification a condition of its enactment. The liberals were horrified, for they had always objected to the plebiscite as a caesarian tool, "that mode of consultation which forces the adhesion of

the voters by offering them the choice between acceptance of the status
quo and the void."[79] They feared the plebiscite as a means whereby the
emperor could bypass parliamentary control. For the same reason,
however, the authoritarians were jubilant, since to them the plebiscite
represented precisely the tool with which the emperor could "dominate
all parliamentary opposition."[80]

When Émile Ollivier presented his proposal for the plebiscite,
however, he included not only the Senatus-Consultum of 1870 but all
the liberal reforms enacted since 1860 as well. This upset the
authoritarians, for whom there was but one way to express the
plebiscitary question: "Do you want parliamentarism, yes or no? Do
you want the Senatus-Consultum, yes or no?"[81] Given the form and
timing of the plebiscite, the choice to be made was between the liberal
empire and no empire at all, Cassagnac charged. Voters had no choice
but to vote "yes," he complained, for "to vote against the
parliamentarism of M. Ollivier would be to vote against the emperor."[82]

Seven and one half million Frenchmen cast "yes" ballots in May
1870, but the great majority do not seem to have weighed the specific
issues proposed by the terms of the plebiscitary initiative. What was
clear from the vote was that they feared revolution and favored
maintenance of the regime.[83] Consequently, it is difficult to ascertain
just how the electorate of the Second Empire did feel at the time about
parlementarisme, or whether the institutions of the liberal empire could
have taken root with the support of public opinion behind them. It is
therefore even more difficult to judge whether the liberal empire might
have outlived its principal sponsor, the ailing Napoleon III, even if his
ministry had not blundered into war with Prussia over the question of
the succession to the Spanish throne. Surely, consummate statecraft
would have been necessary to assure the succession of the young Prince
Imperial in face of an irreconcilable opposition, which took advantage
of every misstep to cast discredit on the regime. Interestingly enough,
none of the historians who have expressed a view on the hypothetical
chances for maintaining the liberal empire have considered the question
with reference to the succession issue.[84] Yet, as has been argued above,
it was precisely the succession that aroused the anxiety of authoritarians
such as Paul de Cassagnac:

> For nearly a hundred years, all sorts of
> governments have succeeded one another in France.
> They have sat in all our palaces -- at the Tuileries, at
> the Luxembourg, at the Élysée. We have seen
> emperors, kings, varied republics, and none has been
> able to endure. Their roots, sunk into the sand, have

not been able to hold them firm against the tempest
and, with the first winds of June, July, or February,
their overturned trunks have covered France.
    For nearly a hundred years, political heritage has
been effectively abolished. No son has succeeded his
father; no uncle has placed his nephew on the throne
he has just vacated.[85]

Given the adverse outcome of the Franco-Prussian war, the Second
Empire foundered before it had even begun to overcome the difficulties
inherent in adjusting to a quasi-parliamentary pattern and before there
was any question of the young prince succeeding his father on the
imperial throne. Cassagnac's gloomy prophecies came true sooner than
anyone, even those irreconcilable republicans who professed to be the
empire's worst enemies, had anticipated.

                              * * *

    When news of the Hohenzollern candidacy for the vacant Spanish
throne exploded during the summer of 1870, public sentiment responded
favorably to the risk of war with Prussia that had been suggested by the
French press. In Le Pays, the Cassagnacs committed themselves with
vehemence to the defense of French honor, by war if necessary; indeed,
for the authoritarians, the prospect of war seemed to offer the emperor a
last chance to abandon the parliamentary experiment, a chance from
which he must profit without delay.[86] No one anticipated that such a
war could be lost, much less be fatal to the regime.
    Only after the setbacks of the French army at Froeschwiller and
Forbach in early August was the alarm sounded. It was then that Paul
de Cassagnac and his friend Robert Mitchell of Le Constitutionnel
volunteered for the army as common soldiers. On 14 August, they
received authorization to join the elite zouaves of the Imperial Guard.[87]
The experiences of the two young journalists during the next few weeks
provided a graphic example of the confusion existing in the French
army at the time. After only a few days of training in maneuvers,
Cassagnac and Mitchell, along with several companions, were permitted
to leave Paris for Châlons-sur-Marne, in an attempt to join their unit at
the front.[88] From Châlons they made their way on foot to Reims, only to
discover that their regiment was blocked at Metz. When, therefore,
they encountered Mac-Mahon's army headed for Rethel on 24 August,
they accompanied it. During the battle of Beaumont, on 30 August,
Cassagnac reported being at the side of the emperor and Marshal de
Mac-Mahon, although his precise role there remains unclear.[89]

Soon the fateful decision was made to fall back on Sedan. In the days following the capitulation, Cassagnac again reported being near the emperor.[90] For Cassagnac and his friends, the days following the capitulation were undoubtedly worse than those of the campaign itself. They spent four nightmarish days as prisoners in the rain-soaked bogs between the river Meuse and the adjacent canal, "the camp of misery," scavenging and foraging off the land. After refusing a safe-conduct pass to Belgium, Paul de Cassagnac remained with the army as a prisoner of war, enduring a fatiguing journey by foot and rail to Silesia.[91] He did not return to France for many months, during which time the political situation of France was completely transformed. The efforts of the Government of National Defense, the convocation of the National Assembly, and the upheaval of the Paris Commune were all experienced by a nation from which Paul de Cassagnac was absent; he viewed these events from afar as a concerned but helpless spectator. When he returned, France was governed by a National Assembly composed largely of monarchists and by a president who was first of all a fervent proponent of parliamentary government.

CHAPTER III

WAR AGAINST THE REPUBLIC AND THE REPUBLICANS
1871-1879

*La République révolutionnaire, je l'ai combattue à
outrance; l'amende, la prison, les injures, j'ai tout
bravé pour combattre les ennemis de la société, ces
radicaux dont je poursuis la chute et la ruine d'une
façon implacable.*

*Entre eux et moi, c'est une guerre à mort, vous le
savez et ils le savent!*

Paul de Cassagnac
Electoral circular, 1877

After his return to France from captivity in Prussia, Paul de
Cassagnac emerged as a distinct political personality. His father,
although still active in the Bonapartist press and politics during the
decade of the 1870s, withdrew from the spotlight, leaving to his son the
editorship of *Le Pays* as well as a fund of his own ideas. From 1871 on
Cassagnac made himself known on his own account as an ardent foe of
things republican and as a champion of an authoritarian monarchy
grounded in universal suffrage which he had christened *Impérialisme*.

Paul de Cassagnac's preoccupation with the form of government
that would succeed the Second Empire was characteristic of many
politically concerned Frenchmen throughout the nineteenth century.
After 1870 political discussion focused obsessively on the issue of
Monarchy versus Republic; then as before, the essential division
between the political Right and political Left was predicated on this
choice between forms of government.[1] One authority on French political
thought has remarked retrospectively that the French Revolution
restricted political thought by narrowing "the field of political
speculation to the main problem raised by the Revolution, that of the
form of the state . . . . The incompleteness of the Revolution caused
men's minds and energies to be directed along the side-issue of external
forms."[2] Such "side issues" dominated French political life until the turn
of the century.

Cassagnac made his principal anti-republican declaration in a
campaign statement in October 1871, when he declared his candidacy

for re-election to the Gers departmental council. While his statement
was highly rhetorical, it is nonetheless interesting as a document
illustrating the themes that characterized provincial elections in the wake
of the Paris Commune and its subsequent repression. Cassagnac made
an unabashed appeal to the conservative instincts of the overwhelmingly
rural, agrarian population of his canton, stressing the lack of patriotism
of the republican opposition and emphasizing the dignity and individual
importance of the rural voter. He played on the peasants' fear of social
upheaval by contrasting the uncertainty and anxiety succeeding the
events of *Quatre Septembre* with the peace and prosperity that had been
theirs under the Second Empire and by pointing to the treachery of the
republican opposition in "abandoning" the imperial regime on the
battlefield. A quotation *in extenso* demonstrates, better than any
paraphrase, both Cassagnac's principal themes and the overall tone of
his manifesto:

> These elections to the *conseils-généraux* are
> solemn ones for you: do not forget that, you country
> populations.
>
> In vain do they [the republicans of 4 September]
> wish to bypass you and try to constitute a definitive
> government without your popular consent [the
> reference is to the National Assembly's vote to give
> itself constituent powers]; in vain do they try to
> dishonor you by treating you as a "vile multitude" and
> as "rustics," and allege that you go to the polls herded
> by the prefect and the gendarmes.
>
> They are afraid of you, for you are France -- the
> France who works, who prays, and who fights, the
> laborious, believing and patriotic France, the France
> who will soon lift herself from her ruins more valiant,
> more radiant than ever, because she never despairs
> either of herself or of God. . . .
>
> I am one of you. Since my infancy I have lived
> with you whom I love and most recently, as you
> know, I left as a simple soldier, one in the ranks
> alongside your sons and your brothers. . . .
>
> Voters! In this day of social danger, when
> everything is caving in about us, when the blessed and
> sacred ideas of the family, of authority, of religion,
> are being trampled underfoot; when the revolution
> snarls and howls from every side; when international
> bands openly preach the pillage of belongings; when

the horizon, ever more somber, is lighted only by the sinister gleam of fires, you must close ranks to defend yourselves. You must place at your head men who fear no peril and who flinch before nothing in order to affirm your political rights, to defend your fortunes, and to protect your existence.

Voters! If you think that I am such a man, elect me![3]

It was clear from this declaration that Cassagnac's emphasis had shifted considerably since 1870. No longer was *parlementarisme* or the extension of liberties the principal danger to stability. Instead the threat lay, as it had before the Second Empire, in the promise of political and social upheaval enshrined in the word republic.[4] Cassagnac's themes of "social danger" echoed those of the conservatives after the June days of 1848, and in fact, this was not the last instance in which that parallel could be invoked. It is uncertain whether it was the candidate's manifesto or his powerful local position that touched the voters more; in any case, Paul de Cassagnac was re-elected to the *conseil-général*.

The Gers manifesto of October 1871 was only the prelude to the campaign Cassagnac launched following his return to Paris, where he rejoined *Le Pays* as editor-in-chief. In his first article he proclaimed war on the republic in the name of the "fifteen communes of the canton that, in hatred of the republic, has just elected me."[5] The crusade against the republic, he announced, was to be the cause to which he would devote his life. His hopes, he proclaimed, were vested in the return of the empire, "not out of enthusiasm for the past, but because of disgust for the present and fear for the future."[6]

* * *

Hatred of the republic became the leitmotif for Paul de Cassagnac's entire subsequent career in public life. His conception of the republic led him to equate it with grave social disorder. Cassagnac himself never took the trouble to formulate his position in an orderly and considered way. Fortunately, however, his many articles in the press provide ample material from which to fashion a synthesis and isolate the basic elements of his political theory.

Paul de Cassagnac might have begun such a synthesis with the analogy he once used, comparing the republic to the temptation of Faust: the ideal of the republic was the aging nineteenth century's "vision of Marguerite."[7] This ideal, with its romanticized notion of self-government, implanted by the classical education of that time, was

extremely dangerous because in practice its fruits in no way
corresponded to the theory.

On leaving high school, your head is filled with the
republican legend; your professors have taught you all
the magic this word can contain, without elaborating
on it. They make sure not to tell you that neither in
Sparta, nor in Athens, Rome, or Carthage, did the
republic signify what our wild imaginations portrayed
in our generous and honest dreams. Everything has
been presented to us in the most seductive colors:
Tiberius and Caius Gracchus, these Roman Vermorels
and Delescluzes, provoke our tears when they
succumb just at the moment their socialist tentative
succeeds. Catilina, that Rossel; Cethegus, that
Cluseret; Marius, that glorious Marat seem almost
sympathetic to us. And thus nourished on false
theories, instructed by a false historical science, where
all the bloody spots have been painted over in pink and
blue, we surge forth into life, each of us with his small
republic in his hand, quite ready to install it in the
street just as one would erect a log cabin.[8]

In Cassagnac's estimation, the reason for the failure of the
republican ideal in practice was simple -- the republic lacked the
essential principle of authority around which any society must be
organized. Thus, the real threat and logical consequence of republican
notions was anarchy, and following from that, the tyranny of the worst
elements in society. The ideal of the republic was constantly subject to
disfiguration at the hands of a less-than-perfect mankind. "Our
Republic, like the sheepfolds of Florian, holds the commonplace, the
dirty and the horrible in horror, and yet it is against such things that we
collide each day."[9]

. . . The republic, by its very essence, by its
nature, will always be the prey of the violent, of the
rascals . . .

Vainly has history shown us that only the
monarchy can protect the honorable and moderate
men, whereas under the republic they are the perpetual
prey and victims of the others.

Sooner or later the violent will take over every
republic.

And this is why this regime which, theoretically
speaking, contains nothing contrary to reason,

becomes, practically speaking, and by the force of
circumstance, the government of a sect against the
majority of the country.[10]
It was the violent, the mob, the rabble, those with insatiable appetites
for power and society's spoils -- the republicans -- who were the
threat.[11]

To Cassagnac, only a regime organized around a principle of
authority could ensure the maintenance of social order: the monarchy
was its obvious embodiment. Its constitutional arms were the army, the
clergy, and the magistracy. Cassagnac explicitly stated that he
preferred any monarchy to any republic.[12] He would rather "be
governed by one lion of good family than by hundreds of rats," as one
of his colleagues paraphrased the expression made famous by Voltaire a
century before.[13] He did not equate monarchy with tyranny as did his
republican counterparts: "Although I am an authoritarian," he once
wrote, "I admit no tyranny, and I would no more accept despotism from
below, from the *canaille*, as a regular and permanent form of
government, than I would from above, be it the despotism of Thiers or
that of Napoleon III."[14] In Cassagnac's frame of reference, however,
tyranny did not constitute a vital point of discussion. He conceived of a
monarch who was the epitome of honorability, of *honnêteté* -- a Christian
prince who was a benevolent patriarch and the chieftain of the forces of
good. "France needs a strong government," he once wrote, "a
government of combat. Dictatorship itself would not frighten us, for the
abuse of power is never to be feared in the hands of an honorable
man."[15]

Cassagnac's conception of monarchical authority is, of course, open
to the same criticism that has been directed at the constitutional
absolutism advocated by Voltaire: "it fails to provide institutions to
determine whether the king is observing the rule of law, and to resist
him if he should disobey it."[16] Put differently, it simply did not provide
for dealing with the very real problem of abuse of power by the
unscrupulous. Cassagnac's notion of monarchy presupposed a
hierarchical system in which access to political power was closed to the
non-honorable, and in which the unruly multitude would be ruled by
Christian gentlemen.[17]

There are two probable explanations for Cassagnac's idealism about
the monarch's use of power. One may be found in the relatively
humane character of political life in France during the mid-nineteenth
century. As Émile de Girardin himself wrote in 1875, "The Empire of
1852 was a despotism without a despot, for of all the sovereigns of
Europe, the emperor was by far the best-intentioned."[18] Another lay in

the still powerful influence of moral restraints placed about the use of power by a religiously-inspired ethical framework, a framework not present in more contemporary and more highly secularized concepts of authority, those that have nurtured totalitarianism and state absolutism of a most oppressive kind.

Paul de Cassagnac was a practicing Roman Catholic and subscribed to a gentleman's code of honor. These facts may have a great deal to do with his illusions concerning the exercise of political power. We are well-informed about certain aspects of his religious belief, which governed his concept of morality. It is clear from his many newspaper articles that he acknowledged the existence of a supreme God, an avenging God who did not hesitate to dispense retributive justice. Cassagnac also recognized the promise of an afterlife superior in quality to terrestial life in which earthly sacrifices would be compensated.[19] These two ideas were, in his opinion, the cornerstones of man's honorability: the self-restraint and the sense of obligation that were fundamental to civilized behavior. These were essential to the "religious idea" which kept man's earthly appetites in check.

To Paul de Cassagnac, this "religious idea" constituted the cornerstone of authority and, therefore, of monarchy. It created and consecrated the human hierarchy -- a hierarchy whose opposite is anarchy:[20]

> Without this hierarchy, which serves as an
> unbridgeable barrier to individual competition, there is
> nothing but an immense and shabby rivalry, where
> crude interest, unavowable appetite, and unhealthy
> ambition dispute avidly with one another for the
> several pleasures of this transitory life.[21]

A republic, being strictly concerned with terrestial matters, opposes the religious idea,[22] as well as its accompanying notion of a social hierarchy. Hence the impossibility of its success in assuring social order.

Cassagnac's harsh theoretical judgment of the republic, which was widely shared by his contemporaries in the upper classes, was grounded in his understanding of French history. He invoked the historical examples of republics previously instituted in France, where tyranny of the mob had become all too frequently a tragic reality.[23] Indeed, his continual invocation of history in support of the war on the republic deserves our attention, for he was but one of many nineteenth-century French political figures who interpreted the politics of his own time through the prism of the French Revolution. Cassagnac had a positivist's confidence in the relevance of history's lessons. He once wrote that "politics is composed of only two things, the study of history and the proper application of its teachings to present circumstances . . . . Men are always the same and events often come to pass with a regular logic; what has happened previously will give us all the probabilities for what is to come."[24]

Cassagnac was in no sense totally opposed to the French Revolution -- as he perceived it. His own attitude is well-expressed in a question he addressed to the republicans in the Chamber of Deputies, concerning their proposal to raise a monument to the French Revolution. Was the monument to honor the Revolution of 1789, he inquired, or the factional revolutions that followed?

> If it pleases you to raise a monument in commemoration of the French Revolution in the exact and defined sense of the word, I will not oppose it, either for my own sake or in principle, for I do not repudiate the French Revolution as the origin of democracy, whose respectful servant I proclaim myself.
>
> We are all agreed here in claiming to the same degree and under the same conditions, the memories of the Revolution of 1789.
>
> We are all its descendants, and we on the Right cannot accept the Left's claims to a monopoly on it.[25]

The Revolution of 1789, Cassagnac continued, headed by royalty and nobility, had established the sovereignty of the people; the remainder of the revolutionary period, beginning with the abolition of the monarchy in 1792 and the substitution of the republic, had brought France only unnecessary difficulties.

Paul de Cassagnac was well-versed in the political history of the revolutionary period. He once boasted of reading through all the legislative records of that era in preparation for his career in journalism, and he was clearly familiar with his father's numerous volumes on the causes of the revolution, the Girondins, and the Directory, as he frequently echoed many of the views expressed in these works.[26] Cassagnac's interpretation of the subsequent phases of the revolution following the abolition of the monarchy was one of the inevitable breakdown of authority and order, followed by a slow and difficult, yet equally inevitable return to authority and order in a new form -- a new monarchy that recognized the principle of sovereignty of the nation. The interim period between old monarchy and new monarchy was characterized by social chaos.

Consequently, Cassagnac held a highly fatalistic view on the degeneration of republics, grounded in the revolutionary experiences of 1792-1799 and reinforced by the events of 1848-1851. Behind the republic of the Girondins lay that of the Mountain; behind that of the Mountain loomed the inevitable republic of the Terror.[27]

> Behind the theoreticians, the pontiffs of the Republic-above-all, those who officiate, those who preach, those who exercise the apostolate, march the indispensable executors, the somber and unpitying rabble -- those who pillage, those who steal, those who kill.[28]

For Cassagnac as for other conservative interpreters of the Revolution, one of the lessons to be learned from this process was that the Girondins, the liberals, were particularly dangerous politically, since they inevitably play the part of dupes for the real revolutionaries. Hence, his constant suspicion of such men in power. He perceived these men to be constantly on the verge of opening the gates to the invasion of the mob, by unconsciously sacrificing the requirements of social order to further their own ambitions.[29] Only the Terror could profit from such a state of affairs.

Following the inevitable Terror, however, Cassagnac saw reason for hope. The republic, he believed, was doomed to cave in, succumbing to its own centrifugal excesses and thereby paving the way for dictatorship and the return of order. His conclusion from this sequence was that the empire represented a necessary and perpetual last resort, the inevitable reprieve from disorder.[30] The implications of this view for Bonapartist politics in the 1870s will be explored in the following chapter. Here, it suffices to remark that Paul de Cassagnac's notion of the empire is clearly "counter-revolutionary," although it had many elements in common with the "anti-revolutionary" tradition depicted by one historian.[31] As Cassagnac put it:

> We are the revolutionaries who made the Code Napoleon.
>
> We are the revolutionaries who consecrated the rights of the people by the rigorous application of universal suffrage.
>
> We are the revolutionaries who shot the scoundrels during the afternoon of December and who sent them to Cayenne and Lambessa, just as we will send them there again if we get the chance.
>
> We are the revolutionaries, who, in short, guarded and protected the sovereign pontiff at Rome

against Italian appetites.
We are the revolutionaries who so protected
Order, Property, Family, and Religion, that during
twenty years no riot dared to trouble   France --
something that had not happened since the beginning
of the century.
If that is what it means to be revolutionary, . . .
we are, and we are proud of it. . . .[32]
We are not revolutionaries in today's sense, and
although we accepted the Revolution of 1789 as the
glorious baptism of our time, we are not
revolutionaries because all that was fertile in the
Revolution of 1789 has already germinated, sprouted,
ripened, and has been harvested.
The gold has been extracted; only the mud
remains. And whosoever calls himself a revolutionary
today wears that mud on his soul and is soiled by it.[33]

In Cassagnac's eyes, the revolution in France had borne its fruits by
returning the monarchy to consciousness of its ultimate basis in the
people, the nation. Divine right was dead. The revolution had
produced a new monarchy, the empire, a new system of authority based
on the principle of sovereignty of the nation: "Caesar is the modern
authority."[34]

Imperialism is the sovereignty of the nation,
which delegates its powers directly, by way of
plebiscite, to a chief with the mandate to impose
respect of the law of the majority and at the same time
to prevent the seditious revolts of the minority.
Imperialism is the antique French monarchy
returned to its origin, always face to face with the
people, being one with them, and owing its prestige
and power to the community that reigns between
them.[35]

Yet Cassagnac did not admit that Caesar had a right to impose his will
upon the nation. "When there is disagreement between the nation and
the prince, the prince has no choice but to respect its will and
disappear."[36]

To anyone accustomed to the liberal interpretation of the
revolutionary period and unfamiliar with the Napoleonic view, Paul de
Cassagnac's conception of the revolutionary gains as simply a
readjustment in the monarchical scheme of things, the recognition of the
sovereignty of the nation as being vested in monarchical authority rather

than in a National Assembly, undoubtedly appears heretical. All the familiar themes -- for instance, the emphasis on the ideas of the Enlightenment, which ostensibly lent the support of natural law arguments to the cause of liberal democracy -- are absent. These are aspects of the revolutionary heritage stressed, during the nineteenth century and since, by the victors in the battle for political liberty and parliamentary participation in wielding the power of the state.[37]

Yet Cassagnac's interpretation offers a full-fledged statement of the Napoleonic plebiscitary tradition, a position that was widely accepted and had considerable impact on French politics and political thinking in the last century. It is impossible to grasp the thrust of monarchist politics or comprehend the strategic and tactical calculations of the Bonapartists themselves after 1870, unless one takes seriously their claim to have countered anarchy and to have fulfilled the revolution in a monarchical context not once but twice during the previous seventy years. It is therefore vital to take account of the credibility their view of the republic and their own significance as saviors of the social order had during the years discussed here.

* * *

Thus far I have discussed the philosophical foundations of Paul de Cassagnac's war against the republic and its historical basis in a particular view of the French Revolution. In the sections that follow, I shall present the three principal themes in Cassagnac's unrelenting anti-republican polemic during the years 1871 to 1879 as they appeared first in the press and, from 1876 on, at the tribune of the Chamber of Deputies.

The first of the three themes was Cassagnac's vendetta against the republicans who, in September 1870, had overturned the Second Empire, and against the regime they were intent on installing as the permanent government of France. The second theme was Cassagnac's equally aggressive campaign to defend the imperial regime against republican insults and thus to aid its return to power as the defender of the social order. The third theme, which made its appearance after 1875, was his personal crusade to demonstrate the wide gap between the theory of liberty and its practice by the republicans in power, particularly in questions of freedom of the press and of religion. The case of the press will be discussed in this chapter, while that of religion will be considered in Chapter V.

Prior to 1875, when the National Assembly consecrated the new constitutional regime as a republic, Paul de Cassagnac directed his fire against the republicans of *Quatre Septembre*, both those who had been active in the Government of National Defense and their colleagues, the communards of Paris, in an effort to prevent their political comeback. Cassagnac summarized his arguments against these men in book form, in a misleadingly titled volume, *Histoire de la Troisième République*, published in 1876. In this lengthy tract, which vividly portrayed the 1870-1871 period, Cassagnac indicted the republican factions for their political activities between 9 August 1870 and the latter part of May 1871. In the last ten pages of the book, he condensed the subsequent two years in order to include the resignation of Thiers in May 1873. Cassagnac's account drew heavily on the documents and depositions gathered for the parliamentary inquest on the Government of National Defense.[38]

The theme of the volume appeared in the opening paragraph of Chapter I (entitled *"Le Crime"*):

> Contrary to what its authors want us to believe, the revolution of 4 September was not the result of a profound and irresistible emotion caused by the sudden news of the disaster at Sedan. It was a surprise raid, premeditated and prepared in advance by the incorrigible instigators of the demogagic conspiracies directed against the Empire. Sedan was only the occasion, not the cause, and the treason of the military governor of Paris [General Trochu] permitted its execution.[39]

Cassagnac then recounted in detail the events and decisions that followed the seizure of power by the Paris deputies, with intent to demonstrate that:

> The presence in power of the Government of National Defense did not prevent disorder. Its maintenance, obtained at the price of adjourning the elections, cost us a war to the finish, two lost provinces, a generation slaughtered, and nameless, countless ruins.[40]

Cassagnac's account contained four principal villains -- Léon Gambetta, for attempting to establish his republic at any cost; Jules Favre, for his equivocation in discussions with Bismarck, which cost France the two eastern provinces of Alsace and Lorraine; General Trochu, for treachery to his sovereign in defecting to the side of the republicans; and Adolphe Thiers, president of the republic, for pursuing his habitual lust for power. The *Histoire* was a moral condemnation of the men of *Quatre Septembre*, who could not be brought to account legally since their actions had been ratified after the fact by the National

Assembly's condemnation of the Second Empire in May 1871.[41] Despite signs of hasty editing, Cassagnac's account provides a veritable handbook of anti-republican propaganda from an authoritarian Bonapartist perspective.

Both in this book and in *Le Pays*, Cassagnac's favorite target was Léon Gambetta, who though only a few years older than Cassagnac was incontestably the outstanding figure of French republicanism in the 1870s. He so personified the republic Cassagnac opposed that when he died prematurely (at the age of 44) in 1882, Cassagnac tolled the death-knell of the republic as well.[42] In Cassagnac's many polemics, Gambetta incarnated the eternal Jacobin element of republicanism: he was "Rabagas," the "Red Dauphin,"[43] the authoritarian democrat *par excellence*. In his domination of other republicans, he was also "Caesar."[44] Gambetta's well-known Grenoble speech of 1872, heralding the arrival in power of the *nouvelles couches sociales*, was greeted by Cassagnac as "the formal declaration of war by the *pures*, the sectarians, the jacobins, the rascals, against all that France possesses of monarchist and conservative beliefs."[45] Cassagnac relentlessly castigated Gambetta as a coward (for his flight to San Sebastian after the demise of the provisional government) and as a liar, and repeatedly condemned his political actions as both self-interested and irresponsible. It must be said that Gambetta, insofar as he was instinctively political in his use of issues and of men, provided an excellent target for Cassagnac's barbs.

Although Cassagnac's anti-republican polemics were often spontaneously generated, his most severe assaults took the form of counterattacks to provocations offered by the republicans themselves. Such assaults usually had serious repercussions, often resulting in prosecutions, in duels, or occasionally both. Consequently, the republicans (who knew their man) would bait the young journalist; this sport was a particular delight of the writers at *La République Française*, who, once, in anticipation of a political duel, went so far as to collect Cassagnac's pistol-practice targets to see whether he was improving his aim.[46]

One of Paul de Cassagnac's fiercest onslaughts took place in early June 1874 when, following the election of a Bonapartist candidate to the Assembly from Nièvre, Gambetta attacked Rouher and the Second Empire from the tribune, as "the *misérables* who lost France."[47] In *Le Pays*, Cassagnac returned Gambetta's insults with a vengeance: the republicans, not the imperialists, were the *misérables*, having overthrown their legitimate government "in order to pave the way more surely for the conquering enemy."

You are the *misérables*, the gang of national
defense, tigers or monkeys, Gambetta or Crémieux,
who, ever at the rear, decamped before the Germans,
thrusting as arms against them your lawyers' robes
and drawing only your pens against them, so that you
might spill only your ink (not your blood)!

You are the *misérables*, cowardly administrators,
Falstaffs of the provinces, who drank, ate, smoked,
and called for girls at Marseille, Lyon, and Bordeaux,
while France expended her last cent and her last drop
of blood.[48]

And when Gambetta was reportedly assaulted by a young imperialist at
the Gare Saint-Lazare, several republican deputies who had mocked the
police during the incident were taken into custody, only to be released
on recognizance.

This incident only whetted Cassagnac's journalistic fury. In his
next editorial, he berated the police, as the forces of order, for
accepting insults from the deputies "elected by the *radicaille*," the
forces of disorder, and for not arresting "these sinister men," "sons of
the rioters of June 1848, murderers of the municipal guard," "grandsons
of the executioners of 1793," on the spot!

You are their natural enemies, as the dog is the
enemy of the wolf, as the gendarme is the enemy of
the rascal . . . you must be inflexible with them, and
tolerate no more on their part. You have right on
your side and you represent us all. Make yourselves
respected . . .[49]

The episode at Saint-Lazare and the ensuing press battle swiftly
came to the attention of the Assembly. The angry republicans
interpellated the Minister of the Interior, whom they suspected of being
"soft" on Bonapartism. Shortly thereafter, the Minister of Justice
announced to the session the suspension of three newspapers which had
been particularly offensive: Cassagnac's *Le Pays*, and the republican
newspapers, *Le Rappel* and *Le Siècle*.[50] In addition, *Le Pays* was to be
prosecuted by the government for "provoking hatred and contempt of
citizens toward their compatriots" and "provoking disorder."[51]

The trial brought new notoriety to Paul de Cassagnac and *Le Pays*.
When the government's case came before the Assize Court in early July
1874, the feisty journalist presented his own defense. Ignoring the
stated charges, he argued that *Le Pays*, as the only one of the three
suspended newspapers to be prosecuted, had been subject to
discriminatory treatment. To substantiate his claim, he read to the jury

item after item of equally provocative material that had appeared in the republican press, thus using the courtroom as a platform from which to denounce republican abuses.[52] This was a technique he would frequently employ from that time forth. The jury acquitted Cassagnac of the charges, and his reputation as a fighter who would stand up to the republicans grew quickly.[53] Soon he was mentioned in the press as a prospective candidate for the National Assembly.[54]

The complement to Cassagnac's war on the republic and the republicans in *Le Pays* and the courts was his equally ardent defense of the record of the Second Empire. Cassagnac did not shy away from championing that record in its most controversial aspects, particularly those that many otherwise committed Bonapartists would have preferred to forget: the *coup d'état* of 2 December 1851 and, more recently, Sedan.

Léon Gambetta had been the first to reopen criticism of the *coup d'état*. In 1868 he had defended in court the man who had opened a campaign for a statue to one of its martyrs, the representative Baudin. After 1870 condemnation of the *coup* continued to be a favorite theme among republicans for attacking their fallen foes. Granier de Cassagnac had, by contrast, been the chief apologist for the *coup*, and his son continued the tradition by celebrating its virtues, as well as its necessity, in the press and from the podium, especially after the election in 1873 of Mac-Mahon as president of the republic.[55] A *coup d'état*, Cassagnac wrote in January 1874, was to be distinguished from an *attentat* in that it was executed on behalf of the nation, which must then be consulted on the act by plebiscite. He was firm in justifying an "illegal initiative that could give life to the nation" in the face of a "smothering legality" adequate for the ordinary working of civil and political life but not for resolving the "great crises of a nation." The *coup* of *Deux Décembre* had, after all, been ratified by the nation; the *attentat* of *Quatre Septembre* had not! "The people are the source of all legality. Only they can make or unmake it. They pronouce as the [court of] last resort. And nine times out of ten, they decide in favor of the one who has proved his energy and resolution."[56] From time to time, Cassagnac elaborated on this theme. One notable occasion was his speech at Belleville, Gambetta's own constituency, in December 1875.[57] Another was his speech in the Chamber of Deputies in early 1877, when he challenged the republicans to public debate on the question of the *coup*: "We have been sent here by our electors to defend the acts of 2 December against outrages and to tell you that what you term a crime was both a right and an obligation!"[58]

Besides justifying Louis-Napoleon's *coup*, Paul de Cassagnac defended the person of the former emperor against the vehement insults of the republicans. In late May 1872, for instance, Cassagnac took on Edouard Lockroy, the radical republican editor of *Peuple Souverain* and son-in-law of the emperor's arch-insulter, Victor Hugo, for calling the former emperor "*bandit et lâche.*"[59] Their exchange of insults ended in a duel, as a result of which both gentlemen journalists were sentenced to spend a week in the Conciergerie.[60]

The capitulation of the imperial army at Sedan, however, was the event for which the republicans most often condemned Napoleon III and the Second Empire. Since 1871 the Bonapartists had published a number of tracts devoted precisely to setting the record straight on this issue.[61] In 1874 Paul de Cassagnac determined to demolish the theme of Sedan as a credible complaint against the former regime. He provoked a quarrel in the press with General de Wimpffen, the unsympathetic officer who had claimed the position of commander-in-chief of the First Army from General Ducrot, following Mac-Mahon's disablement, and who had made the fatal decision to fall back on Sedan. It was Wimpffen, Cassagnac insisted, who by making this decision had assured the army's defeat; the emperor was not responsible. Indeed, the emperor's decision to display the flag of truce -- thereby putting an end to the butchery -- was an act of heroic selflessness. Wimpffen, Cassagnac charged, had tried to place the blame elsewhere when it belonged to him alone: "You shift your faults to others; you deny your acts, and you have played the odious role of a man who betrays the emperor, delivering him to the calumnies, hatefulness and lies of his enemies in order to save yourself."[62] A few days later Cassagnac sharpened his provocation by flatly accusing the general of betraying his sovereign, of giving "the dying lion the kick of the . . . republican," and rebuking him for moral impropriety.[63] The general's reply to Paul de Cassagnac was to file suit against him for libel.

By provoking General Wimpffen, Cassagnac stirred the smoldering coals of a long-standing quarrel between the generals who had been present at Sedan during the last days of the war, following the battles of Beaumont and Mouzon. General Ducrot, whom Mac-Mahon had invested as commander, had advocated a retreat through the Ardennes in order to avoid encirclement by the German army; however, Wimpffen, who had just arrived at the battlefront with a secret order from the Ministry of War, designating himself as commander in case anything happened to Mac-Mahon, overruled Ducrot, preferring to mount one more effort, after which the army had no choice but to fall back on Sedan. Their dispute over the feasibility of a retreat raged in print from 1871 onward.[64] The arguments of Ducrot and his colleagues provided the substance of Cassagnac's defense in Wimpffen's suit, which finally came to trial in Assize Court in February 1875. The *procès de Sedan* swiftly became a trial of the entire issue. Through the generals' quarrel, the Bonapartist party hoped to exonerate the emperor from blame for the defeat. The outcome of Cassagnac's case depended on his ability to demonstrate to the jury that Wimpffen had in fact been responsible for placing the army in an inextricable position, thus rendering the capitulation unavoidable.

During three full days of hearings in a courtroom filled with spectators, all the generals who had played a role at Sedan except Wimpffen -- Ducrot, Lebrun, Douay, Faure, Gallifet, Pajol, and Robert -- testified for the defense. The plaintiff's case was presented, most significantly, by the old republican Jules Favre. But the president of the court, in his summary to the jury, adopted much of the defense argument, attributing a large share of responsibility for the Sedan disaster to Wimpffen and depicting the emperor's display of the truce flag in the most heroic terms. The jury acquitted Cassagnac.[65]

The Bonapartists considered this acquittal a victory. Such a trial, remarked one of the most ardent among them, "was worth more to the cause of the empire than six elections."[66] Critics of the Second Empire argued, however, that the exoneration of Napoleon III from direct blame for the defeat was still insufficient to offset his far greater responsibility for the events that had led to the war and his decisions during the early part of the war itself.[67] But the Bonapartist party with Paul de Cassagnac in the lead set about to capitalize on the acquittal by building a legend of the emperor's martyrdom.

* * *

Newspaper polemics and press trials represented one method of warring on the republic and defending the empire. In 1876, however, another method became available, following the election of a number of the younger partisans of the Second Empire to the Chamber of Deputies.

Already in September 1874 Paul de Cassagnac had announced his intention to run for the assembly and, in August 1875, he had begun an unofficial campaign for a seat with a bitter attack on one of the outgoing deputies of Gers, over the latter's support of the "republican" constitution.[68] Indeed, his chances seemed excellent; a police agent quoted the Prefect of Gers as predicting that "if MM. de Cassagnac [father and son] . . . run for the deputation, they will be elected by 30 or 40 thousand votes majority."[69] Such a report could not have been encouraging to the republicans of Gers.

Paul de Cassagnac chose to run in the *arrondissement* of Condom. At the time he announced his candidacy, no republican had declared against him, and he theatrically bewailed the absence of an opponent:

I hope that the republican party, which I have particularly detested all my life, will, at the last minute, do me the honor every honorable man has a right to have -- the honor of being combatted by it.

Triumph without battle is a terrible thing.

I demand an adversary immediately. If you know of one, please have the goodness to send him to me.[70]

Finally a moderate republican, Sigismund Lacroix, entered the race, as did a legitimist, the Marquis de Cugnac.

The campaign in Gers was bitter. *L'Avenir* led the republican drive, which was both anti-Bonapartist and anti-Cassagnac. The legitimists of *Le Conservateur* accepted the truce offered them by the republicans and also campaigned against the Cassagnacs.[71] This alliance of all forces against the imperialist candidates had been predicted by Paul de Cassagnac in a clever campaign pamphlet entitled *Bataille électorale: la revanche du scrutin*, which he published in late 1875. The pamphlet caricatured the royalist, the Orleanist, and a republican named "Gracchus Latripe," and humorously depicted their alliance to defeat a chivalrous young imperialist.[72]

The five imperialist candidates pledged to respect the *Septennat*, as the seven-year term of President de Mac-Mahon was called, but without renouncing loyalty to the empire. They thereby reserved the right to call for a plebiscite on the definitive form of government. With this program they obtained 43 per cent of the registered vote in Gers. The republicans, however, obtained 33 per cent, a considerable increase over the 19 per cent they had won seven years before.[73] In the district of Condom, Paul de Cassagnac was elected on the first ballot, with 9818 votes to a total of 7914 for his two opponents. Cassagnac had obtained 50 per cent of the registered vote and 55 per cent of the votes cast.[74] "The republicans will not pardon the inhabitants of Armagnac for assuring the election of Paul de Cassagnac," wrote the Condom police commissioner after the election.[75]

If the Gers republicans were disconsolate, the Paris radical republicans were secretly overjoyed at Cassagnac's election to the Chamber. It meant that they could attack him from the tribune in ways they could not do in the press.[76] They anticipated, as did the conservatives themselves, that his presence in the Chamber would create tumult. Even the staid *Le Figaro* remarked, "It is hoped that he will be the d'Artagnan of the tribune, just as he was that of the press."[77] Georges Clemenceau, who was almost exactly Cassagnac's age, was one of the first radicals to bait Cassagnac, in hope of provoking a duel. Already in 1874 he had sent his seconds to Cassagnac in defense of republican honor.[78] It had long been rumored among republicans that Paul de Cassagnac was afraid of Clemenceau, who was reputed to be deadly with a pistol.

Paul de Cassagnac was determined to fight the republicans on new grounds. When Clemenceau launched a polemic against him in May 1876, he addressed a witty reply to the "physician without patients, the journalist without talent, the orator without speeches."

There are, Sir, different phases in life.

I have traversed the first, that of ardor, and am now inaugurating another, that of labor, which will lead to the triumph of a great idea and a sacred cause.

You, Sir, are just beginning. Address yourself to someone who can find a more equal proportion between your skin and his.

As for me, I shall duel no more.[79]

In fact Paul de Cassagnac had fought no duels since 1873 and he would not break his resolution until 1878. Henceforth he would wage a new kind of war on the republicans. In order to make clear the nature of Cassagnac's new strategy, it is necessary to describe the political context of 1876.

The Bonapartist group in the Chamber of Deputies was called the party of *Appel au peuple* because its members demanded a plebiscite to determine the form of government. In the elections of 1876, the group more than doubled its representation.[80] More than eighty deputies had been elected. Nearly half of them, like Paul de Cassagnac himself, had come of age under the Second Empire and had known no other political regime during their adult lives. Many, like Cassagnac, were authoritarians and, agreeing on the virtues of the imperial regime, were in no mood to tolerate further insults from the republicans. They were both impatient and belligerent. Few of them respected the parliamentary system of government established by the votes of 1875: in their eyes, the image of such a system was irreparably tarnished by their experience of it during the brief liberal empire and what they had seen of the National Assembly. Thus, they were not at all reluctant to disrupt the parliamentary process itself in order to demand respect for their beliefs.[81]

The younger deputies, especially Cassagnac, Gustave Cunéo

d'Ornano,[82] Robert Mitchell, and Baron Tristan Lambert, appointed themselves avengers of the Second Empire, issuing systematic reprisals from the floor against its insulters. Led by Paul de Cassagnac, they countered insult with insult and provocation with uproar. Their declaration of intent appeared in *Le Pays* on 21 May 1876:

> The Bonapartist deputies are fully resolved to tolerate no outrage to the empire or to its partisans on the part of the republicans.
>
> For long enough the republicans, profiting from their numerical advantage in the old assembly, have insulted everything we love!
>
> But today, now that the party of *Appel au peuple* counts a sufficient number of defenders in the Chamber, our adversaries must renounce their system of insolence and contain themselves within the narrow limits of politeness and parliamentary proprieties.
>
> Republicans, be advised! The Bonapartist deputies will not restrain themselves in safeguarding their personal dignity and enforcing respect of their constituents' sentiments.

During the year 1876 one incident followed another, as the deputies instituted their system of interventions -- a system that earned them disapproving reprimands from many quarters because it so disrupted the legislative process.[83] Their campaign reached a peak in early July, with Gambetta's reference to *"pourriture impérial"* (in response to which Cassagnac suggested that the republic was a *"fumier"* or dung heap), and another peak in November, when Gambetta extemporized on "the clerical fanaticism which animated that Spaniard whom somebody made empress of the French," in an effort to insinuate a connection between the loss of Alsace-Lorraine and the diabolical influence of the Church.[84] Their arrogance was untempered by criticism. In January 1877 Cassagnac wrote in *Le Pays*:

> We are not in the Chamber of Deputies to play at parliamentarism; on the contrary, we are there to destroy it if need be.
>
> The forms are good for the geese of the trade.
>
> What we must do is speak out to the public, speak out by the windows to the crowd. We must command respect. We must render injury for injury, scorn for scorn. We must rehabilitate the misconstrued acts of the empire, destroy the calumnies and lies, and prepare the return of our Prince Imperial.

This is our duty. There is no other . . . .[85]

The disruptions continued well into 1877, reaching a climax in June of that year following President de Mac-Mahon's dismissal of the Simon ministry, when not only Paul de Cassagnac but also Robert Mitchell and Ernest Dréolle were censured by the Chamber for their provocations and intemperance.[86]

The behavior of the younger deputies scandalized the older and more moderate members of the Bonapartist party. They were shocked by the unbridled audacity of "Captain Fracassagnac" and his troops.[87] But this same behavior appealed greatly to another clientele, admittedly more radical, those to whom Cassagnac and his band were popular heroes, symbols of an ardent, virile imperialism, those who yearned for agitation, movement, and action in what seemed to be an otherwise stodgy parliamentary party and who believed that the strength of Bonapartism lay in its audacity. As certain radical republicans themselves admitted:

> In France, rightly or wrongly, audacity is admired and the appearance of force is irresistibly seductive. There is no country in the world where what is commonly called moderation is more impolitic. Whoever hesitates is seen to be afraid and is scorned . . . . Even when daring has no material results, it has an inappreciable moral result. It is self-imposing.[88]

On the strength of his audacity, Cassagnac had one police agent convinced that he possessed sufficient moral force to summon some twenty thousand Bonapartists into the street.[89] It must be remarked, however, that Cassagnac never used his popularity to incite mob action; he never employed or even threatened to employ mass violence in order to restore the empire. He was convinced that the republic would inevitably dissolve into a state of anarchy, and that the return of the empire was foreordained. He regarded turmoil in the streets as undesirable and unnecessary. Had he been less scrupulous and more power-hungry in his own right, his political career might have taken quite a different turn.

* * *

Instead Paul de Cassagnac chose another approach, shifting his attention from the acts of republican partisans while coming to power to their conduct while in power. From the time of the passage of the constitutional laws that established the Third Republic in 1875,

Cassagnac made it his task to point out the discrepancies between theory and practice of liberty under republican government. The republic claimed liberty as its guiding principle. Therefore, he insisted, the republic must be judged on its own terms. It must not be allowed to practice a double standard, one set of values while in opposition, another while in power.[90] Thus far, he asserted, the record of the republic was miserable. Under the republic, the once-proud goddess of Liberty (whom the republicans had adopted as their symbol) had become a fallen woman, nothing more than a streetwalker.[91] Indeed, the sexual slur, *"la gueuse,"* which translates loosely as "the slut," later became a synonym in Cassagnac's polemical vocabulary for the republic itself.[92]

One of Cassagnac's favorite targets for criticism of this kind was the legislation governing the periodical press during the 1870s, a subject about which many republicans who had long advocated freedom of the press were especially sensitive. Cassagnac was well aware of the embarrassment for republican ministers that could result from enforcing these laws, and he chose to exploit it by inviting prosecution.[93] If the republic stood for freedom of the press, he argued, why did it not practice this freedom instead of maladroitly applying the repressive laws and techniques of the old monarchies? Cassagnac bore down on this point in the months from March 1876 to May 1877 and from February to December 1879, during the ministries of the liberal republicans Jules Dufaure, Jules Simon, and William Waddington.

Although the Chamber of Deputies eventually adopted a new and freer press law, this was not accomplished until 1881. In the meantime the ministers of the new regime were confronted with the dilemma Cassagnac chose to exploit: either they must enforce the provisions of the existing laws, with which many of them disagreed in principle, or they must ignore the challenges to public authority coming from both Right and extreme Left and thereby incur any weakening of the authority of their regime which might result from leaving such abuse unpunished.

The legal framework governing the French press from 1875 to 1881 was an amalgam of laws that included decrees dating from 1848-1849 as well as Napoleon III's decree of 17 February 1852 (minus some of its provisions). These measures had been re-adopted with certain changes by the National Assembly in 1871 and confirmed in their most recent form on 29 December 1875. Although the Assembly had retained many of the press offenses defined in the laws of 1848-1849, which were originally subject to jury trial and punishable by heavy fines and prison sentences, it transferred jurisdiction over most of these from the Assize courts (which the majority regarded as too lenient) to the three-man tribunals of *police correctionnelle*. The Assembly had left only one offense, attack against the government of the republic, to the discretion of the jury.[94] This change in jurisdiction was highly unpopular in liberal circles, where trial by jury was an article of faith. By the following year, therefore, it was on the docket for repeal.

In effect, Paul de Cassagnac had been indirectly responsible for the change of jurisdiction written into the press law of 29 December 1875.[95] Earlier that month he had been acquitted by the jury of Assizes on a charge of "provoking hatred and contempt of the government," a verdict that, as *L'Année politique* remarked, only justified the opinion of those "who thought it illusory to expect the punishment of press offenses by the criminal courts."[96] However, Cassagnac's acquittal was doubtless attributable to two extenuating circumstances. First, the government had placed itself on questionable ground by prosecuting him for remarks made not in the press directly, but in a speech he had delivered to a private gathering -- which had then been reprinted in full by *Le Gaulois* and *Le Pays*.[97] Second, while Cassagnac's remarks concerning the republic were certainly irreverent, the passages chosen for prosecution, which ridiculed the contrast between the ideal republic and the republic in practice, were hardly as seditious as the public prosecutor claimed them to be.[98]

Nevertheless, after this setback, the new premier, Jules Dufaure, who as Minister of Justice in the Buffet cabinet had sponsored Cassagnac's earlier prosecution, was reluctant to sponsor another such abortive prosecution in 1876, especially since Cassagnac had since been elected to the Chamber and could no longer be prosecuted without that body's consent.[99] Dufaure's successor, Jules Simon, did not share Dufaure's reservations; despite Simon's reputation as a liberal's liberal on the subject of freedom of the press, he felt obliged as head of the government to prosecute the worst offenders of the existing press laws in order to assert the new regime's authority. Simon first laid himself open to severe criticism from both the radical republicans and the Right when, in mid-February 1877, he asked the Chamber to stiffen the penalties attached to the laws in force, in order to deal with a provocative press, "which takes the liberty not only of discussing the acts of the ministers who sit on these benches, but of attacking the principle of republican government itself and advocating its overthrow."[100] Later in the month, Simon's government announced its intention to prosecute Cassagnac and *Le Pays* for "offense to the Chamber of Deputies," "provoking hatred and contempt for the government of the republic," "provoking hatred and contempt of

citizens for one another," and "offense to the constitution." These
offenses were all defined under the legislation of 1848-1849.[101] Since
Cassagnac was a deputy, consent of the Chamber to the prosecution was
required, and this circumstance gave rise to a stormy session in mid-
March.

As in 1875 the government's key charge against Cassagnac was that
of "provoking hatred and contempt for the government of the republic."
This was the measure that provoked both Simon's attack and
Cassagnac's defense during discussion in the Chamber, and that
constituted the central issue in the ensuing Assize Court trial. Like
most press offenses, this one depended on definition. As in his 1875
trial, Paul de Cassagnac persisted in arguing that his attacks on the
republic had nothing specifically to do with the government instituted by
the laws of 1875 and the seven-year term of its president:

> For me, the word "Republic" is a kind of general
> unity, a kind of allegory . . . For me, in my way of
> thinking, when I attack the republic, I attack it in its
> moral ensemble, in its historic ensemble. My attacks
> do not apply particularly to today's republic.[102]

Despite such ingenuous disclaimers, neither the Chamber nor the jury
could entirely forget that Cassagnac's criticism of liberty as practiced by
the republic were aimed directly at the ministry and, indeed, at Simon
himself, as when Cassagnac had relentlessly maligned him for hypocrisy
on reaching power. In April the jury convicted Cassagnac for offense to
the government of the republic, although it absolved him on the other
charges.[103] The court sentenced him to two months in prison and fined
him a total sum of five thousand francs.[104]

Neither the conviction nor the penalties it carried with it sufficed to
chasten Paul de Cassagnac. Assessing the results of his encounter with
justice, he wrote:

> On establishing the balance -- having expressed to
> the republic my scarcely affectionate sentiments, to M.
> Jules Simon and others the disdainful pity they inspire
> in me, and having offered the spectacle of an entire
> government hard on the heels of one man -- I declare
> that it was worth it, although a bit expensive. But
> then, as everybody knows, everything is more
> expensive nowadays.[105]

He reserved the right to begin his attacks again, whenever it pleased
him to do so.

Cassagnac's next opportunity to criticize the republicans on their
application of freedom of the press came in 1879, following the political

crisis known to history as *Seize Mai*. A year-long postponement, the invalidation of his election, and his re-election in early 1879 delayed Cassagnac's return to the Chamber. At once he resumed the onslaught he had begun in 1876, this time directing it against the Waddington ministry. Taking his cue from a statement published by the Ministry of the Interior on freedom of the press, he again attacked the gap between republican theory and practice of liberty. The republicans, he charged, were powerless to give liberty or to understand properly the principle of authority. Once their utter incapacity was clearly demonstrated to the country, Cassagnac prophesied:

> when it is clear that you have overthrown the monarchy without being capable of doing better or even of doing differently . . . your Third Republic will meet the same fate as the two others: a wind, a wind of disgust will rise up from the four corners of our country and sweep it away.[106]

For such articles as this, a republican ministry once again brought Cassagnac to trial for offenses against the government of the republic, in a final test case of the enforceability of the old laws.

When the Chamber met to consider the authorization of his prosecution, Paul de Cassagnac presented a masterful defense of his position. Invoking a celebrated analogy, he compared his situation to that of Henri Rochefort in 1870, faced with prosecution under laws which the imperial government had itself declared defunct. He recounted in detail the arguments of Rochefort's defenders in the Chamber, the irreconcilable republicans of only a few years previous, Arago, Picard, Crémieux, and Gambetta himself, who had argued in favor of total freedom of the press and had invoked the utter immunity from prosecution that must characterize the deputy's mandate. Thus he cunningly confronted the republicans in power with the arguments they had used when in opposition, and he challenged the republican Minister of Justice to reply by repeating the speech of Émile Ollivier, against which he himself would employ the arguments of the empire to demolish the position of the republican minister. Cassagnac's clever oratorical strategy provoked tumult in the Chamber. The minister left the Chamber without rising to the bait, and in a second speech Cassagnac let it be known that his trial would serve as a display for all republican press abuse against the conservative party, Christian families, and the clergy, which had been left unprosecuted while he himself was being brought to trial.[107] Despite Cassagnac's diabolical eloquence the Chamber lifted his immunity and authorized the suit. A few weeks later the jury of the Assize Court acquitted him once again, following a heavily-attended trial.[108] It was the last such prosecution to be held under the old press laws.

* * *

Paul de Cassagnac's war against the republic and the republicans was indeed a war of principle -- an ideological war. In retrospect, one may challenge both his philosophical premises and criticize his use of history, but one cannot doubt the sincerity of his convictions. His fear of social disorder stemming from a breakdown of authority was genuine and quite typical in his milieu at the time, although the way in which he expressed it upon occasion may have seemed extreme even to his co-believers.

Cassagnac captured the popular imagination of many in the 1870s by the aggressiveness of his campaigns against things republican. The flamboyant, extravagantly romantic manner in which he dared to challenge the republicans -- the polemics, the duels, the trials, the *tapage* in the Chamber -- won him a sizeable audience and gave him an influence that could not be ignored. By early 1878 one enthusiastic admirer could write: "For the French people, who summarize an entire idea in one man, . . . the unremitting struggle against the republic is called Cassagnac."[109]

CHAPTER IV

IMPÉRIALISME AND THE CRUSADE FOR THE EMPIRE
1871-1877

Voilà la légende, la légende du jour, celle qui
calme les angoisses et fait luire l'espérance chez ceux
qui souffrent et qui ont peur.

Le chapeau du petit caporal s'est retourné sur la
tête de l'empereur et est devenu le chapeau du sergent
de ville. Au lieu d'être en travers, il est en long.

Le deuxième empire est revenu grâce à la légende
militaire du premier.

Le troisième empire reviendra grâce à la légende
autoritaire du second.

Le deuxième avait pour raison Austerlitz.

Le troisième aura pour raison le 2 décembre.

Le sentiment de la fierté nationale a rappelé
Napoléon III.

Le sentiment de la sécurité publique rappellera
Napoléon IV le jour où la France, menacée par la
revanche révolutionnaire qui s'annonce, comprendra
que lui seul est capable de rassurer les bons et de faire
trembler les méchants.

Paul de Cassagnac
Le Pays, 13 February 1877

Paul de Cassagnac's relationship to the Bonapartist party during the 1870s was more complex than historians have recognized to date. It is apparent from Cassagnac's ardent defense of the Second Empire and the imperial dynasty that he was interested in returning them to power in order to counter the republic. It does not, however, follow that he was simply another Bonapartist, working for the restoration of the dynasty. His conception of the empire led to distinctive conclusions, and these gave him a particular place in Bonapartist party politics. To clarify this point has been difficult because of the lack of a comprehensive study of the Bonapartist party and its personnel after 1870.[1] Such clarification must nevertheless be attempted in order to understand Cassagnac's position.

Bonapartists themselves have usually claimed to stand above parties, while historians have commonly spoken of the Napoleonic tradition -- of Bonapartism -- both during and after the Second Empire, as having two wings: a Left or "republican" wing identified with Prince Jerome-Napoleon Bonaparte, cousin of the emperor, and a Right or "monarchical" wing identified with the Empress Eugenie and the Prince Imperial.[2] Each of these categories contains a partial truth. The Napoleonic tradition did combine liberal aspirations and authoritarian organization in various mixtures at different times, leading to widely differing interpretations of the significance of the tradition as a whole.[3]

After Louis-Napoleon founded the Second Empire, the bulk of declared Bonapartists were firmly monarchist, and after the fall of the regime in 1870, they were primarily interested in restoring the imperial monarchy (and themselves to office), much like their counterparts who supported the two other fallen dynasties. The republican elements of Bonapartism fell into disrepute during that time, due in part to identification with the controversial Prince Napoleon. Only after 1877 did republican Bonapartism begin to attract adherents and not until the 1890s would it be represented by an organized party whose platform included election of the president and the Senate by universal manhood suffrage.

Paul de Cassagnac, like his father, was entrenched in the monarchical wing of Bonapartism, but he added to it an original element. When his father's old adversary Émile de Girardin challenged him, in 1875, to a public discussion of whether the "true" Napoleonic tradition was republican or "conservative" (a synonym for monarchical at the time), Cassagnac impatiently dismissed the terms of debate as Girardin had stated them.[4] To the doctrinaire Cassagnac, it was the "Imperial idea" rather than some "Napoleonic idea" that summed up the political contribution made to France by the reigns of two Napoleons; it was authoritarian monarchy tempered by plebiscitary democracy that was the fruit and meaning of the work of Napoleon I and Napoleon III, and no mere cult of personality enshrined in the representatives of a fragile dynasty. Cassagnac's doctrine of *Impérialisme* (which is not to be confused with the later colonial-economic expansionist use of the word "Imperialism" made popular by Hobson and Lenin) can be summed up as a system of plebiscitary monarchy -- a form of political authority that is "not despotic but firm, implacable toward disorder and well-disposed toward all things honest and patriotic."[5]

Both empire and republic were, in Cassagnac's view, democratic systems. Both had their roots in the Revolution of 1789 and thus acknowledged the principle of sovereignty of the nation. He objected to the thesis put forth by Girardin that empires necessarily followed republics and were therefore vassal forms of republics.[6] To Cassagnac, empire and republic were antithetical and irreconcilable forms of democracy. The logical resolution of the first was in a unique authority; that of the latter was in anarchy.

For Paul de Cassagnac, latter-day Imperialism was incarnated for France in the institutions established by the Constitution of 1852 (which was itself modeled on the Constitution of the Year VIII). The full significance of this belief for Cassagnac's subsequent political career becomes clear when one realizes that he did not consider a Bonaparte family member essential to the implementation of the system. Although historically the empire had been represented by the Bonapartes, the survival of the system of authoritarian democracy in no way depended on the fate of that dynasty. In fact, as early as 1872 Cassagnac had proclaimed himself an Imperialist rather than a Bonapartist. "What we desire is a system, not a family; any family is satisfactory, on the condition that it practices the system."[7] "I will rally openly to whatever government gives me the system of 1852, although I would regret not being privileged to see it practiced by the dynasty I love and prefer."[8] In 1873 Cassagnac spelled out his position in even more explicit terms:

> The true definition of an Imperialist is this: you are Imperialist when you are a partisan of the imperial system.
>
> You are Bonapartist when, being a partisan of the imperial system, you insist that the system be practiced by the Bonaparte family to the exclusion of every other.
>
> Thus, to be Imperialist predominates over the extinction of the Bonaparte family and transcends its disappearance; it is a principle, a system independent of persons and extending beyond them.
>
> To be Bonapartist is only a preference, a personal affection -- a sentiment, in a word.[9]

In *Le Pays*, Cassagnac pointedly employed the term "party of the empire" rather than "Bonapartist party" to describe himself and his colleagues.

Paul de Cassagnac's formulation of the doctrine of Imperialism can, in part, be attributed to his dislike for Napoleon III's experiment with the liberalization of the Empire. But it was also the product of his distaste for the person and politics of Prince Jerome-Napoleon Bonaparte. Prince Napoleon (as he was habitually called -- except by Cassagnac, who used the more familiar form, Prince Jerome) would fall heir to the imperial throne if anything happened to the emperor's only son, the Prince Imperial. Since Prince Napoleon, in addition to being considered personally overbearing and offensive,[10] was a proclaimed republican and a confirmed anticlerical, the prospect of his succession was highly unpalatable to the greater number of party sympathizers, who much preferred the monarchist Catholic orientation of Eugenie and her son. Consequently, Prince Napoleon, who had been highly unpopular with the imperialists during the Second Empire, found himself increasingly isolated after its fall and Napoleon III's death, which left the exiled Eugenie as regent for her son.[11]

Paul de Cassagnac cordially detested Prince Napoleon (who reciprocated the feeling) and he frequently attacked the "César déclassé"[12] for his anticlericalism and republican sympathies. "I would break my pen rather than serve such a master," Cassagnac wrote in 1869 during one of his fiercer journalistic onslaughts against the undesirable cousin.[13] Cassagnac's Imperialist doctrine thus allowed him to devote his energies to the promotion of the imperial system while avoiding the prospect of personal allegiance to Prince Napoleon just because he happened to be a Bonaparte. "If the Prince Imperial were to die," Cassagnac wrote prophetically in 1873, "Prince Jerome-Napoleon would become the direct and legitimate heir to the throne. In that case I would remain an Imperialist, but on my honor I would certainly be a Bonapartist no longer!"[14]

Cassagnac's profession of Imperialism was unsettling both to dynasts of various persuasions and to their anti-monarchist foes who, in the words of Daniel Halévy, believed that "monarchy is a man, a dynasty; monarchy is the least abstract of regimes. It is real and personal or it is nothing."[15] By 1873 the dynastic Bonapartists distrusted Paul de Cassagnac for the same reason that Orleanists distrusted Adolphe Thiers, who in 1867 had proclaimed his devotion to the system of parliamentary monarchy without specification of person.[16] Each was considered capable, for the sake of realizing his abstract system, of defecting the princely family that represented that system.[17] From the viewpoint of a dynastic political party, such abstractions of monarchism, exalting institutional principle above personal loyalty to the princes of a particular family, constituted rank heresy. Yet the attitudes displayed by dynastic parties were not representative of popular feeling. After nearly twenty years of imperial government in France, there were unquestionably more imperialists than Bonapartists among the general populace. In the provinces especially, people had become accustomed to see in the political system of the Second Empire the very incarnation of conservative government.[18] Consequently, Cassagnac's Imperialism found its audience among the broader population, if not among the Bonapartist party leaders, the "Pharisees" as he called them, who "consider the return of the empire uniquely as the return of their meal-ticket."[19]

* * *

In consequence of his doctrinal conception of empire, Paul de Cassagnac viewed the role and tactics of the Bonapartist party very differently than did its nominal leaders, of whom the most prominent was Eugène Rouher.[20] As "vice-emperor" from 1863 until 1869, and head of the party following the death of Napoleon III in January 1873, Rouher enjoyed an unchallenged eminence among his colleagues, though he proved to be a less forceful and less imaginative leader than his party required. He had never, as one of his contemporaries remarked, been in "the position of a Cavour or a Bismarck vis-à-vis his sovereign, imposing his opinion as the need arise," but had "preferred to be only the brilliant advocate of the too-often vacillating will of the crown."[21]

Both Rouher and Cassagnac were authoritarians and antiparliamentary in their basic political outlook. But Rouher was the flexible servant of a prince; Cassagnac, the uncompromising partisan of a system. Rouher's aim, the restoration of the Bonaparte dynasty within the reasonably near future, was essentially short-range; Cassagnac's aim, the re-establishment of an imperial system of government, was longer-range and more encompassing. And while Rouher, like a great many Bonapartists, believed that the ambitions of the house of Orleans constituted the greatest threat to a Bonapartist restoration, Cassagnac was far more concerned about the danger posed to the fabric of French society by the republicans, and discounted the Orleanist rivalry as little more than a nuisance.[22] No doubt these differences in perspective can be explained in part by differences between the two men in age and political experience. But there was a temperamental difference too: as Schnerb described it, "Rouher had his moments of bluntness and anger, but he detested the use of polemic as a habitual tactic."[23] In Rouher's view, newspapers and their editors were useful allies to be utilized as needed, but he did not consider it necessary to include them in the councils of the party, where deputies and old notables and family friends discussed actions to be taken.[24] What is more, the conflict between Rouher and Cassagnac may have also been exacerbated by a long-standing personal animosity based on a relationship between the young journalist and Rouher's daughter that could only have made a meeting of minds on political questions more difficult.[25]

Furthermore, Paul de Cassagnac was far more convinced than Rouher that the empire could not be restored by the efforts of its partisans alone. Acting by itself, he declared fatalistically, the party of the empire could do nothing, since the regime could never be restored without majority approval.[26] "The Empire," Cassagnac wrote, "is a remedy to a predictable malady feared by us. If the malady does not develop, the remedy will remain with the pharmacist, sealed in apothecary jars, and nobody will complain in the least."[27] While Cassagnac was skeptical that any true republic could possibly maintain order, he nevertheless challenged the advocates of a "conservative republic" (of whom there were a number in the early 1870s) to do so. During his 1875 debate with Girardin, Cassagnac wrote:

> Our devotion to the Empire is not so blind that we want to impose this form of government on France at any cost; we have often said as much to the republicans. If they render the Empire useless through their wisdom, their intelligence, their patriotism, their honorability, we would be the first to proclaim joyfully, "We do not need to establish the Empire!

> But if -- as has already happened twice in history -- the republic is powerless not only to save the country, but to give her that sum of tranquility, repose, and well-being to which she has a right for her daily life, that would be another matter.[28]

And a few days later he reiterated:

> The Empire, Sir, will return only if your Republic fails to keep its promises of order and security.

> Otherwise it will never return; it would have no reason to do so.

> It's up to you and your friends to fend it off.[29]

The best interests of France, not the immediate interests either of the imperial family or its supporters, must be the criteria governing any return of the imperial system of authoritarian democracy. France herself must choose! Paul de Cassagnac seems to have believed that France *would* choose -- that a plebiscite would one day be held and French citizens would recognize that their interests could best be safeguarded by the return of the empire.

Even before the death of Napoleon III in early 1873, Paul de Cassagnac and his supporters, the imperialists whom he called "*les jeunes*," were in open revolt against Rouher and his coterie, those Cassagnac later accused of decorating their garments with "life-size eagles and violets as big as your fist."[30] But from that time on the dissatisfaction of "*les jeunes*" became far more pronounced. Although Cassagnac constantly criticized inactivity, he was far from pleased with the activity undertaken by Rouher and his colleagues. Time and time again he issued harsh judgments of political actions directed to the exclusive benefit of the dynasty. France's interest, he reiterated, not that of the dynasty, must come first.[31]

Challenging the party leader whose moral dominance was reinforced by his control of funds, both for newspaper subsidies and electoral expenses, could be a risky business. A challenger required a semi-independent position in order to risk such a confrontation. Fortunately for Cassagnac he enjoyed such a position, due to the measured support he received from the empress-regent Eugenie. Although women were barred from occupying the imperial throne, they could serve as regent, and as regent from 1873 on Eugenie was in a position of almost unrestricted influence over the still underage Prince Imperial.[32] She was considered by some as the "legitimist" member of the imperial family, Spanish in her authoritarianism and her ultra-Catholicism, and she was known to be sympathetic to the impetuosity and independent opinions of Paul de Cassagnac, who in turn had sometimes been referred to as the empress's cavalier.[33] It was apparently Eugenie who subsidized *Le Pays* -- which may explain why Rouher had difficulties in bringing Cassagnac to heel.[34]

* * *

The Imperialists and the dynastic Bonapartists disagreed on where to look for allies among existing political factions. The Bonapartist party as a whole seemed to drift toward a "conservative alliance" with the other monarchist parties in the National Assembly. But this tendency troubled the dynastic Bonapartists and virtually split the party into two distinct camps. The conservative alliance question had arisen before the death of Napoleon III, but it became far more acute in the ensuing years as Rouher searched for an orientation that would attract the widest possible popular following behind the Bonapartist cause.

In Rouher's estimation, an alliance with the legitimists and Orleanists had some attractions. But it also appeared to offer a snare that could imperil the very future of the Bonapartist cause by saddling it with unpopular allies, from whom it might be wiser to remain aloof. Moreover, Rouher saw advantages in keeping the party free to contract occasional parliamentary alliances with the republicans, thereby enabling the Bonapartists to navigate a path between the royalists and the republicans without coming down irrevocably on either side. Such a strategy would have to be adroitly engineered to succeed, and it soon became apparent that Rouher was not the man to implement it.[35]

As early as 1872 the Imperialists had begun to exploit the undeniable natural sympathy that existed between them and their royalist (both legitimist and Orleanist) colleagues.[36] This development was hailed as a novelty only by those who ignored the common bonds of religion, social status, and authoritarian ideas that united partisans of the two groups.[37] In fact, after the fall of the Second Empire many members of the royalist Right never demonstrated more than a token hostility to the imperial system. As Pierre de Coubertin (who became famous for his efforts to reinstitute the Olympic Games) later attested:

> If they lacked an attachment to the imperial dynasty, most of the royalists had a taste for the things of the Empire; they liked its manner of governing and regretted, deep in their hearts, that their prince hadn't been the first to make use of it. The "conservative" alliance that formed between the partisans of the diverse monarchic regimes was not as artificial as was believed for a long time. The conservatives were divided by the name much more than by the nature of the solution: their wishes on most points were identical.[38]

They too were Imperialists of a sort. Among legitimists, except the so-called *chevau-légers* (whose mystical personal devotion to the Comte de Chambord precluded any alternative), many would prefer the empire to the parliamentary monarchy that threatened them under the house of Orleans. During the months after the death of Napoleon III, in fact, a group of legitimists enthusiastically supported a fanciful scheme whereby their aging and childless pretender would "adopt" the Prince Imperial, and thereby disinherit his Orleans cousins.[39] This adventure ended later in the summer, when Chambord accepted the "submission" of the Orleans princes.

Even some Orleanists, though hardly sympathetic to the Imperialists' antiparliamentary bias, acknowledged the force of the empire's claims to save the endangered social order by competing against it for that honor.[40] These were the men who, as Cassagnac later put it, "desired an authoritarian coup for a liberal reign."[41] But

Orleanists such as the Duc Albert de Broglie and Louis Buffet, who moderated overt hostilities against the Bonapartists in return for their cooperation in the Assembly, were constantly criticized by anti-Bonapartist Orleanists such as the Duc Edme d'Audiffret-Pasquier, the Duc Louis Decazes, and Jules Dufaure. These men shared the personal hostility felt by the Orleans princes toward the Bonapartes, who had expropriated them in the 1850s. Those Orleanists prepared to cooperate with Bonapartists were sensitive to the demand for "moral order" but also, as committed liberals, to the accusation that they were playing into the hands of the empire.[42] Hence, as long as the Orleanists thought they had a chance to install a liberal, parliamentary regime, most were reluctant to cooperate with the overtly authoritarian Bonapartists.

What brought the Imperialists from all three monarchist parties together was their similar perception of the menace posed by "the revolution" in its most recent incarnation as radical republicanism. Indeed, it was precisely the felt necessity to defend the Catholic and hierarchical social order that had originally enabled the authoritarian empire to take root in France.[43] It was to the same sector of opinion that the Bishop of Orleans, Félix Dupanloup, appealed in his pamphlets against atheism and the social peril during the later years of the Second Empire.[44] And it was likewise this sector of opinion, one well-represented in the National Assembly of 1871-1875, that Paul de Cassagnac addressed when he spoke of "repelling the invasion of the social barbarians, of the republicans," and of "sending this last republic back into that chaos without name from whence it came."[45]

Cassagnac became the staunchest advocate in the Bonapartist camp of a political alliance joining all parties of the monarchist Right -- legitimist, Orleanist, and Bonapartist -- based on the principle of social defense. Indeed, the theme of conservative alliance would become a guiding principle for Cassagnac's political actions throughout his career in French political life. To him, the alliance of conservatives represented the most effective tactic for waging war against the hated republic.

The journalist-deputy first proposed such a tactical alliance in June 1872, in an article entitled "Where are we going?", published in *Le Pays*.[46] Addressing the other monarchist parties, he invoked the results of recent elections that had just sent three more radical republicans to the Assembly. The radicals had won, Cassagnac insisted, only because the conservative effort was fragmented. The monarchist parties insisted on competing with one another. Since the National Assembly, having declared itself constituent, had thereby placed itself *above* the people, the stage was set (in his opinion) for its invasion by the radicals.

Political forces in France were beginning to polarize between republicans and imperialists; Orleanists and legitimists were both destined to disappear from the political scene unless they united their efforts with those of the imperialists. Monarchists, he believed, had no choice but to form an electoral alliance in subsequent elections, to join forces in an effort to deal with the revolutionary threat before it was too late:

> In the presence of the great danger that menaces our country, we must abandon, at least for the time being, the legitimate claims of our political hopes. Will you do as we do, loyally and honorably? Before determining who will reign over France, do you wish to save her?

Cassagnac suggested that in the future, the three parties should decide jointly on the single, strongest candidate in each constituency and unite behind him, irrespective of whether he were a professed Bonapartist, legitimist or Orleanist.

The renunciation of separate party ambitions was both the essence of Cassagnac's proposal and the greatest obstacle to its achievement. Much mistrust did exist within each of the three parties as to the motives of its rivals. Few were disposed to accept at face value the unauthorized disclaimers of ambition that Cassagnac issued on behalf of the imperial cause:

> . . . Even if we had a majority in the Assembly, we would never consent to seize power by means of a parliamentary intrigue. We do not intend to return by other means than the free consultation of universal suffrage. And even if the people should call us back, you are too reasonable to oppose the national will. If France wants the empire, you may perhaps not wish to support it, but your patriotism prohibits you from preventing its return.

Nor were the other dynastic parties disposed to issue such disclaimers on behalf of their own causes. Yet the simplicity of Cassagnac's proposal made it seductive, especially as it offered the only practical electoral solution to the otherwise fatal fragmentation of the monarchist Right. Although no electoral alliances sprang forth in immediate response to Cassagnac's appeal, neither did his idea fall on totally deaf ears.

The legitimists were the first to appear receptive to Cassagnac's advances. During the summer and fall of 1872, they pursued an alliance in the Assembly with the deputies of *Appel au peuple*. By the end of the year, it had an effect. Following Thiers' declarations on the subject of a "conservative republic" in November and the formation of a legislative committee to study proposals for constitutional organization, the Bonapartists suddenly began to oppose dissolution of the Assembly, in order to retain the majority held by the forces for social order in that body.[47] Such was the thrust of a joint manifesto published in early December by the three Bonapartist newspapers, *Le Pays*, *L'Ordre* (which was not yet under Rouher's control), and *Le Gaulois*, urging that the defense of social order be put ahead of the immediate interests of any dynasty. Upon its publication, Rouher had hastened to England to consult with the exiled Napoleon III about the Cassagnacs' deleterious influence on the press (Granier de Cassagnac was then assisting Dugué de la Fauconnerie at *L'Ordre*). Later in the month, Paul de Cassagnac himself scurried to Chislehurst for the express purpose of explaining the politics of *les jeunes* to the emperor.[48]

After the death of Napoleon III, the Bonapartist-legitimist alliance in the Assembly directed its efforts against Thiers, whose flirtation with the republicans had become increasingly pronounced. Another round of by-elections had been scheduled for late April 1873 and one of the vacant seats was in Paris. Consequently, Cassagnac renewed his appeal for a tactical alliance, this time between Bonapartists and legitimists; in Paris the two groups should choose a "neutral" candidate, while in the provinces the predominant group in each department should receive support from the others for its nominee.[49] To the great displeasure of Rouher, who wanted to run a Bonapartist in Paris, both *Le Pays* and *Le Gaulois* pressed for a neutral conservative candidate not favorable to Thiers. In mid-April, nine conservative newspapers sponsored a joint meeting for the purpose of nominating such a man.[50] But by that time the Paris election had already become a race between Thiers' man, the venerable Charles de Rémusat, and the radical republican Barodet, who won by a wide margin.[51] The initiative of the imperialist newspapers, tactically shrewd as it was in principle, thus proved abortive; it merely contributed an insignificant third candidate to an election whose focus had already been determined.

In the National Assembly, the legitimists and Bonapartists soon took their revenge on Thiers, whose professions of conservatism they still distrusted. Led by the Duc de Broglie, they detached a critical number of Center and Center-Right deputies from Thiers' majority and forced him to resign. Thiers was quick to sow the seeds of discord by insinuating that Broglie and his colleagues were dupes, acting in effect for the empire, but the coalition held. The new majority accepted

Thiers' resignation and elected the Marshal de Mac-Mahon president of the republic.

"For several months," wrote Paul de Cassagnac after Thiers' ouster, "The men of the government that just fell before public disgust ingenuously repeated that the republic must be proclaimed, since we, the monarchists were incapable due to our divisions of re-establishing a monarchy in France."

>Thus, we have an imperious obligation to prove to these men that, although we have overthrown their republic, we did not do it in order to satisfy our miserable dynastic ambitions. When the royalists and imperialists came together to rid France of a government that only aggravated her deterioration with every passing day, there was no question of founding a monarchy of whatever kind. Not for a single instant!

>France is not yet ripe for any definitive government, and he who would give her a royal or imperial form at this moment would be as bad a citizen as he who tried only yesterday to impose his abhorred republic. The "*provisoire*" is the only thing that suits us today. We must conserve it, for as the *provisoire* represents the truce of the monarchial parties, it is our supreme guarantee.[52]

Thus did Paul de Cassagnac conceive of the government of "moral order" headed by Mac-Mahon and the Duc de Broglie.

In subsequent issues of *Le Pays*, Cassagnac urged the new government to take firm measures against its republican adversaries. He was unapologetic for his authoritarian concept of what should be done: "it is insufficient to win; we must profit from the victory." He cited the precedent set by the republicans themselves:

>See how they proceeded! Scarcely were they in power when they . . . proclaimed the republic as definitive. They denounced the conservatives on every occasion, excluding them from positions, combatting them to the hilt in elections, and in general, considering France as their own preserve . . . . They intended to establish the provisional government against us; we intend to establish it against them. They chased us out; we will chase them out. They excluded us; we will exclude them. They did everything in the world to annul us; we are disposed to make the same effort so that we hear no more talk of them.[53]

The republicans must be put out of action! "They are the gangrenous limb that must be amputated." They are "public enemies, the Albigensians, the Camisards, the Saracens of our time . . . ." "Between conservatives and republicans, it is war to the death; since they have not and will not spare us, it would be stupid of us to exert ourselves to be nice to them, would it not?"[54]

With this rhetorical call to civil war, Cassagnac brought down on his head a deluge of criticism from within his own party. The liberal Bonapartists were especially incensed, and one of them, Albert Duruy, opened fire on Cassagnac in *La Liberté* for compromising the cause he wished to serve by advocating such extreme measures.[55] Cassagnac countered by arguing, citing examples from the recent history of France, that "all our civil disorders are the unique product of the indecisive, drifting policy represented here by M. Duruy. Those who have practiced an absolute and inflexible policy have succeeded; the others have fallen." All the governments of the nineteenth century, from Charles X to Thiers, had, in Cassagnac's estimation, subverted themselves by making concessions to an irreconcilable minority, and eventually succumbing to that minority, instead of succeeding to woo it.

> Rallying adversaries by concessions is a delusion insofar as we are concerned. We must finish with this system, which has continually betrayed us, because generosity is profitable only with *brave gens*, and unfortunately, the republicans are not *brave gens*.
>
> In a word, we want to govern with those who are for us against those who are against us . . . . One can rally opinions but one cannot rally appetites. And the republicans, generally speaking, have nothing but appetites.

Cassagnac berated the conservatives for their perpetual self-delusion.

> You think that we trouble the calm and repose that you have begun to enjoy under the auspices of a conservative government, and you complain about the unwelcome voice that disturbs your sleep and disperses your beautiful dreams!
>
> Such is the eternal history of the conservative party! One day it awakens on the edge of a precipice, anxious, troubled, terror-stricken, exasperated; it makes a desperate effort and overthrows a Thiers who endangers it, and before the next day comes, it lies down again, swollen with victory and not at all concerned that the peril may return. And to those who

warn it, who provoke it and push it to take radical measures, to finish with the problem once and for all, it replies: "Leave me in peace; you are insupportable!" Cassagnac then deployed a swordsman's metaphor. Since the revolution of 1870, he said, France had been searching for a saber; he himself favored a sharp, pointed sword, drawn and ready for action. But Duruy, he charged, preferred it to be dull and at rest in its sheath. The fact was that Paul de Cassagnac thought he had found a practitioner of Imperialism in President de Mac-Mahon. The illustrious Marshal of France would be the new Louis-Napoleon.

Cassagnac's enthusiasm for the marshal exacerbated his already considerable differences with Rouher over the conservative alliance. Later in 1873 the royalists attempted to restore the monarchy in the person of the Comte de Chambord. In the wake of the Bourbon pretender's refusal to accept the tricolor flag,[56] the Assembly decided to prolong Mac-Mahon's term of office for seven years. This period, the *Septennat*, was intended to provide a time of truce between political factions, a truce that would postpone the establishment of any definitive form of government.

The debate over the *Septennat* offers abundant evidence of the ways in which Rouher and Paul de Cassagnac differed in their conceptions of the Bonapartist party's role. The Bonapartist deputies (then only twenty-nine in number) were badly divided on whether to support the *Septennate*. Most of the party's partisans were greatly relieved by the failure of the royalist offensive and felt that their moment had come. Rouher had been biding time until the departure of the last Prussian occupation forces from French soil and until the Prince Imperial's majority, which would be celebrated in March 1874. He was reluctant to tie the party's hands for as long as seven years in the face of Orleanist aspirations. But in the vote on the *Septennat*, he was only able to convince fourteen deputies to abstain; thirteen others voted for it, while one voted against and another was absent.[57]

Paul de Cassagnac had argued for the seven-year presidential term since June 1873, but beginning in September he had embarked on an aggressive campaign on its behalf, much to Rouher's annoyance.[58] Cassagnac stated his case for Bonapartist support in terms of the highest moral idealism: the Bonapartist party, he contended, had to set an example for the nation. Its partisans must not allow themselves to repeat the recent unpatriotic example of the legitimists, who had selfishly attempted to restore a pretender unwanted by the people. The Bonapartists must therefore appear unremittingly conservative and patriotic. Consequently, he praised those who supported the *Septennat* for their "patriotic abnegation," and condemned the others, who "never stop looking at their watches" to estimate the time of the empire's arrival.[59] Furthermore he urged all the deputies of *Appel au peuple* to perform their patriotic duty in the future, by voting for all laws that could strengthen the authority of Mac-Mahon's government:

> The imperialists are condemned by their past, but more especially by their future, to exemplary behavior in matters of obedience to law and political self-sacrifice. In no case may they depart from the ranks of the larger conservative party. Only at this price can the Empire return within a relatively short time.
>
> The imperialists must resolutely take their part in the present situation and put an end to this state of nervous agitation, which only earns them a deserved discredit in the estimation of all honorable men . . . .[60]

The Bonapartist must even vote for effective measures that might be used against them in the future, Cassagnac insisted, as a token of their duty as conservatives: "A party earns the esteem of public opinion just as a simple individual does -- by its words and by its deeds."[61] In effect, he was preaching possible political suicide to a party that did not want to die.

Throughout 1874 Cassagnac urged a policy of restraint and self-denial in the interest of maintaining the conservative alliance in the National Assembly, while Rouher attempted to main the Bonapartist party's independence by steering a course between the majority favorable to Mac-Mahon and the pro-republican minority. Cassagnac had been highly critical of Rouher's occasional efforts to form tactical alliances with the republicans, especially the previous year when Bonapartist and republican deputies had combined to provoke dissolution of the Assembly.[62] During the summer and autumn of 1874, he was equally critical of Rouher's reluctance to cooperate with the majority's plans for drawing up an organization for the government structure that would succeed the Assembly.[63] In consequence of this criticism, he was attacked, first by friends of Prince Napoleon, such as Jean de la Rocca, editor of *Le Patriote de la Corse*,[64] and later by Rouher's own supporters, who accused him of urging Bonapartists to rally to the empire's desperate enemies, the Orleanists, when there was no "absolute necessity" to do so.[65]

It is hardly surprising, then, to find Cassagnac an isolated voice in the higher councils of the Bonapartist party.[66] During most of 1874 Rouher and his associates were preoccupied with extracting the maximum advantage from the coming-of-age of the Prince Imperial. A ceremonious gathering of the faithful, on 16 March 1874, at Chislehurst, welcomed the young prince, on his eighteenth birthday, to adulthood -- and leadership of the party.[67] Paul de Cassagnac was conspicuous among the celebrants.

The high point in the Bonapartist party's 1874 offensive came with the election in May of a leading Bonapartist in the department of Nièvre. The successful candidate, the Baron de Bourgoing, was a former member of the imperial household and, for the Bonapartist party's opponents, this fact overshadowed the equally notable fact that Bourgoing had announced his support for Mac-Mahon and had been elected with the help of the other monarchist parties.[68]

Later in the year sentiment began to swing behind Cassagnac. By then he had been brought to trial -- and increasing fame -- for insulting the republic.[69] Perhaps more important, pressures within the National Assembly had forced Broglie to abandon the two ministers in his cabinet who were especially sympathetic to the Bonapartist cause, and Broglie's minister of justice had begun an investigation of Bonapartist party organization.[70] Criticism of Rouher began to appear in print. In early November, Robert Mitchell, writing in Le Soir, declared himself firmly in favor of the Septennat.[71] A former director-general of the press under the Second Empire, Pierre Latour du Moulin, in a pamphlet, La France et le Septennat, supported Cassagnac's position and praised the young journalist ("brilliant pen, valiant sword") for "exercising a real influence on public opinion, especially in the departments, where people are exasperated by the progress of radicalism."[72] He criticized the Bonapartists' failure to stand squarely behind the Mac-Mahonien interregnum:

> No party has demonstrated proof of less understanding of the difficulties of the situation or has committed more tactical faults in the Assembly. While reserving its principle of appel au peuple -- which is its strength -- its obligation and interest was never to refuse its aid to the tutelary power of Marshal de Mac-Mahon. By demonstrating its solidarity with him, the party could have made impossible his disengagement . . . from any sign of recognition.[73]

As dissatisfaction with Rouher's leadership and tactics mounted, Paul de Cassagnac acquired increased support from within the party for his own position.

Despite the internal conflict within the Bonapartist party and the opposition it faced from hostile elements in the Assembly, still the imperial cause had never looked more hopeful than in December 1874.

Three recent events raised the morale of the Bonapartists and produced a coalition of their enemies. First, the judicial inquest into the party's activities ended with the dismissal of the case. Second, it was revealed (in Germany, during the trial of the former German ambassador to France) that Bismarck had favored the republic as being the weakest possible government for France, but was not hostile to the return of the empire. Finally, news came of the restoration of the Bourbon monarchy in Spain. The existence of friendly ties between the Spanish Bourbons and the imperial family led partisans of the empire to believe in the imminent triumph of their own cause. All these developments came on top of a string of electoral victories for Bonapartist candidates. Already, in May, Gambetta had sounded a warning note to his fellow republicans: "The truth is," he wrote to his exiled colleague Arthur Ranc, "that the Empire has never ceased to be our principal adversary . . . . The populace seems to be moved by that phrase '*Appel au peuple*,' a well-turned phrase that seems to say something but is only a new lie."[74]

* * *

When the National Assembly reconvened in January 1875, it soon became clear that the Bonapartist resurgence had dislocated the majority supporting "moral order." The defection of key Orleanists made possible the consolidation of the republic as the official government of France by passing the first of two constitutional laws establishing its organizational structure. "It is fear of our party that has reunited our adversaries," wrote Cassagnac, "that has made possible the adoption of the constitutional laws that nobody wanted before, that has overthrown the traditions of the Center Right and the principles of the Left, that has produced the recent proclamation of the Republic."[75] He was entirely correct: the republic had been consolidated in opposition to the empire.[76]

In response to this development, Paul de Cassagnac announced the withdrawal of Bonapartist support from future ministries. "While we will nevertheless conserve our unalterable personal devotion to Marshal de Mac-Mahon, we consider ourselves disengaged from the political alliance that we loyally offered and have practiced since 24 May [1873] . . . . We are conservatives in all matters -- in religion, in authority, in social system -- except in the matter of republics."[77] Future ministries would be fated to look to the Left for support and this, he predicted, would be their undoing.

Paul de Cassagnac persisted in his devotion to Mac-Mahon and in his hope that the marshal would yet "save" France from the republic. In so doing he ignored the opinion of those who considered Mac-Mahon to be both too weak and too scrupulous for such a role.[78] Cassagnac also discounted the objections of Rouher and the other Bonapartists who were interested in asserting the strength of the party. His faith in Mac-Mahon and his utter conviction that the empire lay at the end of the president's term led him to oppose Rouher's efforts to deal with political realities as they arose. It led him, for example, to underestimate the public response to the constitutional laws of 1875, which, as the editor of *L'Année politique* and other republicans were quick to see, denied to the Bonapartists precisely that "clientèle of indifferent voters who, due to weariness with 'provisional' government and a thirst for stability, were predisposed toward caesarian doctrines."[79]

From 1875 on, Cassagnac was on a collision course with Rouher. This became obvious after Rouher's acquisition of a "glorious recruit" for the Bonapartist party in the person of Edgard Raoul-Duval. As Rouher's right-hand man in the Assembly, Raoul-Duval soon became the great white hope of those who advocated a liberal, progressive, and "political" Bonapartism.[80] He was just ten years older than Paul de Cassagnac and, hence, represented a formidable rival for leadership of the younger generation in the party. In contrast to Cassagnac, he was a true son of those "bourgeois dynasties" depicted by Beau de Loménie, being the nephew of Léon Say, the leader of the Center Left, and the grandson of J.-B. Say, the celebrated liberal economist. He had been elected to the National Assembly in a by-election in 1871. At first he had sat with the Center Right, as he was temperamentally much closer to the Orleanists than to the imperialists. He was committed to parliamentary politics, and thereby estranged from the authoritarians, and he was a Protestant, and therefore not disposed to defend Catholic interests with the same concern. He had gravitated to the Bonapartist party because he liked the Prince Imperial much more than the Comte de Paris and because he regarded a national consultation on the constitutional question as a necessity, whereas the Orleanists opposed it. But he was strongly against the truce of "moral order" represented by the *Septennat*, and he dedicated himself to the reconciliation of moderate republicans to the empire.[81]

Consequently Paul de Cassagnac and Raoul-Duval could not have been further apart. Their rivalry from 1875 to 1877 illustrates the tensions within the Bonapartist party, and their clashes took place over the very issues which could escalate those tensions into explosions. Cassagnac supported the conservative alliance; Raoul-Duval regarded it as "fatal." Cassagnac accused Raoul-Duval of leading the Bonapartist deputies in a "revolutionary" politics and turning them into captives of the Left;[82] in turn, Raoul-Duval called Cassagnac "a man who deserves to be called the gravedigger of his party."[83]

Two issues in late 1875 demonstrate the widely divergent viewpoints and strategies of the two rivals. The first was the election of senators for life. The second was the interpretation to be given to the anticipated elections to the new Chamber of Deputies.

In establishing the Senate, the National Assembly had decided to elect seventy-five senators for life from among its own membership. The remainder would be chosen for nine-year terms by a system of indirect election in the departments. The Bonapartist policy was not to put forward any candidates for life terms, as these senators were not being elected by "the people," but instead to offer candidates exclusively in the departmental elections. This decision was criticized by Cassagnac as both inconsistent and impractical.[84] When the voting began in the Assembly, however, it became apparent that the deputies of *Appel au peuple* held the determining votes. Paul de Cassagnac thought they should support monarchist candidates. Like Rouher, Raoul-Duval thought differently and concluded a pact with the republican deputies to vote with them in order to block the Orleanist candidates of the Center Right.[85] Cassagnac attacked this agreement as a direct affront to the empire's natural allies, particularly harmful insofar as it ruined any chance of resurrecting the conservative alliance policy for the approaching national elections to the Senate and Chamber of Deputies.[86] He never forgave Raoul-Duval for this act.

Cassagnac likewise could not forgive Raoul-Duval for his insistence that the elections to the new Chamber, scheduled for February 1876, represented a plebiscitary verdict on the question of the regime.[87] From the Imperialist standpoint, such a claim was heretical, having been invented by Gambetta and employed by the republicans as a strategic response to the Bonapartist *appel au peuple*.[88] It might be called the theory of the "legislative plebiscite," although this term does not appear to have been used at the time. The republicans adopted the idea of the plebiscite, which Napoleon I and Napoleon III had used to obtain consensus and formal legitimacy, but they transformed it to serve their own needs, by posing the question of the regime in each by-election to the Assembly and then interpreting any republican victory as approval of the republic. They employed this technique of "ratifying the republic" during numerous by-elections in 1874 and after. Cassagnac feared that this tactic would mean "the death of the conservative party."[89] and by 1875 he felt obliged to denounce it as a travesty of the true plebiscite.

In his orthodoxy, Cassagnac refused to accept the argument that cumulative results from legislative elections (or, for that matter, from elections to the *conseils-généraux*[90]) could provide a substitute for direct consultation of the nation.

> We affirm that the true plebiscite, the only plebiscite, is that which addresses itself directly to the nation and which is asked on the dynastic question.
>
> Do you want the Empire, yes or no?
>
> That is the plebiscitary formula and there is no other.
>
> It is an aberration to imagine that a legislative election can be transformed into a plebiscite.
>
> It is impossible to say to the voters, "If you want the empire, vote for so-and-so!" So-and-so may displease him and have no local influence.[91]

In late 1875, the nature of an acceptable plebiscite was not strictly a theoretical issue. It had become important because the National Assembly was considering the shape of the electoral system for its successor, the Chamber of Deputies. Led by Gambetta, the republicans were campaigning to retain the *scrutin de liste*, the all-departmental election of a slate of deputies, the method used to elect the National Assembly itself. They believed that such a system would pull the electorate away from questions of personality and local issues and into the realm of abstract political ideas.[92] Cassagnac and the monarchists strongly favored the *scrutin uninominal*, or *scrutin d'arrondissement*, the method used under the Second Empire. They believed that it gave weight to local influence and personal standing, and produced a more "conservative" result. Cassagnac condemned the *liste* in unequivocal terms:

> This system has produced deputies who have no serious attachment to their constituencies and who are incapable of getting themselves elected as municipal councillors. It even so happens that a man who would not be elected in his own *arrondissement* because he is too well-known there, will poll a majority in the other arrondissements for the opposite reason, i.e., because he is not known there at all. Nothing stands in the way of a vote being cast for a nondescript candidate.
>
> The *scrutin de liste* is condemned by all conservatives, for it permits the grouping of

republican minorities and favors them at the expense
of the real majority, which is dispersed and scattered
[throughout the department].

At present [1874] only the republicans favor the
scrutin de liste, for experience has shown [the others]
that, apart from the grand currents of opinion that only
occur rarely and bring everyone out to vote, the
scrutin de liste has never produced anything but the
oppression of the majority by the minority.[93]

In neither case did Cassagnac admit the possibility of a legislative
plebiscite: as he wrote in June 1875, "Even if the *scrutin de liste* were
to give our party every seat, I could not accept that result as a
plebiscitary decision."[94]

Divergence over the form of the new electoral system placed new
strains on the already existing rifts within the Bonapartist party, by
providing another *casis belli* for Cassagnac and the *jeunes* to use against
Rouher. Rouher favored the *scrutin de liste* for two reasons: he
believed that Bonapartists would do better to campaign as such, rather
than to minimize their distinctiveness in order to attract other
conservative votes; and he saw that the *scrutin de liste* would mean
lower campaign costs to the party, since a number of candidates could
be elected with only one campaign per department, where with the
scrutin uninominal a number of separate campaigns would be
required.[95]

Cassagnac opened the debate on the two electoral systems in April
1875 in *Le Pays*. In May he sponsored an inquiry in the provinces on
the question, the results of which filled the pages of *Le Pays* for nearly
a fortnight in June.[96] Meanwhile, the deputies of the Center Left
declared for the *scrutin de liste*, and all but one deputy of the Center
Right voted to support the *scrutin d'arrondissement*. By autumn it was
apparent that the vote on the electoral system might provoke a
governmental crisis, as the radical republicans threatened to topple the
cabinet and replace the *président du conseil*, Buffet, who was
considered mildly sympathetic to the Bonapartists, with Audiffret-
Pasquier, a proclaimed antagonist. All these facts provided Cassagnac
with ammunition.

On 11 November, the Assembly defeated the *scrutin de liste* by a
vote of 357 to 326, on an amendment to the proposed electoral law.
The disunited conservatives obtained the *scrutin d'arrondissement* they
wanted, and upheld the cabinet, which would thus be charged with
conducting the elections. Cassagnac was jubilant.[97] Raoul-Duval was
furious and submitted his resignation from *Appel au peuple*. Rouher, in

turn, was deeply discouraged, and was quoted as saying, "The truth is that everything had been prepared [for the election] in view of the *scrutin de liste*; now it must all be done over."[98] When the final vote on the electoral law was cast at the end of the month, the split in the Bonapartist party was obvious to all: 17 of its 30 deputies voted for the *scrutin d'arrondissement*; two voted against it, and 11 others, including Rouher and Raoul-Duval, abstained.[99]

Nevertheless, Raoul-Duval continued to insist on the plebiscitary nature of the elections. A number of other aspiring Bonapartist deputies, however, felt the need for support from other conservatives in their prospective constituencies and toned down their electoral statements accordingly; these men joined together behind an "Imperialist" *Comité national conservateur*, which issued manifestoes underscoring *ralliement* behind Mac-Mahon, in order to combat antisocial and revolutionary doctrines, and which endorsed candidates in Paris and the provinces who professed varying shades of conservative opinion.[100] Thus, over the strenuous objections both of Rouher and Raoul-Duval, many Bonapartists practiced their own policy of conservative alliance in the elections of 1876. This was a clear triumph for the Imperialists, and it would not be their last.

Throughout 1876 Raoul-Duval persisted in his efforts to reorient the Bonapartist party and to organize it as a compact and disciplined dynastic party, to the great indignation of Cassagnac and the Imperialists. In October of that year, he founded *La Nation*, a daily newspaper intended to provide a voice for "an Empire which is neither that of Amigues nor that of Cassagnac, an Empire of reason, democratic, laic, Napoleonic," as his friend Ernest Lavisse described it to the Prince Imperial.[101] But Raoul-Duval's journalistic venture was short-lived; *La Nation* succumbed to financial failure the following May.[102]

Meanwhile Raoul-Duval had made the mistake of arousing Rouher's resentment of his growing influence with the Prince Imperial, with whom he had cultivated close rapport.[103] By early 1877, when the Imperialists mobilized against Raoul-Duval, Rouher was on their side. Paul de Cassagnac took advantage of an incident in the Chamber to accuse his rival of treason to the party. From Cassagnac's ultra-Imperialist perspective, Raoul-Duval had committed four offenses: he had instigated the vote with the republicans for life senators in 1875; he had accorded a plebiscitary value to the elections of February 1876; he had refused to show solidarity with the *coup d'état*; and he had not supported the monarchist Right on several issues affecting religion. Moreover, Cassagnac charged, Raoul-Duval had tried to line up the deputies of *Appel au peuple* behind the amnesty of the Communards, and after having been elected to the Budget Committee (the only Bonapartist so honored), he had supported Gambetta for president of the Chamber. Cassagnac suggested that Raoul-Duval had "had to effect the delivery of his group" in order to be tolerated on the committee.[104]

Paul de Cassagnac would have occasion to denounce an even greater betrayal later that year when, in June 1877, Raoul-Duval abstained in the historic vote of confidence for the Broglie ministry of *Seize Mai*. The unfortunate Raoul-Duval paid for that abstention with his seat in the Chamber and was effectively driven from political life until the mid-1880s, when he reappeared in the Chamber as a lonely advocate for *ralliement* of monarchists to the republic, arguing once again (however misguidedly) that France had demonstrated her acceptance of the republic by legislative plebiscite.[105]

* * *

The divergences over the doctrine and tactics of Imperialism between Paul de Cassagnac, on the one hand, and Rouher and Raoul-Duval, on the other, were intensified by the degree of personal emnity that existed among them. But these divergences did not create an actual crisis within the Bonapartist party until the *Seize Mai*, at which time Rouher reluctantly committed the party to the support of the conservative alliance, and thereby precipitated the departure of Raoul-Duval and his liberal friends from the Bonapartist camp. In view of this series of developments, which will be addressed in the next chapter, it seems necessary to suspend judgment on the question of whether, in retrospect, a political, dynastic Bonapartism might have succeeded in restoring the empire on its own account. Clearly, such a restoration did not seem possible at this time. We might rather rephrase the question provisionally by asking whether, given the shifting political context in which the Bonapartists were operating between 1874 and 1876, Cassagnac's effort to draw supporters of the three dynastic factions together in opposition to the republic behind a faceless, broadly-defined Imperialism may have in fact offered a more politically realistic strategy for gaining power, in this case by getting votes and winning elections (even without declaring them of plebiscitary value) than that of cut-throat and potentially self-defeating competition at the local level.

CHAPTER V

THE POLITICS OF CATHOLIC DEFENSE AND IMPERIALISM
SEIZE MAI: 1876-1879

Je suis catholique, monarchiste, impérialiste.

Paul de Cassagnac
Le Pays, 26 July 1879

Paul de Cassagnac opened his career as a deputy by speaking out in defense of French Catholic interests in the realm of education. The politically-active Catholic laity or *clericals*, as its members were called by their republican opponents, had just achieved a final triumph in their half-century long challenge to the educational monopoly of the French state. On 12 July 1875, the National Assembly passed a law granting freedom to private bodies such as the Church to establish institutions of higher learning competitive with those of the State. This law included the crucial provision that degrees would be awarded by a "mixed jury," whose examining members must include representatives from these private institutions as well as from the faculties of the State. When the republicans took control of the Chamber of Deputies in 1876, they set out to revise this law--the first step in a more sweeping effort to establish a wholly secular or laic society, in no way subject to the interference of the Church, whose organization and doctrines many republicans considered an obstacle to "democracy" and "progress."[1]

The new Minister of Public Instruction, William Waddington, introduced a measure designed to abolish the mixed jury and thereby restore to the State full authority for granting ng ng degrees. The debate on this issue provided Paul de Cassagnac with the opportunity to make his first speech in the Chamber of Deputies.[2]

The very fact that Cassagnac spoke out on this issue was significant because he was the first leading Bonapartist to declare himself publicly on the pro-Catholic side. His intervention gave opponents of the Bonapartist party the chance to lump its partisans together with those of the other monarchist parties. This was disconcerting to a number of highly-placed Bonapartists who themselves were "laic" and feared that any identification of their cause with the so-called forces of "clerical reaction" would alienate supporters, particularly among the peasants who, because of their instinctive resistance to being patronized by traditional elites, would thus be lost to the anticlerical republicans. Throughout the spring of 1876 these laic Bonapartists had demonstrated their displeasure whenever their colleagues touched on the religious question. When Cassagnac spoke out in committee against the Waddington project, he earned a stern reproach from the liberal Bonapartist newspaper *La Liberté*:

> The conservative union necessitates many sacrifices, but there   are limits and it would be incomprehensible to us that the party,   whose champion, M. Paul de Cassagnac, is often a bit daring, should go beyond these limits without good assurance that outside, in the nation, the party will gain in prestige, and inside, in popularity, in a time when clerical reaction has so frequently seduced and destroyed the conservatives.
>
> As we recently remarked, the Bonapartist party will have an   excellent opportunity in the coming discussion . . . to mark out   its place and the intermediary role which is proper for it in questions of this sort -- equidistant from both clerical reaction   and republican intolerance.[3]

Despite this warning, Cassagnac went ahead with his speech -- delivered, he said, "not as an Imperialist but as a Catholic."

Cassagnac's personal position on the subject of religious freedom in education was by no means new. Already in 1868 he had declared in favor of the right of Catholic institutions to teach on an equal basis with those of the state. In an article entitled "I am a Christian," dating from 1868, he repeated the charge made decades earlier by Catholic deputies, namely that state-controlled higher education was overrun with atheist and materialist teachers whose doctrines did not represent the thinking of the majority of citizens. While "we contest no one the right to be atheist and materialist, we do contest the government's right to make us pay the salaries" of those who preach such doctrines: "we are Catholics and we would appreciate it if the professors . . . did not use their quasi-official situation to defy us and wound us in our convictions."[4] Thus in 1876, Cassagnac only renewed the attack when he charged that:

> . . . at present, the University no longer responds to the ensemble of sentiments and the general state of opinion in France; . . . every day it becomes more entrenched in the direction of materialism and atheism. . . . The *père de famille* is reduced to resort

to the most onerous finegling in order to give his son education and instruction, and in order to avoid seeking these within the University.[5] It was not so much the presence of insidious doctrines that troubled Cassagnac as the fact that they were being taught in the name of the State. Even with a republican majority in the Chamber, Cassagnac reminded his audience, the republicans were not the State: despite their claims, he insisted, "the majority, the Republic cannot say '*l'État, c'est moi*!' No, the State is all of us!"[6]

To Paul de Cassagnac, as to those who, like the Comte de Montalembert, had led the earlier campaign of Catholics for freedom of ideas to compete in the academic marketplace, the issue at hand was construed as one of principle -- an issue of freedom of conscience. Cassagnac underscored the irony of the fact that "we, the authoritarians, are reduced to defending liberty against the liberals" in the education question.[7] As he had done in the case of the press laws, he used the education issue to condemn the intolerance of the liberals and the dissimulation of the republicans. Against both he employed the example of Belgium, where both Catholics and liberals had agreed that the right to grant degrees was central to any meaningful freedom of education.[8]

Paul de Cassagnac's speech on the Waddington project precipitated a schism over the religious question that divided the Bonapartist party as irreparably as it would henceforth divide the nation.[9] In concert with the rest of the conservative press, *L'Ordre*, the official voice of Bonapartism, praised Cassagnac's speech and then concentrated on parrying the charges of *cléricalisme* hurled by the republicans.[10] When the Waddington project came to a vote, the split among the Bonapartist deputies was clear for all to see. The bulk of the deputies of *Appel au peuple* stood firmly behind the law of 1875: 61 of the 123 deputies who opposed the bill were Bonapartists, a group that included Rouher himself; 22 other Bonapartists abstained, including Raoul-Duval, the two Eschasseriaux, and three of their colleagues from Charente-Inférieure. Prince Napoleon and two associates, on the other hand, supported the Waddington project.[11]

This speech of 1 June 1876 was by no means Cassagnac's sole intervention in the Chamber on the religious question. Not for this speech alone did he come to be called the "Catholic hussar" and, more irreverently, "Po-Paul."[12] In 1879 he was one of the first to speak out in the Chamber against republican proposals to laicize education and, in 1880, he was among the first to protest most vehemently against the expulsion of the unauthorized religious congregations. From 1880 to 1882, he presided over the Gers *conseil-général*, spearheading that body's opposition to expulsion of the congregations, and in the Chamber, he opposed the laic laws during the debates.

* * *

A devout Roman Catholic, Cassagnac conceived religious faith as essential for man's morality and a necessary complement to monarchy. The fact that such beliefs as his were shared by men in other monarchist parties certainly contributed to the existence of a climate of mutual sympathy, a climate that underlay the formation of the conservative alliance in politics.[13] But was it merely a case of "throne and altar"? What was the explicit content of these religious attitudes that so undergirded this political relationship?

Paul de Cassagnac spoke the language of "liberal Catholicism." He was not a zealot. He firmly believed that, under the Concordat that had linked Church and State in France since 1801, the State -- whatever its form -- should respect the Church and defend religious interests as its own. Indeed, had the leading republicans not made it their express object to attack Catholic interests, Cassagnac might well have admitted the possibility of their defense even to the Third Republic. However, due to the laicizing actions of the republicans, which the Catholics chose to represent as religious persecution, he came to view the Concordat as unworkable and, as early as 1882, advocated separation of Church and State.[14] Although Cassagnac readily acknowledged that, in principle, the Church was independent of any form of government and could accommodate itself to all,[15] he continued to except the republic, whose partisans seemed to him to be insulting God and outraging religion at every opportunity, under the guise of enforcing the Concordat. In such circumstances, he argued, a Catholic was obliged to resist that form of government with all his strength, irrespective of the position taken by his bishop (whom Cassagnac viewed as little more than a sanctified civil servant under the terms of the Concordat). He was therefore unsympathetic to Leo XIII's conciliatory policy toward the French government. Cultivating the republic while condemning the revolution seemed to Cassagnac an attempt to amalgamate two contradictory, mutually exclusive, positions.[16]

Paul de Cassagnac believed that there was a natural affinity between throne and altar -- that is, that the Church's ultimate interests lay with monarchy -- but he was nevertheless quick to contest the pretensions of any single political party to monopolize religious interests. God cannot be the exclusive property of any particular regime, he frequently argued. By this he meant that the party of the empire had quite as much right as the legitimists to defend religious interests.[17]

Cassagnac's attitudes toward religion and his personal associations drew him toward the men of the *Droite modérée*, or Center Right, who were also liberal Catholics.[18] Like them, and unlike the more ostentatious ultra-Catholic legitimists, for instance, Cassagnac categorically opposed breaking France's alliance with Italy in order to wage a war to liberate the Pope.[19] Like them, he had opposed the resolution voted by the National Assembly declaring that the Basilica of the Sacred Heart to be built on Montmartre was a project in the public interest and granting it the right of eminent domain. As Cassagnac wrote at the time of this vote: "We think that questions of faith necessitate greater restraint on the part of the faithful and that the National Assembly should not be used to make inopportune sermons whose unique result is to incite disrespectful attacks on religion."[20]

Cassagnac was quite willing to give God his due in the spiritual realm, but he insisted that the State must also receive its due in the temporal; in his opinion, the clergy should stay in the cathedral and out of city hall.[21] As he put it in 1882 (although he might have written the same words ten years earlier):

> The bishop is absolute master in the religious
> domain and there I listen on bended knee.
> But when he issues political commands, he enters
> my domain.
> In particular, when he commands disarmament in
> face of the republic, I have the right to admonish him
> as thoroughly as possible.[22]

Cassagnac particularly objected to any interference by the Vatican in French political life. In this respect, his view resembled a variety of the Gallicanism of the eighteenth century. In the nineteenth century, this attitude was often referred to as "Orleanist," although its adherents included many who were not Orleanists in a political sense, being neither partisans of the Orleans dynasty nor advocates of parliamentary monarchy. Cassagnac drew the line between spiritual and temporal power in quite a different place than did the ardent Veuillot of *L'Univers*, the foremost advocate of papal sovereignty within the Church, whose spiritual ultramontanism often shaded off into temporal ultramontanism.[23] While Cassagnac honored Veuillot as a master in journalism and professed to share the latter's distaste for "liberals" and "Gallicans,"[24] his own position on political and religious matters was actually far closer to that of Monseigneur Dupanloup, the Bishop of Orléans, who for years had been Veuillot's arch-antagonist and who was therefore out of favor with the Vatican during the reign of Pius IX.[25]

Dupanloup was one of the men closest to Mac-Mahon during the latter's presidency.[26] Paul de Cassagnac, in turn, seems to have collaborated closely with the old bishop in the cause of social defense. Indeed, it appeared that they were on remarkably friendly terms. One journalist friend of Cassagnac's insisted that during the 1870s Dupanloup had made an effort to find Cassagnac a wealthy wife.[27] Cassagnac himself later bore witness to the closeness of his relationship with the eminent bishop.[28] The extent of their political collaboration, if it could be fully documented, might shed light on much that remains obscure about the politics of conservative alliance in the 1870s. The available evidence, however, is fragmentary -- a few letters, scattered police reports, and occasional clippings from the newspaper inspired by Dupanloup, *La Défense Sociale et Religieuse*, containing complimentary references to Cassagnac.[29]

Among the lay Catholics, Paul de Cassagnac was most closely allied after 1876 with Baron Armand de Mackau, deputy from the department of Orne and member of an old monarchist family who had rallied to the Second Empire.[30] Mackau, like Cassagnac, put principles before persons, and like Cassagnac, he was devoted to the cause of social defense. As he wrote in 1876, in a memorandum to the Prince Imperial on the situation of the Bonapartist party:

> French society is perishing because the principle
> of authority has lost its prestige, (because the slow
> invasion of the human spirit by civil independence has
> led it, by ignorance, to religious skepticism and
> independence), and because a strange interpretation of
> social equality has given birth to every sort of
> ambition and demand; because little by little the stump
> [of society] has been led to claim its rights with ardor,
> while easily forsaking its obligations, thus overturning
> the base on which every society rests.
>
> Thus, these social conditions make light . . . of
> the religious, moral, and social principles which have
> been the grandeur and the   force of every society,
> old or modern. This folly finds its   rationale in the
> search for some ephemeral popularity, some
> immediate success without a morrow, a success that
> lends itself   as little to the establishment of personal
> situations as to the   establishment of a lasting
> government by any party.[31]

Mackau's close relationship with Cassagnac is documented by the remnants of correspondence between the two men from 1876 to 1892, and by the extent of their political collaboration during those years.[32] Cassagnac also appears to have been closely connected with Hippolyte de Villemessant, director of *Le Figaro* and one of the pillars of Catholic and royalist France until his death in 1879.[33] The probable intermediary in this relationship was Granier de Cassagnac, who from 1876 on wrote for *Le Figaro* under the pseudonym of "Mauprat."[34] Their relationship appears to have been personal as well as professional; at the time of Villemessant's death, Cassagnac spoke of his deep admiration for the great editor and for the "charms" of his family life.[35]

Dupanloup, Mackau, and Villemessant were prominent among the proponents of Catholic defense who reinforced Cassagnac in his Imperialism and impelled him, during the political crisis of 1877, known as *Seize Mai*, to urge his Bonapartist colleagues to cooperate in consolidating a conservative alliance against the anticlerical republicans.

* * *

In May 1877 the republican majority in the Chamber, led by Léon Gambetta, opened a frontal assault on *cléricalisme*. By thus choosing a slogan around which all republicans could rally in opposition to all the monarchists, they translated into political terms the irrevocable split over the religious question that had divided France for so many decades. The immediate pretext for the republican onslaught was a petition circulated by the Bishop of Nevers among the civil servants of his district, following a recent papal encyclical. The petition urged the French government to use its good offices with Italy to influence the course of legislation which the Pope considered threatening to his position.[36] The radical republican deputies chose to interpret this petition as an example of interference by the clergy in affairs of the State and they called for an interpellation on "ultramontane affairs," which took place in early May 1877. During the interpellation, Gambetta (whose instincts had long before led him to appreciate the importance of this issue to republican unity) invoked the specter of clericalism invading the State and alleged that if it were not checked, it would attain the double goal of "conquest of the State and direction of the masses . . . . I am only translating the intimate feelings of the people of France in repeating the words of my good friend Peyrat: Clericalism? There is the enemy!"[37] Gambetta's ringing phrase became the watchword for every call to republican unity during the next thirty years.

Whether or not political interference by Catholic clergymen actually constituted a threat in France, either in 1877 or thereafter, is still subject to debate.[38] Certainly the politically-active Catholic laity denied it, and in fact the ministers of *Seize Mai* were so scrupulous in avoiding any appearance of clerical interference during the electoral preparations of 1877 that both *L'Univers* and the Catholic Association of Paris criticized them for it.[39] Paul de Cassagnac scorned the charge of clericalism as merely a bogeyman to be trotted out, "a means of easy eloquence for republican orators." "The 'mud of Sedan' has dried up so thoroughly," he observed in 1878, "that at present it has been completely displaced by clericalism."[40]

Cassagnac's judgement was on the mark. Like Sedan, the word clericalism carried a powerful emotional charge. The republicans deliberately used this popular stereotype to arouse popular feeling, stirring deep-seated political reflexes by engendering fear of a conspiracy of priests that would encroach on the prerogatives of the State. Not only did the word, with its implied threat of elitism, appeal to an assertive levelling instinct, but it also aroused -- in much the same way as twentieth-century anti-Semitism -- a simplistic sort of chauvinism by rendering all Catholics suspect of a prior allegiance to a foreign power, for whose sake they were willing to wage war and drag France with them.[41] As Daniel Halévy pointed out so astutely, the republicans' use of the clerical issue made it possible for them to attack all Catholics, irrespective of tradition or nuance, and "rake them all over the coals together."[42] All these aspects of clericalism were employed by the republicans during the campaign of 1877, as they attempted to convince the electorate "that only through Republicanism, and the eviction of the Church from all influence in politics which was the avowed Republican policy, could the harvest of the Revolution be made secure for future generations."[43]

The events following the so-called ultramontane interpellation of 4-5 May 1877 have frequently been recounted in detail. Here they will merely be alluded to only as they elicited a particular response from Paul de Cassagnac and as they illuminate the actions of the Bonapartist party. The climax came on 16 May, when President de Mac-Mahon addressed a letter to his premier, Jules Simon, which led Simon to submit his resignation. Mac-Mahon replaced Simon with the Duc de Broglie, who promptly called for new elections and suspended any further meeting of the existing Chamber for one month.[44]

Paul de Cassagnac crowed over the new prestige the president had acquired by this move. He cast Mac-Mahon as a "man on horseback" and exhorted him to "finish the job," thereby reinforcing the republicans in their conviction that the president's dismissal of Simon and his call for dissolution were a kind of *coup d'état*, "the struggle of personal government against parliamentary government."[45]

Cassagnac did not ignore the constitutional reality that made Mac-Mahon a prisoner of the Assembly. Indeed, in early 1876, he had acknowledged that a *coup d'état* by Mac-Mahon would be far more illegal than that of December 1851, since the president, elected by the Assembly and not by direct vote of the citizenry, had no independent authority.[46] But from a legal point of view he did not consider the president's action a *coup*; it was merely a *coup* in the moral sense.[47] After all, the president still had to win the approval of the Senate in order to dissolve the Chamber and call for new elections.

Following the Senate's vote of approval in June, Cassagnac cheered the president on. He lauded what he presumed to be Mac-Mahon's determination and exhorted the new ministry to take firm measures and to use to the fullest extent the options at their disposal -- from administrative changes to declaration of a state of siege -- in order to insure a triumph at the polls.[48] As in 1873 and 1876, he constantly criticized "half-measures" and objected to the scruples of Broglie and his ministers in wielding the legal and administrative implements left to them by the Second Empire for the management of universal suffrage.[49] "Well-cut!" he had written following the announcement of the Broglie ministry; "now it must be sewn together!"[50]

In Cassagnac's mind it was utterly clear that there should be a conservative alliance in the elections of 1877, and he urged his Bonapartist colleagues to cooperate in achieving one. Rouher and his associates, on the other hand, had little faith in the outcome of *Seize Mai*; they regarded it primarily as the "triumph of Orleanism," and at first they tried to hold the party aloof.[51] Even after the Senate, with vital cooperation of Bonapartist votes, decided to support the president's decision to dissolve the Chamber, Rouher was reluctant to commit the political forces at his disposal to the cause of social defense without adequate compensation. He preferred the idea of conservatives joining forces only on the second ballot, with each dynastic party for itself on the first. Thus would Bonapartist identity be maintained.

The principal advocates of a conservative alliance, however, desired a united single candidacy in each constituency in opposition to the 363 republicans. On 29 June Monseigneur Dupanloup addressed a letter to Paul de Cassagnac in which he expressed his concern over the Bonapartists' plan, calling it "blameworthy and fatal."

> The terrain of the elections is that of the dissolution
> vote; for the moment there is no other. Radicalism is
> the enemy, and in order to triumph over its powerful
> organization and its fearsome propaganda, all the

conservative forces united are not too many. The other question -- that of a definitive form of government -- is premature; let us wait . . . . First, a conservative Chamber . . . . This is the path of truth, of loyalty and of salvation.

If you share these thoughts, I believe you could perform a useful task, even for the Bonapartist party, in preventing it from so deviating and from indulging in agitation to the liking of the impatient. It would be a work especially useful for France . . . .[52]

On 1 July, Paul de Cassagnac published an editorial entitled "Le terrain des elections," which reads as a direct response to Dupanloup's request. Cassagnac insisted that the electoral issue was quite simply "moral order" versus radicalism; the question of dynastic preference was not at stake. The coalition was concerned with a social, not a political program: "Public peace, order, religion -- these are the things we wish to protect."[53]

During the month of July each of the monarchist parties formed an electoral committee for the purpose of choosing candidates and negotiating with the committees of the other parties. Each party finally agreed to the principle of running a single candidate in each constituency. In addition to Rouher, members of the Bonapartist action committee were Eugène Jolibois (then president of the parliamentary group *Appel au peuple*),[54] the Duc de Padoue,[55] and Baron de Mackau, each of whom favored the policy of conservative alliance. These were the men who met with a committee of royalists headed by Charles Kolb-Bernard, senator from Lille, and with the so-called Catholic committee of the rue de Rennes.[56]

By the end of July, however, their negotiations had reached a stalemate. Mackau wrote Cassagnac a long confidential letter, in which he detailed his woes in working with Rouher on selection of candidates and described the obstacles set up both by Rouher and by the legitimists to the production of a common electoral manifesto.[57] The next day, Rouher's *L'Ordre* printed a letter signed by Rouher, Padoue, and Jolibois -- though not by Mackau -- complaining that the Bonapartists were being "sacrificed, as in the last general elections, to the disquieting cupidity of the other parties."[58] In addition, the authors of the letter upbraided Cassagnac for remarks he had made concerning Rouher and the committee. In *Le Pays*, Cassagnac retorted that Rouher alone was responsible for the difficulties; he alleged that the vice-emperor had "absorbed" the original twelve-man committee established by the party to maintain a balance of opinions. Not only were there only six candidacies at issue, he claimed (having apparently learned this from Mackau's letter), but it had been Rouher who had subverted the joint manifesto. He angrily challenged the committee for affirming that "we know nothing and are informed of nothing," and castigated it for demanding "a DEFERENCE which insufficiently disguises the necessity of servility that seems to be required of all those who add some independence to their devotion."[59]

To this Rouher replied with a public letter to *L'Ordre* in which he requested its editor not to respond to further articles by Cassagnac. Furthermore, he publicly blamed Cassagnac for his provocations:

. . . It hardly displeases me to be attacked, even calumnied, by the editor-in-chief of *Le Pays*. If in so doing he finds an advantage in dissociating himself from me and putting himself in better relief, I acquire a no less precious advantage: the right to attest publicly that I have always condemned a policy whose excesses and transports of anger have too often been inspired by the feelings of a personality who deludes himself.[60]

This was too much for Paul de Cassagnac and he completed the rupture by a personal attack on Rouher:

As for the important role I wish to play, rest assured it does not resemble yours in the least and will not trouble you. I will not compete with you either for portfolios or diamond plaques. My role will be limited to not abandoning my sovereign in the midst of a riot, if ever such lamentable days as those of September 1870 should recur, and to remaining impassively in my seat at the Senate, no matter what, rather than fleeing before the barbarians of Belleville.[61]

Such was the disagreeable state of affairs in the Bonapartist party as the elections approached, a situation which the republicans gleefully exploited.

The language Paul de Cassagnac employed against Rouher was mild compared to that he unleashed to defend *Seize Mai* both in *Le Pays* and in the Chamber from May until October 1877. During these months his polemic against the republicans increased in verbal violence, reaching an extravagant level of exaltation. The republicans delighted in quoting him as proof of the sinister intentions of the ministry itself. His disruptive performance in the Chamber during the mid-June interpellation of the 363 republicans, directed against Gambetta and

Ferry, was only the most notorious example of a pattern that began at the outset of his first term in the Chamber, earning him repeated censures and expulsions. He let forth a further barrage of impassioned prose following the death of Adolphe Thiers in early September 1877. Thiers -- the adopted hero of the 363 was, to Cassagnac, a man "who exercised an ill-starred influence on France;" he was the "renegade of a past which had some value, the unconscious instrument of a dishonored present, the eventual candidate of an odious future, . . . a trembling old man, a crumbling apostate, . . . suspended like a threat over honorable, conservative France, . . . [who] wanted to bind and gag monarchist France, the France of believers, and deliver her over to the eternal republic."[62] This was venomous, insulting and, to some, impardonable language.

Once arrived in Gers, where he would defend his seat in the Chamber, Cassagnac again mustered all his considerable rhetorical facility to castigate the 363 republicans who composed the majority that had censured the Broglie ministry. The 363 represented "the union of the most disparate elements, those most foreign to one another," he told an audience in the arrondissement of Lectoure.

> There the Communard gives his arm to the philosopher; the "pink" joins with the "red;" Marat dances with Vergniaud. There the Mountain embraces the Gironde before devouring it . . . . In sum, there is all that the republic contains of social menaces, of amnestied crimes, of pardoned infamies and of tempting daydreams.[63]

In late September the ministry at last felt ready to decree 14 October as the date for the elections. Accordingly Paul de Cassagnac released his electoral manifesto. He recalled to his electors that in 1876 he had run as an Imperialist, as an adversary of the revolutionary republic, and as a devotee of order, religion, and government as represented by Mac-Mahon, and had likewise called for a plebiscite. In 1877, however, circumstances had altered.

> There is no question of changing the form of government. A more formidable question has presented itself; the question of social health. Before knowing how we will live, we must know if we are to go on living. The enemy is there -- it is the red Republic. It is meditating a sinister and awful revenge. Will you let it take this revenge? No! no! a thousand times no![64]

The Gers republicans were none too optimistic about their chances in the 1877 elections. As Jean David had noted already in August, the change in prefects made by the ministry of *Seize Mai* had once again rendered the Cassagnacs "all-powerful at the prefecture."[65] Only in October did Paul de Cassagnac acquire an opponent, Lacroix, the same man who had run against him in 1876. Lacroix was counting on abstentions as his only hope to win.[66]

The system of official candidacy used by the July Monarchy and refined by the Second Empire was fully employed in Gers in 1877: republican mayors were purged; teachers were displaced; local clubs and cafes were closed; and even musical societies suspected of republican sympathies were dissolved. The archbishop of Auch restricted his efforts to ordering public prayers for the cause of moral order. The ministry, less circumspect, ordered the opening of the newly-completed and very important Auch-Toulouse railway, as an electoral plum. All the republicans could do, besides attempting to reassure the moderates by appealing to the name of Thiers, was to invoke the conduct of the American president, Ulysses S. Grant, who, in contrast to Mac-Mahon, had "no politics to oppose to the will of the nation." More tellingly, their newspaper *L'Avenir* asserted that a conservative victory would result in the return of the tithe, the restoration of Church property nationalized and sold in the 1790s, and the prospect of war with Italy over the issue of temporal power of the Pope.[67]

Paul de Cassagnac was reelected by a margin of 10,896 to 6,750.[68] Since 1876 he had gained some 1,100 votes, while his republican opponent had lost 130. The total number of voters had remained constant. Cassagnac had not gained back many republican votes, but had received the votes previously given to the legitimist candidate.[69] The policy of conservative alliance practiced in Gers had borne its fruits. In the department as a whole, republican votes had decreased since 1876 from 33 per cent to 29 per cent of those registered. All the incumbent Imperialist deputies had been reelected, as had the radical Descamps, who once again defeated a legitimist in the district of Lectoure.[70]

In sum, the department of Gers had held firm behind Cassagnac, Mac-Mahon and the candidates of moral order. However, the nation as a whole had not followed suit. After the first ballot the republicans retained a weaker but nevertheless clear majority, with 315 seats to 199 for their adversaries.[71] Although the conservatives won eleven of the fifteen run-off elections, they were still outnumbered in the Chamber. The republicans were potentially in a position to carry out their previously announced threat to invalidate conservative elections and to overturn the Broglie ministry at the first possible opportunity.

Despite this setback, Paul de Cassagnac and his colleagues favored taking a hard line. Cassagnac urged the president and his ministry to stand firm behind those who, as candidates or as public officials, had risked their careers on his behalf.[72] The Chamber voted, 312 to 205, for a parliamentary inquiry into the electoral activities of the ministry of *Seize Mai*, and the Senate refused to oppose such an inquiry. Following this vote, in mid-November, the ministers resigned. When the Chamber refused to receive the new Rochebouët ministry or to vote the necessary funds, Cassagnac called on the president to demand a second dissolution.[73] Even though key members of the Senate made it clear that they would refuse to support a second dissolution, the president called on Batbie, senator from Gers, to form a ministry that would resist the Chamber. As late as 11 December the president remained disposed to fight. The republicans, in turn, feared a repetition of the *coup* of 2 December 1851, but at the last minute Mac-Mahon backed down before the prospect.[74] Louis-Napoleon found no imitator in the old general.

Thus had Mac-Mahon arrived at the position predicted by Gambetta: he must either submit to the will of the Chamber or resign. When he had first entertained negotiations with Dufaure for a ministry that would satisfy the Chamber, Cassagnac directed a volley of verbal fire at him. Instead of resigning, Cassagnac charged, the president was capitulating: abandonment of his supporters constituted a breach of honor.[75] Following the nomination in mid-December of a Dufaure ministry and the publication of Mac-Mahon's statement of submission, Cassagnac wrote off the president, from whom he had expected so much, as morally dead.[76] Indeed, Cassagnac rarely spoke of Mac-Mahon in print again, except to place full responsibility for the failure of *Seize Mai* on his shoulders.[77] By November 1879, Mac-Mahon had become the president "whose very name I have forgotten;" so deep was Cassagnac's bitter disappointment with the hoped-for champion of *Impérialisme* who had turned out so badly.[78] His companions in arms, who had been so close to victory, were to suffer the wrath of those they had failed to defeat.

* * *

With Mac-Mahon's disappearance, Paul de Cassagnac announced the dissolution of the conservative alliance. He appealed to the former allies to preserve their friendly ties in the face of common peril.[79] Soon thereafter he defined his new political stance -- "prudent but implacable" opposition to the new government. "We will miss no occasion to be disagreeable to our adversaries, knowing full well that they will not stand on ceremony with us."[80]

Indeed, the republicans did not stand on ceremony with Paul de Cassagnac. As a symbol of the staunchest support of *Seize Mai*, he became the target of calculated republican revenge. His election, with those of several other chosen victims, was designated as a sacrifice to be laid on the altar of the republic.[81] By twice adjourning discussion of Cassagnac's election, the republican majority was able to deprive him of his vote (if not of the right to speak) in the Chamber until November 1878, at which time it finally invalidated his election. In the meantime the republicans determined to make their presence felt in Gers by sending an electoral inquiry committee to prove to the countryfolk of Gers (as Jean David had put it in 1876) "that the republic they don't believe in does exist."[82]

Cassagnac was in no mood to submit and, during the year his election hung in the balance, he behaved like a caged tiger, snarling his defiance. "Here is an election," he wrote in *Le Pays*, "with a margin of more than four thousand votes, and which the republicans treat with such off-handedness as to attest to their disdain for universal suffrage!"[83] In November 1878, as he defended his election in a four and one-half hour speech, he defied the republicans to seize his seat: "The morsel is too big for you, gentlemen, and I am here to tell you (Laughs from the Right) that you are taking on the chief of the Imperialist party in this department of mine! I will beat you if you come there -- and not only will I beat you, I will also make probable the victory of conservatives in the other two arrondissements [Auch, where Peyrusse had been invalidated, and Lectoure] by recapturing the strength and complete prestige which . . . were temporarily shaken there."[84] Those who had given depositions against his elections "represent all the unsatiated appetites of my arrondissement, all the dormant hates that ask only one thing -- the chance to make a trip to Paris."[85]

On 2 February 1879 Paul de Cassagnac was reelected deputy of Condom by a much narrower margin -- 9,563 to 8,603 -- against a new republican opponent, the physician Odilon Lannelongue, who was known to be a close personal friend of Gambetta.[86] The electoral battle had been gruelling: the republicans of Gers, including Jean David, were all on the scene to aid their colleague. Their principal technique in one canton at least was to buy off Cassagnac's electoral agents;[87] another was to organize the local royalists against him.[88] Paul de Cassagnac in turn dogged the heels of the republican troop, in order to counteract the effects of their campaign. David was quoted as reporting that Cassagnac might be elected after all, since "the peasants find him more revolutionary and more radical than his opponent, Dr. Lannelongue . . . ."[89] Following his reelection, Cassagnac lavishly praised his constituents for having so valiantly resisted the corruption of the republicans: of all three elections he had won there, Cassagnac declaimed, "this one is certainly the most glorious!"[90] This time the Chamber validated Paul de Cassagnac without discussion.

Back in the Chamber, Cassagnac returned immediately to the offensive against the republic. Taking his cue from a statement by the Ministry of Interior on freedom of the press, he once again pointed to the yawning gap between republican theory and practice of liberty, which he had exploited to such effect a few years earlier:

> You overthrew the Empire in the name of liberty, but where is the liberty you have given us since then?
>
> Where is the journalist who can write with impunity in the name of freedom of the press?
>
> Where is the candidate for the deputation who can be certain of validation in the name of electoral liberty?
>
> Where is the [religious] congregation that can be assured of a future in the name of freedom of association?
>
> Not only is liberty not given us, as the republic ought to give it, but it is diminished in comparison to that of the empire.
>
> The prisons are full of writers, half of France's educational system is about to be suppressed, priests are insulted in the street, the Eucharist has become the public laughing-stock of the *collègiens* of Roanne, all the properties bought by the Catholics at great cost, in order to found free universities decreed by republican law, are ruined, and you ask us -- in your audacious imprudence -- to tell you that this is liberty.[91]

If Cassagnac had learned anything from the adventure of *Seize Mai*, it was certainly not humility in the face of a wily and determined adversary.

* * *

In early 1879, while Paul de Cassagnac was still campaigning in Gers, the republicans had established their dominance in all three arms of the government -- the Chamber, the Senate, and the presidency -- and were, therefore, in a position to carry out their well-publicized program of laicization in education. With the formation of the Waddington ministry in early February 1879, Jules Ferry, a republican long known for his positivist and anticlerical opinions, became Minister of Public Instruction and took the lead in sponsoring laic legislation.[92] Although Gambetta had originally been responsible for invoking the specter of clericalism, it was Ferry who from 1877 on appointed himself its chief exorcist.[93] He thus joined Gambetta as a *bête noire* in Cassagnac's polemical menagerie.

Ferry submitted his first two proposals to the Chamber in mid-March 1879.[94] The first measure, designed to exclude members of the clergy from the *Conseil supérieur de l'instruction publique*, was controversial enough. The second measure, a renewed attempt to revise the law of 1875 on higher education, aroused intense conflict. This latter proposal contained an extremely controversial article that would prohibit members of non-authorized religious orders from teaching in or directing either state or private schools in France. As the two bills were turned over to committees for study, the battle lines began to form in anticipation of a showdown over Article 7. Paul de Cassagnac reminded the president of the Chamber of his desire to speak early in the debate.[95]

When the Ferry proposal on higher education came to the floor of the Chamber on 16 June 1879, Paul de Cassagnac inflamed the proceedings by opening with a deliberate attack on Ferry. As he scored thrust after verbal thrust at the minister, the Chamber teetered precariously on the brink of uproar. Gambetta suspended the session and, enforcing the newly-strengthened rules of the Chamber, had Cassagnac censored and expelled from the body for three days, on grounds that he had insulted the government. Moreover, as Cassagnac departed, hurling a final provocation, Gambetta threatened him with prosecution.[96]

In *Le Pays*, Cassagnac published the undelivered remainder of his speech. He prefaced the text with the boast that the republic "suppresses her adversaries, since she is in no position to combat them," and maintained that he had been the victim of a premeditated attempt to silence him.[97]

The essence of his argument was that the war against the Catholic teaching faculties and religious congregations represented the sole means of maintaining republican unity, by distracting the radicals from attempts to institute a truly republican program: "You are parading the 'black' specter in an attempt to conceal the 'red' specter!" he exclaimed.[98] Cassagnac prophesied that the attack against the congregations was but the beginning of a campaign against Catholicism per se.[99] During the course of his argument, Cassagnac defended the Jesuits, whom the anticlericals always considered the very incarnation of the "black" specter.[100] He concluded by repeating his condemnation of the republicans' betrayal of the principle of liberty they had so sturdily espoused when in opposition.[101]

The republican majority was, however, resolute. Unmoved either by the arguments of Paul de Cassagnac or those expressed by his Catholic colleagues during the ensuing weeks of debate, the Chamber passed Article 7 by a vote of 347 to 143. The entire bill on higher education moved on to the Senate and the Catholics readied themselves for struggle.[102]

* * *

For Paul de Cassagnac, the religious issue had now become the essence of the conflict between republic and monarchy in France. He considered it to be the cardinal point of battle for Imperialism, and goaded his fellow Bonapartists into taking a stand on the defense of "moral order," despite their serious reservations. The failure of *Seize Mai*, however, meant the ouster of the defenders of moral order from their strongholds, allowing the republicans to take the offensive against the positions previously conquered in France by Catholic interests. Henceforth, Paul de Cassagnac would be found among the most intransigent defenders of the Church's prerogatives, even to the point of splitting the Bonapartist party in two to achieve its alignment in the camp of religious defense.

Paul de Cassagnac as a young man

Granier de Cassagnac as porcupine, 1868, by André Gill

Duel of Paul de Cassagnac and Lissagaray, 1868, by André Gill

PRIX : 0.50

LE PROCÈS DE SEDAN

PAUL DE CASSAGNAC

Paul de Cassagnac in zouave uniform
Le Procès de Sedan, 1875

Coming-of-Age of the Prince Imperial, Chislehurst, 1874

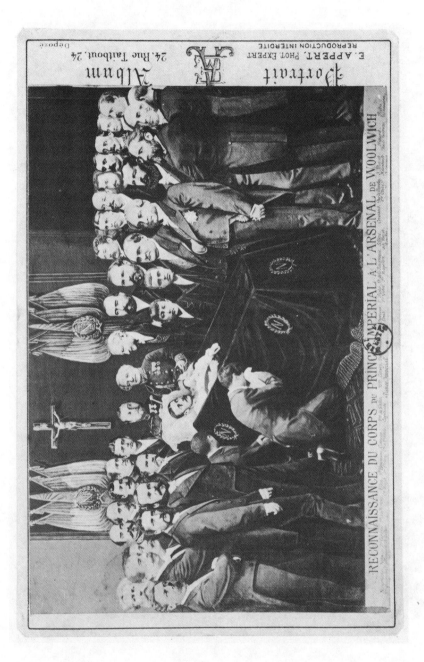

Death of the Prince Imperial, Funeral photograph, 1879

LE LIBÉRATEUR DU TERRITOIRE

Le Libérateur du Territoire, Lithograph, from a painting by J.-A. Garnier, 1877

PAUL DE CASSAGNAC

Caricature of Paul de Cassagnac by Gill, 1878

Caricatures from the Archives of the Prefecture de Police, Paris

"La Rentrée de Paul"
by "Flock" [pseud. A. Gill]
Le Grelot
29 October 1871

Cassagnac as "Po-Paul"
Le Mephisto (Lyon)
10 March 1878

Bouledogue qui pose en vain pour le caniche
En voulant faire croire à la fidélité
A la chaîne rivé, raille la liberté
Tu ne peux la comprendre, étant fait pour la niche.

Alfred Le Petit

Cassagnac as Imperial Bulldog
by A. Le Petit
Les Contemporains
1881

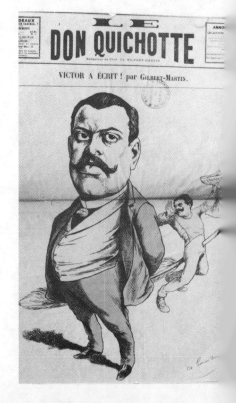

"Victor a écrit!"
by C. Gilbert-Martin
Le Don Quichotte
(Bordeaux)
11 September 1886

Caricature of Paul de Cassagnac, by Blass

Caricatures from the "Parallel March, " 1889

"La Reprise de la Bastille," by Blass

"Dévisseurs de Parlementaires," by Blass

"Pour Faire la Trouée," by Blass

Baisse! Il Baisse!" by Pépin

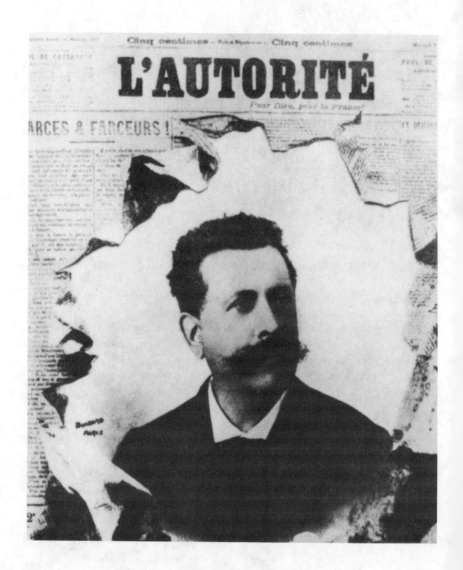

Cassagnac and *L'Autorité*, 1890s

Portrait of Paul de Cassagnac
Photograph, 1890s

Cassagnac as seen by *L'Assiette au Beurre*, 1900s

CHAPTER VI

THE POLITICS OF CATHOLIC DEFENSE AND IMPERIALISM
VICTORISME: 1879-1885

Dieu avant tout, les princes après!

Paul de Cassagnac
Le Conservateur du Gers
12 March 1882

L'Empire n'est plus un opposant, il devient un rival!

Paul de Cassagnac
At the Victorist banquet
Salle Wagram, 15 August 1882

Je suis, en politique, catholique d'abord,
monarchiste ensuite, impérialiste après . . . .

Paul de Cassagnac
Addressing the Chamber of
Deputies, 26 December 1882

On 20 June 1879, Paris received word that the nineteen year-old Prince Imperial had been killed in an ambush in Zululand, where he was serving with the British army. Informed opinion quickly concluded that the death of the young prince had struck a mortal blow to the Bonapartist party.[1]

The tragedy was fatefully timed, for debate on the Ferry proposals was in full swing; the issue of religious defense was paramount in the eyes of the Right. It was clear that the prince's death placed the Bonapartist party in an impossible position, for the anticlerical and republican inclinations of Prince Napoleon, now heir to the throne of the empire, clashed sharply with the monarchist and Catholic sentiments of the party's parliamentary leaders. Bonapartism as an identifiable political force in France required some accommodation among its adherents, divided on an issue which at that very moment was polarizing French political life. Already in 1876 Baron de Mackau had warned the Prince Imperial that if the leadership of the party fell into the hands of the "demagogic Bonapartists" (by which he meant Prince Napoleon and his partisans), conservative Bonapartists such as himself would be forced either to separate themselves from the party or to retire into private life.[2] In 1879, given the dimension of the coming struggle against the laicizers, however, it was apparent that the Imperialists did not plan to retire without a fight.

In a black-bordered edition of Le Pays, Paul de Cassagnac asserted defiantly that although the young pretender was no more, the empire was by no means dead. According to Cassagnac, the Prince Imperial had not designated his father's cousin, the fifty-six year old Prince Napoleon, as the heir, but had bypassed the latter in favor of his elder son Prince Victor, a youth of seventeen, "a young man with an ardent heart, a lively mind, who has been made worthy of us, worthy of France, through the guidance of his pious mother."[3] And, he added, even without a Prince Victor, the idea of the empire would remain to impose itself. "Bonapartism may be in peril, but Imperialism is stronger than ever."[4]

Cassagnac's assertion that Prince Napoleon might be bypassed in favor of his adolescent son was echoed only by Jules Amigues, the editor of the popular Bonapartist newspaper, Le Petit Caporal.[5] Those who interpreted the laws of dynastic succession literally treated the suggestion with disdain, but their disdain soon turned to dismay when on 30 June, Rouher read to the assembled deputies and senators of Appel au peuple the last will of the Prince Imperial -- and its codicil. Much to the joy of some and the scandal of others, young Prince Victor had indeed been designated as successor.[6]

In Le Pays, Paul de Cassagnac elaborated on the reasoning that lay behind the codicil: Prince Napoleon had broken the plebiscitary contract between ruler and ruled. By his pro-republican acts and utterances over the years, particularly by his political campaigns in 1874 and 1876 against Bonapartist candidates endorsed by the Prince Imperial (one of whom had been Rouher himself), Prince Napoleon had morally excluded himself from the succession. In consequence of this, "the Prince Imperial had directly designated the son instead of the father -- but not," Cassagnac added ingenuously, "in opposition to the father."[7] Cassagnac's arguments were not well-received by the less doctrinaire Bonapartists such as Robert Mitchell and Léonce Détroyat, who characterized the Victorist solution as "IMPOSSIBLE, absolutely IMPOSSIBLE," and insisted on the necessity of supporting Prince Napoleon.[8]

In the days that followed, Cassagnac shifted ground slightly, admitting that "we have no moral or material way to make Prince Victor an effective and immediate candidate [for the imperial throne]," and suggesting that Prince Napoleon might still make himself acceptable to the ranking party leaders by giving "formal and categorical guarantees" on the religious question. He attempted to place the prince in a bargaining position by suggesting that the alternative to acceptance of the guarantees was the dispersion of the Bonapartist party.[9]

Although skeptics were convinced at the time that Prince Napoleon would never accept such conditions, Cassagnac nonetheless persevered in his demands. Acceptable guarantees must include: recognition of the principle of authority in government; repudiation of all "false democracy" and of any "revolutionary alliances;" guarantees for complete and absolute respect for religion, from the doctrine to the external forms, and for freedom of education -- both primary and secondary -- and on the university level to the extent afforded by the law of 1875.[10] With the exception of the first proposal, Cassagnac's program of guarantees amounted to an express invitation to Prince Napoleon to recant and repent the errors of his past. It appeared to have some effect; when the 115 senators and deputies of *Appel au peuple* met on 19 July, they did not vote to rally to the prince without guarantees, but adopted a wait-and-see position. Although this was not the whole of the position advocated by Cassagnac and Mackau, it was clearly a step in that direction.[11]

Judging from an unpublished letter Cassagnac wrote to Mackau in late July 1879, it seems apparent that he wanted to reach some accommodation with Prince Napoleon -- or, more precisely, that he would have been satisfied if the prince made the necessary concessions:

I have reason to believe that the prince will come around.

But any show of eagerness and impatience [on our part] would be a deplorable means of getting him there.

The prince must return to our Empire; it would be ridiculous for his friends to think that our Empire has to accommodate itself to him.

He must reassure everybody and win them over.
It is not an easy task . . . .[12]

And, he added ominously, "The Empire is possible only at this price."

The stand-off between Prince Napoleon and the Imperialists continued throughout the winter and into the early months of 1880,

when the Senate rejected Article 7 of Ferry's law on higher education.
The republican majority in the Chamber voted a resolution calling for
the "enforcement of the existing laws" against the congregations,
passing over a proposal by the Imperialist deputies calling for freedom
of association as the sole satisfactory solution to the issue.[13]   On 29
March 1880, the Freycinet ministry issued decrees enforcing these
"existing laws," which dated from 1790 and 1792 and had long lain
dormant.[14]

In *Le Pays*, Paul de Cassagnac poured out his rage against the
decrees in four long columns, predicting that even though the acts called
for were only isolated, localized moves, they represented the beginning
of a war to the death by republicans on freedom of conscience:

> Far from being satisfied, the revolutionary
> appetite will only be whetted by these first
> satisfactions.
>
> Tomorrow, it will call for the other
> congregations; tomorrow it will seek out the Brothers
> of Christian Doctrine, the secular clergy and the
> bishops; tomorrow it will try to close the churches, to
> mock the cult and to obtain its banishment.[15]

In another article entitled "A Common Ground -- Religious Defense,"
Cassagnac declared that the republicans, by their persecution, had
succeeded in giving their opponents a principle around which to unite --
the principle of religious defense. Such an issue, dominating all
political differences, provided assurance of discipline in the ranks.
When the Church was confronted, noted Cassagnac, even Frederick
Barbarossa, Napoleon I, and Bismarck had been checked; how dared the
meager republic pretend to take on such an adversary?[16]

Prince Napoleon was of another opinion, and his response to the
March decrees consummated the schism between his followers and the
Imperialists. On 5 April, in a letter published in *L'Ordre*, the prince
endorsed the decrees as a long-overdue return to the principles of the
Concordat as established by the first Napoleon. They "do not constitute
persecution; they merely represent a return to an unquestionable rule of
public law." The reason "certain Bonapartists" were attacking the
decrees, the prince stated, was because they feared the dissolution of the
conservative alliance, that "disastrous fiction" which had already lasted
too long:

> There is nothing in common between the legitimists,
> who conspire against all that '89 represents, and we
> who have rendered it invincible; between the men of
> the white flag and the faithful of the national flag. It

is time for each to take up his own colors, his
traditions, his principles, and to cease equivocation.
Of all the ways to be untrue to ourselves, the most
deadly would be that which makes us appear in the
eyes of the nation as one with the hopes of the old
regime, which would lead us to deny the legislation
authorized by the Napoleons, and which would make
us the auxiliaries of a party forever condemned, a
party that lowers religion to the instrument of the
passions and calculations of a retrograde politics,
hostile to civilization, to science, and to true liberty.[17]

To the Imperialists this declaration meant rupture: they charged that
Prince Napoleon had thereby declared his solidarity with the republican
government and its program of laicization. "Henceforth," declared Paul
de Cassagnac, "we can pursue freely and without reservation, the
realization of the supreme idea of the Prince Imperial."[18] This
statement was the real beginning of *Victorisme*, through which the
Imperialists committed to a policy of religious defense attempted to
maintain their political identity during the years to come. In retrospect,
this rupture in the dynastic succession, demanded of an authoritarian
monarchy by discontented supporters in the name of a specific set of
sociopolitical values and ideas, can be said to represent a spectacular
advance in the democratization of French political life. Ideas had
triumphed over lineage.

* * *

On 10 December 1880 Prince Napoleon launched a new newspaper,
which he called *Napoléon*. Its director was Adalbert Philis, a close
associate of the prince. On the first page, *Napoléon*'s editor published a
program-manifesto in which he announced the new party's aims: no
hostility toward the republican form of government, but a program
calling for revision of the constitutional laws of 1875 to establish a
presidency elected by universal suffrage, as well as a Senate elected in
the same manner, thereby establishing the responsibility of both to the
electorate.

Napoléon's inspirers advocated the secularization of society and
suggested suppressing the temporal power of the Pope; they also
advocated "democratic" economic reforms such as revision of the tax
structure.[19] These were ideas which, as another staunch supporter of
the prince, the deputy Paul Lenglé, remarked "were of a nature to
astonish a party that had directed itself little by little to the side of the

royalists, toward clericalism, *bourgeoisisme*, and uproar."[20] The following month, Lenglé submitted to the Chamber a proposal for constitutional reform modelled on that of *Napoléon*. This program provided the substance of *Jérômisme*. Or, as Lenglé would phrase it, grandly invoking history: "The consular republic had taken position against the parliamentary republic."[21] The Jeromists had effectively abandoned the imperial plebiscite.

The Imperialists, who constituted the group *Appel au peuple* in the Chamber, responded by published a manifesto of their own in which they stated that if the *appel au peuple* were refused to them they would "demand that the republic re-enter the way of truth . . . by reforming the constitution, stipulating that this be done in the name of national sovereignty."[22] Paul de Cassagnac, however, held out for the empire:

> We ourselves remain true to the *appel au peuple*,
> the motto of Napoleon III and the banner of the Prince
> Imperial . . . . Only *appel au peuple* can give us the
> empire, and the empire is what we want.
>
> Revision of the constitution can only give us a
> republic -- and we do not want a republic, in whatever
> form and with whatever president.[23]

The year 1881 was an election year. It was generally accepted in political circles that, in response to the wishes of Gambetta, the electoral system would be changed to *scrutin de liste*. Consequently, Prince Napoleon adopted a strategy in which he would pit himself against Gambetta in a series of multiple candidacies, thereby providing an informal plebiscite between secular revisionist republicanism and secular parliamentary republicanism. On 19 May the Chamber voted for the *scrutin de liste*, but on 9 June the Senate defeated it. The Senate vote was fatal to the plans of Prince Napoleon.[24]

In the face of this setback, eleven of the outgoing Bonapartist deputies closest to the prince published a manifesto of their own in *Napoléon*, calling for constitutional revision within the form of the republic. Ominously, seven of these eleven, including Lenglé, were defeated.[25] Moreover, of the many other candidates endorsed by Prince Napoleon, none of his closest friends and principal supporters (including Maurice Richard, Ernest Pascal, and Georges Lachaud) was elected to the Chamber. *Jérômisme* as a political force in the Chamber had been nipped in the bud. The prince was convinced, however, that the republican nuance was not to blame for these defeats and he argued instead that it had not been sufficiently stressed. "We must say clearly," he wrote to Lenglé, "that we want the *Republic*, Revision, *the election of the president by the people and that our candidate is the heir of the Napoleons*. We spared the [party's] past too much for the democrats and were too advanced for the old party -- with which *nothing can be done. It is dead.*"[26]

The Imperialists were far from dead, as Prince Napoleon would soon discover to his great regret. Indeed, they returned to the Chamber in numbers far greater than did the Jeromists. Although Rouher had decided to retire from political life and did not run, thirty-three other deputies of *Appel au peuple*, all but three of whom were familiar faces in the Chamber, were elected in 1881.[27]

In the department of Gers, Paul de Cassagnac set the tone for the Imperialists:

> My profession of faith is easy to make.
>
> I have never varied in my political opinions and I will never vary. This fidelity, which no difficulty has been able to shake, which death itself has been unable to bend, shall be the honor of my life.
>
> I shall always carry the banner of the empire, which I have held high over your valiant heads with the same pride and confidence during long and difficult years, after so many misfortunes, so many discouragements, so much treason . . . . I owe you this frank declaration, as I owe it to my adversaries and especially to my generous allies who, without sharing my regrets or my hopes, are nonetheless disposed to give me the mandate to combat for all we share in common -- for the *rélèvement* of France, for the glory of God, for the confusion of the revolutionary idea.
>
> The hour of dynastic complications has not yet arrived: before asking ourselves to whom France will belong, we must first insure that there will still be a France![28]

In this election, Cassagnac changed constituencies, announcing for the *arrondissement* of Mirande, whose seat had formerly been held by his father, Granier de Cassagnac (and since the latter's death in early 1880, by Cassagnac's younger brother Georges). In Mirande, he won a sizeable victory (11,004 to 8,811) over his opponent, Adrien Lannes de Montebello, who being the grandson of the marshal who had served Napoleon I, Cassagnac argued, was not a serious republican.[29] In Condom, Cassagnac sponsored Ferdinand Daynaud, who was elected in the *ballotage* over the republican Lannelongue.[30]

* * *

The Imperialist deputies had consolidated their political base. It remained for them to rebuild the Bonapartist party in their own image, around the youthful Prince Victor. This course of action took the form of a very public campaign, and issued in very curious results.

In 1882 *Victorisme* began to take shape as a political movement. During that spring, Prince Victor had gone to Heidelberg to study, and the press began to follow his movements with keen interest.[31] In the summer months, a number of *Victorien impérialiste* committees had been organized in Paris, thanks to the activity of Jules Amigues and his disciple, Henri Dichard, editor of *Le Petit Caporal* since March 1882.[32] Shortly after the prince's twentieth birthday in July, *Victorisme* was officially launched: six thousand Imperialists gathered in Paris for a banquet at the Salle Wagram to hear Paul de Cassagnac and Jules Amigues proclaim the coming-of-age of *Victorisme*.[33]

Certainly the young prince was attractive to the Imperialists. As even Lenglé, Prince Napoléon's confidant, had to admit, Prince Victor and his younger brother Louis "had been born on the steps of two thrones."[34] This state of affairs was of no small concern to Prince Napoleon himself, and he took precautions lest his sons be set against him by his opponents. When he sent Victor to Heidelberg, he instructed Pugliesi-Conti, Victor's tutor and companion, to intercept any mail that might urge the young prince to undertake any independent political action.[35]

One of the most remarkable aspects of *Victorisme* was the alliance that developed between Amigues and Cassagnac. Amigues had first alluded to the codicil of the Prince Imperial and had most vociferously urged that Prince Napoleon be totally excluded from the imperial succession. Cassagnac had never gone as far in print on that subject, but nevertheless found himself in virtual alliance with this former advocate of the "workers' empire," whom he had treated with contempt for so many years.[36] Their mutual opposition to Prince Napoleon resulted in a slow, cautious *rapprochement* that flourished only after the summer of 1882, when both men were closely associated in arranging the Victorist banquet of 15 August. By the time of Amigues' death in April 1883, they were acknowledged colleagues. Cassagnac served as a pall-bearer and delivered a warm tribute to his fallen "comrade in arms."[37]

With the death of Amigues, Paul de Cassagnac dominated the Victorist movement. At that time he took effective charge of the

Victorist committees, which included both the Parisian *Victorien impérialiste* groups founded by Amigues and Dichard and another cluster of groups established under the auspices of the deputies of *Appel au peuple*.[38] Before long, Cassagnac would give impetus to this new manifestation of Imperialism by effecting the "liberation" of Prince Victor from his father.

In early November 1882, Prince Victor had undertaken to serve in the French army for a year. During that time he was stationed at Orleans, with the 32nd artillery regiment. His supporters had agreed to mute further political activity on his behalf until he had completed his service. Upon his release from the army in November 1883, however, they were quick to act. The Conférence Molé, an important debating society for young lawyers in Paris, invited Prince Victor to speak before their group, but the prince publicly refused the invitation, on the ground that such an appearance might be interpreted as a declaration of political independence from his father.[39] Shortly thereafter he left Paris for Italy, to rejoin his mother, Princess Clotilde of Savoy, and the rest of the Italian royal family at Moncalieri for the Christmas season.

On 2 December 1883 -- the anniversary of the *coup d'état* -- *Le Pays* published an "authorized" commentary on Prince Victor's letter, designed to underscore the fact that the prince's ideas on religion and government were indeed different from those of his father.

> . . . While Prince Victor Napoléon understands and practices filial obedience, he formally intends not to disavow any of the faithful friends who have been inspired by the ideas of Napoleon III and the Prince Imperial to promise France, at the opportune moment, a government that can group together all honest folk around the prestige of a strong power issuing from the national will, by a resolute safeguard of the rights of democracy and conservative interests, and finally, by the protections required for religious beliefs.[40]

This communiqué was hardly calculated to calm Prince Napoleon's fears. He was justifiably suspicious of this sudden public discussion of his elder son, and took measures to put an end to it. Within the fortnight, a letter from Prince Victor to his father appeared in *Le Figaro*. In this letter, Victor repeated that "at this time I have no political role to fulfill," and disavowed any effort "that would have as either its goal or its effect, by dividing our forces, to attribute to me a role which would be as odious in respect to my father as it would be dishonorable for my country." Victor's letter continued:

> You are the head of my family; I remain the faithful

champion of the Napoleonic tradition. My feelings
toward you have never changed and I have never
hesitated to make them known.[41]

In a published commentary on this letter, Paul de Cassagnac once
again underscored the existence of differences in opinion between
Prince Napoleon and his son. Victor's remarks, he argued, only
reinforced the statement of 2 December -- which in fact had had
Victor's "personal adhesion, formal authorization, and preliminary
corrections."[42] A few days later, Prince Napoleon's friend Ernest
Pascal, speaking before a Jeromist gathering in Paris, denied that Victor
could have taken any part in the publication of the note, whereupon
Cassagnac replied that Victor had indeed been involved and, what was
more, that he (Cassagnac) possessed the note in question.[43]

Cassagnac's claim precipitated the publication of a note from Prince
Victor's associate, Baron Brunet, in *Le Figaro*, in which a second letter
from Prince Victor to his father was quoted. In this letter, Victor
responded to three questions put to him by his father:

Did you sign some sort of paper? -- No.

Did you correct in your own hand the note in
question? -- No.

Did it contain one word of your handwriting? --
No.[44]

In a reply to *Le Figaro*, Cassagnac staunchly maintained the authenticity
of the note, remarking that Victor's responses to the three questions,
given their generality, did not amount to a denial.[45] The fact was, he
insisted, that the quarrel over the note was "only a pretext:"

This note, which bears witness to the conservative
and Christian sentiments of Prince Victor, has
exasperated Prince Napoleon.

It proves that the son is a potential candidate for
the throne, whereas the father has always been and
will always be an impossible one.

That is the important point, the only important
point.

In our eyes, Prince Victor has no enemy more set
against him than his own father.

This may be sad and difficult to swallow, but
that's how it is.[46]

The Imperialists had initiated a tug-of-war with Prince Napoleon for
possession of his elder son, but it was clear that the latter had no
intention of letting Victor go. The prince was clearly agitated by the
affair. As one observant journalist remarked from the sidelines:

One fact stands out that has deeply impressed
public opinion: namely, Prince Napoleon's
persistence in demanding that his son certify his status
as head of the family and unique head of the
party . . . . This must indicate that the accord is
highly problematic and that the father lacks confidence
in a son from whom he requires weekly votes of
confidence.[47]

The situation became increasingly aggravated during the next few
months. On 11 January, the officers of the imperialist committees of
Paris met and voted a formal resolution requesting their president, Paul
de Cassagnac, to address himself to Prince Victor for "precise and
public declarations concerning his sentiments and political intentions."[48]
Cassagnac left Paris, abruptly, bound for Italy to see the young prince
with this mandate in hand.[49]

Prince Victor replied to the committees in a note dated 15 January:

What have I tried to establish?

I have tried to establish that I would never
associate myself with the attacks that have been made
against my father, and that I repel indignantly every
association with the thought of a revolt.

Moreover, I have tried to declare that, for the
time being, I have no political role to full.

My repeated intervention has had no other goal.

Does this mean, however, that I cannot have my
own personal views on issues of politics and religion.

Certainly not. And I would not be worthy of the
name I bear, and whose patriotic weight I feel, a name
tightly linked to the destiny of my country, if I was
absolutely disinterested in things that concern it.

I could not summarize my obligations better than
by recalling what I wrote from Heidelberg, notably
that: "I am preparing myself to serve my country well,
on the day that my duty calls me to do so."

Until then, I will maintain the reserve that duty
imposes upon me, while nevertheless acknowledging,
believe me, the affection and devotion you have been
charged to transmit to me.[50]

According to police reports, Prince Napoleon was "furious" at
Victor for this letter and he left Paris for Moncalieri to confront his son
face to face.[51] This visit resulted in yet another letter from Victor, in
which he agreed to undertake no political action whatsoever without the

express agreement of his father; this letter, unlike its predecessors, was not made public until later in the year.[52] The Imperialists must have been aware of this new development, for they cancelled plans for a huge meeting which had been scheduled for 17 February, and soon thereafter, Cassagnac called a halt to all Victorist organizing activities.[53]

Prince Napoleon had won the round. His supporters celebrated this triumph by sponsoring a huge meeting at the Cirque d'Été on 16 February to give new impetus to their program of constitutional revision and to the candidacy of their prince for president of the republic. When the delegates from the meeting called on Prince Napoleon to present their resolutions, Prince Victor appeared at his father's side.[54]

But the Imperialists had not given up. Already in February rumors had begun to circulate that they were attempting to raise funds with which to assure Prince Victor's independence.[55] By early May they had succeeded in raising a capital sum that would produce a yearly income of 40,000 francs for the young prince. At first it was believed that the money had been a legacy from the late Madame Auban-Moët, heiress to the Moët et Chandon champagne fortune, but later it was revealed and confirmed that it had come from a handful of wealthy Imperialists.[56] Such a *caisse* was considered vital since Prince Victor was wholly dependent for funds on his father, who himself was not a very wealthy man, at least by princely standards. Prince Victor could expect to inherit the fortune of Empress Eugenie, who had made him her sole heir, but she appeared to be in good health -- and, in fact, she lived until 1920, dying only six years before Prince Victor.

When Prince Napoleon learned of the Imperialists' fund, he was furious. He confronted his son who admitted that he was indeed receiving this sum and that it came to him through Jolibois.[57] Prince Napoleon and his partisans were convinced that the Orleanists were behind the affair and were set on destroying the Bonapartist party by taking advantage of the youth and credulity of Prince Victor; his friend Lenglé condemned the move as a clear-cut confrontation between reactionaries and democrats within the party. "*Aille qui voudra avec le Roy, Napoléon reste avec le peuple* [Those who wish can go with the King, but Napoleon remains with the people]," he wrote defiantly in *Le Matin*.[58]

On 19 May Prince Victor moved out of his father's house in the rue d'Antin. A few days later he established his own apartment in the rue Monceau. The Jeromists stoutly denied that the move signified a political break, but Paul de Cassagnac insisted that it was, though he cagily refused to elaborate on the point.[59] Prince Napoleon addressed a viputerative letter to Jolibois, following an unproductive encounter between the two men a few days earlier.[60]

By 21 June there could be no further equivocation. Members of the Paris Imperialist committees held a jubilant gathering in Paris to celebrate the "material and moral deliverance of Prince Victor-Napoleon."[61] According to Cassagnac, this had become possible because Prince Napoleon had broken his own agreement with his son to consult jointly on political action, when he issued a manifesto advocating alliance with radical republicans against royalists in the May Paris municipal elections, a strategy to which Prince Victor could never agree.[62] Following Cassagnac's speech, the Victorists enthusiastically reacclaimed Cassagnac president of the committees and voted a resolution applauding Prince Victor's action as a confirmation "that for the Imperialist party he represents Order in democracy and religious liberty, the true politics of the empire."[63]

Thus the Imperialists provoked a new round of publication of private letters. Washing the dynasty's dirty political laundry in public was becoming a habit. *Le Peuple* published Victor's letter of 27 January and Prince Napoleon's letter of 29 May to Jolibois.[64] The Imperialists countered by publishing a letter from Prince Victor to Jolibois, dated 26 June, in which Victor attested to the existence of a pledge between father and son which the father had not kept.[65] The Jeromists capped this sequence by calling a meeting of their own on 2 July 1884, at which Ernest Pascal movingly related the story of the schism and read Prince Victor out of the Bonapartist camp. According to Pascal, Victor was "nothing but the base instrument of those who, by egoistic calculation, are bent on extending their hand to the eternal enemies of his race and his name."[66] This was strong language indeed. The assembled Jeromists then voted a resolution of sympathy and renewed devotion to Prince Napoleon, in face of Victor's act of "moral parricide and political treason."[67]

Not only did the Imperialists capture a prince but they also captured an important newspaper -- both at the expense of Prince Napoléon. The once popular Imperialist newspaper, *Le Petit Caporal*, had been in serious financial trouble during the years 1882 and 1883. Its editor, Henri Dichard, had fought desperately to stave off bankruptcy proceedings, but by the spring of 1884 he was no longer able to avoid court action.[68] Prince Napoleon had entertained high hopes of acquiring the paper -- minus its debts -- following the bankruptcy declaration, but was too late, outmaneuvered by Paul de Cassagnac, whom the prince and his friends suspected to be the intermediary for the princes of Orleans.[69] Following this disappointment, the Jeromists responded by recommencing publication of *Le Peuple* in mid-1884, with Paul Lenglé as editor-in-chief.[70] The Imperialists reconstituted the capital assets of *Le Petit Caporal* and appointed the retired frigate captain, Commander Blanc, as editor.

In sum, the Imperialists had won the second round. On 9 July, they again celebrated victory, Prince Victor's act of independence, with a banquet and reception hosted by Charles Levert, deputy from Pas-de-Calais and a former imperial prefect.[71] No sooner had they triumphed, however, than they found themselves divided once again over the inescapable question: should they participate in a conservative alliance with supporters of the Comte de Paris, or should they seek the empire alone? This question was to divide the Victorists in the 1880s as much as it had divided the Bonapartists in the previous decade.

* * *

Speaking before a group of Bonapartists in late 1880, Robert Mitchell had denounced an Imperialist for "selling out his party to the royalists." Mitchell coyly maintained at the time that he meant Jules Delafosse,[72] but within only a few months he extended the charge to his former friend Paul de Cassagnac, whom many of Mitchell's colleagues thought he had meant all along.[73] This was the first of a series of public accusations made against Cassagnac to the effect that he was in the pay of the Bourbons, the Orleans, legitimists or, alternatively, of the Jesuits, charges which had been whispered privately for several years. These are serious charges, and they take on an added dimension when it is remembered that Cassagnac's father had also been frequently accused of venality during his own political career. Thus, some attempt must be made to evaluate the charges and to arrive at some estimate of their accuracy.

Prior to 1881 most of these charges were recorded in police reports, in the form of rumors reported by police spies. They originated from two principal sources: legitimist circles (reported by agent "P," who frequented the offices of royalist newspapers and certain other royalist groups),[74] and the group of anticlerical Bonapartist who surrounded Prince Napoleon (reported by agents "Bonap" and "Grégoire"). From 1881 on, the charges made their appearance in the Jeromist press, as well as in police reports.

It seems incontrovertible that throughout the 1870s and 1880s certain legitimists were indeed trying to attract Cassagnac and his fellow Imperialists to join the cause of the Comte de Chambord. They were undoubtedly encouraged by Cassagnac's repeated public expressions of sympathy for legitimism; as early as 1872, he had made it clear that in case France, being consulted, preferred Chambord, "he would have no servant more faithful than I."[75] But consultation of the people was a vital caveat. In 1873 Cassagnac had stated publicly that, were it impossible to obtain an imperialist system, he could accommodate himself to a royalist system: "Among all the regimes that do not proceed from the unique principle. . . of *appel au peuple*, it [the royalist system] is the only clean and honorable one. Moreover, it is the only one that represents the old and precious religious traditions of our country."[76] The obstacle was, of course, that the Comte de Chambord rejected the principle of *appel au peuple*.

Following the death of the Prince Imperial in 1879, the royalists redoubled their efforts. Chambord himself invited the discouraged Imperialists to rally to his cause at that time, but met with little success. Cassagnac replied to this invitation by reaffirming that he was not a legitimist and did not plan to become one.[77] Serious as the situation in the house of Bonaparte might be, he pointed out, it was still less critical than in the house of Bourbon, where the traditional monarchy seemed destined to end with the childless Chambord. As for the latter's eventual heirs, the Orleans branch, Cassagnac dismissed them with a public shrug: "Voltairianism and parliamentarism are the foundations of the Orléans family; the Christian and authoritarian king is doomed to be replaced by *that*!"[78] The Orleanist princes provided no attractive alternative to most of the Imperialists, nor indeed to the legitimists. But the legitimists persisted in their efforts to convert the Imperialists.[79] As the Imperialist Loudun remarked during the spring of 1880:

> I find myself in a singular position with respect to the legitimists. Feigning to believe that one cannot be religious without being in their party, they make advances to me and solicit me to come to them. Some even affect to consider me as already won over, and they let me in on their hopes and sometimes even on their projects.[80]

From 1880 on, the legitimists were encouraged in their hopes by the concerted efforts of Prince Napoleon and his associates to exclude the Imperialists (particularly Cassagnac) from any future Bonapartist party.[81] Especially after the Imperialists' success in "liberating" Prince Victor in 1884, Prince Napoleon's entourage became the principal source of stories attesting to Cassagnac's "treason." In their hostility to everything associated with the princes of Orleans, they seemed convinced that the Victorist schism had been engineered by the Comte de Paris as a means of dividing and conquering the Bonapartist party. They portrayed Paul de Cassagnac as the royalist pretender's principal agent and the conservative alliance as anti-Bonapartist collusion. This attitude, which verged on paranoia, is everywhere evident in the articles and speeches of Lenglé, Pascal, and others in the group, as well as in the police reports.

The most specific allegations of an actual financial deal, however, are found in the police reports. According to various agents, a deal had been struck in May 1884 between Cassagnac and the Comte de Paris during a dinner held at the home of Lacave-Laplagne, the senator from Gers. "Grégoire" reported that Prince Napoleon had even hired a domestic servant in the senator's household to spy on Cassagnac's meetings there with the Orleans princes.[82] Other reports, written long after the fact, allege that both personal monetary gifts and election subventions had been given to Cassagnac by the royalists.[83] From 1884 until 1904, Cassagnac's adversaries threatened intermittently to publish the proof of his alliance with the Orleanists, but the only evidence they ever provided consisted of published press statements of his insistence on conservative alliance and of his equally public refusals to act in any way against the royalists.[84] No documentation of any actual deal has come to light.

Credence was lent to rumors that the royalists might be tempting Cassagnac with funds by the undisputed fact that during the years following his election to the Chamber, Cassagnac suffered from serious financial embarrassment.[85] It seems safe to say that Cassagnac, like many of his contemporaries, had always taken a cavalier attitude toward fiscal management; like Balzac and many other nineteenth-century gentlemen, he was constantly being hounded by his creditors. Indeed, it took a good deal of money to move in the society of the Faubourg Saint-Germain, to which Cassagnac was irresistibly attracted.[86] When in the summer of 1878, he married the wealthy Julia Acard, the size of her substantial dowry -- as well as her clerical connections -- became topics of public discussion.[87]

Beside a wealthy and very Catholic wife, however, Paul de Cassagnac also acquired a financial benefactor during the year 1878. A rich Marseille industrialist, Victor Julien, who had made his fortune in the Saint-Louis sugar refineries, offered to cover Cassagnac's election expenses that year -- as an advance on the inheritance he planned to leave to the young deputy.[88] It is impossible to say what forces may have been at work to determine Julien's decision -- Julien did not seem to have royalist or legitimist connections. On the surface it appears that he simply took a fancy to Cassagnac, whom he had never met personally. As he wrote to the fiery journalist in 1881:

You didn't know me either by name or by sight
when, out of admiration for your political faithfulness
and a sympathy for your disinterested character, I
decided to offer you both my fortune, honestly gained,
and my paternal tenderness . . . .

I owe nothing to the empire; I am independent of
it, but its cause has become dear to me in its
misfortune. I believed that I could best serve the
imperial idea by putting you, whom I knew to be
without fortune, at ease to fight for it with more
liberty and even greater power.[89]

Paul de Cassagnac maintained that at first he resisted this
extraordinary display of generosity, but later accepted on behalf of his
first son, who was born in April 1880. Victor Julien stood as godfather
to the boy, who was named Paul-Julien.[90] Later that year Julien bought
the Cassagnacs a house on Boulevard Malesherbes.[91] But he did not die
until late 1884 and, in the meantime, reports of Cassagnac's financial
difficulties continued to flourish.[92] This windfall was nevertheless a
great boon to Cassagnac, who had no prospects for family wealth.
Indeed, when his own father died in early 1880, he left an estate
burdened with great debts; the remaining assets were finally auctioned
off to pay his creditors. Only the chateau of Couloumé, which had long
been held in the name of his widow, was saved.[93]

Cassagnac's achievement of financial independence through his
marriage and M. Julien put no stop either to Jeromist suspicions of his
fidelity or to royalist aspirations to acquire his support. Yet
Cassagnac's conciliatory brand of monarchism, his close relationship to
leading French monarchist Catholics, and his defense of Catholic
interests both in the Chamber and in the press continued as before.
Thus, it is difficult to regard his financial difficulties as determinant in
questions concerning his allegiances.

Indeed, the only -- and best -- concrete refutation of the charges of
venality made against Cassagnac is the very consistency of his own
stated opinions from 1872 on concerning Imperialism and the
desirability of a conservative alliance. Even if one makes the
assumption that Cassagnac did accept money from legitimist and/or
Catholic sources for services rendered -- and I have come across no
effective proof that he did, although I have not found explicit proof that
he did not -- his polemic arguments continued in precisely the same vein
as before. His stated political principles did not alter in the slightest.
If, as one writer suggested during the controversy between Cassagnac

and Mitchell, "A *vendu* is one who for money writes the contrary of
what he believes, or for money believes today the opposite of what he
thought yesterday at a lower rate,"[94] then certainly Cassagnac was no
vendu. In order to convict him, one must invent a more subtle charge.

It is a fact that Paul de Cassagnac defended the Catholic and
monarchical cause long before anyone charged him with having sold out
his party; moreover, he never renounced the doctrine of *appel au
peuple*, which for so many years had distinguished the imperialists from
the royalists. Although speculation persisted in dynastic party circles
throughout Cassagnac's career that he was on the verge of a political
conversion, Cassagnac maintained his imperialist affirmations to the
end. His public pronouncements on this subject leave no room for
equivocation. As late as 1897 he wrote:

> I have always considered consistency in political
> life as the most enviable honor.
>
> Born Imperialist, I will die Imperialist, that is to
> say, partisan of a monarchy whose foundation is
> national consultation and which, moreover, exercises
> the authoritarian regime that can only be legitimized
> by delegation [of power] by the nation.[95]

The Comte de Paris himself acknowledged that Cassagnac was not
a royalist and said so in a private letter to Cassagnac. In 1887 he wrote
to the Imperialist deputy: "You are not a royalist. But you are more.
You are *un homme de coeur* and a good Frenchman. I know it, but
your letter . . . proves it to me once again."[96] And in 1892 he wrote
again:

> Certainly I do not reproach you for understanding
> the word Monarchy in a vaguer and more general
> fashion than I do, for you are concentrating on the
> most urgent task, which is to demonstrate once and for
> all that the present republic is necessarily the enemy of
> the conservative and religious cause. For that I thank
> you. Then it is up to me and my friends to prove that
> this cause will find no solid guarantees except with the
> monarchy I represent. With God's help we shall
> succeed.[97]

Thus, in the final analysis, the charges circulated against Paul de
Cassagnac by the suspicious dynasts may simply indicate how far from
general acceptance was the notion of *Impérialisme*, and its corollary, the
conservative alliance. Neither dynastic party found Cassagnac's
position reassuring. This was doubtless due both to the continued
strength of personal loyalties to a dynasty among many of the most

active monarchists themselves, and to the ingrained prejudices of the politically-minded populace at large, where dynastic rivalries represented a fundamental psychological truth susceptible to exploitation by the type of propaganda that could denounce the conservative alliance as "the union of three frogs huddled under a cowhide, pretending to be a cow."[98] Even in the 1880s, the extreme legitimists, the adamant Bonapartists, and most republicans rejected the politics of conservative alliance practiced by the monarchist deputies, interpreting it simply as evidence of the latters' discouragement with and abandonment of their respective dynastic traditions.[99]

Such a judgment, however, ignores another dimension of Cassagnac's politics, his long view of the future. His formulation of a systematic and, more important, an impersonal monarchy was radical. The next generation would pick up many of the threads of Cassagnac's impersonal, antiparliamentary, and plebiscitary authoritarianism and pull them together under various rubrics. In the 1880s, however, there were some who understood the devastating implications of Cassagnac's political system for the existing dynastic parties. One of these was the Victorist Henri Dichard, who acknowledged that the logic of Cassagnac's position of "*Catholique d'abord, monarchiste ensuite, impérialiste après*" did lead "even to royalty, if the empire defaults." It was not Cassagnac, he wrote, but the others -- "those who, although they don't think as he does, want to have him on their side for fear of having him against them" who were in an embarrassing situation.[100]

None of the other Catholic Imperialists behind Prince Victor were willing to admit publicly that Imperialism could be practiced by anyone other than a Bonaparte. For these men -- Padoue, Jolibois, Levert, and the lesser lights of Victorism -- the propulsion of Prince Victor into political action represented the only way of holding the Catholic Bonapartists (and their own electoral positions) together and keeping them outside the royalist camp until such time as Prince Napoleon disappeared. They, not Cassagnac, were the desperate dynasts. They were traditionalists, while Cassagnac was, in Mirecourt's astute characterization, "a real temperament of radical opposition misplaced in the conservative party."[101]

CHAPTER VII

WAR AGAINST THE OPPORTUNIST REPUBLIC
1881-1885

Au point de vue militaire, la République nous a donné le déshonneur national dans toutes les questions extérieures qui se sont présentées; au point de vue administratif, c'est le désordre partout, quand ça n'est pas le vol; au point de vue religieux, c'est la persécution haineuse et bête; au point de vue financier, c'est l'abîme qui se creuse tous les jours sous nos pieds et avec la faillite au fond.

Il est donc naturel que l'on en ait assez, et, effectivement, on en a assez.

Paul de Cassagnac
Le Pays, 18 September 1882

N'importe qui! n'importe quoi! tout, plutôt que la République! Voilà le cri général.

Paul de Cassagnac
Le Pays, 29 August 1883

The legislative elections of 1881 marked the low point in the political fortunes of the monarchist parties. Although Gers returned three out of five conservative deputies to the Chamber of Deputies, this department provided virtually the only example of conservative alliance on the first ballot in all of France.[1] Elsewhere, the candidates of the monarchist parties took a severe beating: in the first round, only eighty monarchists had been elected, as compared to 403 republicans; in the *ballotage*, the monarchists won eight more seats, while the republicans added 56 more deputies to their already strong majority.[2]

Several factors had contributed to their crushing defeat. One of the most important was the extremely high (31 per cent) abstention rate; the Ferry ministry had scheduled the elections for late August, during the height of the harvest season. Moreover, the ministry made a conscious effort to direct the elections to its advantage. The Minister of the

Interior, Ernest Constans, proved adept at wielding the resources of his administration in a thoroughly Bonapartist manner.[3] In anticipation of this probability, many of the monarchist deputies had supported the *scrutin de liste*. Paul de Cassagnac had predicted accurately that with the *scrutin d'arrondissement* employed in such a manner, no more than forty Imperialist deputies would be elected.[4]

Within the year, however, both royalists and imperialists had begun a new phase of political activity. By 1885 they could take advantage of republican dissidence and exploit a growing dissatisfaction with the lack of achievement under republican government, to which they constituted a serious political threat. What they did to achieve this goal comprises the subject of this chapter.

* * *

During the legislature of 1881-1885, the remaining monarchist deputies of both parties formed a parliamentary group in the Chamber known as the *Union des Droites*. Its object was to debate the important questions that came before the Chamber and to decide on a common vote.[5] This attempt at adopting a common parliamentary strategy was a step forward in "conservative alliance" over earlier efforts, restricted as these had been to electoral cooperation on the departmental level.[6]

The group had been consolidated originally by the issue of religious defense, since many of its members had taken an active role in opposing the decrees of 1880 against the congregations, both in Paris and in the provinces. Indeed, one of the group's first public actions was to issue a protest against the law of 28 March 1882, Ferry's law creating an obligatory and wholly secular primary instruction.[7] During the next three years the deputies of the *Union des Droites* spoke out against various other laicizing measures, which the republican majority nevertheless enacted. However, religious defense was by no means their only concern; in fact, the replacement of a politics of principles by a politics of "interests" was a key development in the emergence of the *Union des Droites*, particularly after the advent of the second Ferry ministry in 1883.

The deputies of the *Union des Droites* consecrated the politics of interests by electing Baron Armand de Mackau as their president. Mackau, while a man of principle himself, was unquestionably a political realist: his unpublished memoirs begin with the statement: "With only a few exceptions, I scarcely believe in people's political opinions; I believe much more in their political interests -- which are not the same thing . . . . I have constantly seen political interests dominate even the most elevated questions, carrying with them even the most honorable of men . . . ."[8] If, as the elections of 1881 had indicated, France was about to listen only to her stomach and the rumblings in her pocketbook, then the Right must address material concerns. In addition to religious defense or aspiring to restore a monarchy, the Right must concern itself with concrete problems -- finances, foreign affairs, agriculture -- all of which were to provide ample opportunities for challenging republican ministries as well as issues to exploit in the next elections. In other words, they must learn to play a new political game.

Cassagnac's response to the politics of "interests" was somewhat diffferent from Mackau's. To him it constituted an affront to his romanticized view of the French people. The possibility that the citizenry would not rise up either to defend its religion or to cast off the republic filled Cassagnac with gloom and, in the years 1882-1883, his wounded idealism expressed itself as a consuming conviction of national moral decadence.[9] Somewhere along the way this generation of Frenchmen had lost touch with the old values; their punishment for forgetting God and French national traditions was the republican regime, *la gueuse*, with her baggage of immorality and vice. Nevertheless he continued to hope that someday France would have drunk the bitter cup to the bottom and would then seek out someone "to come save what still remains of the French *patrie*."[10] He was willing to admit the politics of interests as an expedient if nothing else. The sole means to reawaken the initiative of decadent France against the republic, he wrote soon afterward, was for her citizens to find themselves vitally threatened in their economic interests. "In a country as completely decadent as our own, *les esprits abaissés* can be dominated and tyrannized, but the imperative claims of stomachs and guts can never be silenced."[11] From 1883 on this theme appeared in Cassagnac's editorials and speeches with increasing frequency, as he grew more and more discouraged with France's continuing failure to rise to the real task at hand. By 1889 his denunciations of his compatriots' preoccupation with material gain and speculation made him sound like an angry Old Testament prophet denouncing his people's worship of the golden calf. By 1893 Cassagnac had reached a point of utter despair and disgust.[12]

Among the deputies who constituted the *Union des Droites*, there appear to have been broad differences of opinion on the group's proper role in the Chamber as well as on the behavior of the Right in general. Some thought that the group should function as a "loyal opposition," republican practices and attitudes toward the Right notwithstanding. Such a conception was totally unsatisfactory to Paul de Cassagnac, who repeatedly insisted that the ultimate aim of the Right must be the overthrow of the republic and that the deputies should vote with this end in mind. During debate on a new municipal law in 1882, for example, Cassagnac criticized his monarchist colleagues' failure to vote for the proposal of the radical republicans. It was impossible, he remarked, to "habituate them to the role of opposition . . . . The Republic is asking you for a cord to hang herself with and you refuse to give it to her . . . . Why preserve her from herself; why protect her from her follies?"[13]

By late 1882, however, certain basic principles of opposition had been agreed on by the Right. One of these was opposition to the republican ministry's budget. The deputies of the monarchist parties opted *en bloc* to oppose the Budget of 1883 as a general indication of their discontent with various policies of the republicans and, in particular, as an expression of their dissatisfaction at being totally excluded from the Budget Committee (the only permanent committee of the Chamber prior to 1890).[14] As their spokesman, Dufort de Civrac, explained their position in the Chamber:

> Excluded for six years from the Budget Committee by decree of the republican majority, and thus deprived of effective control over finances, denied the most important of our rights as deputies, a right with which we are invested, as are you gentlemen, by the will of our electors, . . . we believe we should leave it to those who prepared it the responsibility of voting a budget in such conditions of deficit . . . .
>
> We declare before the country that the finances of the State are in peril . . . unless a prompt remedy is brought about by profound reforms, by important reductions in expenses, the exaggerations of which, due especially to thoughts of a purely political order and not to those of the general interest, strike the least partial minds.[15]

The position of the deputies of the *Union des Droites* on the budget, which they maintained throughout the legislature of 1881-1885, was both symptom and symbol of the systematic exclusion practiced against them by the "republic of the republicans."[16]

Exclusion from the Budget Committee offered only the most striking example of the political isolation of the monarchist deputies in the new Chamber. Well before the elections of 1881 the republicans had also "expelled" them from the third vice-presidency of the Chamber, which had traditionally awarded to the Right, even after *Seize*

Mai.[17] The practice of invalidating monarchist elections, which had been carried to extremes in 1878, was continued in 1881, although on a considerably smaller scale.[18] The republicans claimed that their regime would be open to all, Cassagnac pointed out, but they were practicing a policy of systematic exclusion.

Moreover, outside the Chamber, Cassagnac charged, the republican ministries had been presenting a poor parody of the empire with their attempts at administrative purges -- from the personnel of the Ministry of the Interior (especially mayors and prefects)[19] to two of the three institutional arms of social order, the army and the magistracy.[20] The republicans, Cassagnac charged, were interested only in satisfying the appetites of their clientele, not in reconciling the nation to the new regime: perhaps they should be encouraged, he speculated, to play out their historic role, to effect their own self-destruction and thus allow the return of authority.[21]

As if to aid the opportunist republicans -- the Gambettas and the Ferrys -- in their work of auto-destruction, Cassagnac invoked the aid of their arch-antagonists, the radical republicans. Following the amnesty of the Communards in 1880, he addressed the returned exiles as his "allies," whether they liked it or not. "We have need of you," he wrote, "to take charge of all the evil passions of the revolution."[22] It is noteworthy that although during Mac-Mahon's presidency, Paul de Cassagnac had opposed any amnesty whatsoever on the ground that the return of the communards posed a threat to social order,[23] he changed his position in 1879, publicly announcing his intention to vote the full amnesty in the hope that the return of the radicals would mark the beginning of the opportunists' fall.[24]

Such moves as this, however informed by historical precedent, lent themselves with little difficulty to opportunist accusations that Cassagnac -- and by extension, his colleagues of the monarchist Right -- were practicing a *politique du pire*, or seeking salvation by precipitating catastrophe. This charge seemed to gather substance with each common vote by both the Right and the radical Left in the Chamber, despite the fact that no purposeful entente existed between the two groups. Certainly such a policy, although not to the liking of a good number of Cassagnac's colleagues, did appear to be the logical fruit of the fatalistic rhetoric with which Paul de Cassagnac constantly invoked the inevitable course of the revolution. As he had written in 1872, dismissing the notion that a "conservative republic" could ever prove lasting: "A durable government is never founded except by public exasperation, and we in France have scarcely begun to be nervous."[25]

In retrospect, one of the most striking aspects of Cassagnac's political career is the extent to which he shared the radicals' criticism of the opportunist republic.[26] From 1877 on he openly exhibited expressions of kinship and admiration for the members of the radical Left, expressions that assumed a permanent place in his polemical repertoire. He often referred to himself as a radical in his own party, a *Jacobin de droite*; were he ever to become a republican, he once wrote, he would be a radical. "Radicals of Right or Left, we have the same enemies -- the Centers -- those havens of cowardice, envy, and vanity . . . . The Centers have always benefitted from the events created by the courage of the radicals of Right and Left."[27] Unlike their opportunist colleagues (and by extension, Cassagnac's own "opportunistic" colleagues on the monarchist Right), radical republicans remained true to their ideals and their doctrines; they retained an "honorability" and a consistency in their politics that offered a visible contrast to the "*politique habile*" practiced by the opportunists.[28] It was in this context that, in 1880, Cassagnac had praised his longtime colleague in the press, the intransigent polemicist Henri Rochefort, and the latter's friends as "men of action," "true republicans" -- and therefore, in Cassagnac's estimation, worthy republicans, not to be confused with the "liars and humbugs who for ten years have exploited the republic, living off the sacrifices made by others."[29] Likewise, Cassagnac singled out for admiration radicals such as Arthur Ranc ("one of the few dangerous men of the republican party"), Henry Maret, editor of *Le Radical*, and Anatole de La Forge,[30] and he treated Georges Clemenceau, the foremost radical in the Chamber at that time, with great respect.[31]

Indeed, these men did have much in common with Cassagnac: like him, they were doctrinaires who preferred to keep their cause free from compromise; like him they were inclined to be idealistic and intransigent rather than pragmatic in their demands on political life. And in fact, when Cassagnac's political career is considered in its entirety, striking parallels emerge between his views and those of his radical republican counterparts.[32] Despite the gulf that existed between them on two subjects -- the form of government and the place of religion in modern life -- they shared a common viewpoint in many other areas. They were antagonistic toward liberals and *parlementaires*: this was perhaps a matter of temperament. But their economic views were similar as well. Like the radicals, Cassagnac advocated the income tax (a tax which many opposed because it would strike at revenues from *rentes*, or state bonds, which hitherto had been exempt), although he disagreed with their various legislative proposals to that effect.[33] In later years he was at one with them in opposing state socialism as a solution to economic problems. Both Cassagnac and the radicals steadfastly opposed any threat to private property,[34] just as they agreed in their concern for rural interests during the 1890s.[35]

During the legislature of 1881-1885 Paul de Cassagnac continued to be one of the most relentless critics of the republic. For over a year after the elections of 1881, when the republican work of laicization was at its peak, however, Cassagnac held himself in a position of extreme reserve in the Chamber, having learned that on religious issues the intervention of the Right was a sure way of consolidating the unity of the republicans. "We must leave them free to devour each other," Cassagnac remarked on one occasion in November 1881.[36] Only in December 1882 did he again speak in the Chamber. At that time he made a firm declaration of his political faith: "In politics," he proclaimed, "I am first of all Catholic, then monarchist, and imperialist after that."[37]

In 1883 he moved once again into the national political spotlight, constantly criticizing the republic and conscientiously working to further the conservative alliance. It was not altogether coincidental that Gambetta's death, which to the historian Hanotaux and others seemed to symbolize the end of the heroic age of the republic, also spelled the end of the heroic opposition to the republican form of government by the bulk of the monarchist Right. Not for Cassagnac however; he provided the major exception to this general rule. He continued to prophesy that the end of the republic was imminent. As he wrote following the fall of Gambetta's ill-starred ministry in 1882, the event marked a step toward the day

> when we will sweep it [the republic] from French soil, after having successively chopped off all the heads. The highest held,   proudest head -- the lion's head -- is already in the basket . . . . It was difficult to obtain and required a hatchet. The others -- the Leon Says, the Ferrys, the Freycinets -- are only calves' heads, and a fork will suffice.[38]

Cassagnac's evocative language varied little in this respect. Gambetta's death only confirmed his impatience to arrive at the historic finale, which must necessarily be near.

Following the publication of a manifesto by Prince Napoleon and his subsequent arrest in January 1883, the republicans sought passage of a law that would not only expel the heirs of former reigning houses and their direct descendants from French territory, but would also bar them from holding civil or military positions.[39] Since the latter provision directly affected the Orleans princes, three of whom still held active commands in the French army (Prince Napoleon had been deprived of his command in the 1870s), Paul de Cassagnac utilized this issue to promote monarchist unity in face of republican oppression and to appropriate for the Right the defense of military patriotism in France. The army, he declared, was not the republic's army; it was the nation's army, France's army. "*Vive la France!*" was the only battle cry that could transcend the cries of "*Vive le Roi!*" and "*Vive l'Empereur!*"[40] The Senate's defeat of this proposal in late February 1883 brought Jules Ferry to the premiership for the second time, and once again Ferry employed decrees to achieve his purpose, "expelling" the princes from their commands.[41]

Ferry's second ministry lasted nearly two years, during which he and his colleagues bore the brunt of criticism from both the *Union des Droites* and the radical republicans. During those two years Paul de Cassagnac established himself as one of Ferry's most relentless critics, making a series of speeches and interpellations which, insofar as they dealt with "interests," were calculated to undercut Ferry, but were also designed to undermine the republican regime as well. Cassagnac thereby hoped to arouse the French people to the realization that only in return to a monarchy could they find governmental stability and sound management of the nation's affairs. Cassagnac treated matters ranging from finance to foreign policy, from conversion of the state's bonded indebtedness (by reducing the interest rate on bonds from 5 to 4 per cent) to management of the *caisses d'épargne*, the state-run savings banks.[42] His most fiery interventions, however, targeted Ferry's colonial policy in Tunisia and later in Tonkin, both issues that drew the fire of the oppositions, Right and Left, in the Chamber.[43]

The question of intervention in Tunisia had drawn Cassagnac's attention from 1878 on, following Bismarck's offer to French delegates at the Congress of Berlin, allowing France free rein to expand in that direction.[44] In 1881, subsequent to the Chamber's authorization of a French expedition to Tunisia, Cassagnac had come out firmly against the "terrible adventure" of Tunisia, and had employed it as a campaign issue.[45] Indeed, the monarchists had learned in 1877, much to their regret, just how effective a war scare issue could be in an election year. Cassagnac charged that the republicans had undertaken the Tunisian expedition because they were speculating in Tunisian currency (which was, in fact, administered by Charles Ferry, brother of Jules). On various occasions Cassagnac asserted that the ventures in Tunisia -- and later in Tonkin (the area since known as North Vietnam) -- were designed primarily to distract the nation from its problems at home, to fill the pockets of the few at the expense of young Frenchmen, and to provide further employment opportunities for the ever-avid republicans.[46]

As for intervention in Tonkin, Cassagnac charged that it was merely an attempt to restore "face" following France's "humiliation" by England in Egypt in 1882:

> The fact is that the government of the republic, maligned in Europe, humiliated and used as a doormat by serious powers, is trying to re-establish its prestige by assuming swaggering airs toward several samples of the yellow race.
>
> Ridiculous at Berlin, ridiculous at London, ridiculous at Vienna, the Republic wants to take revenge by making itself fearsome at Shanghai and Hué.[47]

Consequently, as Cassagnac wrote in July 1883, for the Right to be faithful to its mandate, "we are obliged to survey closely the use they [the republicans] wish to make of our military forces, our pecuniary resources, even the honor of the flag -- all things that seem forever on the verge of compromise whenever, by some misfortune, they fall into the hands of the Republic."[48]

Paul de Cassagnac was by no means hostile to colonial efforts per se, nor did he share the attitude of Déroulède's *Ligue des Patriotes*, which opposed all colonial expansion on the ground that it took France's eyes from the "blue line of the Vosges" and the prospect of achieving *revanche* against Germany for the loss of Alsace-Lorraine. Consider, for example, Cassagnac's attitude toward Madagascar, which he perceived to be France's Australia, a rich and valuable complement to the mother country.[49] Colonies, he wrote in 1886, give "besides prestige, outlets to commerce, industry, agriculture, and all the other resources and products of the *métropole*."[50] This statement was typical of pro-colonial opinion and is hardly surprising, given Cassagnac's close family ties with the French colonies in the West Indies. Cassagnac did, however, make other distinctions; in his view, a country like France had no business pursuing colonies in unhealthy areas, in "pestilential swamps" such as Tonkin.[51]

Not only did Cassagnac argue that Tonkin was an unhealthy place, but he also believed that French presence there entailed a very real risk of war with China. In 1882 members of a French expeditionary force had been ordered by the governor of France's colony in Cochinchina to proceed up the Red River in Tonkin to clear out a group of marauding river pirates known as the *Pavillons Noirs*. The troops had taken control of Hanoi, leading China to protest and to mass troops of her own on the border. In May 1883 the expedition leader and a number of his men were massacred by the *Pavillons Noirs*, an act which greatly aroused French opinion.[52] In response to Ferry's call for credits to mount an additional expeditionary force for the purpose of reestablishing order, most of the deputies of the Right rallied. Cassagnac was an exception. He roundly scolded his colleagues for responding to Ferry's appeal:

> It is not simply an issue of reestablishing order in a province troubled by a gang of pirates and withdrawing the province from an Annamite empire that is incapable either of keeping it free from pirates or of defending it against us.
>
> China is behind Annam -- China with its millions of combatants who, several years ago, weren't dangerous, who even seemed ridiculous when they were armed merely with sidearms, old arquebuses, even bows and arrows. But today they possess modern guns, a modern artillery, and in the bargain they are instructed by European officers . . . .
>
> Nobody knows where this Tonkin affair will lead us, and those of us who do not engage in shady deals, who are not profiteers, who do not enrich ourselves and who, unhappily, sacrifice our best men, ought to disengage ourselves at any price, I say, completely, absolutely, not letting ourselves be blinded by a falsely patriotic sentimentalism.[53]

By July, with the news that Ferry planned to send more reinforcements and establish what amounted to a protectorate in Tonkin, the monarchist Right grew more critical. Ferry's propensity to deal with colonial affairs by presenting the legislature with a step-by-step series of *faits accomplis* created what has since been called a "credibility gap" that only fuelled their suspicions.[54] In July 1883 Cassagnac's colleague, Jules Delafosse, addressed a major interpellation to the ministry on the Tonkin question; during the course of the debate Paul de Cassagnac charged that the war in Tonkin, like the war in Tunisia, was motivated by considerations which the ministers "try to decorate with the label of patriotism" but which "are absolutely unspeakable." It was "financial intrigue," he charged, appropriating the term used by Henri Rochefort, involving the Credit Foncier and probably also grants of mining concessions in northern Tonkin "which are still at the disposition of the republicans who await them."[55] Furthermore, he accused Ferry of making war without consulting the legislature, of engaging the country's honor, its soldiers, and its funds without permission; he charged that the earlier "protectorate" had turned into a conquest. Ferry called on Cassagnac to furnish proofs of his accusations. Cassagnac replied by insulting Ferry, calling him the *"dernier des laches et des menteurs,"* to which the republican majority replied by voting Cassagnac's expulsion from the Chamber for yet another time.[56] The following month, French guns bombarded Hué, and the French concluded a treaty of protectorate with the new emperor of Annam, a move which activated the machinations of the war party in the Chinese imperial court.

During the ensuing campaign in Tonkin, Cassagnac bore down hard on the seemingly double-faced nature of Ferry's policy. In spite of Ferry's attempts to come to a peaceful settlement with the Chinese, by late 1884 he had effectively broken relations with them and was indeed engaged in an undeclared war.[57] Consequently, Cassagnac treated with scorn Ferry's attempts to explain his way out of the situation: in early 1884 he remarked that while it might not be essential to be completely frank and sincere in politics, it was nevertheless essential not to be regarded as a liar:

> While Mazarin was cunning, Cavour shrewd, and Bismarck prudent, none of these three statesmen of different epochs could be said to have persisted in lying. Alone among them all, Jules Ferry has claimed this monopoly.[58]

Cassagnac continued to oppose the granting of further financial credits for the Tonkin operation throughout 1884 and well into 1885, when the sensational news of the French defeat at Lang-Son precipitated the fall of Ferry's cabinet and, seemingly, justified all Cassagnac's prognostications.[59] The headlines in *Le Pays* for 31 March 1885 read: *"DESASTRE AU TONKIN," "INVASION de 200,000 Chinois," "Mensonges de M. Jules Ferry."* Paris crowds demanded the head of the "Tonkinese" (as Ferry had become known), and the Chamber felled the cabinet the following day.[60] Some deputies even threatened to prosecute Ferry for his role.[61]

* * *

Before discussing the great impact of the Tonkin affair and of the monarchist deputies' "politics of interests" on the elections of 1885, it is necessary to examine two developments that took place outside the Chamber and that were of great importance in realizing a tighter alliance between the monarchist parties.

The first of these was a change in the political course of the royalist party, following the death in August 1883 of the pretender, the Comte de Chambord. His successor, the Comte de Paris, was the forty-five year old grandson of Louis-Philippe. The new pretender offered a well-educated and capable, if by no means charismatic, heir to the throne of the Bourbons.

Sometime prior to April 1882, Paul de Cassagnac had become personally acquainted with the Comte de Paris, who was his senior by only a few years. Cassagnac was particularly impressed by the prince: years later, he wrote that "since the death of the Prince Imperial, I have never seen anyone here on earth who was as great in heart and mind, and who more completely incarnated old French honor . . . . Indeed, he was a man who commanded one's esteem and forced one's admiration."[62]

Just when or how they met is uncertain. It is likely that they were introduced by mutual friends among the royalists such as Lacave-Laplagne, the senator from Gers, or perhaps even by Isabelle de Bourbon, the former queen of Spain, who was a close friend of Paul de Cassagnac and also the aunt of the Comtesse de Paris.[63] An April 1882 letter from the prince to Cassagnac, accepting an invitation to hunt at Noyalles, reveals that a personal relationship was already in place, despite political differences:

> Even the reservations that you expressed concerning politics, with a loyalty which I appreciate and a sincerity which I honor, only increase the value of our personal relations.
>
> I regret to warn you that at Noyalles you will find something like the image of present-day politics: a terrain full of quagmires and deep mud, over which one can walk only warily and in zig-zags, whether one wishes to or not. But who knows? Perhaps one day we will meet one another on solid ground.[64]

Less than a year later, following Cassagnac's speech of December 1882 in the Chamber, the Comte wrote again to Cassagnac:

> Believe me, when each follows a line of conduct loyally, with disinterestedness and perseverance, a moment always arrives when, in the midst of political vicissitudes, these lines meet. God alone can foresee this moment and prepare this meeting.[65]

The Comte de Paris had long shared his Orleanist supporters' antipathy for Bonapartists and their methods. As late as 1880, he had written that "solidarity with or complaisance for the Bonapartist party must be rejected; it must be well-understood that the *'constitutionnels'* [i.e., those who support the constitution of 1875] will never prefer the empire to the republic."[66] Cassagnac interpreted these remarks as both a gesture to the republic by a prince who feared expulsion and as evidence that Henri V (as some royalists referred to Chambord) had no real heirs.[67]

Following Chambord's death, however, it appeared that the Comte de Paris might be persuaded to modify his attitude. In any event, Paul de Cassagnac applied himself to this task in the press. During the last stages of Chambord's illness, Cassagnac issued a warning to the princely pretenders, the Comte de Paris and Prince Napoleon: "If one lets the other surpass him in inspiring confidence in France, in giving her hope, in letting her catch a glimpse of salvation, he who remains behind is finished -- perhaps finished forever."[68] Prince Napoleon, Cassagnac asserted, was weak on the subject of Catholicism; the Comte de Paris, on the subject of authority.[69] In the interval a Parisian newspaper revealed that Cassagnac had been seen dining with the Orleans princes at the home of Lacave-Laplagne. This news item provoked speculation in the press that a possible political agreement between Cassagnac and the Orleanists might emerge. Brushing off the report, Cassagnac did not discount the possibility that such an agreement might be possible -- but only on his terms: "It could happen only if Orleanism came over to my side, that is, to the side of fierce and implacable authority." He was highly amused "at the thought that I pass for half-converted to the parliamentary and constitutional regime, a regime I have always found absurd but that seems particularly stupid in the epoch in which we live."[70]

In early September 1883, the royalist journalist Edouard Hervé of *Le Soleil* argued that royalty accept the plebiscite. Paul de Cassagnac publicly expressed his enthusiasm for such a program, and attached a warning meant for the Bonaparte princes to his praise for Hervé's suggestion:

> If Hervé's grandiose idea were accepted by the heir of the Comte de Chambord and if our princes of the Bonaparte family do not make haste to parry this fearsome blow with prompt and energetic determination, it will be the end of us as a party. We would no longer have a monopoly on the *appel au peuple*; we would no longer be the only government that claims the national will for its base. The empire would be cut from beneath our feet.[71]

The prospect of a plebiscite for royalty was by no means new; indeed it had been promoted during the late 1840s by a group of monarchists, of whom the most prominent was the Marquis de La Rochejacquelein. Although the Comte de Chambord had rejected this suggestion of *"Droit national"* in favor of *"Droit divin"* in his Wiesbaden circular of 1850, his decision did not bind his successor.[72] That the proposal should be revived in the 1880s gave reason to hope that royalists and imperialists might yet reach a meeting of minds. "M. Hervé," Cassagnac observed some time later, "is a man who loves his king and who understands his times."[73]

Such discussions as these in the press were ripe with implications for the future. In the meantime, however, certain royalists continued to court Cassagnac. One of these was Jean-Joseph Cornély, the brilliant young editor of *Le Clairon*, who continually urged Cassagnac to adhere publicly to the royalist cause as represented by the Comte de Paris.[74]

The second important development arose from the changing relationship between the Vatican, the French republic, and the monarchist parties. The issue of religious defense had been originally responsible for bringing the deputies of the two parties into a closer functional working relationship, just as it had served to unite the republicans against them. As the opportunist republicans achieved the secularization of education, however, they themselves had begun to pursue a more conciliatory relationship with Rome. Jules Ferry, "the archbishop's cabby," as Cassagnac had called him, who had presided over the expulsion of the congregations in late 1880, was -- ironically -- one of the most successful in this respect. Ferry wanted the Vatican to support his colonial ventures and, therefore, during his second ministry he paid particular attention to mollifying the Holy See which, in turn, set great store on maintaining an amicable relationship with the French government.

When Ferry returned to power in the early months of 1883, relations between the republic and the Vatican were strained, due to a series of incidents which had resulted when Rome placed on the Index a number of French laic school morality manuals.[75] During the summer the Pope had addressed a letter to President Grévy, detailing his grievances at the government's attitude toward the church in France.[76] Relations continued to deteriorate until about the time Ferry took over the ministry of foreign affairs. During the debate on the budget in December 1883, the ministry made a public stand conciliatory to the maintenance of the French embassy to the Vatican -- a stand Paul de Cassagnac was quick to congratulate as "very Catholic," in order to demonstrate to the radicals the extent of the "opportunism" being practiced by their ministerial colleagues.[77] Relations remained tense, however, until Ferry moved to settle a number of outstanding complaints and made known to the Vatican his express wish to retain the Concordat.[78]

In May 1884 Leo XIII replied with an encyclical letter, *Nobilissima Gallorum Gens*, addressed to the clergy of France, in which he directed the bishops to pursue their work of defending the Church without opposing the established government. At least for the time being, the Concordat seemed safe in Ferry's hands. And even though the work of secularizing French society continued (with the final passage of a law reestablishing civil divorce in July 1884, and the suppression of public prayers in July-August 1884), relations between the government of the republic and the Vatican improved to the point where, by early 1885, the Pope and Ferry were openly exchanging compliments.[79]

Clearly, this situation portended difficulties for the monarchist minority, whose members had traditionally been the exclusive defenders of religious interests in France. In fact, however, the broadening of responsibility for religious defense sought by the Vatican fitted in quite well with the plans of the leadership of the *Union des Droites*. If it seemed essential to the Vatican to separate religious defense from the issue of form of government, it seemed equally essential to the monarchist Catholics who led the conservative alliance to relegate religious defense to the status of one among other concerns in their "politics of interests." It was to their advantage, as well as to that of the Vatican, to reject the identity between throne and altar that had characterized royalism under Chambord (and that had nettled Catholic imperialists such as Cassagnac) for the simple reason that this identification had facilitated republican attacks on the Church.[80] Consequently, the advocates of conservative alliance agreed with Church leaders that religious personnel must maintain a stance of neutrality in political matters. This policy, which had far-reaching implications for practical politics, has frequently been considered by historians within the context of discussions of the *Ralliement*, but it has rarely been discussed in connection with the policy pursued by the royalists themselves.[81] Such a policy, however, was actually encouraged by the Comte de Paris: as he wrote to Mackau in 1888, expressing a view he had long held, "Political solidarity between throne and altar has always been equally compromising for the Church and for the Monarchy."[82] The Church must get out, or be gotten out of politics.

During the year 1884, Mackau and his colleagues (in conjunction with leading prelates such as Cardinal Guibert, the archbishop of Paris, and Monseigneur d'Hulst, rector of the *Institut Catholique* of Paris) made a serious effort to transform the religious issue into a question of "interests" like any other. In pursuing this course of action, they ran headlong into the opposition of the intransigent Catholic press, as exemplified by L'Univers. This newspaper, since 1883 under the direction of Louis Veuillot's brother Eugène, remained faithful to its founder's legacy, and thus to the ultramontane tradition of Pius IX. Following a particularly bitter polemical outburst in L'Univers during the summer of 1884, first Mgr. d'Hulst, then Mackau journeyed to Rome to discuss with the Pope himself the problem of toning down that paper and thereby reducing its potential for putting new weapons into the hands of the anticlerical republicans.[83] The Pope replied by addressing a brief to his nuncio in Paris in which he blamed the press for spreading dissension and thereby hindering efforts at pacification.[84]

The intransigent Catholic press, however, was not the sole obstacle to political neutrality for the Church. Both the Vatican and the leaders of the Union des Droites, including Paul de Cassagnac, criticized and attempted to restrain the activities of certain intransigent monarchist members of the clergy, notably Mgr. Freppel, the fiery bishop of Angers, who was also the deputy from Brest and one of the foremost orators against the laic laws.[85] They likewise discouraged the efforts of monarchist Catholic laymen, notably Albert de Mun, to found a purely Catholic party along the lines of those in Belgium and Germany, on the ground that a confessional party would not work in a situation where its members had not achieved consensus on the question of regime.[86] In the meantime, Leo XIII was at work on an encyclical intended to underscore further the Church's indifference to the form of government of the State. The pontiff had already sketched the outlines of this encyclical at the time of Mackau's visit to Rome in October 1884; in deference to the opinion of Mackau (and, presumably, of others as well) he agreed to postpone its publication until the following year, after the French legislative elections of 1885, in which the Right anticipated substantial gains. Consequently, the important encyclical Immortale Dei appeared only in November 1885, "retarded but not renounced," as Mackau put it.[87]

* * *

In mid-May 1884 Paul de Cassagnac called once again for the formation of a conservative alliance in anticipation of the next general elections, and he proposed as the first step the formation of a conservative press committee.[88] Cassagnac's proposal stimulated considerable discussion in the press: the editors of the diehard legitimist Gazette de France, as might be expected, stood alone in preferring the notion of a wholly royalist committee which would then treat with an equivalent imperialist committee. The remainder of the conservative press, however -- *Le Gaulois, Le Soleil, Le Moniteur Universel, Le Francais* -- enthusiastically endorsed the idea, as did *Le Monde* and *L'Univers*, though with the condition that defense of religious interests occupy the forefront in any prospective electoral program.[89]

This proposal corresponded with a new stage in the development of Cassagnac's doctrine of Imperialism -- namely, the doctrine that became popularly known as "*n'importequisme*," or variously as "*solutionnisme*," "*Bourbonapartisme*," and "*bimonarchisme*."[90] The theory was that while both royalists and imperialists clung to their hopes that the prince of their preference would be the one to succeed, each would accept whichever prince would act first: "*N'importe qui! n'importe quoi!*" in place of the republic.[91] But the princes must act to stir the current of public opinion hostile to the republic. The elements of discontent within the population would not call out for the pretenders without a bit of prodding.[92] The coming elections would modify nothing, Cassagnac maintained, "unless princely lips address a powerful appeal to what still remains of courage and honorability in France."[93] Cassagnac sought nothing less than a messianic monarch to lead France out of the republic.

Many of the Victorists were not disposed to follow Cassagnac down the path of *n'importequisme* into an even more binding conservative alliance with the royalists -- "this new Holy Alliance," as Prince Napoleon's friend Maurice Richard later called it.[94] Despite their estrangement from Prince Napoleon, the Victorists nevertheless retained the suspicion and distrust of the Orleanists that had so long characterized dynastic Bonapartism.[95] From late 1884 on, the ubiquitous Robert Mitchell, who had charged his former comrade-in-arms Cassagnac with selling out the party to the royalists and had since become his political opponent, emerged as the principal spokesman for the anti-solutionist element in Victorism. His arguments first appeared in the pages of *Le Matin*, then, after the elections of 1885, in *Le Pays* (which he edited after Cassagnac's departure in late 1885) and *Souveraineté Nationale*.[96]

As the elections drew near and Prince Victor's "anti-solutionist" supporters began to step forward, urging him to avoid any sort of alliance with the royalists, relations between the young prince and Paul de Cassagnac grew strained.[97] Since the summer of 1884 and Prince Victor's act of independence, Cassagnac had become increasingly discontented with the prince's lack of political action, as well as with his aversion to the conservative alliance. In October 1884, therefore, he issued a solemn warning to Victor:

> In face of social peril, formerly opposed political viewpoints are coming together; the strength of words is diminishing, party labels are going under. And while I believe that the Imperial doctrine is incontestably the only doctrine of the times for modern monarchy, it is also incontestable that the empire can be restored by someone other than the emperor -- this is our weakness.
>
> Napoleon is no longer indispensable, even though the empire is indispensable.[98]

Despite Cassagnac's exhortations to act, to take advantage of the political situation, the prince's position remained much the same well into 1885. His failure to take some positive action soon condemned him in the opinion of many as a do-nothing pretender.

In August 1884 the Chamber and the Senate met as a National Assembly to consider partial revision of the constitutional law of 24 February by striking the clause in Article 8 that allowed for revision of the form of government in the future. Henceforth, the republic was consecrated; it could no longer be altered by constitutional means. Paul de Cassagnac boycotted the Assembly, calling it a "comedy prepared in advance, whose slightest incidents have been foreseen and decided on by a domesticated majority."[99] Writing from a summer vacation retreat in Brittany, he predicted that this change would only tighten the bonds of conservative alliance. It "renders union easier by suppressing every impulse of competition, and by obliging us to come together . . . on the only profitable electoral platform, hatred of the republic."[100] Furthermore, he added, "the pretenders can kiss their "legal combinations" goodbye; they will have to fall back on truer and more virile resolutions. [The republicans] shut the door on us? So be it! We will go in through the window.[101]

This significant revision of the constitution did indeed change the electoral ground on which the parties of the monarchist Right would henceforth operate. Cassagnac had anticipated this with the proposal he had submitted to the Union des Droites in early June, advocating that the parties adopt a strictly electoral approach to the coming elections, based on issues and not on cries of "Vive le Roi" and "Vive l'Empereur."[102] This strategy, subsequently adopted, was heavily criticized by the republicans, who charged that by running as "conservatives," the monarchists were "hiding their flags."[103] Since the monarchists denied any plebiscitary significance to the legislative elections, however, this charge seemed meaningless, except as a propaganda device for use by their republican opponents. Cassagnac's vision of conservative alliance for the elections of 1885 went far beyond that which he had previously advocated. This time he called for "Conservative Union" -- with unity in candidates, unity of program, and unity of campaign funds.[104] Achieving unity in candidates was perhaps the most complex challenge, particularly after restoration of the *scrutin de liste* in the spring of 1885. Although Cassagnac did not enthusiastically favor the *liste*, he nevertheless campaigned for it among the deputies of the monarchist parties, arguing that with it, given the strong current of discontent in the nation, a unified Right would win some 140-150 seats.[105] As it became apparent that discord among the republicans would result in the formation of a number of competing lists in their camp, the advantages of a single list on the Right became increasingly obvious. In July 1885, the Comte de Paris authorized his supporters to proceed in this direction. Soon thereafter, the *"Comité électoral des Droites,"* headed by Sosthène de La Rochefoucauld,[106] president of the *Droite royaliste*, and Baron de Mackau, president of the *Union des Droites*, established a campaign headquarters on the rue de Mailly.[107] This committee was publicly compared to that of the rue de Poitiers in 1848, which had helped topple the Second Republic.[108]

The imperialists had already formed their own electoral committee in January, the *Comité central impérialiste de l'appel au peuple*, known in the political shorthand of the time by its location on the rue d'Anjou. The venerable Duc de Padoue presided over this committee, assisted by Cassagnac, Jolibois, a senator Poriquet from the department of Orne, and a representative from the imperialist committees of the department of the Seine.[109] In June the imperialist central committee issued an electoral manifesto which some royalists interpreted as a separatist proclamation.[110] That it did not preclude conservative alliance, however, became clear from subsequent events.

The monarchist deputies of both parties did cooperate to produce a single list of candidates in all but four departments.[111] This was more difficult in the larger, more populous departments, such as Nord, where twenty deputies were to be elected, and in the department of the Seine itself, where thirty-eight places were to be filled. In the Nord, the imperialist committee, through its envoy Robert Mitchell, demanded eight of the twenty available places on the list, and the incumbent monarchist deputies appealed to Cassagnac for his help in "defending local interests" against demands they considered excessive. In the dispute, Cassagnac went so far as to submit his resignation from the imperialist central committee, but he had his way, provoking Mitchell to insist, with his now-habitual rancor, that the Bonapartist majority in the

Nord had been sacrificed to benefit the Comte de Paris.[112]

In the department of the Seine, which included Paris and its immediate suburbs, Paul de Cassagnac (acting in his capacity as president of the Paris imperialist committees[113]) took charge of negotiations with the royalists' equivalent group, the *Comité conservateur de la Seine* (rue des Pyramides), headed by Ferdinand Duval, to form the list. By mid-September, the list had been completed. It included twelve imperialists: the deputies Cassagnac and Delafosse; three members of the Paris municipal council, Bartholini, Maurice Binder and Marius Martin; and six notables and former imperialist deputies, Padoue, Baron Haussman, Henri Chevreau, Camille Godelle, Frédéric-Barrot, and Clement de Royer. The entire list was made public during a large private gathering at the *Cirque d'Hiver* on 16 September, three weeks before the elections.[114] With this, one faction of the Parisian Victorists revolted. As one of them wrote in *Le Peuple*:

> We will endure the alliance you have made in the departments to conserve our seats, sacrificing the general interests of our party to your personal interests -- but there wi]l be no alliance in Paris. You can conclude it if you wish, but we will not ratify it with our votes.[115]

On the eve of the elections, the Victorists disavowed the conservative alliance list and circulated one of their own.[116]

Despite these difficulties, unity of candidacy had for all practical purposes been achieved. By late September the Duc de Padoue was able to report that in the great majority of departments, the parties had reached agreement, while in some others, the imperialists had been accorded satisfaction in principle, that is, acceptance by another candidate of the plebiscitary principle, when they did not obtain their own man. Only in a very few departments, Padoue remarked, could imperialists not support the conservative list without betraying the flag of the empire.[117]

Cassagnac's second objective, unity of program, was somewhat easier to obtain: so many complaints had been lodged against the government of the republic during the previous four years that the only problem was one of choice. In early September, the outgoing deputies of the monarchist Right published a joint manifesto, the "*Déclaration des Droites*," which served as the electoral program for the Conservative Union. This document, which was signed by seventy-eight outgoing deputies (some thirty of whom were identifiable as Bonapartists),[118] detailed their grievances -- budgetary, domestic and foreign policy decisions made by the opportunist ministries and the republican majority of the previous four years. Cassagnac's hand in its drafting is apparent, for it was an angry document, an indictment of "deficit, violence, and war" under republican rule, from which had resulted the stagnation of agriculture, commerce, and industry, as well as the politicization of the nation's administration and institutions. Nowhere did it mention changing the form of government or restoring the monarchy; it was purely a *programme d'affaires* designed to win France away from "her worst enemies."[119]

Cassagnac's third objective, unity of funds, was by far the most problematic. In fact, there seems to be very little information available on the extent to which it was realized. Some police reports indicate that, at least for the Seine, a major obstacle to the formation of "Conservative Union" lists was the imperialists' inability to carry their weight financially.[120] One opponent of the alliance later wrote that "in the famous Conservative Union, the Orleanists contributed the money, their Bonapartist allies furnished the voters, and in the last analysis a royalist was chosen."[121] While this may have been true in the department of the Seine, it is by no means certain that the same was true for the provinces.

Despite problems in certain departments, the Conservative Union was singularly successful. On the first ballot, the Right more than doubled its previous representation in the Chamber, with the election of 177 deputies. Their opportunist republican antagonists elected only 127, with some 270 seats requiring a run-off. More impressive were the actual figures. The candidates of the Conservative Union polled some 3.5 million votes in the nation as a whole (44 per cent), up 1.6 million since 1881; they even attracted 25 per cent of the Parisian vote. They won back eleven departments which had returned republican majorities in 1881.[122] It was truly an impressive comeback. In Gers, the conservative list -- Cassagnac, Faure, Daynaud, and Peyrusse -- won by a wide margin on the first ballot. All the candidates had campaigned on the grievances expressed in the *Déclaration des Droites*, giving particular emphasis to local agricultural miseries and the republicans' squandering of public funds. Although all four candidates were imperialists, they consolidated the conservative alliance by stating their willingness to accept "*n'importe qui*" who would save France and raise her up once again. In contrast to the unity of the conservatives in Gers, their republican opponents were deeply divided by local quarrels.[123]

The extent of the success enjoyed by the Conservative Union put Paul de Cassagnac in an exalted mood that was quickly reflected in his newspaper articles. Fired with elation over the conservatives' success, he heralded the defeat of the republicans' policies as the beginning of the end for the Third Republic. The nation had begun to "vomit" the republic, he exulted.[124]

On 9 October *Le Matin* printed Cassagnac's editorial, "Le Balai [literally, the broom] ," perhaps the most controversial and strategically inopportune piece he ever published. Considered in the context of Cassagnac's previous editorials, "Le Balai" contains no surprises; it was a characteristic piece of Cassagnaquist allegory and rhetorical prophecy, portraying the triumph of conservative good over republican evil and proclaiming the demise of the latter. However, some of Cassagnac's more cautious colleagues on the Right considered its publication prior to the run-off elections as a first-rate tactical blunder. They feared that Cassagnac's indiscretion -- and indiscipline -- would cost them greatly on the second ballot, despite the fact that he had repeatedly said the same thing in print before.[125] By raising the question of the regime, they argued, Cassagnac had provided the sole stimulus capable of spurring the quarreling republicans to close ranks on the second ballot in defense of the established political order, a position from which they could portray the Right as "revolutionary." The *Comité électoral* sent instructions to friendly provincial journals to counter Cassagnac's remarks as best they could.[126]

The republicans quickly took advantage of the situation. The moderate republican *Le Temps* tellingly commented on Cassagnac's article: "It authorizes one to believe that in reality all members of the coalition have the same thought -- to overthrow the republic . . . . The voters must make no mistake on this point."[127] And, in the interim before the run-off ballot, the ministry strategically announced that the Tonkin problem had been resolved.

In the run-off elections, the candidates of the Conservative Union won 26 additional seats, while their republican opponents, who now professed to recognize no enemies on the left, won well over two hundred.[128] In response to his critics Paul de Cassagnac contended that, in fact, the conservatives had won six more seats in *ballotage* than they had counted on, and that the policy of republican concentration lay in the logic of the elections, and was not caused by him. He anticipated a "solutionist" alliance of some 150 deputies in the Chamber, excluding the 40-odd dynastic "intransigents."[129] Before long, however, there were 18 fewer deputies on the Right, due to the invalidation of five Conservative Union lists.[130] This left the Right with some 180 deputies, about one-third of the new Chamber, of which one-third was opportunist republican and one-third radical. There was no majority.

Although the Right had greatly increased its representation in the Chamber, its leaders were even happier with the greater increase in their share of the popular vote. The candidates of the Conservative Union had attracted 44 per cent of the 8,000,000 votes cast -- less than a million votes behind the republicans. If they could capture 500,000 more votes in the future, they would have a majority. This was to be the key to the Right's strategy in the legislature of 1885-1889, a strategy which would lead them straight into the fatal alliance with General Georges Boulanger.

* * *

Paul de Cassagnac played a singular role, both in the press and behind the scenes, in advancing the organization of the monarchist forces against the opportunist republic. His initiative in stimulating a policy of conservative alliance, both in the Chamber of Deputies and without, was amply rewarded by the results of the elections of 1885. Cassagnac would have preferred to see the conservative alliance develop furthler on lines of principled opposition -- frankly anti-republican and pro-religious defense. But he was enough of a political realist to see the possibilities inherent in the "politics of interests," despite his personal distaste for it, and to exploit such interests against the republicans with the same zeal he had formerly devoted to the advocacy of principles. His efforts to bring imperialists and royalists together through the practice of *n'importequisme* were also of evident value to the achievement of Conservative Union in 1885, even though his *n'importequisme* often appeared to his imperialist colleagues to be incompatible with his position as a leader in Victorism. Within the next few years, however, this seeming contradiction in Cassagnac's position would be eliminated, as he devoted himself ever more exclusively to the politics of *solutionnisme*.

CHAPTER VIII

WAR AGAINST THE RADICAL REPUBLIC
1885-1888

Si la France, fatiguée du chaos dans lequel elle se perd, déchirée par l'anarchie républicaine, réclame l'Autorité, c'est qu'elle en a soif, depuis qu'elle ne la voit plus à aucun des degrés de l'échelle sociale, pas plus en haut qu'en bas.

Paul de Cassagnac
L'Autorité, 25 February 1886

The Conservative Union of 1885 between the royalists and imperialists represented a remarkable, albeit fragile, political achievement. That it had been realized at all was due to the sheer force of personality of Paul de Cassagnac, Baron de Mackau, and those of their colleagues who were determined to maximize conservative electoral strength in each department by eliminating inter-party competition. Its members were far less divided on the subject of immediate aims and goals than were the disparate elements that composed the new Chamber's fragmented republican majority.[1]

Although the alliance represented a significant step forward in meeting the pragmatic challenges of electoral politics, however, it was unquestionably far from perfect. As the swelled conservative minority entered the Chamber of Deputies, factional dissent quickly reemerged. The imperialists drew back from their entangling alliance with the royalists, and the royalists disagreed among themselves on the attitude they should adopt toward the existing regime. The Conservative Union would quickly reveal its deficiencies as a viable political organization.

These deficiencies quickly became apparent, and the first severe fissures in the façade of the Conservative Union appeared in mid-February 1886, during the balloting to replace the deputies whose elections the previous October had been invalidated. Reciprocal distrust and governmental pressure caused the erstwhile allies to lose eighteen deputies to the republicans in one sweep, salvaging only the four members of the list in Tarn-et-Garonne.[2] The fissures consolidated when the imperialists reorganized their former parliamentary group,

Appel au peuple,[3] and the royalists likewise organized a separate group, the *Droite royaliste*. A third element, including the now dynastically-unaffiliated deputies Raoul-Duval and Jacques Piou,[4] contemplated the formation of a frankly "constitutional," that is to say, republican group. Each of these factions had its reasons for resisting a more tightly structured organization.

The situation of the imperialists was perhaps the most difficult. Many rank-and-file Victorists had severely chastised Prince Victor for cooperating with the royalists in the elections; indeed, the Jeromists' scornful reference to the young prince as the "Vicomte de Paris" would have struck them (as it did Prince Napoleon himself) as uncomfortably apt.[5] They damned Cassagnac's *n'importequisme* as inimical to party interests and complained that they had been cheated of seats in Paris by their erstwhile allies, the royalists.

Such complaints came from outside the ranks of the deputies, Prince Victor was nevertheless sensitive to them and in early January 1886 he issued a programmatic statement that was distinctively dynastic in tone.[6] Yet he did not wish to alienate his principal supporters either, and consequently he never dared to disavow Paul de Cassagnac or the latter's policies. Henri Dichard cruelly underscored the prince's dilemma:

> Don't you owe it to M. de Cassagnac that you still have so many partisans? By whom would you replace him? Who among your present or former friends commands such prestige and possesses so great an influence? Overthrow M. de Cassagnac and Victorism will have lost its principal champion.[7]

The deputies were also sensitive to this popular pressure and although most of them were disposed to support further cooperation with the royalists, the establishment of a separate parliamentary group seemed necessary as an affirmation of independence. They underscored the Victorist nuance of the group -- and its pro-conservative alliance bias -- by electing Jolibois as their president. This act provoked the resignation of Baron Dufour, deputy from Lot, an old friend of Prince Napoleon, and one of the few Bonapartists who had stood aloof from the Conservative Union in 1885. Dufour had opposed the Victorist schism from the beginning and, following his resignation from *Appel au peuple*, he addressed to the press a series of articles and letters in which he blamed the "solutionist" politics practiced by the imperialist chieftains. "Never will I go," he wrote in the first of these communications, "as has a certain member of the group *Appel au peuple* to young Napoleon to give advice, and to the Comte de Paris to receive

it."[8] The angry exchanges provoked by Dufour's letters echoed for
weeks in the Parisian press. They were amplified by the controversy
that followed the publication of Dichard's *La Fin d'un prince*. By the
end of February, republican spokesmen were already proclaiming the
demise of the Bonapartist party.[9]

During the year 1886, relations between Paul de Cassagnac and
Prince Victor went from bad to worse.[10] By June, when the princes
were expelled from France, Cassagnac was conspicuously absent from
the group that accompanied Prince Victor to his departure for exile in
Belgium; indeed, available evidence indicates that Cassagnac never saw
Prince Victor in person again until 1895, after the deaths of both Prince
Napoleon and the Comte de Paris.[11] With Victor in Brussels,
surrounded by counselors who opposed "solutionism," their relationship
deteriorated all the faster.[12] In November 1886 Cassagnac resigned
from the *Comité central* (of which he was still vice-president) and from
the presidency of the Seine imperialist committees. Never again, he
vowed, would he be part of a committee: "I insist on conserving my
absolute independence so that I can serve my party as I please."[13] It
was understood at the time that nothing less than an unrestricted
invitation to head the party could tempt him back.[14]

Despite such flare-ups of bitter internal strife, the various elements
that composed the conservative minority of the Right in the Chamber
coexisted within the loose framework of the *Union des Droites*, which
continued to flourish under the leadership of Baron de Mackau. This
union provided the framework for legislative action. It never succeeded
in regularly gathering all the deputies from each group for strategy
sessions; personal antipathies and diversity of political convictions were
still too strong for such meetings to be effective.[15] Most of the
decisions on parliamentary strategy were therefore made by a steering
committee whose members included a delegate from each group or sub-
group. The actual legislative work was done at the secretariat, where a
small staff aided the deputies in formulating policy by collecting
materials for the study of legislative questions.[16] A few years later,
when Mackau described to the Comte de Paris the difficulties that had
plagued the Right during the legislature of 1885-1889, he assured the
pretender that "the only appropriate single reunion is the *Secrétariat des
Droites*, to the support of which everyone contributes, where everyone
meets on a working basis without feeling offended and, consequently,
where there is no reason to fear a rupture."[17]

The unity that did exist among the deputies of the monarchist Right
was reinforced by the republican campaign for the expulsion of the
pretenders during the first half of the year 1886. That June, the

Chamber enacted a law enabling the ministry to expel members of former reigning families from French territory. The pretext for passage of the measure had been a magnificent reception given in mid-May by the Comte de Paris to honor his daughter's engagement to the heir-apparent of Portugal. The guest list had included so many dignitaries that *Le Figaro* had played up the occasion as the manifestation of a counter-government. Republican leaders once again leaped to the defense of the regime.[18] Far from being sorry, Paul de Cassagnac was publicly jubilant about the prospect of expulsion, and he voiced the hope that the princes would finally be roused to action (his colleague Delafosse insisted that Cassagnac's opinion was widely shared by the deputies of the Right).[19] The expulsion measure became law on 22 June, and within only a few days the Comte de Paris, Prince Victor, and Prince Napoleon had all left France for exile in other lands.

Cassagnac exulted in the effects of the expulsion, both for the conservative alliance and for the cause of monarchy generally:

> Thanks to you republicans, . . . all eyes can see . . . two men . . . who, erect, dominate with all their sovereign haughtiness the powerless barriers of the frontier, awaiting the signal, hands on their sword-hilts, to deliver the *coup de grâce* . . .
>
> They could still hesitate when the only question for them was one of regaining a throne.
>
> But to reconquer the lost fatherland, to deliver by a final crusade their God and their France, they will risk all . . .
>
> Imbecile republicans, thank you once again![20]

* * *

During the legislature of 1885-1889, Paul de Cassagnac came to be considered -- especially by the republicans -- as "the leader *par excellence* of the monarchist opposition."[21] Thus both his newspaper articles and his public statements are of special interest to anyone who wishes to understand the politics of the Right in those years.

From late February 1886 on, Cassagnac's newspaper articles appeared primarily in *L'Autorité*, the newspaper he founded as a personal organ following the elections of 1885. The establishment of *L'Autorité* was the last in a complicated series of events that had forced Cassagnac to abandon *Le Pays*. Gibiat, the proprietor of *Le Pays*, had died in May 1885, and his nephew, Albert de Loqueyssie, a large shareholder in the company that owned the paper, was a partisan of

Prince Napoleon. He was determined to oust Cassagnac.[22] In September Loqueyssie acquired control of the paper and Cassagnac realized it would be impossible for him to remain as editor. In late November, therefore, he left *Le Pays*, accompanied by the key members of his staff.[23] Succeeding Cassagnac as editor of *Le Pays* was his constant rival Robert Mitchell, who made it his mission during the next few years to combat "solutionism" and promote Bonapartist autonomy.[24]

Cassagnac's *L'Autorité* would be a fixture in the Paris newspaper scene until the outbreak of war with Germany in 1914.[25] As a distinctively personal organ, the paper was a considerable success: it never attained the press runs of the two other personal newspapers with which it was later constantly compared (Rochefort's *L'Intransigéant* and Edouard Drumont's *La Libre Parole*), but it often exceeded 100,000 copies per issue while Cassagnac was a deputy and sometimes achieved 75,000 or more thereafter.[26] The paper's readers included a range of groups from the aristocracy to the *petit peuple*, including a notable portion of the French clergy, which it had drawn away from *L'Univers*.[27]

Paul de Cassagnac proclaimed his new paper to be the voice of the *Union des Droites*, and indeed, if any newspaper could have been said to speak authoritatively for the group's leadership, certainly it was *L'Autorité*. This paper became the platform from which Cassagnac advocated the reestablishment of the rule of authority in France by means of the conservative alliance. In a letter introducing *L'Autorité* to the public, he appealed to all conservatives who, while conserving their specific governmental preferences, were prepared to "make all concessions compatible with the rights of the nation and, patriotically, put the immediate interests of France -- her salvation, in a word -- ahead of their dynastic preferences . . . ."[28]

Thus far, Cassagnac's appeal provided no basis for quarrel: even Raoul-Duval could have agreed to this statement. Cassagnac differed, however, from others on the Right in his view of the means to achieve France's salvation. He defined that means in a seemingly unequivocal way -- "to rid ourselves of the republic, to get out of it at any cost and as soon as possible . . . ."[29] But it was unclear whether he was actually advocating overthrow of the Third Republic or simply waging another war of words against the allegorical republic espoused by the radicals. In this statement and in subsequent ones, it was often exceedingly difficult to tell which Cassagnac actually meant without carefully examining the context.

Cassagnac complemented his articles in *L'Autorité* by frequent speeches, most of which were delivered in the Chamber of Deputies. One extra-parliamentary address, however, stands out as a more general statement of Cassagnac's actual political position: this was his speech at Armentières (Nord) on 11 July 1886. Several weeks after the expulsion of the princes, on the eve of elections to the *conseils-généraux*, Cassagnac's colleagues from the Nord invited him to address the conservatives of their department. This private gathering attracted an audience estimated at ten thousand persons, "the most colossal gathering ever seen in France," Cassagnac later boasted to the editor of *Le Figaro*.[30]

The Armentières address was a paean to the conservative alliance as the "national party" that would rid France of the republic and all it stood for. Dynastic interests must not stand in the way of this task of social reparation.[31] The princes were only candidates for leadership of this party, and in the case of either one, the systems of monarchy they represented were separated neither by their origins in the popular will nor in their method of government, centered in the principle of authority. The new royalty, he claimed (a full year before the Comte de Paris outlined just such a conception in a public document) had discarded its former faith in parliamentarism and false liberties and had returned to the authoritarian principle.[32]

Although Cassagnac insisted that only a traditional, monarchic government could accomplish such reparation, he was not optimistic that such a monarchy, royal or imperial, would return "solely by political persuasion." Instead, he foresaw that "the republic will be felled because she unleashed against herself the redoutable coalition of all menaced, injured interests,"[33] and he elaborated on all the points of discontent common to the partisans of both monarchies, from state concerns like the army and the administration of justice, to the state of agriculture, industry, and the institution of the family itself. To bring such injured interests together for the task ahead, he exalted the conservatives to fulfill a duty, to act with their votes to elect representatives at all levels to speak for their wishes and complaints. Once the conservatives had a majority -- and only after France had spoken -- Cassagnac emphasized, could her champion take steps to enact her wishes, "if necessary, by the sword."[34]

Cassagnac constantly referred to the republic in language which could easily be construed as revolutionary and hinted at possible extralegal acts to put an end to the republic. But the plan of action he actually advocated was to exert pressure on and perhaps obtain control of the governmental process within the established order. This was the main significance of the speech. For, simultaneously with his denunciations of the republic, Cassagnac explicitly acknowledged that the *form* of government was overshadowed in importance by its social content. For a hundred years, he remarked, France had experienced "so many revolutions, so many disorders, so much agitation that she has become almost indifferent to the form of government . . . . The label no longer signifies a thing. The republic itself would be accepted, had it rendered itself possible and acceptable."[35] These statements reflected an attitude that was becoming increasingly widespread among the monarchists, but which seems particularly important coming from Cassagnac, the arch-foe of the republic, at this point in time.[36]

* * *

Following the expulsion of the princes, the opportunist and radical republican groups that together constituted a majority in the Chamber found themselves at odds on a wide variety of subjects, thus making difficult the formation of effective republican ministries. This led the leaders of the Right to consider closely the tactical possibilities of the situation. In August 1886, early in the parliamentary recess, *Le Soleil* had proposed that by following a "certain program," a moderate republican ministry might find itself able to count on support from the deputies of the monarchist Right. An acceptable program would entail ending the war against the Catholics, in particular by combatting the provisions in the proposed law on military organization which would require military service by religious personnel and seminary students.[37] The following month, the Comte de Paris, in a private communique, advocated a similar program.[38] By the time the Chamber reconvened in October the idea of supporting a moderate republican ministry -- without renouncing their monarchist identity -- had gained considerable ground among the deputies of the monarchist Right.

In a parallel move, two unaffiliated members of the Right, Raoul-Duval and Auguste Le Poutre, a new deputy who had been elected on the Conservative Union list in the Nord, once again solicited the formation of another sort of Right, which they termed "constitutional" or *Droite républicaine*, uncommitted to either of the existing dynasties.[39] Far from opposing this development, as he had done earlier, Cassagnac professed to welcome it, characterizing the new venture as that of "decoys," by providing a group that would serve "as a waiting room for all those who wish to change trains, from the republican car to the conservative car."[40] This was quite a different welcome than he had given to Raoul-Duval's earlier effort to form a "national party" within the republican framework.[41] But from the perspective of the Catholic monarchists, Raoul-Duval's much-remarked speech of reconciliation came at a most inopportune time -- in November -- following a period during which relations between the Right and the republicans had been severely strained by the passage of yet another laic law, proposed this time by Paul Bert, a fervent proponent of secular education. This law not only barred religious personnel from teaching in the state primary schools but also provided for the construction of a number of new schools, which the Catholic conservatives insisted only rivalled existing schools run by the religious orders.[42] In Cassagnac's opinion Raoul-Duval, the Protestant and "eternal liberal," had chosen an extremely inauspicious moment to launch his attempt at pacification. Coming as it did on the heels of the *loi scélérat*, as the conservatives referred to the Bert law, Raoul-Duval's declaration amounted to adherence to republican religious policy as well as to republican form.[43] The *Union des Droites* was anxious to avoid this latter position at all cost.

When the Freycinet cabinet fell in December 1886, however, the leaders of the Right put their own plan into motion by convoking all the deputies of the Right to meet together and affirm publicly an attitude of conciliation, to demonstrate that their object was not to create blind opposition. Unlike Raoul-Duval, they specified that they could not rally to the regime because of the religious persecution, which they associated with the republican principle, Nevertheless they registered their disposition to support a constructive program. The leaders of the Right then drafted a statement of position, the "*Déclaration des Droites,*" which included this summary of intentions:

> Whatever the ministerial combinations that may come about, the deputies of the Right are resolved more than ever to cling to the political attitude they have always had and which can be summarized as follows:
>
> First of all, to create no systematic opposition;
>
> Secondly, to support all conservative and liberal measures.
>
> To combat energetically all antireligious and antisocial measures.
>
> To maintain firmly their financial program: no borrowing; no new taxes; economy.[44]

This declaration stirred up considerable discussion in the conservative press.[45] During the weeks that followed, the position affirmed by the deputies received public support from the Comte de

Paris.[46] In January 1887, in a speech to the assembled deputies of the *Union des Droites*, their president, Baron de Mackau, reiterated the points presented in the *Déclaration*.[47] The following month, Mackau met confidentially with Jules Grévy, the president of the republic, to make the point that a moderate ministry which did not attack religious interests would have a chance of survival.[48]

The conciliatory effort of the Right had a great strategic importance. Within the Chamber, it was designed to drive a wedge between the warring republican factions and to open the way for a realignment of political forces by freeing the moderate republicans from their former dependence on the radicals. That a receptive republican audience awaited such a move was suggested by the remark in *L'Année politique -- 1886* that a ministry formed with the support of the Right seemed to be the only alternative to dissolution.[49] Within the nation at large, it was designed to have a wider impact -- to convince a half million additional voters, whom the minority needed in order to become a majority, that the conservatives were the stuff of which good government in France could be made. The intention was clear; what remained to be seen was how such an attitude would manifest itself in practice. The principal difficulty was the deputies' stated refusal to rally to the republican regime.[50] This refusal amounted to a specific repudiation of the concept of a republican right as envisioned by Raoul-Duval. Henceforth, it was precisely this adherence which the more doctrinnaire republicans would demand as the prior condition of any cooperation between themselves and the monarchist Right, and which would play such a vital role in *ralliement* discussions during the years to come. Paul de Cassagnac continually insisted, both in the Chamber and in the press, on the distinction between useful political collaboration with the republicans and any unconditional adherence to the republic -- the latter notion still implied to him a betrayal of principles.[51]

Under the new Goblet cabinet, the Right's declaration of cooperative intent was put to the test several times on foreign policy questions. During the war scare that followed Bismarck's speech to the German Reichstag in January 1887, in which he depicted the French Minister of War, General Boulanger, as a threat to peace, the *Union des Droites* presented a solid front with the moderate republicans, agreeing with them that preserving the radicals' protégé in the ministry was hardly worth the risk of war. Writing in *L'Autorité*, Cassagnac branded Boulanger "a public menace."[52]

Following this episode, the moderate republicans seemed more kindly disposed toward the deputies of the Right, even entertaining the notion of allowing them a certain number of places on the Budget

Committee, from which they had been excluded for so long. This was at least indicative of a changing attitude on their part, for even the previous year when the *Union des Droites* had purposely presented candidates for the committee in each *bureau*, not one had been elected: radical republicans had obtained the majority of seats.[53] In 1887, however, the final outcome was the same, for even as the Right dickered with the moderates for a proportional share of the seats, the Chamber voted to change the method of selecting members for the Budget Committee to *scrutin de liste*. Once again the deputies of the Right were passed over in the final vote, provoking Cassagnac's associate Paul de Léoni to remark in *L'Autorité* that the Left sought not "associates," but "accomplices."[54]

In April a flare-up of tensions in Franco-German relations due to the so-called Schnaebele incident brought the moderates and the Right closer. Frenchmen were at least learning to present a united front in the face of foreign threats. As the crisis drew to a close, it had become evident to both groups that Boulanger must be forced to abandon the War Ministry, lest he provide a continual source of embarrassment. When the Chamber reconvened in early May, the moderate republicans and the deputies of the Right combined to defeat the Goblet ministry in a vote of confidence over a budget proposal: they made little attempt, however, to disguise the fact that their real target was Boulanger.[55] As President Grévy sought another cabinet, the groups of the Right once again publicly reconfirmed the conciliatory stance they had assumed the previous December.[56]

There were only two possible replacements for the Goblet cabinet, Paul de Cassagnac observed: a ministry that would include Boulanger or one from which he would be excluded. The essential condition for forming the latter would be the tacit assistance of the Right, for the radical republicans were committed to keeping the general in office. Cassagnac repeated the Right's offer of assistance, "provided that the situation be made possible and honorable."[57] As far as the public knew, no republican hands stretched forth to request such assistance: Cassagnac complained in *L'Autorité* that, in breach of good parliamentary practice, the president of the republic had not even asked to consult with the leaders of the Right before he authorized a first attempt at cabinet formation.[58] In private, however, the leaders of the Right, including Cassagnac, met several times with President Grévy to discuss the terms of their support.[59]

The memoirs of Baron de Mackau provide the major source of information on these meetings in February and again in May 1887. According to Mackau, these meetings took place at the private request of Grévy, despite a public denial that he had taken any such initiative.[60] On 20 May, Mackau, accompanied by La Rochefoucauld-Bisaccia and Paul de Cassagnac, met with the president at the Elysée palace. Grévy, wishing to acquire the unconditional support of the Right, fenced with Mackau over the conditions concerning internal policy proposed by the latter.

To acquire the Right's support, Mackau insisted, any prospective ministry must envision a liberal application of the education laws and must not push the military law, certain provisions of which threatened the draft-exempt status of priests and seminary students. Such conditions seem mild enough in themselves, but it must be remembered that for the moderate republicans, meeting them would be interpreted as a slap in the face of their radical colleagues, and would threaten "republican unity." Mackau insisted on the Right's desire for a cabinet that would exclude Boulanger in the interest of peace, but nevertheless he reiterated the importance of these internal questions. No agreement was reached at this meeting; Mackau recorded that he left feeling "very discontented" and with a low opinion of President Grévy.[61]

On 24 May it was rumored that Floquet was expected to form a cabinet that would include Boulanger. Rouvier, who knew of Mackau's meeting with the president on 20 May, urged Mackau to return to the Elysée. After meeting with the other leaders of the Right, Mackau returned to see Grévy on the 25th, to inform him that a Floquet cabinet of such composition would be construed as defiance of the Right. He repeated the conditions under which the Right would make its support available. That evening, Mackau recorded, he was informed that the Floquet cabinet attempt had been abandoned.[62] Had the Floquet cabinet been named, the Right was rumored to have laid plans for an immediate interpellation, to be led by Paul de Cassagnac.[63]

After a ministerial vacuum of nearly two weeks' duration, Maurice Rouvier, financial expert and deputy for Bouches-du-Rhône, formed a cabinet with Armand Fallières at Interior and Jacques Spuller in the sensitive post of Beaux-Arts et Cultes. This cabinet rested principally on a truce between republicans and the Right on the subject of institutional religion: the leaders of the *Union des Droites* had insisted on a liberal application of the laic laws, restoration of clerical salaries cut off earlier by Goblet, and cabinet opposition to the offending portions of the law on military recruitment.[64] The Right had asked for no cabinet posts; they did offer the support of their votes for positive measures in other areas. From the viewpoint of the *Union des Droites*, Cassagnac later wrote, the agreement represented an armistice, not a capitulation.[65] It implied neither "*ralliement*" to, nor "participation" in the government. The Right's intention was to make possible the functioning of the country in the critical areas of agriculture, commerce and industry, and to preserve credit and moral order.[66] The Rouvier cabinet, said Cassagnac, was the "last possible cabinet;" beyond it lay dissolution.[67] That the Right was not anxious to risk dissolution at the time was attested to by the Comte de Paris, who wrote to Mackau that the newly-constituted ministry *must* last until the end of the legislative session.[68]

The tactic of the *Union des Droites* was clever, but its position was vulnerable. The historian Adrien Dansette colorfully portrayed the situation from the republican point of view when he wrote, "the natural enemy . . . has been admitted to the household following the departure of the prodigal child [the radicals]; when the latter returns, the former will be cast out."[69] The Right had to tread warily as the radicals went on the offensive. One misstep could compromise the positive results its leaders had so far obtained. The survival of the cabinet depended on the degree of courage the moderate republicans would display in standing up to the radicals' anticlerical demands as well as on the radicals' continued support of Boulanger.

During the summer months of the session, the radical republicans took every opportunity to place the ministry in conflict with the Right. They were well aware of the danger to themselves inherent in the Right's new position: as Arthur Ranc himself pointed out, the Cassagnac-Mackau operation, if it succeeded, would act as a solvent within the republican party.[70] The first onslaught came during June with the discussion of the law on military recruitment, which the Right fought bitterly. As a gesture to the *Union des Droites*, the ministry had avoided taking a stand on the controversial articles, which the Chamber nevertheless passed on 9 July.[71]

Even social events could be charged with political significance, as the Comte de Paris had discovered the previous year. Following a reception given by Baron de Mackau for the new papal nuncio, the radical republicans launched a second attack. Pelletan and Clemenceau interpellated the Rouvier ministry on "menées monarchistes et cléricales." Pelletan charged the deputies of the Right with being "permanent enemies of the republic," and Clemenceau insisted that the only hope of the deputies of the Right was "to present themselves to universal suffrage as conservatives, not as monarchists," and appealed to all republicans to prohibit them from realizing their hopes. All the emotional symbols peculiar to *concentration républicaine* -- hostility to throne, altar, aristocracy -- were present in his speech, in which he concluded with a call to war on the oligarchies and the accomplices of the Pope.[72]

The *président du conseil*, Rouvier, ably counter-charged, however, by shifting the question back to Boulanger. The radicals' opposition, he charged, was based solely on the general's absence from the ministry. A few days later, the radicals rectified their position; following the scene made by Boulanger when he departed from Paris for his new command in Clemont-Ferrand, Clemenceau disowned him in the Chamber. Thus, the ostensible barrier to republican concentration was eliminated prior to the close of the session. Signs of severe strain in the ministerial majority were not long in appearing, as the radicals concentrated their fire on the religious question. On 19 July they interpellated the ministry again, this time concerning the nomination of a curé in the department of Isère who had previously been fined for involvement in a civil incident. Although the cabinet won a republican majority in the vote of confidence, a number of deputies of the Right refused to vote with the forty of their colleagues who supported the cabinet.[73] When the session closed, the Right was badly split on the question of further support for Rouvier and his colleagues, who they felt had let them down.

During the parliamentary vacation, the entente was subjected to even more strain. Cassagnac put it bluntly: "On the top level, they [the republicans] disarm; below, they remain armed to the teeth."[74] The leaders of the Right had hoped that the ministry would make certain conciliatory gestures, such as issuing an order from the Ministry of Interior to calm the anticlerical, anti-monarchist zeal of provincial civil servants. But as Mackau soon noted, the attitude of the prefects during the August meetings of the *conseils-généraux* was disillusioning in this respect. One disruptive incident followed another: in Poitiers, for instance, local administrative officials cancelled a traditional religious procession. Mackau made an unscheduled visit to Paris "to inform the government of the dangers involved in leaving our friends in face of a whole series of provocations and discontents . . . ." "I said to them," he wrote to Cassagnac afterward, "that we wanted nothing more than to support [the government], but that they must not make it impossible for us."[75] Soon after, in *L'Autorité*, Paul de Cassagnac issued a warning to the ministry:

> It is apparent that the Catholics, despite their good
> will, can scarcely count on a republican government
> whose chiefs dare not resist the passions that stir
> below. Once more it is evident that the revolutionary

spirit is incapable of coming to terms with the
Christian spirit.
The one must necessarily destroy the other.[76]
In light of such incidents as these, Cassagnac refused to take seriously
the apprehensions of others of his colleagues that, as a result of the
Right's support of the republican cabinet, the conservative voters would
become comfortable with the republic.

In the midst of the dissension within the Right over the question of
continuing their support of the Rouvier cabinet, the Comte de Paris
published his important "Instructions" to the representatives of the
monarchist party in France, which were intended in part as a gesture of
inter-party conciliation and as a statement of support for the politics of
the *Union des Droites*. The "Instructions," whose political impact will
be discussed below, had the immediate effect of adding another divisive
element to the already strained relations that existed within the Union.

Faced with the restlessness of his colleagues, Paul de Cassagnac
grew increasingly determined in his defense of the ministerial entente.
Even though the cost might be great, he believed, the ministry must
survive until the end of the legislature's term. Accordingly, he chided
the impatience of the entente's critics on the Right (notably the factions
represented by *La Gazette de France* and *Le Gaulois*), and defended the
evolution accomplished by the Right and the moderate republicans as
"one of the most considerable, most unparalleled political facts of this
century," one which required time and patience to bring to fruition.[77]
He maintained this position vociferously, long after other firm
supporters of the entente -- including Mackau -- had altogether lost
patience with their erstwhile allies.[78] It seemed as though he really
believed that by sheer willpower, he could hold the Right in line behind
the ministry.

When the Chamber reconvened in late October, the Rouvier
ministry still stood, however reluctantly backed by its allies of the
Union des Droites. Had no other irritations arisen, the Right still might
have had difficulty standing behind the cabinet for long; as it was, the
Third Republic's first major scandal broke open at this very moment.
The revelations of the *Affaire Wilson*, the accusations of corruption
directed at President Grévy's son-in-law over the "sale" of state
decorations, pointed to an astonishing lack of scruple in high political
places.[79] Many of the deputies of the Right, already impatient with the
accord, seethed with indignation on hearing of the scandalous dealings
of Wilson, and they determined to fell the cabinet as a disclaimer of
solidarity with messy republican affairs. In the Chamber, other
members of the *Union des Droites* shouldered the moral initiative. The

Bonapartist deputy Cunéo d'Ornano demanded that a parliamentary commission be established to investigate the decorations scandal. As a result of their increasing impatience with the situation, the deputies of the *Union des Droites* nearly toppled the ministry on 3 November, over the issue of converting state bonds. The leaders of the *Union* fought desperately to hold the deputies in line; according to Mackau, this adverse vote was staved off only by the sheer force of Cassagnac's personality.[80] In Mackau's estimation (which was shared by the Comte de Paris), it was of the utmost importance that both the ministry and the president of the republic be left in office to discredit themselves and, in particular, that the Right not be responsible for precipitating a ministerial crisis.[81] As the deputies' indignation mounted, however, this strategy became increasingly difficult to maintain. One further annoyance came when the republicans excluded the Right from any seats the 22-man investigating committee established by the Chamber to probe the Wilson scandal. "It's a matter to be handled by the republicans themselves," affirmed the staunchly doctrinaire republican paper, *Le Siècle.*[82]

The attitude exemplified by *Le Siècle* triggered a vehement outburst of Cassagnac's contempt for republicans and republics, which had lain dormant since the previous year. In *L'Autorité* he vented his indignation by painting a vivid tableau of the cavern of iniquities to which no one had access except certified republicans:

> There must be no torch lighted in the cavern of the Republic. You must not see in its depths, seated on a thick layer of Dreyfus guano, the austere and venerable president of the republic, the light-fingered son-in-law at his side, both recalling those great red slugs that you are afraid to step on, mornings, in the damp woods. All around, hanging as on the nails at the rag-man's, are the *Légion d'honneur*, the general receipts, the commissions, and in the midst of all that, republicans clinking their *pots de vin* together, in the manner that one clinks glasses at the end of an orgy, and saying: "Here's to you, beloved Radical Left! to you, adored Far Left![83]

In the following weeks, *L'Autorité* served up the details of other current republican scandals, in the manner observed by Cassagnac's papers since 1876 (in *Le Pays*, the series on scandals in the United States "model" republic in 1876; the misdeeds of the "prefects of the R. F." in 1878; the dossier of M. Gent in 1879, and the "Livre d'or de la Libre (?) Pensée" in 1882). Cassagnac once more raised the question of regime, of whether France would "long support this regime which brings her not only material misery but squanders and jettisons the entire accumulation of nobility, virtue, and honor amassed by our kings and emperors during twelve centuries."[84] Such outbursts notwithstanding, Cassagnac never called into question the continued existence of the cabinet.

On 9 November, it became known that several fraudulent letters by Wilson had been substituted for others in the dossiers seized by the prefecture. From that point on, public indignation directed itself not only at Wilson but at his protector and father-in-law, Jules Grévy as well. In L'Autorité, Cassagnac (in chorus with a good many of his colleagues in the press) called for Grévy's ouster as president of the republic: the old man seemed too compromised to lead the nation.[85] Still Cassagnac avoided calling for the ouster of the cabinet. In the meantime, the Chamber voted to lift Wilson's parliamentary immunity, but against Grévy it had no other means to strike except to topple his ministry and to refuse to provide him with a new one. Seizing on this course of action, the radical Clemenceau took the initiative of interpellating the cabinet.[86] Rouvier accepted the challenge ("imprudently," judged Cassagnac) by seeking to postpone the interpellation and, on 19 November, the Chamber toppled the cabinet by a vote of 317 to 228, the majority being composed of the radicals and the Right. The deputies of the Right had overridden the better judgment of their leaders in order to achieve a momentary satisfaction.

Cassagnac was bitter over the vote of the Right -- whose alternative had been to abstain -- for, as he pointed out, it was in the interest of the radical republicans to liquidate the messy situation as fast as possible, while the Right's interest was to allow it to continue in view of the next elections.[87] Cassagnac was not alone in holding this view. In a letter addressed to Mackau a few days later, the Comte de Paris qualified the vote of the Right as a "capital mistake."[88]

In all fairness to the deputies of the Right, it must be acknowledged that their position was difficult: supporting the cabinet, even by abstention, in the stormy circumstances of the moment and with the knowledge of how often the cabinet had disappointed them in the matters they cared most about, seemed utterly distasteful to many. In Dansette's words, "they gave their vote of defiance the significance of a protest against the whole messy business."[89] Encouraged in this path by Le Gaulois and La Gazette de France, many of the deputies were less than ever willing to consider the implications of such a vote on long-range strategy, despite Cassagnac's arguments to that end. In a meeting prior to the vote in the Chamber, the deputies of the Right had voted by an overwhelming majority to overthrow the ministry. Albeit reluctantly, the minority went along for the sake of unity.[90]

During the weeks that followed, Grévy was forced to resign and Sadi Carnot was elected president of the republic in his place. From a governmental point of view, at least, the scandal had been liquidated. In *L'Autorité* (7 December), Paul de Cassagnac published a bitter post-mortem "to shed light on the mistake committed by the Right" in precipitating the cabinet crisis, and to condemn the short-sightedness of the deputies who had urged that move.

> This mistake . . . is the reason that we have not profited, as certainly we would have profited, from the scandalous events just traversed by the Republic.
>
> If we had not overthrown the Rouvier cabinet so rapidly, the ignominies of which the Elysée was giving such a spectacle would have penetrated more quickly, more profoundly into the popular masses, carrying with them the discredit of the present regime.
>
> Never had the situation been better for us.
>
> A bit more President Grévy, a bit more Wilson agency, and the Republic would have been irremediably destroyed in the public conscience.
>
> The Right was too impatient. It obeyed sentimental considerations which were most honorable, but devoid of political foresight.
>
> And at this time we see clearly the results of the mistake committed.
>
> We aided the republicans to liquidate their situation -- which had been inextricable.[91]

The Comte de Paris agreed fully with Cassagnac's assessment of the situation, and wrote to his friend, Montesquiou-Fezensac, senator from Gers, in praise of the deputy's attitude during the crisis. "He has displayed exactitude, good sense, and a political clairvoyance that have never been contradicted," wrote the pretender, adding: "If those who think they are serving the cause of monarchy when they let themselves be guided uniquely by their passions or their prejudices would listen to me, they would follow [Cassagnac's] counsel, and this would be a great good for us in our cause."[92] He later wrote to Cassagnac personally, lauding his devotion to France and remarking how their rapprochement had led to the discovery of further common points. During the November crisis, he remarked, "I had the pleasure almost every time of finding my own thought in what you wrote with so much sense and talent."[93]

The mistake had been made, and the Right had to live with it. After the formation of the Tirard ministry, the Right resumed a conciliatory position. In his capacity as spokesman for the group, Cassagnac specifically repudiated systematic opposition and *politique du pire*, or the notion that excessive evil, "the politics of adventure," might lead to good.[94] As token of their agreement, the deputies of the Right re-elected Mackau president of the *Union des Droites*.[95] The Right had gained several seats in the Senate elections of 1888, and the prospect of dissolution seemed to recede before this minor gain.[96] The only parliamentary initiative taken by the Right during this ministry was in pursuit of the Wilson affair.[97]

* * *

The program statement made by the Comte de Paris during the autumn of 1887 created a tremor of sizeable magnitude within the Right. His *"Instructions aux représentants du parti monarchiste en France"* were published in mid-September. In this document the prince presented a radically new conception of the structure for a future monarchy. "The country," he wrote, "disgusted with republican parliamentarism, wants a strong government, because it understands that even the real parliamentary regime is incompatible with an assembly elected by universal suffrage."[98] The king should rule on mandate from the nation, obtained either from a constituent assembly or by direct consultation of the electorate. He should rule with the assistance of the representatives of the people -- but the budget, traditionally the issue over which the fight for parliamentary sovereignty has been waged, would be voted permanently and thus removed from annual contention. There would be two legislative houses, the first to be elected by universal suffrage (the recognition of universal suffrage by an Orleans prince was considered very significant), while the second would represent the great social interests of the nation. The judiciary would be independent; civil and religious liberties would be guaranteed, as would freedom of association. Responsibility for schools and education would be delegated to the communes, thus removing from the national arena its most controversial issue.

In a private letter to Paul de Cassagnac, the Comte de Paris explained the intention of his program statement:

> The constitutional theory is new; I believe it to be true
> and practical. It is sincere. It is the reply I was not
> yet willing to give you several years ago when, in our

first conversation, you spoke to me of the abuse of
parliamentarism. Then the question was not yet
ripe.[99]

He then sketched for Cassagnac's benefit the effect he intended the
"Instructions" to have:

The deputy of the Right will find there, first of all, a
complete approval of the parliamentary politics he
defends with so much talent. The imperialist will
perhaps find that I place myself in a position close to
his: to him I would recall that I have only renewed an
antique tradition and that I gather the political
patrimony of the House of France wherever I find it.
He cannot hold this against me, and will see, on the
contrary, larger grounds for rapprochement in the
future than he ever dreamed existed.[100]

Cassagnac understood the Comte de Paris, and in L'Autorité he
applauded the modern monarchy conceived by the prince, lauding his
wisdom for following the path of the empire in meeting the needs of the
age. "Thanks to exile," he wrote, "the union of conservatives in ideas
has been achieved; that which was believed impossible has been
realized." He qualified the newly-achieved unity of ideas as "the most
terrible blow the republic has ever received."[101]

Cassagnac's response was the exception, however. Among the
traditional monarchist factions, the "Instructions" were considered
scandalous. While the Bonapartists moaned publicly over the
appropriation of their dearest doctrines,[102] L'Univers, which still
mourned the death of "divine right," concluded that there was no longer
a king worthy of the name. The liberal republicans, on the other hand,
who believed the Orleans family to be irrevocably committed to
parliamentary monarchy with its principle of ministerial responsibility
and devotion to restricted suffrage, considered the Comte de Paris'
"national monarchy" to be a betrayal of the Orleanist heritage; their
reaction was well expressed by the editor of L'Année politique, who
insisted that "the Comte de Paris has passed over to caesarism, bag and
baggage."[103] No representative of the old dynastic factions seemed
capable of abandoning his preconceptions sufficiently long to agree with
the later judgment of Charles Maurras, who qualified the theories
embodied in the "Instructions" as "profound."[104]

In reality, the antiparliamentary and quasi-authoritarian inclinations
so in evidence in the "Instructions" were hardly as heretical as they
appeared to believers in old-fashioned divine right or, for that matter, to

the parliamentary republicans then in power. As one historian has concluded, "the parliamentary regime, with the predominant role of elected representatives, controlling a responsible ministry itself endowed with broad initiative, does not correspond to French political tradition."[105]

Indeed, the parliamentary regime had become firmly established in France only after President de Mac-Mahon's statement of submission to the will of the Chamber, following the crisis of *Seize Mai*. From that time forth, defense of the republic had become identical with defense of the parliamentary regime, while anti-parliamentarism became an increasingly prominent characteristic of the opposition, both of the monarchist Right and of the radical republican Left, to the opportunist republicans and the regime they seemed to exploit with such ability.[106] By 1887 antiparliamentary sentiment had spread far beyond the circles of Bonapartism and traditional monarchism to permeate the climate of political opinion in France.[107] What a change from the era of the liberal empire, when Paul de Cassagnac and his father had stood virtually alone in opposing the parliamentarization of Napoleon III's regime! After less than twenty years of experimentation with parliamentary government, it appeared that authoritarian antiparliamentarism was becoming almost fashionable.

Public discussion of the inadequacies of the parliamentary system as practiced by the opportunist republic had, of course, begun with the founding of the regime in 1875. From the beginning, one of the most damning critiques was that the opportunists ignored the fundamental principle of ministerial responsibility -- both to the Chamber and to the Senate -- established by the constitutional laws.[108] Another was that the president, by not calling on the most prominent republican leaders -- the Gambettas and the Clemenceaus -- to head cabinets, also violated the rules of the parliamentary game.[109] In the early 1880's, however, the antiparliamentary criticism gained impetus from discussions going on in England, where Gladstone was campaigning for further extension of the suffrage.[110] From that time on, the basic theoretical premise for all French opponents of the parliamentary regime, monarchists and republicans alike, was that such a system, because of its aristocratic nature, was incompatible with the reign of universal suffrage (i.e., with democracy). Since in France universal suffrage was a fact of life, parliamentary government was, therefore, an anachronism. This premise was explicitly stated by the Comte de Paris in his "Instructions." Furthermore, ran the argument, in a republic, where there was no hereditary executive to resist, parliamentary government made no sense whatsoever. Even Émile Ollivier, who had so favored parliamentary limitation of the power of Napoleon III, wrote in 1885: "A parliamentary republic is a contradiction [in terms]. Where there is neither king nor emperor, the parliamentary system is no longer comprehensible. A parliamentary regime and a republic are logically incompatible."[111] In radical republican and socialist circles, moreover, the argument took on an added dimension insofar as the practice of parliamentary government became closely associated in their minds with the defense of oligarchical bourgeois interests and, therefore, with exploitation abroad and opposition to meaningful socio-economic reforms at home.[112]

All these currents of antiparliamentary thinking, common to the monarchist and radical republican opposition alike, were to culminate in a movement for constitutional reform that would find its focus in Boulangism.

* * *

From 1885 to 1888 the leaders of the ever-fragile *Union des Droites* waged a campaign against the radical republic by reaching an entente in the Chamber with a group of conciliatory opportunists, in an effort to prepare ground for their hoped-for triumph in 1889. Although Paul de Cassagnac was not personally responsible for initiating this new approach, he loyally accepted it as a strategic necessity. Moreover, he became one of the principal spokesmen for it, muting his campaign against the republic accordingly. The Rouvier ministry marked the culmination of this enterprise, but it fell, due to the additional strain imposed on an already delicate undertaking by the Wilson scandal.

In the meantime, Cassagnac's pursuit of *solutionnisme* took a new turn, as he became increasingly estranged from Prince Victor and found further evidence of the growing community of ideas that existed between himself and the Comte de Paris. It appeared to Cassagnac that the monarchical solution he so desired for France might well be realized by the royalist pretender, who had adopted a democratic authoritarian and antiparliamentary program quite acceptable to the first practitioner of Imperialism. At this point, however, the Right -- along with the nation generally -- was transfixed by the appearance of a new star in the political heavens: General Georges Boulanger. For the Right, the principal problem was how to transform this potential rival into an ally that could sweep the hated republic into the dustbin of history -- by legal means.

CHAPTER IX

WAR AGAINST THE PARLIAMENTARY REPUBLIC: *BOULANGISME* AND THE "PARALLEL MARCH" 1888-1889

*Le nom de Boulanger n'a rien qui vise un homme
plutôt qu'un autre, c'est une formule géométrique, c'est
l'X cherché. . . . On a soif d'être gouverné.*

Paul de Cassagnac
L'Autorité, 1 March 1888

The political phenomenon known as *Boulangisme* was both an antiparliamentary and an authoritarian movement. It encapsulated and expressed the widening range of grievances, social, political, and economic, some of which had earlier found political expression in 1885 as votes hostile to the stagnancy of opportunist republican rule. It also encompassed a certain nostalgia for a heroic past, a golden age, a secular savior -- a man on horseback -- that had come to be associated with the Napoleonic tradition. Adrien Dansette once characterized it this way: "The call for a man is secreted by certain temperaments in predetermined conditions: the year VIII, 1852, 1888. *Boulangisme* was one of these manifestations of the authoritarian tradition, which have been episodic in France since the Revolution."[1]

In 1888 General Georges Boulanger, long the darling of the Paris crowd as well as the protégé of the radical republicans, had offered himself as a protest candidate in a series of provincial by-elections. Soon he became the focus and embodiment of protest and, consequently, a serious threat to the status quo. The story of *Boulangisme* has been recounted by others from a wide variety of perspectives.[2] Here I shall be concerned primarily with the response from the authoritarian Right as highlighted through the political activities of Paul de Cassagnac. I will first examine Boulanger's electoral successes, and the reaction of Cassagnac to the man and his success in mobilizing public discontents into an electoral force. Following this, I will analyze Cassagnac's role in the efforts of the Right to harness *Boulangisme* and to capitalize on its political momentum for purposes of its own.

* * *

When Paul de Cassagnac heard the results of the by-elections of 26 February 1888 -- in which Boulanger's name appeared as a write-in choice on some 54,000 ballots in seven scattered departments[3] -- he instinctively recognized the vote's significance. "It's small change," he wrote in *L'Autorité*, "but it's the currency of Bonaparte."[4] From the first, he underscored the impersonal, authoritarian content in the votes. "Nothing about the name of Boulanger points to one man rather than another," he wrote soon afterward; "It's a geometric [did he mean algebraic?] formula -- the unknown X . . . . People thirst to be governed."[5]

Others on the Right soon added to Cassagnac's colorful metaphors, offering their own equally picturesque variations. In March the royalist Cornély of *Le Gaulois* suggested that Boulanger was "the microbe that will transmit the mortal illness to the Republic."[6] In May the imperialist central committee released a manifesto entitled *"Le Césarisme -- et pourquoi pas?"*[7]

Such characterizations effectively dismissed the cult of personality that had grown up in certain circles around Boulanger, which the general himself had shamelessly cultivated (both his dashing good looks and his black horse Tunis were contributing elements), and which his opponents would eventually take so many pains to demolish. But this aspect of *Boulangisme* did not directly impress either the leaders of the monarchist Right or their clientele. It was not the general's personal qualities or charisma that commended him to their attention but his potential political usefulness. Neither Cassagnac nor his colleagues were "Boulangist," because for them Boulanger could never be more than an expedient -- this much was clear from numerous articles Cassagnac had written during the general's sojourn at the Ministry of War.[8] Well before the general's well-staged appearance at the Longchamps review in 1886 had made him a popular hero, Cassagnac had branded him as both ambitious and unscrupulous:

> Renegade from monarchist opinion, apostate of the Catholic religion after having been the servant of princes and the servant of God, he has sold himself to the Revolution and to the Devil.

> And having neither conscience nor conviction, being a scoundrel of a republican, he would not hesitate, if the occasion should arise, to re-enact the

18 Brumaire or the 2 December for his own personal benefit.[9]

In spite of this history of skeptical hostility, however, Paul de Cassagnac came to the general's defense when, only days after the February elections, the ministry revoked Boulanger's command without prior hearing, on the ground that he had come to Paris without obtaining leave. The government's excuse, Cassagnac wrote, was "petty;" moreover, he estimated, Boulanger freed from his army responsibilities had the potential of becoming a serious danger.[10] In the Chamber, Cassagnac took the opportunity presented by Boulanger's revocation to denounce the government's "politicization" of the French army and to deliver a ringing indictment of the ministry for acting against the general out of fear. He characterized the recent vote as the expression of a reawakening within the country directed against *parlementarisme* and favoring a plebiscitary consultation. He reeled off his complaints against the republican government in France during its years in power, invoking the words of Napoleon I before the Council of 500 -- "What have you done to France?" -- and asserting that the accomplishments of the republicans consisted solely of fomenting religious persecution and civil war.

Is it surprising that in this situation, this "mess" -- there is no other word -- in this anarchy, the people are seeking something and, finding no relief in the ideas, the principles, the traditions that you represent, is it surprising that they seek out a man?

They seek him because they are fed up with you in this country -- fed up with your regime, with your system, and with your government.[11]

And quoting Clemenceau's remark of the prevous year, that "the popularity of General Boulanger is nothing more than the result of [the Chamber's] prodigious unpopularity," he reminded the deputies that the republican regime had arrived at that ominous eighteen-year barrier which had spelled the end of other regimes throughout the century. He concluded with a supplication for France's escape from the republic, through which she would regain her prosperity, security, and honor. His words were far from the conciliatory phrases that had emanated from the Right only the previous year. Cassagnac's speech signalled that the *Union des Droites* had once again cast its lot with the opposition.

Within a short time Boulanger was brought before a committee of inquiry and dismissed from military service. This coincided with the acquittal of the scandalous arch-opportunist Daniel Wilson, whose corrupt activities in the shadow of the Elysée Palace had so recently brought down his father-in-law, President Jules Grévy.[12] The moral of these two judgements seemed clear to the monarchists. Politically more important, however, was the fact that Boulanger's enforced retirement from the army made him a free agent. Promptly thereafter, a new newspaper, *La Cocarde*, appeared, presenting a "Boulangist" political program -- *"Dissolution, Révision, Constituante"* -- and announcing the general's candidacy in two more by-elections, both scheduled for 27 March. When the returns from these elections came in, Boulanger had captured 45,000 votes in one contest alone, running far ahead of both his opponents, a republican and a monarchist.[13]

Three days later, in early April 1888, the republican majority in the Chamber split over a proposal by the radicals to revise the constitutional laws so as to elect the Senate by universal suffrage, thereby felling the makeshift Tirard ministry. It was replaced by a cabinet headed by Charles Floquet, a fact which by itself virtually guaranteed the Right's continued opposition.[14] It was a cabinet paralyzed at birth on all significant doctrinal issues. During the ten months of its duration, Cassagnac sarcastically criticized the Floquet ministry for the breach that existed between the radical ideas of its leading members and its inability to act on them. The only thing that kept the Floquet government in office, Cassagnac assured his readers, was the threat of Boulanger.[15]

More elections were scheduled during the Chamber's spring recess. On 8 April, Boulanger was elected deputy of Dordogne. "Dissolution and Revision" had triumphed once again. In assessing the victory, Cassagnac went one step further in his appreciation of its significance for monarchist politics:

> M. Boulanger finds himself to be the motor that
> moves public opinion.
> By himself he represents nothing . . .
> He has become the occasion for a national
> awakening from which he is doubtless incapable of
> profiting personally or definitively.
> He is the springboard. He is the bridge by which
> we will cross the torrent -- which was uncrossable up
> till now.[16]

The following week, Boulanger was elected in the populous department of Nord, and Cassagnac became even bolder in depicting the meaning of the general's victory for the Right. Success, he affirmed, would be with those who took a resolute position and marched to the assault of the parliamentary republic.[17] The great neutral mass of citizens had finally been set in motion, he declared, and would come to rest on the side of the Right. The conservatives -- and the pretenders -- must take charge of this movement and master it.[18] *Boulangisme* was succeeding with the themes of the Right. As Cassagnac colorfully depicted the situation: "We are not astride his [Boulanger's] horse, for the horse he has mounted, whether he calls it *dissolution* or *révision*, is plainly from our stables."[19]

* * *

Since the latter months of 1887, certain leaders of the Right had been in secret relations with General Boulanger himself. This was not known publicly at the time, although one radical journalist had made allegations to that effect long before their first meeting actually took place.[20] Since March 1888, however, the monarchists had been requested to contribute to the general's campaign coffers by comte Arthur Dillon, Boulanger's confidante and campaign manager, who assured them that Boulanger had plans to restore the monarchy. They had done so without the knowledge of the Comte de Paris, who was then in Spain.[21] In early April six of the deputies who had been directly engaged in the contacts with Boulanger, or who knew of them -- the Baron de Mackau, Paul de Cassagnac, Jacques Piou, Albert de Mun, the Marquis de Breteuil,[22] and the Comte de Martimprey[23] -- constituted themselves as a secret committee of six to meet with the Marquis de Beauvoir, official representative of the Comte de Paris in France, and with Dillon and Boulanger himself to coordinate the details of any further cooperation.[24] The only other monarchist who certainly knew of the relationship at that date was the journalist Arthur Meyer, editor of *Le Gaulois*.[25]

In mid-April Mackau, Breteuil, and several other members of the secret committee met in London with the Comte de Paris, who had by then returned to England, in order to bring the prince up to date and to urge him to approve a course of action that would actively exploit Boulanger's electoral successes for the benefit of the monarchy.[26] The monarchist deputies' plan was to organize an electoral "parallel march" with *Boulangisme*, aiming at dissolution of the Chamber, new elections, and eventual constitutional revision. Cassagnac argued that, in addition, the Right should go beyond the call for constitutional revision advocated by the Boulangists to demand a national consultation, or plebiscite. "Revision . . . ," he wrote to Mackau, "is nothing but a word, as 'reform' was formerly."

Each wants it in his own fashion. And it would
be difficult to agree among ourselves on its
application.

And then, the people don't know and will never
know precisely what it means.

But accompany 'revision' with a demand for
'appel au pays,' and they will grasp it easily. The
plebiscite will give them the exact sense of the word
'revision.'[27]

Soon thereafter a second committee of six deputies formed to
implement the revisionist campaign. Mun and Armand de Maillé from
the *Droite royaliste*; Piou and Cassagnac, representing the *Union des
Droites*; and Léon Chevreau and Eugène Berger from *Appel au Peuple.*
Cassagnac envisioned calling a congress in which each canton of France
would be represented, to be subdivided into departmental committees
and governed by a central committee,[28] and in mid-May the six
organizers submitted to the Comte de Paris for his approval a plan
conforming to Cassagnac's suggestion.[29] A few days later the
presidents of the three parliamentary groups declared their resolution to
proceed with the organization of a grand committee, following the
Pentecost holidays.[30] On 25 May 1888 the deputies of the Right
assembled at the Hotel Continental to celebrate the founding of the
Ligue de la Consultation nationale, which would be the public vehicle
for the "parallel march" and the conservative counterpart and opponent
of the republican and anti-Boulangist *Société des Droits de l'Homme*,
founded the same day by Clemenceau and the governmental radicals.[31]

The *Ligue de la Consultation nationale* never became the all-
encompassing organization Cassagnac had advocated, but took a more
modest form. As in the conservative alliance in the Chamber, the *Ligue*
had to contend with suspicion and jealousy within the existing
monarchical party organizations. For instance, when during the
summer months the directors of the *Ligue* sought the adherence of
existing party groups, royalist and imperialist, to its program, their
efforts were met with extreme suspicion by the more staunchly dynastic
members of the groups who were waiting, as one of them remarked, "to
see who was going to profit from it."[32]

The *Ligue*'s immediate role was therefore restricted to issuing
propaganda for the "parallel march" -- for "Dissolution, Revision,
Consultation." It sponsored publications and organized public
conferences and private meetings, in which the emphasis was always on
the use of "legal means."[33] In short, it served as a campaign
clearinghouse and center for coordinating efforts. This league, it should

be pointed out, was quite distinct from the political leagues of the early twentieth century, which acquired so much notoriety for street agitation. The *Ligue de la Consultation nationale* was above all else a promoter of political education. Its efforts were restricted to recruiting dues-paying members among conservatives,[34] and to spreading the revisionist message in the provinces.[35]

In its final form, the *Ligue* was headed by a committee of twelve members, the six deputies mentioned previously with, in addition, the presidents of the three parliamentary groups, Mackau, Jolibois, and La Rochefoucauld, and three members at large, Breteuil, Delafosse, and Martimprey, two of whom were also members of the secret "Six". In all, there were five royalists, five imperialists, and two "unaffiliated" deputies.[36] This was the group that became known as the *Comité des Douze*, the committee of Twelve which coordinated the "parallel march."

The Twelve obtained the services of another young monarchist, Jules Auffray, as administrator of the *Ligue*. Auffray was not a deputy at the time (he was elected to the Chamber much later, in 1902) but had compiled a brilliant record for a man of 36 years.[37] He proved to be an able administrator, gaining the reputation of being "the great elector" of the Right.[38]

* * *

The Comte de Paris had decided to support the Boulangist venture, but he himself did not possess the requisite funds. Some monies came from well-connected bankers. Only in late June, when the Duchesse d'Uzès put three million francs at the prince's disposal "to place on Boulangism," were the monarchists able to make a substantive long-range arrangement with the general. They agreed to support Boulanger's own candidacies both with funds and votes. They were, however, unwilling to support his lieutenants such as Paul Déroulède, who ran in Charente as a Boulangist in mid-June and, losing in the first round, threw his support to the opportunist republican candidate. In their view, Boulanger alone provided the rallying-point for public discontent. Mackau and Mun interceded with Dillon, threatening to cut off the funds if Boulangism did not once again resume its plebiscitary course.[39] From that point on, the royalist involvement in Boulangism became increasingly pronounced, restrained only by the monarchists' mistrust of Boulanger[40] and by the intense hostility of a few members of the general's radical republican committee who had begun to suspect their hero of dealings with "the reactionaries."[41]

Boulanger's fortunes waned during the summer months of 1888, with his lackluster appearance in the Chamber in June, when as deputy for the Nord he called for constitutional revision, a ludicrous duel with Floquet, the pompous republican premier, and an electoral defeat in the Ardèche in July. But in August he staged a remarkable comeback when he ran and was elected simultaneously in three departments, Somme, Nord (for a second time), and Charente-Inférieure. One key to the general's spectacular victory appeared to be his explicit renunciation of religious persecution in response to a query by *La Croix*, the newspaper published by the Assumptionist fathers. As Paul de Cassagnac wrote in *L'Autorité*, Boulanger's statement on religion constituted an adequate reason for conservatives to prefer his candidacy to that of the republicans.[42] Cassagnac and his colleagues continued to insist on the impersonal character of their support: "It's not General Boulanger who won," quipped his lieutenant Deflou after the elections, "it's general opposition."[43] The moderate republicans were shocked at the dimensions of the victory. Jules Ferry wrote to the journalist Joseph Reinach, director of *La République Française*: "This is a rude blow . . . . Henceforth, Boulanger is the formula [for monarchist concentration] and the '*N'importequisme*' predicted by Cassagnac is taking place."[44]

As Boulanger's challenge grew once again, his radical partisans became increasingly suspicious that he might be colluding with the monarchists and called on him to clarify publicly his relationship with them, urging him to take an explicitly republican position. The Jeromists, who were themselves publicly supporting the general, called on him to break all ties with the monarchists and even sought to provide him with alternative funding.[45] In early December, Boulanger attempted to placate both groups to some extent by attacking the principle of monarchy in a speech at Clichy.[46]

This speech, whose effect was compounded by the *comité national*'s insistence that future Boulangist candidates explicitly accept the republic, precipitated yet another confrontation between the monarchists and Boulanger in mid-December. The Comte de Paris had written to Mackau, urging that Boulanger be forced to come down firmly on either the Left or the Right. Boulanger, in glib fashion, reassured the indignant monarchists of his good intentions.[47] Still, the relationship between the royalists and Boulanger remained tense, and might have deteriorated further, had it not been for the death of a Parisian deputy on 24 December.

For Boulanger, this unanticipated opening in Paris represented quite a different test of his drawing capacity than the provincial departments in which he had earlier been winning election; for years Paris had appeared to be republican to the core. Nevertheless, the general swiftly announced his candidacy for the seat. The contest was to be between Boulanger and the republic. With this thought in mind, the Comte de Paris counseled Mackau that the Paris royalists should abstain yet not oppose Boulanger's candidacy in any way.[48]

The election in Paris had been scheduled for 27 January 1889. It was considered by one and all to represent the ultimate confrontation between the parliamentary republic and the mobilized forces of discontent. This election was to be the prelude to the national legislative elections that would be called later that year, and the monarchists had great hopes for the success of their "parallel march." Yet they were anxious also, for 1889 carried a tremendous symbolic value, both to monarchists and to republicans: it was the centennial of the Revolution. It might also be the monarchists' last chance to restore the monarchy. Such was certainly the thought of Paul de Cassagnac, as he greeted the new year by dramatizing the symbolic meaning of the election to be fought: "the supreme battle that will decide our fate and after which, if we lose it, we must lock ourselves forevermore in the republic . . . abandoning all hope from without." The year 1889, he assured his readers, would be either "the time of deliverance or the time of the final disaster."[49]

Deliverance from the parliamentary republic in 1889 -- as before -- was contingent on two unknown quantities: the extent to which the monarchists could convincingly present a united front with Boulanger in the effort for revision and with each other, and the degree of unity that the republicans themselves could achieve in their attempts to counter the challengers.

The Paris election of 27 January did not provide a promising example of cooperation between the monarchist parties. The Victorists had flung themselves openly and enthusiastically behind Boulanger.[50] The royalists, on the other hand, remained divided in their attitude toward Boulangism and toward any compromise with it. When the Comte de Paris counseled an attitude of neutrality, on the theory that the election represented a contest between republicans, he quickly confronted revolt from below. Both *Le Soleil* and *Le Figaro* encouraged the royalists to run a candidate of their own as evidence of their displeasure with the "parallel march." They were dissuaded only by the personal intervention of the prince himself, who deplored any sort of royalist competition in the election.[51]

On election day, the "battering ram"[52] General Boulanger was elected deputy for the department of the Seine over his sole opponent,

the "candidate of the republic." The story of election night and
Boulanger's so-called failure to seize power need not be retold here;
indeed, in the light of subsequent scholarship, it appears that the *coup
manqué* story was in fact a product of retrospective wishful thinking on
the part of several of Boulanger's nationalist republican supporters.[53]
Certainly there is no evidence to suggest either that the leaders of the
"parallel march" were preoccupied with the possibility that Boulanger
might attempt a *coup* at that time, or that Boulanger's committee had
made any plans of the sort themselves.[54] More significant, the Right
attempted to exploit the general's victory in the weeks that followed.
The nature of their campaign clearly indicates their intention of working
within the system, at least until after the general elections.

Royalists, imperialists and Boulangists all agreed on the
significance of the Paris victory. To them it meant that new elections
must precede any legislative attempt to revise the constitutional laws. In
the Chamber, the monarchist deputies launched an onslaught on the
Floquet ministry, with Paul de Cassagnac as one of the principal
orators. On 31 January the Right called for dissolution of the existing
Chamber. Cassagnac confronted Floquet with a long, merciless
indictment, predicated on the electoral verdict four days earlier. It was
one of his most dramatic orations.

In the course of his speech, Cassagnac demanded that the
government account "for its conduct, the conduct of factionalists and
insurgents against the national will." The verdict had gone against the
republic, he insisted, against the very republicans who had argued
earlier that Boulanger's preceding victories were meaningless as long as
he had not achieved a victory in Paris. With this victory, the Right and
Boulanger had become the defenders of French liberties and the popular
will against the republicans. "We, those whom you call reactionaries,
have now come to be the trustees of all violated liberties, of all
unrecognized rights, due to your abandonment and your desertion!"[55]

Henceforth, Cassagnac proclaimed, revolution in France would be
accomplished by the ballot, and he called for immediate dissolution of
the Chamber. By remaining in session in order to undertake revision,
he insisted, the legislature would be defying the national will. New
elections must be held for the deliberative body which would concern
itself with the revision question. ". . . With the moral authority left to
you, you are no longer qualified to accomplish [revision], and you are
condemned to leave it to your successors . . . . Clear out! Clear
out! . . . or, if you prefer, let us all clear out!"[56]

But bravado was not enough. The Right lacked the critical votes to
effect dissolution on their terms. All that the monarchist deputies were

able to do was to strangle any further projects for constitutional revision by the existing legislature. When Charles Floquet, who had headed the cabinet since April 1888, called the question of confidence on a revision bill quite different from those the Right envisioned, both the Right and radical republican deputies voted for indefinite adjournment of debate and thereby toppled the ministry.[57]

* * *

With the divisive issue of constitutional reform temporarily shelved, the republicans were again able to present a façade of unity before the imminent threat of *Boulangisme*. The Floquet ministry was replaced by a cabinet headed by Pierre Tirard, but actually masterminded by Ernest Constans, the agile republican deputy who once again took the post of Minister of the Interior and rapidly put the coalition on the defensive.[58]

Constans began by initiating judicial action against the revisionists, first against the three deputies of the *Ligue des Patriotes* who were active members of Boulanger's *comité national*. Subsequently, he initiated judicial action against Boulanger himself for "conspiracy," thus impelling Boulanger to flee France for Belgium.[59]

Paul de Cassagnac applauded Boulanger's flight and dismissed the accusations of cowardice directed against the general by the anti-Boulangist press.[60] In the Chamber, Cassagnac led the protests against Constans' kind of justice, charging that the suits were primarily an electoral maneuver.[61] Such protests have subsequently been justified by historians, who similarly regard the suit against Boulanger as a political trial.[62] Cassagnac denounced the indictment brought against Boulanger as a "a heap of lying, stupid fables," and the prosecutor who had signed it as "the lowest of valets."[63] When the republicans proved eager to convoke the Senate as a High Court to prosecute the Boulanger case, the deputies of the Right as a body exhibited their scorn by denouncing the court as a "parody of justice," which "menaced free expression of the national will."[64] Cassagnac called on the senators of the Right to boycott the court, and in August, when the High Court finally convened, fifty-two senators of the Right withdrew, charging that the court was incompetent to try the case.[65]

Throughout the spring of 1889 Cassagnac continued his blistering attacks on the High Court and the prosecutions. In late May and again in June, he was censured by the Chamber for his intemperate outbursts. The June incident also ended is his expulsion from the Chamber for the third time in his career, for a personal attack on the Minister of Justice.[66] "I have just been expelled from the Chamber . . . ," he wrote in *L'Autorité*, "like a mere unauthorized congregation, like a mere prince, and with a unanimity that both touches and honors me."[67] Indeed, Cassagnac's eruptions in the Chamber during the 1889 session were to be his last virtuoso performances before that body. His vehemence and arrogance, his sarcastic and fiery oratory were at a peak, comparable only to his activity in 1877 (during the *Seize Mai* crisis) and 1883. In the theatre of French political life, Paul de Cassagnac was at his best in the opposition.

Since the monarchists had staked all on winning at the polls, their leaders were able to do little but issue declamatory protests. They had no alternative plan of action -- and this would be their downfall. The parliamentary republicans, on the other hand, with their majority in the Chamber, could alter the electoral situation to their own advantage while delaying the legislative elections.

The previous year, Boulanger's first successes at the polls had led some republican deputies to propose changing the method of election, once again establishing the *scrutin d'arrondissement* instead of the *scrutin de liste*.[68] In February 1889, under the impact of Boulanger's election in Paris, Floquet succeeded in pushing this significant change through the Chamber. The passage of this measure provided further ammunition for the Chamber's critics. Cassagnac argued that, having thus denied its own origins, the Chamber was morally defunct and should be immediately dissolved.[69] In public, the monarchist deputies opposed this change in the electoral law, but privately they were relieved. The *scrutin d'arrondissement* would greatly simplify their task, by eliminating the problem of forming joint lists with Boulanger and his colleagues.[70]

A second change in the electoral law forbade multiple candidacies by a single individual. The parliamentary republicans had first attempted to change this law in late February 1889. Speaking for the opposition, Cassagnac qualified the proposal as a *"coup d'état* against the people."[71] There was considerable justification for his allegation, since the republicans had long used the procedure of multiple candidacies both to enhance the stature of their own leaders and to ensure the election of certain candidates who ran both in Paris and in the provinces. With public opinion shifting to favor the opposition, their attempt to remove the prospect of a plebiscite on the name of one man was at once clever and cynical. Cassagnac complained to his readers:

> Previously, you were not consulted about the form
> of government you were given -- or rather, which was
> imposed on you . . . .
> This time it's worse.

You will no longer have the right to choose the
deputy you prefer.
You will not even be able to vote for the man who
pleases you most.[72]

The measure was not brought to a formal vote, however, until July,
when the Chamber enacted it over the protests of Cassagnac and others
on the Right.[73]

This clever change in the law meant that Boulanger himself could
run only in one constituency of one department in the general elections.
Besides eliminating the multiple candidacies of Boulanger, the law also
made impossible those planned by other coalition candidates, including
those of Cassagnac himself.[74] Thus the cause of revision found itself in
dire need of additional candidates to represent the cause before the
electorate. This law effectively beheaded *Boulangisme* and severely
crippled the "parallel march." It was undoubtedly more detrimental to
the coalition and, therefore, to the aspirations of the monarchist leaders,
than either Boulanger's flight in April or his indictment and trial for
conspiracy.

Meanwhile the ministry postponed setting the election date, hoping
that the Boulangist impetus, which had been so strong in January and
February, would slowly dissipate with the passage of time. In the
interim, Constans implemented the various means of administrative
pressure at his command in the departments to counter the revisionist
thrust, and in late July he made his first test of the administrative
apparatus in the elections to the *conseils-généraux*.[75]

By this time the monarchists realized that the success of the
"parallel march" was seriously jeopardized. Yet there seemed to be no
other course left open to them, for they had not only effected a "parallel
march" but had virtually absorbed the Boulangist political apparatus.
As they secretly funded Boulanger and his lieutenants, they drew the
latter increasingly under their dominance. The monarchists, in contrast
to the Boulangist *comité national*, possessed both an electoral
organization and funds.[76] These assets were particularly important
following the changes in the electoral laws. Since the Boulangist
committee had planned that Boulanger himself would be their candidate
in most districts, its members had put together no electoral organization
of their own (with the notable exceptions of Paris, Nancy, and
Bordeaux), and the monarchists were able to dictate the choice of
Boulangist candidates in the constituencies where they themselves were
weak, at the same time ensuring that they would not be challenged in
their own strongholds.[77] In mid-June the *Comité des Douze* of the *Ligue
de la Consultation nationale* constituted itself arbiter in the choice of

local candidates.[78] Its members were successful in imposing their conditions. This became apparent from Comte Dillon's electoral notebook, published in 1891 by a disenchanted Boulangist as evidence of Dillon's "treason."[79] The Boulangists' resentment of the Right's effective dominance increased dramatically when they discovered the actual extent of their captivity, but their last-minute efforts to organize in behalf of exclusively Boulangist candidates proved to be both too little and too late.

The monarchists' funds enabled them to exert virtual control over the Boulangist press as well: by mid-1889, they held a controlling interest in every Boulangist newspaper except Rochefort's *L'Intransigéant*. Not only had they acquired *La Cocarde* and *La Presse*, but they had even achieved indirect control over the formerly anti-"solutionist" Victorist papers, *La Souveraineté* and *Le Pays*, which had been acquired by Lenglé early in the year with money obtained from Dillon, who in turn had obtained it from the royalists.[80] *L'Autorité* and *Le Gaulois* were, of course, already engaged in the "parallel march," their respective editors being among its most enthusiastic advocates. The monarchists also published a satiric weekly, *Le Pilori*, which carried cartoons depicting the revisionists' assault on the fortifications of the parliamentary republic, as well as a prodigious amount of revisionist campaign literature directed to the "politics of interests" -- finances, agriculture, education, religion, foreign affairs, republican scandals, and the record of the *Union des Droites* in the Chamber.[81]

Despite the outward display of assurance given by the monarchists as the elections drew near, many of them were privately worried. Both the Comte de Paris and Prince Victor issued pre-election statements to underscore (with differing emphases) that the French nation must be consulted on the disposition of its destiny,[82] and Baron de Mackau stressed the conservatives' insistence on returning to power by legal means.[83] But what they really wanted was a dramatic flourish to end the campaign -- a finale that would reawaken public interest in the revisionist program -- General Boulanger must return to France. The royalists sent a delegation to England to plead with him to come back. But Boulanger refused to come.[84]

Spokesmen for the Right, including Cassagnac, were bitterly critical of Boulanger's behavior. After the elections, Cassagnac admitted: "We had foreseen everything -- except that this general, this soldier, had no courage. A soldier who saves himself! Such a thing has never before been seen."[85] In Cassagnac's judgment, Boulanger had fled from his political responsibilities; later, the journalist assessed the general's suicide as a similar effort to flee from the difficulties of life.[86]

Had the general returned to France, he might possibly have offset, by his personal appeal, the handicaps faced by the revisionist coalition due to the changed electoral laws and severe administrative pressures, although it is impossible to judge to what extent. In his absence, the assembled monarchists and Boulangists still captured 210 seats altogether. This result was insufficient to constitute a revisionist majority, but it nevertheless represented 45 per cent of the greatest popular vote since 1877.[87] For the parliamentary republicans, the defenders of the constitutional status quo, this was victory enough. But the results were still such as to enable Cassagnac to call them a "relative success" for the cause of revision, despite Boulanger's absence.[88] The Right would never have accepted the later verdict of historians that the elections of 1889 had been "the decisive defeat of the traditional Conservatives."[89] This became clear only in retrospect.

In Gers, Paul de Cassagnac was returned to the Chamber without opposition. His opponent withdrew from the race a few days before the election, giving Cassagnac the opportunity to suggest tongue-in-cheek that a reward be posted for his return.[90] The other incumbent conservative deputies were also re-elected. *Cassagnaquisme*, not *Boulangisme*, dominated the elections of 1889 in Gers.[91] Elsewhere, the Right recouped its 1885 invalidations in the departments of Ardèche, Corsica, and Lozère, and in coalition with the Boulangists they made spectacular gains in departments where, in 1885, republicans had swept the field: Aisne (the coalition won 6 of 8 seats); Dordogne (4 of 8); Gironde (6 of 11); Ille-et-Vilaine (8 of 8); Haute-Marne (2 of 3); Seine (18 of 42), and Seine-et-Oise (6 of 9). But they suffered heavy losses in other traditionally conservative areas: Charente-Inférieure (losing 4 of 7 seats); Finistère (7 of 10); Lot (4 of 4); Nord (11 of 21); Oise (4 of 5); and Pas-de-Calais (9 of 11).

Despite the symbolism of the revolutionary centennial evoked by Paul de Cassagnac and others at the beginning of 1889, what was clear in October of that year was only that the revisionist coalition had registered no gain in percentage of votes over the Conservative Union of 1885. Mackau firmly defended the coalition policy which he and his colleagues had pursued. The monarchists, he insisted optimistically, had effectively maintained their previous position, with the difference that "the alliances contracted will give us points of support within the majority and on the extreme Left which we did not have before." In the countryside, "this policy gave us the additional support we needed almost everywhere . . . . Without it we would be 60 in the Chamber -- as we were formerly [1881-1885] -- that is to say, those of us whose strongholds are impregnable."[92] Mackau even anticipated rallying

Boulanger's own supporters to the cause of the monarchy as *Boulangisme* went into decline.

* * *

The political calculations that had prompted the monarchist deputies and the Comte de Paris himself to undertake the "parallel march" with Boulanger in 1888-1889 have since been obscured by the recriminations arising from the effort's failure.[93] These calculations, as well as the limits which both prince and deputies imposed upon themselves, must, however, be taken into account in order to evaluate their decision and its consequences.

It is important to underscore that neither the deputies nor the Comte de Paris himself believed that a lasting restoration of monarchy could be effected in France by other than legal means. Thus, their immediate aim was to seek an electoral victory, a majority in the Chamber capable of achieving their desired end by means of constitutional revision. For an electoral victory, they had to win 500,000 votes more than they had mustered in 1885, and this could not be accomplished without appealing to disaffected republicans.

With the advent of Boulanger as a political force in the spring of 1888, the monarchist leaders saw that Boulanger was capable of rallying the essential votes and that in alliance with him they might will achieve their aim. Neither Mackau nor Cassagnac believed that *Boulangisme* offered any real threat to the conservatives' own previously manifested strength, although not all their colleagues agreed with them on this point. As Cassagnac bluntly put it in *L'Autorité*, "What have we got to lose?"[94] The members of the *Comité des Douze* could even rationalize that Boulanger's clearly republican declarations of December 1888 and March 1889 enhanced his attractiveness to the necessary republican protest votes, without splitting the already assembled conservative forces.[95] With Boulanger's name added to conservative lists in the borderline departments, the monarchists could foresee victory in areas where they had been pessimistic about succeeding alone.

Implicit in Mackau's attempt to acquire a majority by rallying discontented republicans was the aim of broadening the base of support of the Comte de Paris in the event of a restoration. The monarchist activists like Mackau and Cassagnac were disturbed by the self-righteous inactivity of many of their co-believers who seemed content (as Drumont later put it) to remain "faithful to their most deeply-rooted principle --that of imposing no sacrifice on themselves for their cause."[96] "One must pay for them, think for them, act for them," complained Mackau to the Comte de Paris.[97] Faced with such inertia, the activists thought it better "to cross the Boulangist bridge" rather than to be "held back, immobile, on the banks by exaggerated scruples of political virtue."[98] This course of action was clearly risky, but that of inertia was deadly. Mackau therefore sought to recruit the young men of action, both Boulangist and Bonapartist, whose presence might bring fresh enthusiasm and vigor to the cause of monarchy, men like Lenglé (who by that time was estranged from Prince Napoleon) and Maurice Barrès. Following the elections, Mackau urged the Comte de Paris to continue, as he himself had been doing,

> to augment Monseigneur's troops without being disturbed over the difference in uniforms, rather than closing myself within too small a circle by demands which were too great . . . . Undoubtedly, not all will respond to every call. But even those who hold back will cease to be adversaries and will at least be more or less advanced allies, if not friends.[99]

The Comte de Paris opted to support the initiative advocated by these activists -- the "parallel march" -- over the strenuous objections of members of his own family (notably, several of his uncles) and from among the old Orleanists ("*les vieux jeu*" as the journalist Terrail called them[100]), who criticized the "parallel march" as "compromise with an adventurer," the kind of alliance that only victory could excuse, and a stain on the honor of the dynasty.[101] After the failure, these critics depicted the pretender as having been coerced into the alliance against his own better judgment. But their apologies are undermined by the prince's own statements. The Comte de Paris insisted on accepting full responsibility for the decision, and defended it as the only sound one. In an unpublished letter addressed to Paul de Cassagnac in 1891, the prince wrote:

> Since the elections of 1889, I have been violently attacked. Among so many criticisms, only one has wounded me -- that which represents me as having been led into error, dragged along and compromised in spite of myself, and afterwards covering out of generosity acts which I am supposed to have disapproved deep in my heart. When I trace out a policy for the party, whose chief I am honored to be by hereditary right, I can make a mistake. But whether I am right or wrong, I do not intend to share with anybody the responsibility for this direction . . . . I am persuaded that if we had adopted another

electoral policy, our defeat would have been crushing,
and that we have emerged with the least possible
damage from a situation which had become very
bad.[102]

In the electoral campaign of 1889, the leaders of the Right were
scrupulous in professing respect for legal means of achieving
constitutional revision and, thereafter, eventual restoration of the
monarchy. Indeed, one can direct at these men the Machiavellian
criticism that Dansette made of Boulanger -- namely, that they
"committed the capital error of believing in the legal conquest of power
and . . . launched an assault on the ground chosen by the regime."[103]
Neither Boulanger nor his monarchist allies were truly "revolutionary."
Had they been, they would hardly have missed the psychological
moment for dissolution and revision -- in early 1889 -- in order to wait
for the calling of regular elections by their opponents. Even Cassagnac,
who was undoubtedly the most radical of the monarchists in this respect
as in others, was not prepared to invoke civil war on behalf of a
dynasty. He continued to invoke the *coup d'état* of 1851 upon occasion
and to chide the Comte de Paris for confining himself voluntarily within
the bounds of "legality."[104] but during the actual campaign his own
utterances were very restrained.

Cassagnac's reserve was not due entirely to good will. It must be
remembered that since the constitutional revision of 1884, open
advocacy of changing the form of government was illegal. To do so
would have provided grounds to invalidate, if not to prosecute,
monarchist deputies. The amended article (to quote Cassagnac in 1889)
"forbids us to say what government we want and what government we
don't want."[105] As the republicans developed their formula of
"concentration," or no enemies to the Left, even the governmental
radicals came to the defense of the parliamentary republic, charging that
their opponents on the Right were actively conspiring against the
regime.

One such incident took place in the Chamber in 1886, when
Clemenceau charged that republican stability was confronted with the
menace of revolutionary monarchism: "Today the masks have fallen;
the veils are torn aside. There are now but two parties in the country --
those who desire the maintenance and consolidation of the republican
order and those who desire a political revolution to the profit of the
monarchy."[106] Cassagnac countered Clemenceau's charge by summing
up the program of the monarchist Right since 1882, and that would be
theirs through 1889:

Not by insurrectional procedures, not by armed
conspiracy, which you republicans have often used
youselves, will we try to return and to reconquer
France. We will use a means you know already, for
you furnished us with it. This means consists of
profiting from all the faults you have committed and
which will increase in number, and at a given moment
to reap the ripened fruit of general public misery, of
the despair that fills the workshops and the
countryside, of the urgent need everyone feels today
and manifests loudly -- of finally finding a government
that can protect the worker and reassure the believer!
That is what France demands . . . .[107]

Another incident in early 1889 began with the proclamation, by the
governmental radical, Madier de Montjau, that "the Republic has
no . . . divine right, but she is [nonetheless] above the law of majorities,
because she is the government of all by all. Against this government,
nobody can protest. . . ."[108] The monarchist conservatives' reply to
such reasoning was summed up by Cassagnac later in the year. If the
Republic was really the government of the people, he wrote, then the
people have a right to change it when they please, without having their
efforts referred to as "*attentat*" or "*complot.*" Such an act . . .
"becomes the licit and permanent manifestation of real democratic
freedom under the republic."[109]

Thus, the Right's campaign strategy, consisting of attacks on the
faults of the parliamentary republic and its personnel, was dictated in
advance. This was set forth explicitly in the manifesto published in late
June 1889 by the twelve-man directorate of the *Ligue de la Consultation
nationale*, which was subsequently endorsed both by Prince Victor and
the Comte de Paris.

The text began with the words, "The party that has held the reins of
government for twelve years is condemned." The manifesto catalogued
the various affronts to the national interest committed by the
parliamentary republicans and convoked all "honorable men" to unite
for the salvation of France, by delivering her "from the parliamentary
feudal system which discredits, oppresses, and ruins [her]." Beyond
that, the document contained only vague references to revision of the
"powerless" constitution and the sovereign verdict of the national
will.[110]

In accordance with the Right's strategy, Cassagnac's own
statements concerning the future of the regime remained remarkably

pacific as the election date drew near. In contrast to his threats against the republic only a few years previously, he struck a note that sounded almost conciliatory. In 1887 he had still maintained reservations about a form of government "whose name alone . . . is the equivalent of moral disorder and political instability," but he had acknowledged that ". . . the value of governments is found not in words, that is, in the form, but in the content itself, that is, in the ideas."[111] On a number of occasions during the 1889 campaign, he stated frankly that his preoccupation was "not to change the form of government, but to change the men who compose it."[112] Like Mackau, he had seemingly resigned himself to the notion that "the country had become indifferent to the form of government" as long as there were no revolutions; the single theme which could stir the electorate was "Down with the thieves; long live the honest men!"[113] Law and order above all.

Indeed, during the spring of 1889, Cassagnac even attempted to reply directly to the republicans' insinuations of revolutionary intent. He provided a scenario for the cautious course of action that the coalition would have to pursue if it won at the polls.[114] "The most vulgar common sense," he reasoned, indicated that neither the imperialists nor the royalists would benefit sufficiently from the victory to permit a restoration, particularly in the face of a powerful "Jacobin minority." Such an attempt would be "a prodigious stupidity, . . . given the diversity of our coalition majority," he asserted. For the time being, *Boulangisme* alone would have to provide the pivot for action by the majority, which would concentrate on purging government personnel as it prepared the terrain for a national consultation.[115] The new majority's next steps would be to lay siege to the Senate and the Presidency.

> We will use neither force nor violence. . . . We
> will make no revolution . . . . We will render
> ourselves master of the government by the normal and
> regular functioning of institutions and without stepping
> outside legality for a single second.[116]

What Cassagnac described in these articles was a sort of *Seize Mai* in reverse. The Boulanger elections had shown, he stated in a later article, "that it is no longer necessary and indispensable to have recourse to violence . . . , to trouble the public peace in order to overthrow the parliamentary republic: the ballot suffices."[117] Certainly he had come a long way toward moderation from his earlier and more extreme position; it remained to be seen whether he could be wholly convincing in this new posture. It was indeed difficult to separate this moderate, conciliatory-sounding Cassagnac from the Cassagnac who, only the following week, wrote these paragraphs:

A man has appeared. He is worth what he is worth. I shall neither praise him nor denigrate him.

But suddenly he has become the pivot for all resistance against the evil from which we suffer and die -- revolutionary *parliamentarisme*.

He is the living synthesis of everyone's repugnance, disillusionment, and disgust.

The conservatives, who verged on rupture, can agree to work with him for a transitory task.

What do we risk to march at his side, under our own flags, with our own autonomy, in our complete independence?

Wherever he leads us, it will always be beyond what is, out of this sea of mud.

Whatever he gives us, he will give us something else than what is -- shame, ignominy, forced labor.

One does not quibble over the hand that is held out to the drowning man. One does not make difficulties about the means of escape for a prisoner.

One saves himself in the way he can.

I defy the future to inflict a government on us that is not infinitely better than the present government . . . .

Can one have anybody more odious than Floquet or Goblet? Stupider than Tirard or Freycinet? More rascally than Thévenet or Guyot-Dessaigne?

This is why I plunge, without hesitation, into the unknown, for that unknown can only offer me pleasant and unanticipated surprises; what I have known already has exhausted every possibility under the heavens for what is foul, *immonde*, and mortal for the destinies of the *patrie*.[118]

"*N'importe qui, n'importe quoi! Tout plutôt que la république!*"

* * *

To Paul de Cassagnac, the politics of the "parallel march" represented a new twist in the *n'importequisme* or "solutionism" he had advocated since the early 1880s. He threw himself into it with his customary zeal, convinced that if the consolidated Right rode the current of *Boulangisme*, it would lead to their victory, and to the eventual re-establishment of a monarchical, authoritarian government in France under the leadership of the Comte de Paris. The "parallel march" was clearly more to Cassagnac's taste than the Right's previous policy of cooperation with the opportunist republicans had been, despite his ardent defense of the latter in late 1887. His active participation in the secret group of the "Six," in the *Comité des Douze*, and his oratorical role in the Chamber during 1888 and 1889 all provide ample evidence of this truth.

Despite all Cassagnac's calculations and expectations, however, the "parallel march" suffered two major handicaps. The first of these, its leaders' failure to anticipate and counter the parliamentary republicans' defense of the regime by legal and administrative measures, was extremely serious. But the second, Boulanger's weakness of character, which determined him to remain in England instead of returning to France to brave his opponents, was mortal. Indeed, this latter failure underscored for many the basic flaw in any call for *n'importe qui,* a flaw that had already been demonstrated by Mac-Mahon in 1877: the lesson was that although Frenchmen might ardently desire the arrival of a political messiah, they could not depend on his successful arrival. As Edouard Drumont wrote in 1890, "During the last eighteen years, there has always been someone who was supposed to mount his horse and never mounted."[119] Drumont belonged (in spirit) to a new generation of political realists which recognized that Frenchmen must finally take their destiny into their own hands. To this group, after the failure of the "parallel march," Cassagnac's rhetorical appeals to a delivering authority figure perhaps appeared increasingly outmoded, if indeed not pointless.

CHAPTER X

WAR AGAINST THE PAPACY AND ITS POLICY OF *RALLIEMENT* TO THE REPUBLIC 1890-1893

On nous invite à l'union, mais si c'est pour adhérer à la République actuelle, c'est inutile, car ce serait l'union pour le suicide.
Mgr Lavigerie nous engage à respecter la République.
Nous la respecterons quand elle sera respectable, et quand elle nous respectera . . . .
La question est close.
Les catholiques n'iront pas à la République, quoi qu'on fasse et quoi qu'on dise.

Paul de Cassagnac
L'Autorité, 22 January 1892

On 12 November 1890, in celebration of a visit by the French fleet to Algiers, Cardinal Lavigerie, archbishop of Algiers and Oran, lifted his glass to toast the French republic. His move marked the beginning of a new phase in the diplomatic policy of Pope Leo XIII, that of assuring the *ralliement*, or formal adhesion by French Catholics, to the republican government of the nation. The policy was confirmed little more than a year later, in February 1892, when the Pope issued his encyclical letter to French Catholics entitled "*Au Milieu des Sollicitudes.*"

At the time of the encyclical, the Vatican still pursued a favorable resolution of the Roman question. This matter necessitated the cultivation of a close alliance with France. The reaffirmation of the Triple Alliance of Germany, Austria, and Italy in 1887 made it impossible for the Vatican to achieve any satisfaction on the Roman question from either of the two northern powers. The new Vatican secretary of state, Cardinal Rampolla, persuaded the Pope that "close liaison with France" was "the only course left open to the Papacy by the current conjuncture of circumstances," in which Vatican-Italian relations were steadily deteriorating and France and Italy were engaged in an acrimonious tariff war.[1] To achieve close ties with France, "a high price would have to be paid, and Rampolla was ready to pay it: papal support for the republican regime in France."[2] This was a step beyond the policy of political neutrality that which had prevailed during most of the 1880s, a policy that has frequently been referred to as the prelude to the ralliement, but which was in fact as acceptable to the monarchists as to the republicans the Vatican was attempting to cultivate.

The Vatican was disposed to conclude a definitive peace with those in power. Hence, the attempt of the monarchist Right to enter into the "parallel march" with *Boulangisme* in 1888-1889 was not viewed with favor in Rome. In the eyes of the Papacy, the monarchists' effort had led them "to compromise not only themselves but France and the religious cause they claimed to serve."[3] Following the defeat of constitutional revision at the polls, therefore, the Vatican was quite prepared to sacrifice these monarchist leaders who, however aristocratic and wealthy they might be, still nurtured their inconvenient distaste for republics in general and for the current anticlerical and parliamentary republic in particular. Leo XIII had made up his mind on this point and no amount of persuasion would move him. His decision cannot be attributed to having been "misinformed" by his nuncios on the state of Catholic opinion in France, as Paul de Cassagnac and others charged, since many leading French Catholics -- men like Émile Keller and Monseigneur d'Hulst -- were frank with the Pope both in interviews and letters.[4] By design Leo XIII and Rampolla subordinated monarchist Catholic outcries, which they considered discredited, to the achievement of the new policy. Indeed, if a serious accusation can be lodged against Leo XIII's policy of *ralliement*, it is that his priorities were unwise. He placed his hope of resolving the Roman Question favorably upon France's help, the price of which was maintainance of the Concordat, ahead of the discomfiture and damage which still threatened the Church in France at the hands of the anticlerical republicans.[5]

The parliamentary republicans were jubilant at the new development in papal policy, which effectively confirmed their narrow victory at the polls in 1889 by calling for the unilateral disarmament of their opponents. They had long been eager to obtain papal aid to neutralize Catholic elements hostile to the republic. Indeed, in 1885, they had formally solicited such aid, in President Grévy's letter to Leo XIII.[6] Consequently, the papal demand for formal adhesion by French Catholics to the republic could not have pleased them more. Their radical colleagues were, however, far from pleased.

The point of view put forth by the "African," Lavigerie, and shared both by the parliamentary republicans and by Leo XIII has dominated the historiography of the *ralliement*.[7] As one might expect, the proponents of this view have been most unsympathetic to the arguments employed against the *ralliement* by the French monarchists, and have habitually blamed the failure of the policy on the latter's intransigence in refusing to follow the papal instructions.[8] They have discounted the powerful argument employed by so many of the monarchists, from Paul de Cassagnac to the Comte de Paris himself, that the papal action represented a clear instance of interference by the Vatican in French political life, a right they had insistently denied to the Papacy under any and all circumstances. The Pope could give his counsel to Catholics on political matters, the monarchists argued, but his advice could not be construed to impose an obligation of conscience.[9] Historians have likewise taken little account of the irreparable cleavages created by the *ralliement* in French monarchist and Catholic circles. As one *rallié*, Fernand Laudet, acknowledged in his memoirs, "The *Ralliement*, both for those who desired it and for those who combatted it, was a terrible political trial that unchained the most violent passions and upset entire families."[10]

No lay opponent of the *ralliement* policy was more outspoken than Paul de Cassagnac. Lavigerie was infuriated by Cassagnac's treatment of the issue, and of the persons involved as well, from bishops to the nuncio in Paris, and even the Pope himself. The Cardinal charged that monarchist journals such as *L'Autorité* only used religion for political purposes.[11] The Cardinal's arguments which, in effect, accused Cassagnac of bad faith, have dominated subsequent treatments of the latter's role in contesting the *ralliement* to the republic.[12]

In the context of Cassagnac's earlier political career, however, Lavigerie's judgments seem a little too polemical, too facile and too peremptory. Indeed, Cassagnac's propensity for independent action and single-minded opposition to policies he was convinced were wrong was certainly not new in 1890. The difference was that in the political situations where he had previously demonstrated his mettle, there had been no organizational structure capable of dominating him. The Bonapartist party, for example, had been unable to thwart or silence him. Not so with the Church, however. As a lay Catholic, Cassagnac confronted an overwhelming obstacle when he determined to resist the *ralliement* -- namely, Leo XIII's claim, increasingly effective during his papacy, to subordinate every political program that defended religious interests to the approval and control of the ecclesiastical authorities.[13]

Thus, Cassagnac, in opposing the *ralliement*, was in effect challenging the authority of the papacy itself. His challenge resulted in a running battle between his brand of politics and the Catholic hierarchy, a battle that lasted until well after Cassagnac's own death in 1904.[14] Cassagnac refused to desist in spite of heavy criticism from *L'Osservatore Romano*, the official newspaper of the Vatican,[15] and despite interdicts against the distribution of *L'Autorité* in some dioceses.[16] He remained undaunted by such actions. As far as he was concerned, the bishops were captives of the Concordat, "accomplices in the persecution," as he put it, and therefore lay Catholics must take the lead.[17]

* * *

There had already been some movement toward the formation of a "constitutional" opposition in the Chamber of Deputies prior to the Algiers toast of November 1890. Early in 1889 Baron de Mackau had warned the Comte de Paris to expect such a development in the event that the "parallel march" did not attain its electoral goals.[18] Following the elections, therefore, when the moderate republicans made overtures to members of the Right, offering them a "habitable republic" in exchange for their support in forming a ministry, many seemed receptive.

Paul de Cassagnac sought to brake any precipitate move in this direction by invoking the Right's earlier experiences with the Rouvier ministry, opposing any more such bargains with the republicans that did not include firm guarantees on the religious question.[19] There were signs, however, that a conciliatory attitude was gaining ground on the Right: in November 1889, the deputies elected a provisional steering committee of eleven members˜ from which the leaders of the "parallel march" were conspicuously absent.[20] In mid-December, two sub-groups formed within the Right, the *Groupe royaliste* and the *Réunion indépendante de Droite*; the latter group was devoted to continuing the policies of the earlier *Union des Droites*.[21] By late January 1890, however, the deputies of the Right had formed a single group, under the rotating presidency of La Rochefoucauld, Mackau, Jolibois, and Piou, representing the royalist, independent, imperialist, and conciliatory tendencies respectively.[22] "There is no 'Constitutional Right,'" Cassagnac proclaimed, referring his readers to the charter of the new group.[23]

There were, however, other signs of conciliatory activity as well. In December 1889, the Right and the moderate republicans formed a 300-member parliamentary group to consider agricultural policy, and elected Jules Méline as its president.[24] The following month, the Chamber elected 50 republicans and five deputies of the Right to its tariff committee,[25] and in March, four deputies of the Right were elected to the Budget Committee, the first to be so chosen in over a decade.[26]

Following the formation of a moderate ministry by Freycinet in March 1890, a small group formed on the Right which called itself the *Droite indépendante* and soon became known as the *"Droite constitutionnelle."* Its leading members were Jacques Piou and Jules Delafosse, both former members of the *Comité des Douze.* While the *Droite indépendante* disclaimed any opposition to the republic on principle, neither was it "constitutional" in the sense of accepting the republic. Its members desired to place the constitutional question on hold in order to oppose the individual acts of the republicans as they arose, acting in conjunction with the existing Right, and to seek reform within the existing structure. Cassagnac voiced his skepticism about their chances of being well-received by the republicans.[27] As the year wore on, however, and other deputies of the Right appeared to be gravitating increasingly toward such an "independent" politics, Mackau felt obliged to warn the Comte de Paris that these deputies might be provoked to break with the monarchists if pushed too hard by the intransigent royalists.[28]

As far as religious interests were concerned, most deputies of the Right were still convinced that the republic remained the enemy.[29] One attempt to organize conservatives on a more rigorous basis was made by Cassagnac in the late spring of 1890, when he founded a social action group known as the *Ligue de Défense Sociale.* Although little information is available on the eventual development of the organization, it was designed initially to unite conservatives in defense of their social interests by pledging them to hire employees and buy from businessmen of "conservative" opinion only. The police considered this *Ligue* to have another, more important goal of providing a tighter basis for electoral action throughout France.[30]

In late 1890 conservative opinion was discouraged by the publication of various revelations concerning the monarchist involvement in Boulangism. Even Cassagnac had to admit that never in the last twenty years had spirits been lower.[31] But he still considered the prospect of unconditional *ralliement* to the republic as impossible. The republic would first have to guarantee religious liberty.[32]

* * *

Cardinal Lavigerie's toast to the republic astounded Frenchmen generally, and Paul de Cassagnac was no exception. Cassagnac argued that the toast had been the cardinal's own idea and betrayed a total lack of understanding of the situation in France.[33] In France, he contended, the republic was not simply a form of government, as in Switzerland and the United States (the two examples invariably cited by advocates of *ralliement*), but comprehended an anti-Christian doctrine. To adhere to such a republic as that in France was to betray the faith. The heads of the Church, he insisted, were capitulating.[34] Cassagnac refused to acknowledge that Lavigerie's action had been authorized by the Pope, but argued that even if it had, the papal advice on such a subject was restricted to the right of paternal counsel. Neither Pope nor bishops, he insisted, had authority over the consciences of the faithful in politics. "In matters political, the Catholic is completely free and entirely independent with respect to the Pope."[35] He pointed to the reaction of the minor clergy "who have never been more independent, more firm, more bold, more heroic," and who responded to such as Lavigerie by a respectful but significant silence.[36]

Less than a month later, Cassagnac spoke in the Chamber on the "causes of the opposition by the Right," repeating his argument that the Right, however conciliatory its members might be, could not come closer to the republic unless the latter were to allow religious liberty. The dynastic question, he proclaimed, was now nothing more than a fond memory; the religious question remained the sole barrier to a *rapprochement*. Two concessions would suffice, Cassagnac allowed: 1) that the seminary students be allowed to perform their military service in the medical corps, and 2) that the communes be allowed to decide whether the communal school would be secular or Christian. It was not the Right that prevented unity in France; the actions of the *Droite indépendante* were certainly proof of that. It was the republicans "who do not wish to share with newcomers the favors and benefits of power" who were to blame. "There are many in the republican party . . . who oppose their insatiable appetites to the pacification, the civil peace, and the health of France." It was these republicans who kept the doors to the republic shut -- or who had "made them so low that one must bend over to enter," by the sacrifice of religious belief, a cause for dishonor. The conservative minority would continue to fulfill its mandate, Cassagnac stated, but the republicans must make the next move toward conciliation.[37]

Some organs of the republican press treated Cassagnac's proposals as reasonable, but others -- and particularly Cassagnac's old enemy, the radical republican senator Ranc, writing in *Paris*, branded Cassagnac's demands as attacks on the very principles of the republic, that is, on the secularized society. Cassagnac's speech, he allowed, was a parliamentary tactic designed to reap certain modest benefits; at base, however, it "only amounts to a conditional adhesion, and what conditions! That the Republic abandon all its principles, that it cease to be itself. At this price, their adhesion to the form of government is too costly . . . ."[38] Ranc's response exemplified the opinion of the radicals.

Thus, by December 1890, the lines of the *ralliement* debate were drawn. During the next twelve months, little would be added beyond clarifications and elaborations of existing positions. Much of the debate centered on the statements and activities of Piou's *Droite indépendante*, whose members were slowly evolving toward a more explicitly republican position. The more skeptical members of the Right like Cassagnac (and Comte d'Haussonville, the new representative of the Comte de Paris) estimated that the members of the Piou group would alienate both monarchist-conservative and republican voters in the next elections and would thus be driven from public life.[39] They considered the *essai loyal* as impossible in a time of religious persecution and Piou as hopelessly naive. "I know you," wrote Cassagnac of Piou; "I have seen your kind before under the Empire. Then your name was Émile Ollivier."[40] In the eyes of the masses, Cassagnac pointed out, one is either republican or one is not. "To borrow the word without borrowing the thing would appear to them entirely incomprehensible."[41]

Meanwhile the lines of resistance began to form within the episcopacy itself. In February 1891, Monseigneur Freppel, bishop of Angers and deputy from Brest, journeyed to Rome with a mandate from forty-four monarchist deputies (drafted by Cassagnac) to present their objections and to entreat Leo XIII to proceed no further in the direction indicated by the Algiers toast, which (they argued) risked irreparably dividing French Catholics.[42]

In March the archbishop of Paris, Cardinal Richard, published his "Response to the eminent Catholics who have consulted him on their social obligations," a document which was sufficiently oblique to win the applause both of those who frankly favored rallying to the republic and of opponents of the policy.[43] In May, a new, ostensibly apolitical Catholic lay organization, the *Union de la France Chrétienne* -- led by Mun, Mackau, Chesnelong, and Keller -- was formed. As Dansette has remarked, however, concerning this group, "Since the men were the same, the result amounted to the creation of a Catholic monarchist party alongside the monarchist Catholic party."[44] In July, Leo XIII replaced his nuncio in Paris, sending Mgr Ferrata, an avowed supporter of *ralliement*, to contend with the monarchists' reluctance to conform wholeheartedly to papal wishes.

One by one, a trickle of *ralliés*, led by Cardinal Lavigerie himself, formalized their committment to the republic. In July, Fava, the bishop of Grenoble, joined Lavigerie, and in August, Achille Fould, a deputy from Hautes-Pyrénées, made his adhesion.[45] But the vast majority of Catholics, clergy and laity alike, remained aloof from the movement, and Cassagnac trumpeted defiance on their behalf:

> We will never disarm. We will continue the battle, ardent and keen, without flinching, without becoming discouraged.
>
> *L'Autorité* will remain -- and this will be its glory in this time of cowardice, treason, and desertion -- the rendezvous for all the anger, indignation, and hates amassed in the hearts of honest men by the Republic.
>
> Others may capitulate, but we will remain in the front ranks, where one can be hit, 'tis true, but also where -- and only where -- one may win honor.[46]

An incident in November 1891 provided ample ammunition for the opponents of *ralliement*. The government prosecuted the archbishop of Aix, Gouthe-Soulard, for insults to a government official, insults provoked by a communiqué from the Minister of Cults to French bishops.[47] This incident, however deplorable it may have been, served to unleash the clergy's hostility, which had remained largely unexpressed, and likewise gave the radical republicans an opportunity to make trouble with the ministry by sponsoring yet another interpellation on *menées cléricales*, all too reminiscent of that of 1877. During the interpellation in the Chamber of Deputies, Cassagnac took the opportunity to call for either a genuine application of the Concordat or separation of Church and State. The Church, he contended, had been jeopardized by prosperity but never by persecution.[48]

Such calls to renewed strife did not bode well for any *ralliement* by French Catholics to the republic. Rumors flew that Rome had threatened *L'Autorité* with an interdict, although Cassagnac hotly denied them.[49] Nor were the chances for pacification success improved by the joint declaration published in January 1892 by five French cardinals (the sixth, Lavigerie, had not, for obvious reasons, been asked to participate). The cardinals' declaration protested the many abuses to which the Church in France had been subjected at the hands of the "sect" in power, and stated that the form of government was not in question but rather its doctrine and program.[50] The statement, as Mgr. d'Hulst (who drafted most of it) remarked to a colleague, was intended to unify the French clergy and head off further intervention from

Rome.[51] Paul de Cassagnac applaided the declaration as the fulfillment of his call for leadership on the part of the hierarchy.[52] Despite the evident criticism of the regime apparent in the declaration, advocates of *ralliement* still found it sufficiently conciliatory to attract their praise as well.[53]

During the weeks that followed the cardinals' statement, Catholic feeling in France was subjected to further strain by governmental action. The Freycinet ministry introduced a bill dealing with associations, which was heralded as a preliminary to separation of Church and State. Nearly every article of the proposal, as Cassagnac carefully pointed out in *L'Autorité*, was aimed at strangling the religious orders.[54] Even though the Chamber overthrew the ministry in a vote on this proposal only a few days later, feeling continued to run high in both Catholic and radical circles.

In this climate of extreme tension between Catholics and republicans, Leo XIII's encyclical, *Au Milieu des Sollicitudes*, fell like a bombshell. It was published on 20 February, following a sensation created by the Pope's interview with a republican journalist, which had been published in a popular Paris newspaper. The encyclical made a clear distinction between accepting the form of government and accepting the legislation that accompanied it.[55] This distinction was quickly denied by the radical republicans, who insisted on the solidarity between republican form and laic legislation.

In *L'Autorité*, Paul de Cassagnac greeted the encyclical as a "development and a confirmation" of the cardinals' declaration of the previous month. He carefully pointed out the comparison to be made between the position of the monarchists in France and the Pope's own position in Italy, which he cleverly interpreted to the advantage of the French monarchists' freedom to act:

> Indeed, while resigning himself to accept the government of the Quirinal, which is also a *de facto* government and as legitimate as the government of the [French] republic, the Pope does not abandon the thought of a temporal revenge and does not renounce the realization of his hopes as concerns the spoilation of which he has been the victim. Thus, the Pope, by logic and by his own example, must necessarily recognize the same rights for the monarchists of France with respect to the government of the republic, a government which owes its installation to fraud, violence, and crime, just like the government of King Humbert.[56]

The Pope, Cassagnac argued, has instructed us to "accept" the form in order to combat the bad doctrines and men who dominate it; he has not ordered "adhesion, ralliement to the republic without conditions or guarantees, as some have tried to make us believe."[57] The republican press, he noted in a subsequent article, has gotten only one thing from the encyclical -- that the Pope had officially recognized the republic. Such an interpretation was silly, he argued, insofar as the papacy had been recognizing the republic for years, having accredited a nuncio to it.[58] He estimated that the overall effect of the encyclical would be to weaken the moderate republicans in the eyes of the radicals, thus compromising them, by placing them under the patronage of Rome.[59]

Cassagnac was certainly correct in interpreting the letter of the encyclical, although he purposefully neglected its spirit, thereby infuriating the papal nuncio, Ferrata.[60] To counter such resistance, Leo XIII subsequently took great care to clarify his position further. In May 1892 he addressed a letter on the subject to the French cardinals and, during the remainder of the year, in letters to other prelates, he condemned certain recalcitrants for "putting their party interests first."[61]

On 9 June 1892, the deputies of the *Droite royaliste* published a statement in which they detailed their understanding of their obligations as Catholics and as citizens. This statement, which Cassagnac had a hand in drafting,[62] is of fundamental importance for understanding the monarchist response to the papal *ralliement* policy. The text (reproduced here in French) clearly summarizes their position:

> En présence des divergences de sentiment que des manifestations récentes ont révélées parmi les catholiques, les membres de la Droite Royaliste se croient tenus de dire comment ils comprennent leurs devoirs de catholiques et de citoyens.
>
> Comme catholiques, ils s'inclinent, avec respect, devant l'autorité infaillible du Saint-Père, en matière de foi.
>
> Comme citoyens, ils revendiquent le droit qu'ont tous les peuples de se prononcer en liberté sur toutes les questions qui intéressent l'avenir et la grandeur de leur pays.
>
> La forme du gouvernement est, par excellence, une de ces questions. C'EST EN FRANCE ET ENTRE FRANÇAIS qu'elle doit être résolue.
>
> Telle est la tradition nationale.
>
> Le Saint-Siège a reconnu tous les gouvernements qui se sont succedé en France, depuis le

commencement du siècle. C'était une nécessité politique qui s'imposait à lui; mais en traitant avec ces gouvernements, il n'a jamais demandé aux partisans des régimes anterieurs l'oubli de leur fidélité et la renonciation à leurs espérances.

La République est aujourd'hui le gouvernement de fait, reconnu par le Saint-Siège au même titre que les précédents, et ne saurait être l'object d'un privilège qu'aucun d'eux n'a jamais obtenu: L'ACCEPTATION OBLIGATOIRE.

D'ailleurs, la Constitution est perpetuellement revisable. Ceux qui exercent un mandat politique, en vertu de cette constitution, ne peuvent être tenus de renoncer à un droit qu'elle leur confère expressément.

Cette détermination de maintenir l'intégrité de leurs droits politiques n'infirme rien, chez les auteurs de la présente déclaration, leur volonté constante de rechercher l'union avec tous ceux qui voudront défendre les intérêts religieux et nationaux sur le terrain de la liberté. Ils feront au maintien de cette union tous les sacrifices compatibles avec la fidélité aux convictions politiques de toute leur vie.

Si, par un motif de déférence, ils renoncaient aujourd'hui à ces convictions, ils fourniraient à leurs adversaires un prétexte pour dire que les catholiques ne sont point des citoyens comme les autres et qu'il ne leur est pas permis d'avoir, sur les affaires intérieures de leurs pays, UNE OPINION QUI LEUR SOIT PROPRE.

Ils ne s'exposeront pas à cette calomnie, estimant, en outre, qu'ils apporteront à la défense religieuse un concours d'autant plus efficace qu'ils auront su conserver leur dignité plus intacte.

La Droite Royaliste n'entend pas faire une oeuvre exclusive, en prenant l'initiative de cette declaration, à laquelle peuvent s'associer les catholiques de tous les partis, soucieux de mettre, en ce qui les concerne, au-dessus de toute atteinte et de tout soupçon, CETTE INDÉPENDANCE DU CITOYEN QUE LA FRANCE EXIGE DE TOUS SES ENFANTS.[63]

Henceforth, the position of the monarchists as "intransigents" and worse, as "Gallicans" with respect to obedience to papal instructions, was clearly defined. The Vatican was apparently unable to discover who had been responsible for the declaration.[64]

On 22 June, Leo XIII replied directly to the points raised by the monarchist declaration. In a letter addressed to the bishop of Grenoble, the Pope denounced the behavior of those who

> while protesting their Catholicism, believe they have the right to show themselves refractory to the guidance of the Head of the Church, under the pretext that this is simply political. Well, faced with these erroneous claims, we maintain in their entirety all the acts we have issued, and we say once again: No, undoubtedly we do not seek to enter into politics, but when politics are closely bound up with religious interests, as at present in France, if anyone has a mission to determine the conduct that can effectively safeguard the religious interests which are the supreme end of all things, it is the Roman Pontiff . . . .[65]

Following this ultimatum, and despite repeated and authoritative warnings by republican spokesmen that the laic legislation and the republican constitution were inseparable, the *ralliement* began in earnest.[66]

The *Union de la France Chrétienne* had disbanded in May, when several of its most prominent leaders could not agree to rally. Soon afterward, Albert de Mun made his submission to the papal instructions, as did Jacques Piou. In October Baron de Mackau likewise made his *ralliement* declaration.[67] Mackau's move must have been a great shock to Cassagnac, for although he addressed a clever article to the public congratulating Mackau on his "Trojan Horse strategy," expressing his regret that the two of them had not rallied together in order to illustrate the patent ridiculousness of the policy,[68] the personal letter he wrote to Mackau revealed that he was deeply disturbed.

> My dear friend. I understand your reasons and I give you your freedom. But I must tell you frankly that all this discourages me terribly . . . . Having done all that I have done for the conservative alliance, it is a bit hard to be repaid like this. I will address an article to my colleagues for form's sake, and I will remember what has happened and stay in my corner from now on. With much affection, Paul de Cassagnac.[69]

His ill humor was evident during subsequent weeks. Reverting to a favorite theme, he insinuated that for most people religion was only a pretext and the encyclical only the excuse to rally to the dispensers of positions, honors, and favors.[70] As *ralliés* began to proliferate, Cassagnac became increasingly intransigent, alleging that French Catholics had been delivered over to their adversaries by Rome, and denouncing the *ralliement* as "that fatal policy which has disorganized the conservative party and which will lead the Church to its ruin."[71] The Vatican, whose deployment of invective was no less skillful than that of its lay adversaries, in turn, denounced Cassagnac's remarks as perhaps inspired by "a tribune's bile, a Jansenist's hypocrisy, . . . or a Voltairian's irony."[72]

* * *

During 1892-1893, Cassagnac found another important lay ally in his campaign against the republic. This was none other than the journalist and writer Edouard Drumont, who had attracted a wide following in Catholic circles since the publication, in 1886, of his sensational book, *La France juive*.[73] Though both were journalists and polemicists, they were unlike in many respects. In particular, Cassagnac never shared Drumont's antagonism to Jews, and he once qualified Drumont's anti-Semitism as a monomania; he argued that if Catholics wished to retain their right to protest religious persecution, they had an obligation not to persecute others.[74] Nevertheless, Cassagnac admired Drumont as "one of the rare Frenchmen who can still become angry for the sake of an idea."[75] Cassagnac did come around to voicing some of Drumont's anti-Semitic attitudes only in late 1891, when there were charges that Jewish bankers were interfering with the Russian loan.[76] By this time the Jewish question had become, in his mind, a socio-economic rather than a religious question. But even then, he was never blinded by anti-Semitism as were a number of conservative Catholics in France.[77] His attitude during the early stages of the Dreyfus affair provides ample evidence of this: in 1894, and again in 1896 and 1897, Cassagnac stood apart from the Catholic journalists of his day for his willingness to entertain the thought that Captain Dreyfus might have been convicted in 1894 without sufficient proof.[78] Indeed, three months before the publication of Zola's celebrated letter, "J'accuse," Cassagnac demanded revision of Dreyfus' trial. On 14 November 1897, he would write: "Dreyfus has been condemned by the *Conseil de guerre* on the strength of a piece of evidence that he knew nothing about, that no one had ever showed to him, and that his honorable defender, M. Demange, had never even seen! Now, in a civilized country, the fact of being a Jew gives nobody in the world the right to treat you like that!"[79] A few years later,

Cassagnac's remarks would sharpen and one writer would make the case that during the elections of 1898 he had become a rabid anti-semite.[80] This poorly-documented charge must be weighed with respect to the earlier evidence cited here.

Perhaps the principal difference in this respect between Cassagnac and Drumont (and later, between Cassagnac and Charles Maurras) was that Cassagnac never systematically attempted to externalize the causes of national decadence by blaming the infiltration of "foreign" or "un-French" influences.[81] To Cassagnac, the cancer was within and consisted, quite simply, of the destruction of the traditional religion by the sectarians of the republic.

This position is indicative of a further difference between Drumont and Cassagnac. Drumont no longer shared the vision which underlay Cassagnac's desire for an alliance of all conservatives -- that is, that the forces of good, "the true Frenchmen, honest, generous, proud of the grandeur of the patrie, could ever overcome the forces of evil, "the exploiters, cynical republicans, shameless schemers, who persecute and oppress the true honorable Frenchmen." As Drumont put it:

> This conception is absolutely erratic. In reality there are not two political parties, but only a general regime, a system -- the capitalist, Jewish system -- with which the representatives of both parties that dispute power are equally affiliated . . . . The conservatives are as attached to the regime as the republicans.[82]

For Drumont, the "parallel march" with *Boulangisme* had been the experience that had opened his eyes, disillusioning him permanently as to what he could expect from the Right. Drumont was far more skeptical and pessimistic than Cassagnac could ever bring himself to be. Yet neither of these differences overshadowed their joint campaign against the *ralliement*.

It was Drumont, writing in *La Libre Parole*, who brought public attention to the latest republican scandal, over the bankrupt Panama Canal company's "purchase" of votes in the Chamber of Deputies during the legislature of 1885-1889.[83] This scandal provided further arguments against *ralliement* by the Right, giving its opponents additional ammunition to use against the opportunist republicans and fanning the flames of antiparliamentary sentiment. Ever since the Panama Company's bankruptcy in early 1889, the Right had ardently defended the small investors who had been hurt; in May of that year, Cassagnac had proclaimed that "*L'Autorité* will break its last pen before it abandons the victims of Panama."[84] In 1890 the deputies of the Right had pressed for a judicial investigation of the company's activities, but the government dragged its heels for over a year before reluctantly proceeding. In November 1892, Jules Delahaye, a deputy of the Right, interpellated the ministry concerning the Panama affair with the objective of provoking a full-scale parliamentary investigation.

During the Panama scandal polemics over the identity of the compromised deputies, some even tried to single out Cassagnac, in an attempt to discredit him and drive him from political life. But Cassagnac was successful in clearing himself. Like other newspapers, *L'Autorité* had published paid advertisements for the Panama Company loan. Apart from that, its editor insisted, his newspapers, in Paris and in Gers as well, were untainted by corruption.[85]

After testifying before the parliamentary inquiry committee in January 1893, Cassagnac was formally cleared of suspicion, and promptly sent his seconds to the committee member who had singled him out.[86] Cassagnac was well aware of the impact any such taint could have in an election year, particularly when the conservative forces were split over the *ralliement* issue and an opponent would exploit even the slightest hint of compromise against him.

Despite the campaigns carried on in the press by Cassagnac and Drumont to discredit the *ralliement* by exploiting conservative indignation over the Panama scandal, their efforts were insufficient to heal the breach previously created in the ranks of the Right. Consequently, the results of the legislative elections of 1893 bore out Cassagnac's most pessimistic predictions. He had long feared that the *ralliement* would have a dire effect on the elections, and the results of municipal and departmental elections during the year 1892 did nothing to encourage him. *Rallié* candidates in crucial departments went down to defeat, dragging conservative candidates with them.[87] In face of this pattern, the principal concern of the intransigent monarchist deputies like Cassagnac was whether the *ralliés* intended to oppose candidates to their former companions-in-arms in their own districts. In July 1893 the monarchist deputies sent a delegation to the *ralliés* to inquire about their intentions in this respect. Ominously, they received no reply.[88]

Paul de Cassagnac's fate in the department of Gers exemplified the divisive effect of *ralliement*. The papal instructions and the successful regrouping of local republicans combined to work against the Gers conservatives. In 1892 they lost twelve seats from their former majority on the *conseil-général*.[89] Their republican opponents were therefore hopeful of gaining substantially in the legislative elections.[90] In 1893 Cassagnac had two opponents for his seat in Mirande -- in contrast to 1889, when he had been unopposed for re-election. One was a republican named Bascou, whom Cassagnac characterized as a radical disguised as an opportunist; the other was the *rallié* Fernand Laudet.[91]

Laudet came from a Catholic monarchist family long established in Gers. For a time, it appears, Cassagnac considered him as a protégé and possible political successor. But in 1892 Laudet had declared himself a candidate for a vacant seat on the *conseil-général* for which Cassagnac had another, more markedly monarchist candidate in mind, and would not desist. This provoked Cassagnac to denounce him as an *ambitieux*, particularly after he won the election. Thus Laudet had been marked as an opponent for Cassagnac himself.[92]

In June 1893, several months before the elections to the Chamber were scheduled, Laudet announced his intention, in the event of a run-off election, to withdraw in favor of the republican candidate. This move infuriated Cassagnac, who responded by subjecting Laudet to a verbal thrashing in *L'Autorité*.[93] This action was but the prelude to a violently-fought campaign.

Cassagnac knew that this campaign would be one of the most difficult he had ever waged. Already in 1892, he had reorganized his press base by founding *La Voix du Peuple*, after the editor of his previous paper (*L'Electeur du Gers*, which in 1891 had succeeded *L'Appel au Peuple*) announced his own *ralliement* to the republic.[94] From the beginning of 1893 Cassagnac made monthly trips to Gers in order to keep abreast of the electoral situation. The *ralliement* press was, of course, hostile to him. Piou's paper in nearby Toulouse asserted that Cassagnac was falsely campaigning as a *rallié* himself, a claim that Laudet also plcked up; the now pro-*ralliement* religious publications *L'Univers* and *La Croix* (in Paris) both opposed his candidacy.[95]

In fact, Paul de Cassagnac campaigned on the platform that he had not changed his political preferences, which indeed he had not, and in addition -- much as he had done since 1885 -- he appended a series of agricultural, financial, and religious demands directed against the republicans in power.[96] His was no conciliatory program. It was utterly frank and characteristic of him. No one familiar with this political past could have mistaken its thrust.

On the first ballot, Cassagnac led with over 9000 votes to 7400 for Bascou and some 2000 for Laudet, but he did not quite have a majority. He attributed his loss of a majority to administrative tampering with election results, qualifying it as "outright robbery."[97] He had at least survived; his former allies Piou and Mun, now running as *ralliés*, had not.[98] Neither had his colleague Daynaud in Condom.

In the run-off, Laudet performed true to his word and threw his support to the republican candidate. Cassagnac lost to Bascou by a margin of 600 votes, after watching the *rallié* Catholics follow Laudet's directives, voting openly for the radical candidate. "I was beaten," he wrote in *L'Autorité* soon after his defeat, "not by the republican party, which I left behind by some 1600 votes during the first ballot, but by the defection of a segment of the conservative party . . . ."[99]

Being conquered by one's natural adversaries, by those one has braved for so many years, is the game of war.

But when your coreligionaires strike you in the back and attack you from behind in order to second the common enemy -- the radical and the freemason -- it is a spectacle both sorrowful and unforeseen, reserved to be offered for the first time by our sad and shameful epoch.

All that because it didn't please me to deny my monarchic past and abandon my faith in a future atonement.

I fall, wrapped in my banner, without regrets.

A devout Catholic, profoundly respectful of the religious teachings of the Papacy, I cannot renounce my right to remain a free citizen in my own country and to find my inspiration in political matters, in national questions, in my conscience as a Frenchman, which I affirm to be a true Catholic conscience . . . .

The assault which the Republic has delivered against me . . . has lasted twenty-three years.

And the enemy, constantly repulsed, always crushed, was unable to penetrate the stronghold -- this is my pride and my honor -- except by treason, by the apostasy of some of our own, by the *ralliés* who sold us out and delivered us over by opening the door to him, while we stood guard, facing him without failing . . . .

My only regret is for Gers, the Gers that I love so. Heavy is the   responsibility of those who have caused her loss . . . .

But now . . . we must only look ahead and once again begin the implacable march, for God and for France, toward the conquest of the future.[100]

Cassagnac then served notice on his adversaries that ". . . Although I no longer have a tribune, I still have a pen -- and its point is sharp."[101]

* * *

"'Absurd is he who never changes,' runs the oft-quoted French proverb, but consistency is not always due to narrowness and stubbornness." So wrote Albert Guerard of the poet, Alfred de Vigny. "It may come from genuine strength of mind, and from such a lead over one's contemporaries that their progress fails to overtake the pioneer."[102] Indeed, change can take place in many aspects of one's beliefs, but one of the places where it is least forgiven is in the realm of political convictions. A writer in *Le Figaro* summed up this counter-perspective in 1889, on the eve of *ralliement*, when he wrote: "There are persons . . . who do not have the right to change their opinion and who are respected precisely because of the firmness of their convictions."[103]

The *ralliement* indeed confronted convinced monarchists in France with a grave dilemma. For men like Paul de Cassagnac, whose anti-republican position was not merely anti-opportunist and antiparliamentary, but closely tied to the defense of religious interests against the radical republicans, the papal instructions appeared as an invitation to capitulation. The only real alternative to accepting the republic left open by the Vatican was to retire from political life, an alternative chosen by many of the less combative Catholic monarchists like Chesnelong, albeit with regret. Combatting the instructions was quite another matter. Leo XIII and his advisors, of course, interpreted such opposition as strictly self-interested, since they were convinced that their policy was the wisest for the Church both in France and at large.

In retrospect, it does not seem at all clear that Cassagnac was wrong to impose conditions on the cooperation of the Right with the moderate republicans. In 1898, after many years of unrequited support by the *ralliés* in the Chamber, the then *président du conseil*, Jules Méline, refused to grant them any concessions on revision of either the school or the military laws as a precondition of their electoral cooperation. This decision led to defeat for many of the surviving *ralliés*, and to the fall of Méline's moderate ministry.[104]

The supreme irony of the papal policy was that it demonstrated the increasing will of Rome to intervene in national politics generally. While professing "neutrality" the Vatican practiced an "ultramontanism" on behalf of the republic that succeeded in turning leading monarchist Catholic laymen into "anticlericals." Paul de Cassagnac's denial of the

Papacy's right to intervene in French political matters would find frequent echoes in "integral" Catholic circles (as they came to be called) during the next forty years, as the Vatican chose to intervene even more firmly against other political groups to separate Catholics from them.[105]

However promising the papal policy may have seemed in the short term -- or in the hindsight of historians, it was a failure in the intermediate term. One author who defends the policy has argued that "due to Leo's efforts, the Concordat of 1801 remained in effect, and the French embassy at the Vatican continued to function, with advantages to the Papacy in regard to the Roman question. But in refusing to heed the Pope's sound advice French Catholics brought destruction upon their own heads."[106] Perhaps. But separation of Church and State in France was only postponed for a decade, and the solution of the Roman question was only achieved in 1929. In 1904-1905 the republic severed diplomatic relations with the Vatican and proceeded to the liquidation of the Concordat. By that time Leo XIII was dead. He "did not live to witness the final debacle."[107] In any event, his successor, Pius X, was not disposed to continue the experiment and, in fact, it was not renewed until years after 1918. In the meantime, the reality that many Frenchmen remained unreconciled to the republic was attested to in the early twentieth century by the growth of the neo-royalist *Action Française* and by the subsequent conflict between the Vatican and this organization that took place during the 1920s.[108]

The Vatican and leading moderate republicans pressed for *ralliement* at the highest level of politics. But the fundamental obstacle to the policy's success was the absence of reconciliation between anticlerical, anti-Catholic republicans, and Catholic monarchist conservatives. This reconciliation could only take place on the local level, in each canton and each village. It was there that the polarization was most acute and republican administrators constantly harassed Catholics and conservatives. No temporary adoption of an "*esprit nouveau*" by the republican leadership in Paris could provide sufficient justification or incentives to break the local pattern of stereotypes and harassment. Certainly this was no new phenomenon; conservative leaders had complained about it throughout the era of laic legislation. Even the seasoned Bonapartist Dugué de la Fauconnerie, who himself had rallied to the republic on several occasions during the 'eighties, returned each time to the monarchist-conservative fold complaining of the reception he had received "from the ranks," even when, as on the eve of the Rouvier ministry, it had appeared their leaders were momentarily conciliatory before the threat of radicalism.[109] At the time, Delafosse wrote tellingly of the behavior of the republicans in the countryside, based on his own experiences in Normandy and on his conversations with conservatives from other regions.[110] Cassagnac likewise cited examples of such harassment whenever they came to his attention, thus reinforcing his conviction that there could be no ultimate reconciliation between conservatives and the republic without the offer of formal guarantees on the religious question.[111] The republicans' great mistake, he had written already in 1886, had been to establish the republic on a base of religious hatred; had this not happened, he argued, the conservatives might well have come over to the regime long before.[112]

In any event, 1893 marked the effective end of Cassagnac's career in political life, although his influence in the Catholic and conservative press continued to be strong for another decade.[113] From the pages of L'Autorité he relentlessly critiqued the behavior of the rallié Right during that legislature of 1893-1898. He considered his former colleagues, with only a few exceptions, to be acquiescing in every respect to their erstwhile republican friends who desired their help to "stop socialism" but would in turn make no concessions of principle to religious interests. Cassagnac was particularly harsh on them during the first days of the Méline ministry (1896-1898), to which the rallié Right lent decisive support. He even criticized his former ally, the Baron de Mackau, who had underscored the gratuitous nature of the rallié support in Le Gaulois, for "having a singular conception of your obligations as a patriot, citizen, and Catholic, since you took refuge in the skirts of la gueuse."[114] He called on the ralliés to require the immediate replacement of the Minister of Cults, the filling of empty bishoprics, and to insist on some accommodation on the most recent laic laws, which imposed state controls over Church accounts and belongings, instead of preoccupying themselves to oppose the radical republicans' proposals for income tax.[115] But the ralliés asked nothing, thereby abandoning themselves to Cassagnac's scorn.

In 1898 Cassagnac was re-elected to the Chamber, but he never again played a role comparable to that of his earlier career. This was primarily due to ill health.[116] He was not yet sixty years of age in 1898, but a photograph taken at that time reveals significant physical alterations. His black, bushy mustache is still in evidence, but his hair is grayed. His formerly fleshy cheeks and jowls have receded sufficiently to reveal the chiseled line of the jawbone.[117] He appeared to have lost both his strength and his illusions. Even before his death in 1904, he had been described as a campaigner whose day had passed. As the Paris correspondant for the Swiss Journal de Génève remarked, reflecting the opinion of many French republicans: "The Republic has lost an irreconcilable enemy, but one who already for a long time had ceased to be a threat."[118]

Cassagnac's sudden death in early November 1904, while hunting with friends, deprived him of any last chance for grandeur comparable to that achieved by his more robust contemporary Georges Clemenceau, who had also been temporarily eliminated from political life in 1893. Despite Cassagnac's many gifts and successes, wrote Drumont, he had died "among the vanquished; . . . Like most men of his generation, he had been badly served by events. A sort of bad luck, an adverse fortune, a fatality, seemed to have dogged him . . . ."[119] Paradoxically, Drumont observed, Cassagnac was detested most by those he had always defended -- the conservatives themselves, who had been unable to accept Cassagnac's unremitting independence.[120]

Perhaps the most poignant appreciation of the significance of Paul de Cassagnac's contribution to French political life was provided by the writer H. de Gallier, in an article on Cassagnac and Rochefort published in late 1902. In one brief passage, Gallier captured the tragic element implicit in the journalist-deputy's unceasing yet ultimately unfruitful quest. Invoking an image from France's greatest heroic epic, *Le Chanson de Roland*, Gallier provided a fitting epitaph for Cassagnac's extraordinary political career:

> Le clairon sonne bien encore, mais il a des notes
> d'angoisse. C'est le cor de Roland qui retentit.
> Charlemagne n'apparaît, hélas! ni son armée . . .[121]

CHAPTER XI

UNDERSTANDING BONAPARTISM, NATIONALISM, AND AUTHORITARIAN DEMOCRACY IN FRANCE

Paul de Cassagnac's political thought and action had a definite impact on French political life. His activities are characterized by certain distinctive features which serve to individualize and to date them. The more general features of his career nevertheless suggest several conclusions about the historical relationship of Bonapartism, nationalism, and authoritarian democracy, and thereby contribute to a more balanced account of the Third Republic.

What is, perhaps, most immediately startling to a twentieth-century observer is how Cassagnac, as an opposition figure, managed to survive in the arena of national electoral politics for nearly three decades. Whether he would have been able to do this without his family's political base in the department of Gers, established firmly under the Second Empire, is a matter for speculation. That he did so is a fact.

Cassagnac was a *Jacobin de droite*, a non-conciliatory doctrinaire rather than an unprincipled and power-hungry politician of the type all too familiar to modern democracies. He was a militant leader who seemingly aspired neither to place nor to position beyond that of speaking out and convincing his followers. He believed firmly in the power of the word to exhort, to moralize, to guide, and he chose the press as his vehicle. At bottom, although he was certainly a political pragmatist when it came to controlling elections, *à l'impériale*, his thought appears fundamentally idealistic. He was, in many respects, a child of the French romantic tradition in its Catholic counter-revolutionary guise. It is this quality that at once seems to explain his appeal to his contemporaries and, as Frenchmen became more urban, more industrialized, and more cynical, accounts for its fading. He was perhaps the last popular spokesmen for the monarchist-imperialist form in the French authoritarian tradition. However one may ultimately judge his politics, one cannot help admiring his energy, his tenacity, his stalwartness and devotion in pursuit of his cause.

Cassagnac is historically significant as a transmitter of several of the elements that comprised the authoritarian tradition from a firmly monarchist and Catholic generation to members of a new generation, some of whose members, republican in habit and secular in instinct, renewed the authoritarian critique of liberal aspirations within the ranks of the Third Republic itself, while others devised a new strategy and style for monarchist politics. Cassagnac's own militant campaign against the parliamentary republic failed to achieve its central goal, but many of its ingredients nevertheless spilled over into the republican revisionist tradition. Indeed, many of the criticisms made against the Third Republic by critics of the following generation ranging from Maurice Barrès and Charles Maurras to Georges Sorel, were fully anticipated by Cassagnac in his campaigns against the republic in the 1870's and 1880's.[1] Had Cassagnac developed his arguments in books, rather than in the daily press, he would doubtless rank among these distinguished enemies of the Third Republic in the judgment of later historians.

Cassagnac's political career spans the period 1879-1899, which René Rémond considers an interim period between two distinct coalitions of Right-wing elements -- that of *l'ordre moral* of 1871-1879 and that of the nationalism of 1899-1902.[2] Thus it is inviting to test Rémond's suggestive hypothesis that the political temperament represented by Bonapartism prior to 1879 found its spiritual successor in the nationalist movement of the early twentieth century. In Rémond's words, "nationalism inserted itself into the Caesarian, authoritarian, plebiscitary, popular, and antiparliamentary tradition of the two empires."[3]

Surface similarities support this comparison. Certainly the Napoleonic heritage from the French Revolution centered on the concept of an appeal to the nation and to things French. The notion of *appel au peuple* itself, where the term *le peuple* is considered synonymous with *la nation*, is a Bonapartist idea. Both Napoleon I and Napoleon III emphasized as fundamental the principle of consulting the nation on its destiny.

But there were significant differences. As Rémond points out, the appeal of Bonapartism was typically rural, while the nationalism of the early twentieth century was mainly urban in character.[4] The massive migration of rural Frenchmen to the urban centers during the late nineteenth century might, however, provide an explanation for this apparently contradictory development.

There is another, far more problematic discrepancy. As has become clear in the preceding chapters, Bonapartism during the 1870s and 1880s had become increasingly monarchist and Catholic in character (and constituency); indeed, during the 1880's its evolution at the leadership level -- had been matched by a corresponding "imperialization" of the other two traditions of the monarchist Right. In contrast, the nationalism discussed by Rémond tended to be firmly secularist and republican in nature, represented as it was by Paul Déroulède's action-oriented *Ligue des Patriotes*, with its lower middle-class appeal, and the more elitist and intellectual *Ligue de la Patrie Française*. Although most historians classify the nationalist movement as a movement of the Right, it must be emphasized that the political Right they discuss is, until the advent of the *Action Française*, a firmly republican and secular Right.[5] Monarchists and former monarchists were, in some cases, party to the nationalist coalition and hoped their cause would benefit from it, but they were in no case its dominant members.

Indeed, during the 1880s, the monarchists had come close to succeeding in the construction of a "nationalism" of their own, identified with Catholic, conservative, and rural France. Both the politics of the *Union des Droites* in the Chamber and the electoral coalitions of the *Union Conservatrice* in 1885 and the "parallel march" of 1889 exemplified attempts to build an electoral coalition in which national interest was emphatically touted as transcending individual party interests. Insofar as Paul de Cassagnac had been both prophet and prime mover behind these attempts, he may be considered a contributor to the later nationalism; indeed, Edouard Drumont at the time credited Cassagnac's "*solutionnisme*" or "*n'importequisme*" of 1885 as the ancestor of *Boulangisme*, of the *ralliement* coalition, and of the nationalist coalition itself.[6]

Cassagnac himself, however, never felt entirely comfortable with the new nationalism. He formally declined to adhere to the *Ligue de la Patrie Française*, founded by Barrès and a stellar group of *académiciens*, because of its bias in favor of the parliamentary republic, even though he acknowledged his agreement with its general goals.[7] Moreover, he carried on a bitter feud with Déroulède and his *Ligue des Patriotes* for the same reason.

In fact, the feud with Déroulède highlights an important nuance in the ostensible kinship between Bonapartism and the new nationalism. In 1898-99, close organizational links developed between the *Ligue des Patriotes* and the left wing of Bonapartism, links which had originally been forged during the Boulangist experience. Following the death of Prince Jérôme-Napoléon Bonaparte in 1891, the "republican-revisionist" Bonapartism that he stood for was adopted as official policy by the Victorists themselves, under the leadership of Gustave Cunéo d'Ornano and Baron Jules Legoux.[8] These Bonapartists no longer advocated national consultation on the form of government, but rather constitutional revision to elect the president of the republic by universal suffrage, and they put forth Prince Victor as their candidate for the office. The new program was not monarchist, even less imperialist in nature, and in fact remained formally antagonistic to the politics of conservative alliance. It therefore aroused the scorn of old imperialists like Paul de Cassagnac, who held out for what he later called the "integral plebiscite."[9]

The newly-reorganized *Ligue des Patriotes* also advocated constitutional revision to institute popular election of the president, and during the 1890's the neo-"plebiscitary" Bonapartists of Paris had gravitated to the *Ligue* to the point of being virtually absorbed by it. In early 1899, however, at the height of civil disturbances in Paris, Déroulède made it clear that, as far as he was concerned, defense of the existing republic took precedence over aid to any monarchist pretenders. This impelled Cassagnac to denounce him as a political adversary and created serious difficulties within the revisionist Bonapartist committees, whose members remained, in the final analysis, devoted to the person of Prince Victor.[10] Following this episode, Cassagnac attempted to reorganize purely "imperialist" committees, and thereby separate the cause of Prince Victor from that of Déroulède.[11] For a time it appeared that he might succeed, but Cassagnac was outmaneuvered by representatives of the "plebiscitary" republican faction (headed by the automobile magnate, Marquis Albert de Dion), who triumphed in late 1903 and who, following Cassagnac's death the next year, completely dominated organized Bonapartism from that time forth.[12] In the meantime, Cassagnac carried on a bitter personal polemic against Déroulède, who had gone into exile in Spain following the trial of the *Ligue* in 1899. In 1901 he even stood as a second to the personal representative of the royalist pretender, André Buffet, in a duel with Déroulède, thereby underscoring his monarchist sympathies.[13]

Thus, the more secular pro-republican Bonapartists had installed themselves triumphantly in the vanguard of the new nationalism, while Catholic imperialists like Cassagnac still preferred to preface their proclamations of patriotism with a tribute to God: "*Pour Dieu, pour la France!*" remained the slogan of *L'Autorité*. When he did praise the nationalist movement, Cassagnac qualified it by adding the reservation that while "faith in the fatherland" was a sacred faith, it must necessarily stand second to faith in God.[14] He found it difficult to conceive of a purely secular nationalism as anything other than "false chauvinism." "Religion and *patrie* are two inseparable words," he had written already in 1887.[15] His idea of *la patrie* was inseparable from a specific notion of a traditional, religiously-inspired France, a notion not shared by the republican nationalists, whom he accused of attempting to appropriate patriotism for their own exclusive use.[16] It is this very traditionalism that distinguishes Cassagnac's kind of authoritarianism from the later "fascist authoritarianism" described by later psychologists and sociologists.[17]

Although Rémond cites examples of Cassagnac's viputerative polemical style as evidence of the Bonapartist-nationalist kinship,[18] it seems clear, in light of this study of Cassagnac's political career, that he and his journalistic successors were linked more by the polemic temperament than by more specific similarities in their political positions. That in each case their talents should find employ within the most ardent movements of their respective generations should come as no surprise; Henri Rochefort as well as Léon Daudet ranked among the scribes of early twentieth-century nationalism.

Polemical violence constitutes a shared characteristic of men in both movements, but their modes of action remained distinctive. The Bonapartists of the 1870s were raucous young gentlemen, engaged in creating an uproar in parliamentary assemblies for the ostensible defense of their cause. The neo-nationalists of the early twentieth century were, however, agitating in the streets of Paris -- an activity formerly considered, even by young gentlemen, to be the prerogative of the *canaille*.

Indeed, one of the dangers encountered in positing such connections as those attempted by Rémond is the likelihood of becoming ensnared in the trap of historical overlay, in which the features of later developments are overlaid on earlier, superficially similar phenomenae. In the particular case at hand, a major preoccupation in scholarship since the Second World War has been to project the roots of fascist action of the 1930s back to the street action of the nationalists of the early 1900s and, from there, back to the Bonapartists. One example among others is provided by the British historian David Thomson, who has written that "in methods and appeal, the post-1870 Bonapartists were the ancestors of those later semi-fascist, authoritarian movements, such as the Croix-de-Feu of Colonel de la Rocque."[19] Attempts to find historical precedents for later developments (or "root-stretching") can be enlightening when pursued with care, but they can also be treacherous, as they may obscure fundamental differences and lead the historian to draw misleading conclusions. The literature on Nazi Germany and Fascism more generally provides abundant documentation of this point.[20] The historian who attempts this sort of evaluation must be constantly on guard against his or her own assumptions and prejudices, as well as sensitive to those of others, including one's very subjects. Otherwise the shadow of later developments (or the preoccupations of one's own culture) will find ways of overpowering the essential and distinctive elements of the preceding movements.

In retrospect, it appears clear that the neo-nationalists' proclivity for the agitation they called "direct action" was not a style of action appropriated from earlier Bonapartists, but from their contemporaries, the revolutionary syndicalists.[21] Both nationalists and Bonapartists were antiparliamentary, as were all those groups that by the early twentieth century had embraced "direct action" to achieve their goals; it does not necessarily follow, however, that all groups -- or individuals -- hostile to parliamentary institutions automatically favored direct action.[22] Even within the Bonapartist tradition itself, the style of the young imperialists was quite different from that of the later *plébiscitaires*.

The problem of historical overlay is particularly difficult with respect to the most important political movement to grow out of the neo-nationalist context: the *Action Française*, and the neo-royalist philosophy of Charles Maurras. Indeed, studies of this movement, particularly those of Eugen Weber and Ernst Nolte, have done a great deal to stimulate reexamination of the late nineteenth-century Right with respect to the debate about fascism.[23] The *Action Française*, as it emerged from the ashes of the Dreyfus case, long dominated the historiography of the post-1900 period, thus blotting out consideration of the Catholic dilemma posed by the *ralliement* as well as of the evolution of the rest of the monarchist Right. Only with the recent work of Jean-Marie Mayeur and Maurice Larkin on Church-State relationships, and Ben Martin's biography of Albert de Mun, which details the development of the *Action Liberale Populaire*, has this problem begun to be systematically addressed.[24]

Had Paul de Cassagnac lived to witness the flowering of the *Action Française*, he would doubtless have been at odds with the movement. Although one can only speculate on this point, there is good reason to believe that he would have contested the movement for its insufficient appreciation of France's "traditional" values as he understood them. One index of his probable feeling on the subject was provided by his son Paul-Julien, who, having taken over the editorship of *L'Autorité* with his brother Guy, championed his father's political ideas and who, in 1912, fought a duel with Maurras over this very point.[25] As the younger Cassagnac wrote in his unpublished memoirs, "[the program] of the Action Française represents only the personal views of its directors, that is, of Charles Maurras. As a basis for a monarchist restoration, this is perhaps insufficient."[26]

Yet the leaders of *Action Française* and Paul de Cassagnac did have certain ideas in common; as in Shakespeare's play, *Henry the Fourth*, not the least of their preoccupations was with the institution of monarchy as distinct from the person of the king. It is difficult to determine whether or not Cassagnac's campaigns might have directly influenced Maurras's thinking in this respect; certainly Maurras never claimed him among his intellectual masters.[27] But clearly in 1885, when Maurras arrived in Paris, and ten years later, when he began writing in the monarchist press, such ideas as Cassagnac's certainly permeated the climate of opinion. After all, Maurras's point of departure for his *Enquête sur la monarchie* in 1899 was the plan for national monarchy sketched by the Comte de Paris in his "Instructions" of 1887, the plan that Cassagnac had enthusiastically endorsed at the height of his "solutionism."[28] It seems more than coincidental that among those who arrived at a rational acceptance of monarchy by way of nationalism after 1900 were some of the men who, like Barrès, had been cultivated in 1888-89 by the monarchist leaders of the "parallel march." The seeds planted by the monarchists may have been slow to germinate, but once they had done so, the new plants flourished. It is significant that in the 1890s a Maurras, through a study of French classical literature, could reach many of the same conclusions about the necessity of monarchy for France as a Cassagnac had reached in the 1860s through a study of the French Revolution.

There is an operational similarity as well. Like the doctrinaires of the *Action Française*, Cassagnac teetered constantly on the verge of disavowal by a prince who stood to benefit from his program, as well as by the Catholic Church he professed to serve. Each in his own way represented the radical, ideological fringe of monarchism and, therefore, each was in jeopardy of alienating its more traditionally-minded, less adventurous, less ideologically-conscious constituents. But the difficulties that could be caused for an acknowledged beneficiary by an organized political movement operating outside his direct control were considerably greater than those that might be raised by a single individual. Cassagnac's independent ideas could be tolerated by a Napoleon III and even applauded by the Comte de Paris, and his opposition to the *ralliement* could be criticized though never subjected to formal censure by the Vatican, but Maurras's *Action Française* was formally disavowed by the Catholic Church in 1927 and by the royalist pretender in 1937.

The fundamental difference, however, is located in their contrasting appreciation of modern democracy as incarnated in the institution of universal suffrage. Cassagnac and his conservative alliance colleagues remained authoritarian democrats. They still hoped for redress -- and even restoration -- at the hands of the all-male electorate, provided it was given a chance to pronounce on the subject. The royalist Louis Teste remarked in 1891:

Indeed, universal suffrage is master. The Comte de Paris, like Prince Victor, General Boulanger, the conservatives, and the republicans, awaits its investiture. He asks it to restore to him the monarchist heritage, and promises, if the legislature calls him to the throne, to ratify his election by plebiscite. Thus, if the people should refuse to ratify, the Comte de Paris would be obliged to renounce the crown.[29]

Not so Maurras, who had no faith in the efficacy of universal suffrage as a vehicle for meaningful change and considered the judgment of the sovereign people to be both erratic and fickle. As he wrote for the *Dictionnaire politique et critique*, that was compiled by his movement: "The masses have feelings but they have no memory. To depend on the initiative of their judgment and their votes is the greatest folly that can be committed under the guise of nationalism and philosophy."[30] With the *Action Française*, French royalism virtually ceased to flirt with the will of the people. It denied, as one of its opponents pointed out, not only *parlementarisme* but the electoral system itself.[31] Its elitism was anti-democratic and, therefore, utterly foreign to the thinking of the successors of Cassagnac and his colleagues. Authoritarian democracy would have to make its peace with the republic.

* * *

Both the contrasts and the similarities between Paul de Cassagnac's political inclinations and those of the later neo-nationalists, however, underscore their mutual kinship -- unfriendly cousins within a larger clan, not unlike Cassagnac and his cousin Lissagaray themselves in an earlier period. They can be seen as successive manifestations of an ongoing, broader tradition of authoritarian thought and political action in France. In the perspective of over half a century, Cassagnac's brand of authoritarianism appears as an less elaborated and less intellectually self-conscious sort than that of the *Action Française*. His ideas represent a bridge between the anti-republican and antiparliamentary inclinations of the *notables*, the party of order of 1848-1877, and that of the less aristocratic nationalists of the early twentieth century. The antiparliamentarism common to both of them remains, even under the Fifth Republic, a critical index of kinship within this tradition. So does the appeal to a unifying national authority.

The overt monarchism that characterized the French authoritarian tradition in the nineteenth century has, however, receded in favor of an authoritarian republicanism, and its strongly Catholic flavor has been muted by the settlement of the Church-State quarrel. The French authoritarian tradition has, in keeping with changing times, become increasingly secular and increasingly urban, yet has managed to retain the sympathies of religious and rural elements. It has survived the monarchies and the several attempts to revive them. It has survived the Third and Fourth Republics and, despite the passing of Charles de Gaulle from the political scene, it appears to live on. Such endurance depends, in the final analysis, on the ability of authoritarian proclivities among the French people to reshape their forms of expression in response to ever-changing conditions. In the evolution of this authoritarian tradition in France, the political career of Paul de Cassagnac, and his conception of "*Impérialisme*", consolidating Bonapartist notions of authority and Catholic monarchism in an impersonal democratic formula, illuminate a critical transition. Antiparliamentary and authoritarian, indeed counter-revolutionary and Catholic nationalist he may have been, but pre- or proto-fascist are not simply not appropriate labels for the politics Paul de Cassagnac represents.

NOTES - INTRODUCTION

[1] See my entry on Paul de Cassagnac in the *Historical Dictionary of the Third French Republic, 1870-1940*, ed. Patrick H. Hutton, 2 vols. (New York, 1986), I, 167-68. What follows immediately hereafter is an amplified and revised version of this entry.

[2] "Monarchist" was the more general term. David Shapiro is correct in insisting that: "In contemporary usage 'monarchists' covered both Bonapartists and royalists, the latter term, both legitimists and Orleanists." See his "The Ralliement in the Politics of the 1890's," in *The Right in France 1890-1919: Three Studies*, ed. David Shapiro (London, 1962), p. 8.

[3] In fact Cassagnac probably did more than any other deputy to insure strengthening of disciplinary measures in the Chamber after 1876; see Chapters III-VI below.

[4] Quoted by Alfred Baudrillart, *Vie de Monseigneur d'Hulst*, 2 vols. (Paris, 1912-1914), II, 362.

[5] As I will argue subsequently, there are good grounds for seeing this grouping as a projection into the later nineteenth century of the "party of order" of 1849-51, the coalition of conservatives known by their meeting location on the rue de Poitiers. Not only is there overlap in personnel and mentality, but there are striking similarities in the tactics envisioned by the two groups.

[6] A. Mels, *Wilhelmshoehe 1871: Souvenirs de la captivité de Napoléon III* (Paris, 1880), p. 64.

[7] *Le Pays*, 1 March 1878.

[8] Charles Seignobos, *Le Déclin de l'Empire et l'établissement de la IIIe République* (Paris, 1921), and *L'Évolution de la IIIe République* (Paris, 1921), vols. 7 and 8 of Ernest Lavisse, ed., *Histoire de la France contemporaine*. The titles of the chapters dealing with internal politics are indicative of Seignobos' emphasis: "L'évolution de l'Empire vers le régime parlementaire;" "L'établissement de la république parlementaire;" "L'avènement du parti républicain;" "La scission et les luttes entre les républicains." For a discussion of the political and constitutional preoccupations of Third Republic historiography to 1955, see Auguste Soulier, "La Troisième République entre dans l'histoire," *Revue internationale d'histoire politique et constitutionnelle*, V (1955), 151-172.

[9] Daniel Halévy, *La Fin des notables* (Paris, 1930); now in English as *The End of the Notables*, ed. Alain Silvera (Middletown, Conn., 1974). See also Halévy's *République des ducs* (Paris, 1937). John Rothney, *Bonapartism After Sedan* (Ithaca, N.Y., 1969).

[10] See, in particular, Alphonse V. Roche, *Les Idées traditionalistes en France de Rivarol à Charles Maurras* (Urbana, Ill., 1937).

[11] In particular, the work of the Israeli scholar J. L. Talmon, *The Origins of Totalitarian Democracy* (London, 1952). For France, the controversy now swirls around the work of another Israeli scholar, Zeev Sternhell. See his *Maurice Barrès et le nationalisme français* (Paris, 1972); *La Droite révolutionnaire, 1885-1914; les origines françaises du fascisme* (Paris, 1974), and *Ni Droite ni Gauche. L'idéologie fasciste en France* (Paris, 1983) [now translated by David Maisel as *Neither Right nor Left: Fascist Ideology in France* (Berkeley and Los Angeles, Calif., 1986)]. See also the numerous publications on French nationalism by Raoul Girardet in the 1950s and 1960s, which argue against a nationalist-fascist connection, and from an opposing perspective, the biographically-focused work of Robert Soucy, *Fascism in France: The Case of Maurice Barrès* (Berkeley and Los Angeles, Calif., 1972), and *Fascist Intellectual, Drieu La Rochelle* (Berkeley and Los Angeles, Calif., 1979).

[12] See the early articles by René Rémond, "Droites classiques et droite romantique," *Terre Humaine* (June 1951), 60-69, and "Y a-t-il un fascisme français?," *Terre Humaine* (July-August 1952), 37-47. My thanks to Emily Goodman for sharing her copies of these articles.

[13] Jacques Néré, "The French Republic," *The New Cambridge Modern History*, XI (London, 1962), 300; Eugen Weber, "Introduction," to Hans Rogger and Eugen Weber, eds., *The European Right: A Historical Profile* (Berkeley, Calif., 1965), pp. 2-3.

[14] René Rémond, *La Droite en France de 1815 à nos jours; continuité et diversité d'une tradition politique* (Paris, 1954); and the second, revised edition, on which I have relied: *La Droite en France: de la première restauration à la Ve République*, 2nd ed., revised (Paris, 1963) [in English translation as *Right Wing in France: From 1815 to De Gaulle*, transl. James M. Laux (Philadelphia, 1969)]. A third edition, with a supplemental volume carrying the story to June 1968, was published in 1968. Many of Rémond's students have since explored topics on the political Right in the post-1914 period, as have those of Gordon Wright and Eugen Weber.

[15] See Pierre Renouvin, "Research in Modern and Contemporary History: Present Trends in France," *Journal of Modern History*, XXXVIII (1966), 1-12, and the subsequent lament of Josef Konvitz in 1976: "Biography: The Missing Form in French Historical Studies," *European Studies Review*, VI (1976), 9-19. See also Barrie M. Ratcliffe, "The Decline of Biography in French Historiography: The Ambivalent Legacy of the 'Annales' Tradition," and William Arthur Bruneau, "An Apologia for Biography in French History," both in *Proceedings of the Western Society for French History, 1980*, ed. Edgar Leon Newman (Las Cruces, New Mexico, 1981), pp. 556-67 and 568-76.

[16] René Rémond, "Introduction," in René Rémond, *Pour une histoire politique* (Paris, 1988), pp. 18, 22.

[17] See especially Philippe Levillain, "Les protagonistes: De la biographie," in Rémond, ed., *Pour une histoire politique*, pp. 121-59. See also the reports by Ernst Engelberg and Hams Schleier, S. L. Tikhvinsky, R. F. Ivanov, and T. A. Pavolva, and John A. Garraty, in the methodology session, "La biographie historique," at the 1990 International Congress on the Historical Sciences (Madrid): *Grands Thèmes, Methodologie, Sections chronologiques 1: Rapports et abregés* (Madrid: Comité internationale des sciences historiques, 1990), pp. 209-25.

[18] See Jean-Marie Mayeur's thoughtful reinterpretation of the 1870's, *Les Débuts de la Troisième République* (Paris, 1973) and, most recently, Philippe Levillain, *Boulanger, fossoyeur de la monarchie* (Paris, 1982).

[19] In addition to my own unpublished dissertation, "The Political Career of Paul de Cassagnac" (Stanford, Calif., 1971), works by American scholars that adress aspects of monarchist politics between 1880 and 1900 include Robert R. Locke, *French Legitimists and the Politics of Moral Order in the Early Third Republic* (Princeton, N.J., 1974); Marvin L. Brown, *The Comte de Chambord* (Durham, N.C., 1967); and Marvin L. Brown, *Louis Veuillot* (Durham, N.C., 1978). An important, as yet unpublished study is Alan Grubb, "The Politics of Pessimism: A Political Biography of Duc Albert de Broglie during the Early Third Republic, 1871-1885," Ph.D. dissertation (Columbia University, 1969). For the 1880s, see Benjamin F. Martin, Jr., *Count Albert de Mun, Paladin of the Third Republic* (Chapel Hill, N.C., 1978), and William D. Irvine, *The Boulanger Affair Reconsidered* (New York and Oxford, 1989). More will be said about these studies in the ensuing chapters.

Work by American-based scholars on the twentieth-century Right includes the distinguished study by Eugen Weber, *Action Française* (Stanford, Calif., 1962). In Great Britain, the interest in Bonapartism of Oxford historian Theodore Zeldin led him to a more strongly social and cultural interpretation of French history. See his chapters on the dynastic groups in *France 1848-1945*, 2 vols. (Oxford, 1973 and 1977) in the Oxford History of Modern Europe.

[20] Eugen Weber, *Peasants into Frenchmen: The Modernization of Modern Rural France 1870-1914* (Stanford, Calif., 1976).

[21] Cassagnac appears to have coined the term "*n'importequisme*," but this attribution was not picked up by subsequent writers such as Charles Benoist, "Le n'importequisme," *RDM* (15 December 1925), 801-18 [the third article in a series on "les maladies de la démocratie].

[22] Edouard Drumont, in *La Libre Parole*, 8 November 1904.

NOTES - CHAPTER I

[1] Quoted by police agent "6" in a report dated 18 June 1874. A.P.P., B^A 998.

[2] "Notice historique sur Granier de Cassagnac," in preface to Vol. III of Bernard-Adolphe Granier de Cassagnac, *Souvenirs du Second Empire*, 3 vols. (Paris, 1879-1882), III, 1. Except where other works add to or clarify aspects of Granier de Cassagnac's career, my account is based on this "Notice." Supplemental material has since become available in William Evan Duvall, "Bernard-Adolphe Granier de Cassagnac and Right-Wing Bonapartism under the Second Empire, 1860-1870" (unpublished doctoral dissertation, University of California at Santa Barbara, 1973), and in Gilbert Sourbadère, "Un polémiste du XIXe siècle: Bernard-Adolphe Granier de Cassagnac," 2 vols. (mémoire de maîtrise, Université de Toulouse-Le Mirail, undated [mid-1980s]).

[3] Warren C. Scoville, *Capitalism and French Glassmaking* (Berkeley, 1950), p. 83.

[4] J. Mastron, "Les verreries dans le Gers," *BSAG*, V (1904), 290. Many of these details are also included in the biographical notice on Paul de Cassagnac's elder son, Paul-Julien, in Jean Jolly, *Dictionnaire des parlementaires*, 8 vols. (Paris, 1960-1977), III, 889.

[5] On the litigation, see *Le Figaro*, 6 July 1878, and *Le Pays*, 7 and 11 July 1878. See also the article, "La famille Cassagnac," in *L'Autorité*, 18 February 1902. The family's full name was and is Granier de Cassagnac. However, many articles and references to the family are indexed under Cassagnac, since the shortened name was used by Paul de Cassagnac, his sons, and later generations of the family. In this study I have adopted the nineteenth-century convention of referring to Paul de Cassagnac simply as Cassagnac, and to his father as Granier de Cassagnac.

[6] Scoville, *French Glassmaking*, p. 83.

[7] Granier de Cassagnac's uncle later fathered the revolutionary H.-P.-O. Lissagaray, who became well-known for his history of the Paris Commune. The young Lissagaray declared himself the sworn enemy of his cousin, Granier de Cassagnac. Their feud will be described in Chapter II. On the family relationship, see Z. Baqué, "Les origines vicoises de Lissagaray et sa parenté avec Granier de Cassagnac," *BSAG*, XLIX (1948), 126-31. On the political climate in Toulouse during the Restoration, see David Higgs, *Ultraroyalism in Toulouse* (Baltimore, 1973).

[8] Baqué, "Origines vicoises de Lissagaray," 131; J. Dagnan, *Le Gers sous la Seconde République*, II (Auch, 1929), 364.

[9] Rémusat later regretted sponsoring Granier de Cassagnac. See his *Mémoires de ma vie*, III (Paris, 1960), 187. In 1838 Victor Hugo had recommended Granier de Cassagnac for the *Légion d'Honneur*, which was awarded on 1 May 1838. Hugo remained friendly until his departure into exile, in protest against the *coup d'état*. The original of Hugo's letter of recommendation was last in the possession of the late radio personality and chansonnier "Saint-Granier" (Jean de Cassagnac) of Paris.

[10] Granier de Cassagnac, *Souvenirs*, III, 15. The Adour is the river that traverses Gascony.

[11] Le duel Beauvallon et d'Ecquevilley (1845). Duel Dujarier," in Armand Fouquier, *Causes célèbres*, II (Paris, 1859), cahier 10, 2.

[12] *Histoire des classes ouvrières et des classes bourgeoises* (Paris, 1838); *Histoire des classes nobles et des classes anoblies* (Paris, 1840). Delphine Gay, writing as the Vicomte de Launay, praised the *Histoire des classes ouvrières* in Lettre XXXVI (16 December 1837), reprinted in her *Lettres Parisiennes*, I, pp. 287-88. A long review by J.-P. Rossignol appeared in *RDM* (1839), 471-514.

[13] Granier de Cassagnac published a variety of articles and brochures on the slavery question between 1837 and 1844. These have been recuperated and analyzed by Sourbadère, "Granier de Cassagnac," I, chap. 3.

[14] His account of the trip was published as *Voyage aux Antilles* (Paris, 1842). According to André Tudesq, in *Les Grands notables en France*, II (Paris, 1964), 837, Thiers actually subsidized Granier de Cassagnac's trip while at the same time he encouraged the work of the Broglie commission on abolishing slavery.

[15] In 1840 Guadeloupe was governed by a military governor and had no parliamentary representation. Tudesq notes that delegates to the Conseil des Delegués des Colonies were paid a handsome twenty thousand francs per year. On Granier de Cassagnac's work for the *colons*, see Rufz de Lavison, "La Martinique sous le gouvernement de M. le contre-amiral du Val d'Ailly (1840 à 1844)," *La Revue Brittannique*, V (September 1882), pp. 103-42, esp. p. 118.

[16] Information on Rosa Beauvallon from her school dossier was graciously furnished by Mme Vandevoorde, Surintendante des Maisons d'Éducation de la Légion d'Honneur, Saint Denis. I am grateful to Professor Rebecca Rogers, University of Iowa, for assistance in accessing this material.

[17] In 1838, Rosemond de Beauvallon edited the short-lived *Revue Coloniale (intérêts des colons, marine, commerce, littérature, beaux-arts, théâtres, modes).* He also published several books, listed in the catalog of the Bibliothèque Nationale.

[18] The marriage contract between Granier de Cassagnac and Mlle de Beauvallon, dated 20 January 1841, is discussed in Duvall, "Granier de Cassagnac," pp. 63-64. The groom brought assets worth 80,000 francs (including his chateau, his apartment in Paris, and his library) to the marriage.

The bride's dowry was 100,000 francs. See also Sourbadère, "Granier de Cassagnac," I, 95-96 and 149 concerning the original marriage contract and its revision in 1847 from community property to *séparation de biens*.

[19] Eugène de Mirecourt, *Histoire contemporaine. Portraits et silhouettes au XIXe siècle. No. 93 - Paul de Cassagnac* (Paris, 1870), p. 9. In later years, Cassagnac's own enemies frequently referred to him in print as *le Nègre*, thus transferring to him the "insult" originally addressed to his mother. See Cassagnac's careful distinction between *créole*, the general term for French colonists in the New World, and *métis*, or mixed race, in *L'Autorité*, 1 October 1888.

[20] Cassagnac's place and date of birth were confirmed by the discovery of a facsimile copy of his birth registration, obtained by the police, in A.P.P., B^A 1000. Other sources, including the *Dictionnaire biographique française*, erroneously place his birth in Guadeloupe. According to family sources, there were three younger brothers, Louis, twins Albert and Georges, and a sister, Jane, who married a M. de Saulcy, and lived in Metz. Louis, who became a career officer in the French army (a brigadier general and, from 1871 on, a fervent republican), and Georges, a banker, now have biographies in the *DBF*, fascicule 95 (1986). Albert also served in the army.

[21] For a lengthy and detailed account of the Dujarier-Beauvallon affair, which began in March 1845 over a gambling debt, see Fouquier, *Causes célèbres*, II, cahier 10, 1-32. Maurice Reclus qualified this duel as "*la plus ténébreuse peut-être et certainement la plus balzacienne des affaires d'honneur du XIXe siècle.*" See the preface to Maurice Reclus, *Émile de Girardin* (Paris, 1934), p. 9.

[22] Constant Hilbey, *Vénalité des journaux, révélations accompagnées de preuves* (Paris, 1845); *Plaidoyer de Constant Hilbey en réponse à l'assignation de M. Granier de Cassagnac* (Paris, 1845); *Réponse à tous mes critiques* (Paris, 1846); and *Nouveau procès des quatre couverts et des six petites cuillères d'argent* (Paris, 1846).

[23] On the affair of *L'Époque*, see Rémusat, *Mémoires de ma vie*, IV (Paris, 1962), 130-131, and Hippolyte Castille, *Les Journaux et les journalistes sous le règne de Louis-Philippe* (Paris, 1858), pp. 44-47. See also Sourbadère, *Granier de Cassagnac*, I, chap. 4.

[24] For a discussion of the French position on the Italian question during later 1847, see P. Thureau-Dangin, *Histoire de la monarchie de Juillet*, VII (Paris, 1892).

[25] For details, see Granier de Cassagnac's *Histoire de la chute du roi Louis-Philippe, de la république de 1848 et du rétablissement de l'Empire* (Paris, 1857), I, 214. For a sketch of his activities in Paris during the next two months, see the "Notice," preceding his *Souvenirs*, III, 28-29.

[26] In 1838 Granier de Cassagnac purchased the east half of the chateau of Couloumé, which at one time belonged to the Abbé de Montesquiou, for 57,000 francs. Thereby he established himself as a *grand seigneur* in Gers, gilding his aristocratic claims with the purchase of land and manor house. Paul de Cassagnac acquired the other half in the 1880s. Couloumé remained in the Cassagnac family until the 1960s. For further information on Granier de Cassagnac's land holdings, see Sourbadère, *Granier de Cassagnac*, both vols.

[27] *Histoire des causes de la Révolution française*, 3 vols. (Paris, 1850); 2nd ed., 4 vols. (Paris, 1857).

[28] Quoted from Granier de Cassagnac's preface to his *Souvenirs*, I, vii-viii.

[29] Jules Barbey d'Aurevilly, in *Le Constitutionnel*, 9 February 1880.

[30] These articles were published in the issues of 14, 16, 20 and 23 April, and 1 and 9 May 1850. See Granier de Cassagnac, *Souvenirs*, I, 35.

[31] See his *Récit complet et authentique des événements de décembre 1851* (Paris, 1851). According to Cassagnac family folklore, plans for the *coup d'état* were laid during a meeting at the chateau of Couloumé. However, I have found no evidence to substantiate this story. Granier de Cassagnac made no mention of this possibility in his *Souvenirs*. In fact, he repeatedly stressed his ignorance of any details of the president's plan. Nor do the other principal accounts of the *coup* lend support to the story; see, for example, Howard C. Payne, "Preparation of a Coup d'État: Administrative Centralization and Police Powers in France, 1849-1851," *Studies in Modern European History in Honor of Franklin Charles Palm*, eds. Frederick J. Cox et al. (New York, 1956), pp. 175-202.

[32] Details of Paul de Cassagnac's itinerary as a law student were conveyed to me by Monsieur P. Champagne, secrétaire-général adjoint, Faculté de droit et des sciences économiques de Paris. Letter to the author, dated 13 March 1969.

[33] In pursuit of the sources of Cassagnac's political ideas, I initially consulted the following works, listed here in order of their publication: Alphonse V. Roche, *Les Idées traditionalistes en France de Rivarol à Charles Maurras* (Urbana, Ill., 1937); Peter Viereck, *Conservatism* (Princeton, N.J., 1956); Roger H. Soltau, *French Political Thought in the 19th Century*, new ed. (New York, 1959); and J. P. Mayer, *Political Thought in France from the Revolution to the Fifth Republic*, 3rd ed. (London, 1961). For further detail, I had recourse to Richard Lebrun, *Throne and Altar: The Political and Religious Thought of Joseph de Maistre* (Ottawa, 1965), and to the important work by Juan Donoso Cortés, *An Essay on Catholicism, Authority and Order Considered in their Fundamental Principles*, tr. from the Spanish by M. V. Goddard, new ed. (New York, 1925). Donoso Cortés was close to the imperial family, especially to Eugenie. A recent study of his ideas is John T. Graham, *Donoso Cortés: Utopian Romanticist and Political Realist* (Columbia, Mo., 1974).

More immediate parallels for Cassagnac's political philosophy are found in works such as Raymond Troplong's *Du Principe d'autorité depuis 1789, suivi de nouvelles considerations sur le même sujet* (Paris, 1853). Troplong was editor of the *Revue de législation et de jurisprudence* from 1834 to 1853 and subsequently presided over the Imperial Senate. See also Granier de Cassagnac's important tract, *L'Empereur et la démocratie moderne* (Paris, 1860), and Evariste Bavoux, *La France sous Napoléon III: l'Empire et le régime parlementaire*, 2 vols. (Paris, 1870). A new study of Granier de Cassagnac's colleague, Jules Barbey d'Aurevilly, by Brigitte Guillouet, *Le Royalisme de Barbey d'Aurevilly* (Maule, 1983) has also clarified some points.

[34] Particularly striking is the resemblance between Granier de Cassagnac's pose as a patrician of the Roman Republic, lauding rural virtues and castigating urban vices, and Rousseau's description of the Roman Comita, in Book IV, chapter IV of the *Social Contract*. Indeed, the Cassagnacs' arguments for plebiscitary democracy appear initially to lend support to the position of J. L. Talmon concerning the Enlightenment (or at least Rousseauian) roots of totalitarian democracy. See his two books, *The Origins of Totalitarian Democracy* (London, 1952), and *Political Messianism: The Romantic Phase* (London, 1960).

[35] As will be seen in subsequent chapters, Paul de Cassagnac never became an ultramontane on the model of Louis Veuillot or Émile Keller. He identified more closely with the liberal Catholic politics of Félix Dupanloup, bishop of Orléans.

[36] *L'Indépendance Parisienne, revue des théatres, du monde, des lettres, des arts et de la finance.* Twelve issues were published between mid-May and mid-October 1862. Cassagnac wrote under the pseudonym of Paul Valter. Two of his articles (1 June and 16 July) savagely attacked Victor Hugo's new novel, *Les Misérables*, for striking at the pillars of the social order, the judiciary and the clergy.

[37] From January to May 1863, *La Nation* (under Granier de Cassagnac's editorship) was devoted to campaigning for official candidates. On *Diogène* and its counterparts, see Philippe Jones, "La presse satirique illustrée entre 1860 and 1890," *Études de Presse*, no. 14 (1956), 47; see also the scattered reports concerning this publication in A.N., BB[18] 1679.

[38] Mirecourt, *Cassagnac*, pp. 21-22.

[39] *Ibid.* I have also consulted the reports on the creation of the Fifth Bureau, its duties, and its personnel in A.N., F[1b], dossier 10[12].

[40] Pierre Dominique, *Les Polémistes français depuis 1789* (Paris, 1962), p. 9.

[41] In 1868 the journalist Edmond Texier was already lamenting the demise of militant political journalism in face of commercial pressures. "*Le journal a été une force, une puissance; on l'appelait le quatrième pouvoir de l'État. Il ne sera bientôt qu'un poteau d'annonces.*" Edmond Texier, *Le Journal et le*

journaliste (Paris, 1868), p. 12.

[42] H. d'Alméras, "Paul de Cassagnac," *Avant la gloire: leurs débuts*. Second series (Paris, 1903), p. 108.

[43] The literary critic Barbey d'Aurevilly classed Granier de Cassagnac with Louis Veuillot and Jacques Crétineau-Joly as one of the three great men of journalism in the nineteenth century. See the article cited in footnote 27. Another sympathetic critic, René de Lagarde, classed him with Armand Carrel and Chateaubriand as one of the three foremost "*journalistes lettrés*" of the century. Lagarde's article, which appeared in *Le Figaro*, was reprinted in *Le Pays*, 11 February 1880.

[44] Quoted in an interview, "Chez M. de Cassagnac," *Le Matin*, 14 November 1899.

[45] D'Alméras, *Avant la gloire*, pp. 99 and 107.

[46] H. de Gallier, "Deux polémistes," *Le Carnet*, VI (October 1903), 107.

[47] See especially the articles on Cassagnac by Charles Laurent -- such as his "M. Paul de Cassagnac," in *La France*, 2 April 1875. See also the various obituary tributes, including that signed "Un Parisien," in *Le Radical*, 7 November 1904, and another signed "J.B.", in *La Croix*, 6 November 1904.

[48] Quoted in *Le Pays*, 7 March 1877. Cassagnac made these remarks before a committee of the Chamber of Deputies charged with examining a request subitted by judicial authorities for his prosecution for violation of the press laws.

[49] "Chez M. de Cassagnac," *Le Matin*, 14 November 1899.

[50] "E.D." in *L'Express du Midi* (Toulouse), 7 November 1904.

[51] Lenore O'Boyle has remarked how distinctive France was in this respect. See "The Image of the Journalist in France, Germany, and England, 1815-1848," *Comparative Studies in Society and History*, X (1967-68), 290-317, esp. 300.

[52] Rémond, *La Droite en France*, p. 317.

[53] *Le Pays*, 3 August 1873.

[54] "E.D." in *L'Express du Midi*, 7 November 1904.

[55] Paul de Cassagnac, "Souvenirs de 1870," p. 3. A collection of articles found pasted into a notebook, Cassagnac family papers.

[56] André Maurois, *Olympio: The Turbulent Life of Victor Hugo*. Tr. from the French by Gerard Hopkins. Pyramid ed. (New York, 1968), p. 131.

[57] *Le Radical*, 7 November 1904.

[58] Gallier, "Deux polémistes," 108.

[59] Jules Richard, *Le Bonapartisme sous la République* (Paris, 1883), p. 54.

[60] See, for example, the testimony of a Marseille Bonapartist:

> *Cassagnac était un homme superbe. Sa carrure athlétique*
> *de beau géant, était comme une incarnation de la devise:*
> *'Qui s'y frotte, s'y pique'. A voir la longueur de ses jambes*

> *'Qui s'y frotte, s'y pique'. A voir la longueur de ses jambes*
> *et de ses bras, on comprenait ses succès de duelliste. Mais,*
> *plus encore que la vaillance qui se lisait dans ses yeux, était*
> *remarquable leur expression de bonté. C'est, sous des traits*
> *pareils, qu'on se représente un Hercule, redresseur de torts.*
> *Dieu, quand il créa Cassagnac, dut avoir, un instant l'idée*
> *de nettoyer nos écuries d'Augias! Pourquoi Dieu a-t-il*
> *changé d'idée?*

Paul Corticchiato, *Les Corses et le parti bonapartiste à Marseille en 1870 et pendant les premières années de la République* (Marseille, 1921), p. 168.

[61] For information on Eugenie's cult of Marie-Antoinette, which included arranging an exhibition of her possessions in 1857 and plans to restore the royal residences, Trianon and Malmaison, see Comte Maurice Fleury, *Memoirs of the Empress Eugenie*, vol. 1 (New York, 1920), pp. 453-57. In *Gossip from Paris during the Second Empire* (New York, 1903), pp. 154-55, Anthony B. North Peat reported Eugenie masquerading as Marie-Antoinette at a pre-Lenten ball in February 1865.

[62] See Olympe Audouard, *Silhouettes Parisiennes* (Paris, 1883), pp. 250-51.

[63] The Cassagnac family papers contain sixty-five letters from Queen Isabelle to the Cassagnacs, dating from 1878 to 1902. In March 1868 a mysterious girl baby was born and recognized by Paul de Cassagnac as Rose-Pauline de Granier de Cassagnac; the mother's name was given as Rose-Eugenie-Claire Pourchey. The child was raised in the Cassagnac household. Family legend has it that she strongly resembled the Spanish Bourbons and was, perhaps, the child of Isabelle de Bourbon. Family papers contain information about her marriage in December 1892 to a cousin in Tahiti, the birth of a son the following October, and notice of her death in late November 1893.

It is worth mentioning in this connection Paul de Cassagnac's insistence on men's taking responsibility for paternity, at a time when *recherche de paternité* was illegal in France. In 1890 he wrote:

> *Personne, en effect, personne, en face de Dieu et des*
> *hommes, n'a le droit de décliner la responsabilité de la*
> *paternité. Celui qui seduit une femme, donne la vie à un*
> *enfant et les abandonne pour se soustraire aux nouveaux*
> *devoirs qui s'imposent à lui, est un lâche, un misérable, pour*
> *lequel il ne saurait y avoir de pitié.*

"La recherche de la paternité," *L'Autorité*, 24 June 1890.

[64] His relationship with Castiglione is documented in Alain Decaux, *La Castiglione* (Paris, 1959). The original correspondence between Cassagnac and Castiglione was last known to be in the possession of "Saint Granier" (Jean de Cassagnac) of Paris.

[65] See Marie Bashkirtseff, *Journal de Marie Bashkirtseff*, 2 vols. (Paris, 1887), and *Cahiers intimes inédits*, ed. Pierre Borel (Paris, 1925). Bashkirtseff's frank revelations created a literary sensation when they were first published. There are many accounts of her life, based on these publications. See, among others, Albéric Cahuet, *Moussia; ou la vie et la mort de Marie Bashkirtseff* (Paris, 1926); Dormer Creston (pseud. Dorothy Julia Baynes), *Fountains of Youth: The Life of Marie Bashkirtseff* (London, 1936); and, most recently, Colette Cosnier, *Marie Bashkirtseff: un portrait sans retouches* (Paris, 1985).

[66] Many stories circulated during 1878 and subsequently about Cassagnac's marriage to Julia Acard. It was widely rumored in Paris that Mlle Acard, who had been on the brink of becoming a Carmelite nun when the engagement was arranged, was in fact not the legitimate daughter of Comte Acard but of Cardinal Antonelli, the late papal secretary of state. Mme Acard was reputed to have been the mistress of this cardinal who, having never been ordained a priest, was not bound by vows of celibacy. See the series of police reports concerning Mme Acard and her mother, dating from spring 1877, in A.P.P., B[A] 999, especially "P," 11 June 1878. See also *Le Rappel*, 12 June 1878, and the article on the Cassagnacs in *Le Gaulois*, 14 November 1878. On the womanizing Antonelli, see Frank J. Coppa, *Cardinal Giacomo Antonelli and Papal Politics in European Affairs* (Albany, N.Y., 1990). In *Le Libéralisme catholique* (Paris, 1969), Marcel Prélot claimed (p. 307) that Mme Paul de Cassagnac was reputed to be a granddaughter of Antonelli and had thereby acquired his papers, which her husband passed on to Abbé Barbier in the early 1900s. I found no correspondence concerning such papers in the Cassagnac family archives, or on any other aspect of the marriage. Two sons were born to this union, Paul-Julien (1880) and Guy (1882). Mme Paul de Cassagnac lived into the 1930s and was listed in *Tout Paris*.

[67] See *Le Gaulois*, 14 November 1878. "He has the instinct of the *épée* to an almost divinatory degree, a prodigious quickness of the hand and a gay calm; the most foxy could be undone." The same observer remarked that with a schedule of regular workouts, Cassagnac could have quickly achieved the level of Ferry d'Esclandes or of Aldama, two of the outstanding amateurs of the day, not to mention Cassagnac's brother, lieutenant of the *dragons*, "one of the three or four first *épées*, not of France, but of the world."

[68] Quoted by Ben C. Truman, *The Field of Honor* (New York, 1884), p. 73.

[69] For Cassagnac's opinions on duelling, see his articles "Le Pape et le duel," and "Contre le duel," in *L'Autorité*, issues of 3 October 1891 and 20 November 1903. Both articles have been reprinted in his *Oeuvres* (Paris, 1905), VI, 225-28 and 413-18. See also his preface to Jules Jacob, *Le Jeu de l'épée* (Paris, 1887).

[70] On Cassagnac's duel with Scholl, I have consulted Mirecourt, *Cassagnac*, pp. 16-18, and a collection of reports in A.N., BB[18] 1679.

[71] Truman, *Field of Honor*, p. 455.

[72] In a letter from Cassagnac to Franceschini Piétri, 5 October 1869; reproduced in *Oeuvres*, I, 59-60. Cassagnac had been reprimanded for his criticism of the emperor's decision to reconvene the Corps Législatif.

[73] From Cassagnac's long apology for independence in *Le Pays*, 15 January 1869; *Oeuvres*, I, 36-37. See also his later editorial, "Question personnelle," *Le Pays*, 23 September 1874; *Oeuvres*, I, 147-52.

[74] *Le Pays*, 30 June 1873.

[75] See, for instance, the tributes by Edouard Drumont, in *La Libre Parole*, 2 November 1904; *Le Courrier du Soir*, 6 November 1904; and the *Sunday Times* (London), 6 November 1904.

[76] *Le Pays*, 27 August 1883. See Cassagnac's speech in the Chamber of Deputies, 26 December 1882, and *L'Autorité*, 4 February 1897.

[77] Quoted by Cassagnac in *Le Matin*, 14 November 1899.

[78] The two newspapers shared a building at 4, rue de Valois where, as Arthur Meyer remarked, they "stood watch over the authoritarian empire." Arthur Meyer, *Ce que mes yeux ont vu* (Paris, 1912), p. 223.

[79] Many reports pertaining to the early administrative history of *Le Pays* are available in A.N., F[18] 400. See also Jean Morienval, *Les Créateurs de la grande presse en France* (Paris, 1934), pp. 185-86; Guy-P. Palmade, *Capitalistes et capitalisme françaises au XIXe siècle* (Paris, 1961), p. 162, and "Fidus" (pseud. E. de Balleyguier, called Loudun), *Journal de dix ans*, I (Paris, 1886), pp. 344-47.

[80] Information concerning the contract and subsidy arrangements made in 1868 between the *Société* and Granier de Cassagnac became public knowledge in the 1870s, due to several lawsuits. In October 1868, a potential sale of *Le Pays* was forestalled by the last-minute negotiation of a new contract between Gibiat and Granier de Cassagnac. The agreement stipulated that, in exchange for Gibiat's renunciation of his right to change the editorship of the newspaper at will, Granier de Cassagnac would guarantee to the newspaper 50,000 francs per year over and above its net gain: this amount was to be paid into the treasury in monthly installments.

The contract, effective 1 November 1868, was scheduled to run until February 1874, but was interrupted by events connected with the fall of the imperial regime in 1870. The 50,000 franc guarantee was to be provided from the secret funds of the Ministry of Interior. An order providing 250,000 francs payable to the publisher of *Le Pays* was drawn up and was honored by the Ministry of Finance until the advent of the Émile Ollivier cabinet in January 1870, at which time the new government refused to continue payment of the subsidy. The lawsuits were provoked by this refusal.

The first suit, for breach of contract, was brought by Gibiat against Granier de Cassagnac, and came to court in July 1875. The second suit was brought by the publisher, Gibiat, and Granier de Cassagnac, against the ministry to obtain execution of the order that had provided the subsidy. Extended coverage of the court proceedings appeared in *Le Rappel*, 25 July 1875, as well as in other newspapers. Other occasional reports on the lawsuits can be consulted in A.N., F^{18} 400 and in A.P.P., B^A 997. In later years, the affair of the subsidy re-entered public discussion, as, for instance, in an acrimonious exchange between Robert Mitchell and Cassagnac in 1881. See *Le Pays*, issues of 29, 30, and 31 March and 1 through 6 April 1881.

[81] J. Dagnan, "Le Gers sous le Second Empire," *La Révolution de 1848*, XXIX (1932-1933), 61.

[82] D'Alméras, *Avant la gloire*, p. 99.

[83] *Le Temps*, 24 December 1866. Bismarck had employed this argument himself a few days earlier, in his speech before the Reichstag urging support of the bill that would allow legal annexation of the two duchies.

[84] *Le Courrier Français*, 9 December 1866; cited in *Le Temps*, 30 December 1866.

[85] *Le Pays*, 9 December 1866; likewise cited in *Le Temps*, 30 December 1866.

[86] *Le Temps*, 30 December 1866. I have also consulted the copy of the verdict in A.N., BB^{18} 1743.

[87] The Malespine case was heard by the court on 11 January 1867. The verdict was published in *Le Temps*, 13 January 1867. The court merged the sentence in this case with that from the earlier Guéroult case.

[88] *Le Pays*, 29 December 1866. Quoted in Alexandre Zévaès, *Henri Rochefort, le pamphlétaire* (Paris, 1946), p. 34. Other versions of the story indicate that Joan of Arc had been the victim of Rochefort's insuits. In a much later article published in *Le Matin*, 26 January 1886, Cassagnac indicated that during his youth he had celebrated a sort of cult for the mystic dead whose saints included both the maid of Orleans and the bride of Louis XVI. This would seem to be another manifestation of the chivalric idealism discussed above.

[89] The best account of the Cassagnac-Rochefort duel is that by Mirecourt, *Cassagnac*, pp. 26-36. Shorter accounts appear in Ernest Vizetelly, *Court Life of the Second French Empire* (New York, 1907), pp. 218-19, and in the brief biographies of Cassagnac by d'Alméras, *Avant la gloire*, and Albert Croquez, *Paul de Cassagnac* (Paris, 1911). The account by Roger Duchaussoy, "Duels et duellistes du XIXe siècle: les Cassagnac," in *L'Escrime française* is strictly second-hand. Roger L. Williams, *Henri Rochefort: Prince of the Gutter Press* (New York, 1966), p. 23, takes his account of the duel from Zévaès, *Rochefort*, p. 34, where the anecdote of the religious medal is not mentioned. Other

references to the medal are found in an article on Cassagnac in *Le Gaulois*, 14 November 1878; in Cassagnac's own article in *Le Matin*, 26 January 1886; and in Truman, *Field of Honor*, p. 491.

[90] Mirecourt, *Cassagnac*, p. 25. Years later, Cassagnac indicated that he had been dismissed from his position at the ministry because of a duel he had fought with a republican journalist who had insulted the emperor. "A la Place Beauvau," *L'Autorité*, 17 July 1897. As far as I can discover, however, the duel Cassagnac fought in defense of the emperor only took place after his dismissal.

NOTES - CHAPTER II

[1] Bernard-Adolphe de Granier de Cassagnac, *Souvenirs du Second Empire*, 3 vols. (Paris, 1879-1882), III, 166. See also Theodore Zeldin, *Émile Ollivier and the Liberal Empire of Napoleon III* (Oxford, 1963), pp. 102-4. Zeldin views the concessions of 19 January as mere half-measures. A detailed study of Granier de Cassagnac's opposition to the liberalization of the Second Empire is William Evan Duvall, "Bernard-Adolphe Granier de Cassagnac and Right-Wing Bonapartism under the Second Empire, 1860-1870" (unpublished doctoral dissertation, University of California at Santa Barbara, 1973).

[2] Hostilities erupted more than once into open conflict, as in the incident during the visit of the Russian czar. During a tour of the Palais de Justice, certain prominent members of the republican opposition greeted him with cries of *"Vive la Pologne, Monsieur!"* in a defiant reference to Russia's suppression of the Polish insurrection. This incident provoked two duels between the Cassagnacs and the republican provocateurs. Another incident, incited by a series of articles in *Le Courrier Français* that were extremely insulting to Granier de Cassagnac, provoked both court action and additional challenges to duel. On these, see Eugène de Mirecourt, *Paul de Cassagnac* (Paris, 1870), pp. 39 and 41, and the relevant issues of *Le Pays* and *Le Temps*. For an extensive treatment of the republican opposition under the Second Empire and its alliance with the liberals, see Georges Weill, *Histoire du parti républicain en France, 1814-1870* (Paris, 1900), pp. 498-523.

[3] Cassagnac regularly reiterated the distinction between "de luxe" and "necessary" liberties in various articles and speeches. For other examples, see *Le Pays*, 14 October 1872, and Cassagnac's speech at Belleville in late November 1875.

[4] *Le Pays*, 28 July 1867; *Oeuvres*, I, 11.

[5] *Le Pays*, 29 July 1867; *Oeuvres*, I, 15-16.

[6] *Ibid.* See also Granier de Cassagnac's remarks on the *ambitieux* in his *Histoire de la chute du roi Louis-Philippe, de la république de 1848 et du rétablissement de l'Empire* (Paris, 1857), I, 110-13. Indeed, Granier de Cassagnac's attitude toward the liberal bourgeoisie is strikingly similar to that expressed in the 1940s by Emmanuel Beau de Loménie, *Les Responsabilités des dynasties bourgeoises*, vols. 1 and 2 (Paris, 1943-1947). A sample: "The Girondins were the truest expression of that portion, at once skeptical and ardent, of the bourgeoisie, ready to support any regime that would promise it domination." Granier de Cassagnac, *Histoire des Girondins et des massacres de septembre*, 2nd ed. (Paris, 1860), I, 2.

[7] Roger Bellet, *Presse et journalisme sous le Second Empire* (Paris, 1967), p. 67; "Les droits de la majorité," *Le Pays*, 28 August 1867; *Oeuvres*, I, 23-26.

[8] Indeed, Granier de Cassagnac aspired to be the Marcus Varro of the Pyrenees, according to his *Souvenirs*, I, 1-2. Varro was a noted Roman scholar of classical times who glorified country life in his work, *Res Rusticae*.

[9] The phrase was used by Robert Schnerb to describe another staunch supporter of the authoritarian empire, Eugène Rouher, in *Rouher et le Second Empire* (Paris, 1949), p. 164.

[10] See Granier de Cassagnac, *Histoire de la chute du roi*, I, 372.

[11] The few legislative initiatives sponsored by the Cassagnacs were directed to meet the agricultural needs of their constituents. In November 1876, for example, Paul de Cassagnac introduced an amendment to the budget that would would distribute a sizeable credit to be shared among winegrowers struck by frost damage. See *J.O. 1876, Ch.D., Débats*, 8275, session of 14 November. From 1889 on, when agricultural difficulties became a prime political issue, Cassagnac devoted many articles to the subject in *L'Autorité*. He was one of the founders of the agricultural group behind Jules Méline in the Chamber of 1889-1893, and in 1901 he endorsed the newly-formed Comité du Vin de France. On these later activities, see E. O. Golob, *The Méline Tariff: French Agriculture and Nationalist Economic Policy* (New York, 1944), pp. 170-71.

[12] Granier de Cassagnac headed the Agricultural Inquiry commission for the three southwestern departments of Gers, Tarn-et-Garonne, and Haute-Garonne. See *Le Pays*, 8 December 1875.

[13] *Le Pays*, 29 July 1867; *Oeuvres*, I, 16-17.

[14] *Ibid.*

[15] "Notre démocratie," *Le Pays*, 20 August 1867; *Oeuvres*, I, 19-23. See also *Le Pays*, 28 August 1867.

[16] See Granier de Cassagnac's tribute in his *Histoire de la chute du roi*, I, 89-90.

[17] See the discussion by Pierre Guiral of the "permanence and deficiencies" of liberalism in France, in which he notes that the liberals generally did not take society and its requirements into account. "Le libéralisme en France (1815-1870): Thèmes, succès, et lacunes," in *Tendances politiques de la vie française depuis 1789* (Paris, 1960), p. 34.

[18] For an instructive discussion of the contest between the *thèse royale* and the *thèse nobiliaire*, centering on the role of Voltaire, see Peter Gay, *Voltaire's Politics* (Princeton, 1959), pp. 89-116.

[19] The Cassagnacs' position on liberty can be contrasted with that of Arthur Loth, Veuillot's assistant at *L'Univers*, who argued that man is spiritually unfit for liberty. See *L'Univers*, 8 July 1867. A recent study of Veuillot is Marvin L. Brown, Jr., *Louis Veuillot: French Ultramontane Catholic Journalist and Layman, 1813-1883* (Durham, N.C., 1978).

[20] But Voltaire, as well as Burke, argued in such terms. Gay, *Voltaire's Politics*, pp. 109-10.

[21] *Annales, C.L.*, 1863-64, III, 214. Session of 22 January 1864.

[22] *Ibid.*, 220.

[23] *Annales, C.L.*, 1868, IV, 117-23. Session of 31 January 1868. La Gorce qualified Granier de Cassagnac's speech as "the real manifesto of authoritarian imperialism." P. de la Gorce, *Histoire du Second Empire*, V, 5th ed. (Paris, 1903), 353.

[24] La Gorce, *Second Empire*, V, 358.

[25] On the nomination, see *Le Temps*, 19 August 1868, and the article by Robert Mitchell in *Le Gaulois*, 6 November 1904. I have since retrieved certification of Cassagnac's nomination from the files of the Grand Chancellery of the *Légion d'Honneur*.

Isidore-Hyacinthe-Marie-Louis-Robert Mitchell (1839-1916). Born in Bayonne to a Spanish mother and an English father, but opted for French citizenship. Don Carlos, the Spanish pretender, was his godfather, and his older half-sister married the composer Jacques Offenbach. Active in journalism from his 17th year, Mitchell became editor-in-chief of *Le Constitutionnel* in 1868. After 1870 he founded *Le Courrier de France*, then in 1874, *Le Soir*. From 1876 to 1881 he was a Bonapartist deputy for La Réole (Gironde). During the 1880s he wavered between rallying to the republic and playing a role in Bonapartist politics. He then feuded with Cassagnac over the issue of "conservative alliance," of which more will be said in a later chapter.

[26] Irene Collins, *The Government and the Newspaper Press in France: 1814-1881* (London, 1959), pp. 147-48; La Gorce, *Second Empire*, V, 351-52, 359-62.

[27] Collins, *Newspaper Press*, pp. 150-51.

[28] Zeldin, *Ollivier*, p. 107.

[29] Guy-P. Palmade, "Évolution de l'opinion publique dans le département du Gers de 1848 à 1914," unpublished *mémoire* submitted for the Diplôme d'Études Supérieures, Faculté des Lettres de Paris, 1949, pp. 4-5 and 11. For an excellent study of the economic geography of the region that include Gers, see Roger Brunet, *Les Campagnes toulousains: étude géographique* (Toulouse, 1965).

[30] Guy-P. Palmade, "Le département du Gers à la fin du Second Empire" (Auch, 1961), p. 16. Offprint from *BSAG*, LXII (1961), 73-95 and 177-99.

[31] Palmade, "Évolution de l'opinion publique," pp. 6-9; Palmade, "Département du Gers," pp. 16-17.

[32] J. Dagnan, "Le Gers sous le Second Empire," *La Révolution de 1848*, XXIX (1932-33), 60.

[33] J. Dagnan, *Le Gers sous la Seconde République*, II (Auch, 1929), 370-73. For an example of the petty concerns that troubled provincial politics

during the 1850s, see P. Tallez, "Adolphe Granier de Cassagnac et la Société d'Agriculture du Gers," *Revue de Gascogne*, nouv. ser. XXIX (1934), 123-33. This article details a dispute between Gers notables over awarding an agricultural prize.

[34] Jean-Justin-Fritz-Étienne David (1834-1885). David was the son of Irénée David, a representative to the National Assembly in 1848. After the revolution of 1870, David was named mayor of Auch. He was the republican candidate for Auch in the legislative elections of 1869, 1871, 1876 and 1877, and served as deputy for Auch from 1878 to 1885. For a more elaborate sketch of David, see Dagnan, "Gers sous le Second Empire," 53-58.

[35] Hippolyte-Prosper-Olivier Lissagaray (1838-1901) was a militant republican during the Second Empire and a revolutionary socialist during the Third Republic. He took an active role in the Paris Commune and then lived in exile in London until the amnesty of 1880. While in London, he unsuccessfully courted Karl Marx's sixteen-year-old daughter, Eleanor. His history of the Commune, first published in 1876, has been reissued in a number of editions during the last century. The best sketch of his life I have located is that by Amédée Dunois, "Notice sur Lissagaray," in the Librairie du Travail edition of Lissagaray's *Histoire de la Commune de 1870* (Paris, 1929), v-xxxvi.

[36] *Le Temps*, 18 August 1868.

[37] Dagnan, "Gers sous le Second Empire," 106.

[38] Granier de Cassagnac did not acquire a local organ until 1869, when he took over *Le Courrier du Gers*. Dagnan, "Second Empire," 103.

[39] *Ibid.*, 106; quoted from *Le Pays*, 19 August 1868. The term "a necessary ulcer" alluded directly to Louis-Napoleon's celebrated remark in his *Idées Napoléoniennes* that government is not a "necessary ulcer," but rather "the beneficient motive power of every social organism." See Napoleon III, *Napoleonic Ideas*, ed. Brison D. Gooch (New York, 1967), p. 28.

[40] *Ibid.*, 107; quoted from *L'Avenir*.

[41] *Ibid.*, 107-8; quoted from *Le Pays*, 24 August 1868.

[42] *Ibid.*, 109; quoted from *L'Avenir*, 25 August 1868. The qualification of the article is Dagnan's.

[43] *Ibid.*, 110.

[44] *Ibid.*

[45] Lissagaray claimed that his article had been reproduced in some 250 French and foreign newspapers and that he received some 4,000-5,000 letters of approval. Dagnan, "Second Empire," 110, accepts his claim. The actual circulation of *L'Avenir* was only 500 copies, of which some 40 per cent were distributed outside the department of Gers. Prefect (Gers) to Interior, 27 September 1868, "Journaux du département du Gers. État de distribution par arrondissement et hors du département," A.D. Gers, dossier "Famille Cassagnac."

[46] Fuller accounts of the duel can be found in Dagnan, "Second Empire," 110-12, and in Mirecourt, *Paul de Cassagnac*, pp. 46-48.

[47] Quoted by Mirecourt, *Paul de Cassagnac*, p. 48.

[48] Dagnan, "Second Empire," 161-62, quoted the issues of *L'Avenir* for 19 September, 27, 29, and 31 October, and 3 November 1868. I have subsequently consulted the voluminous file on *L'Avenir* in A.N., BB[18] 1771b. At one point the Minister of Interior was urging the Garde des Sceaux to prosecute Lissagaray and *L'Avenir*, but it was decided to stand aside and leave legal action to Granier de Cassagnac.

[49] Dagnan, "Second Empire,' 172-73, 176.

[50] *Ibid.*, 162-63. A collection of newspaper clippings concerning this trial are filed in A.N., F[18] 400.

[51] Prefect (Gers) to Interior, 27 September 1868. A.D. Gers, dossier "Famille Cassagnac."

[52] Dagnan, "Second Empire," 229-37.

[53] Dunois, "Notice sur Lissagaray," ix.

[54] Dagnan, "Second Empire," 236-40. The necessary precautions were detailed in *L'Avenir*, 22 October 1868.

[55] For details on the reunions and subsequent prosecution, see Dagnan, "Second Empire," XXVII, 241-45, and XXIX, 44-54.

[56] *Ibid.*, 162-63.

[57] *Ibid.*, 164-67. I have also consulted the brief correspondence between the imperial prosecutor and the Ministry of Justice concerning this matter in A.N., BB[18] 1784.

[58] Procureur-général (Agen) to Justice, 4 December 1868. A.N., BB[18] 1784. See also Palmade, "Département du Gers," pp. 40-42.

[59] Palmade, "Département du Gers," pp. 33-43, provides an extensive analysis of the 1869 election in all three districts of Gers.

[60] Sub-prefect (Mirande) to Prefect (Gers), 28 June and 4 July 1869. A.D. Gers, dossier "Paul de Cassagnac."

[61] *Le Conservateur* (Auch), 29 July 1869. Following the election, a group of voters filed a lengthy protest concerning certain electoral procedures allegedly employed by the Cassagnacs. The text, dated 31 July 1869, has been preserved in A.D. Gers, dossier "Paul de Cassagnac."

[62] French historiography long sanctioned the popular notion that the constitutional evolution of the Second Empire was toward parliamentary monarchy. See, for instance, Charles Seignobos, *Le Déclin de l'Empire et l'établissement de la IIIe République* (Paris, 1921), Book One, and Félix Ponteil, *Les Institutions de la France de 1814 à 1870* (Paris, 1966), pp. 366-70. However, Theodore Zeldin, in discussing the theory behind the liberal empire, has pointed out that the intent was not, in fact, to establish parliamentary government with the ministry solely responsible to the legislature. The correct

comparison, according to Zeldin, is not with the English constitution of the nineteenth century but with that of the late seventeenth century, when the ministry was responsible both to the king and to parliament; see his *The Political System of Napoleon III* (London, 1958), pp. 151-53.

[63] "Le passé et l'avenir," *Le Pays*, 23 May 1869; *Oeuvres*, I, 43.

[64] *Ibid.*

[65] *J.O. 1876, Ch.D., Débats*, 3770. Session of 1 June 1876.

[66] *Le Pays*, 23 May 1869. See also Cassagnac's letter to the emperor's private secretary of 5 October 1869; *Oeuvres*, I, 60.

[67] *Le Pays*, 1 August 1869.

[68] Napoleon III (ed. Gooch), *Napoleonic Ideas*, p. 75.

[69] Both Zeldin, *Political System of Napoleon III*, pp. 101-2, and John Rothney, *Bonapartism after Sedan* (Ithaca, N.Y., 1969), p. 20, make this point.

[70] Seignobos was most emphatic about this: "As the political education of this generation resulted from parliamentary life, every attempt at liberal reform led to the re-establishment of some practice of the parliamentary regime." *Déclin de l'Empire*, p. 4.

[71] See the remarks of Émile Ollivier in the Corps Législatif, 22 January 1864, when he noted that both the proponents and opponents of the extension of liberties in France invariably invoked the English experience and cited English precedents. *Annales, C.L.*, 1863-64, III, 221.

[72] "Par force!" *Le Pays*, 19 April 1870; *Oeuvres*, I, 87. See also Granier de Cassagnac, *Histoire de la chute du roi*, I, 85: "Although one cannot absolutely insist that the parliamentary regime is impossible in France, experience authorizes us to state that its establishment encounters more difficulties here than elsewhere. Having been tried three times since 1789, it has always led by its own free play to revolution." In addition, see the latter's apologia for the Constitution of 1852, also in *Chute du roi*, II, 451-55.

[73] Louis Andrieux, *Souvenirs d'un prefet de police* (Paris, 1885), II, 136.

[74] "Les deux constitutions," *Le Pays*, 19 April 1870; *Oeuvres*, I, 91.

[75] The correspondent for the London *Times* wrote following Cassagnac's death that the deceased "was delightfully obstinate in his Anglophobia. No power on earth would induce him to say a word in favor of *perfide Albion* . . . ." See the *Sunday Times* (London), 6 November 1904. For samples of Cassagnac's remarks on the English, see "Nos amis les Anglais," *L'Autorité*, 3 July 1892, and "De Français à Anglais," *L'Autorité*, 29 August 1900.

[76] "L'Empire parlementaire," *Le Pays*, 29 March 1868; *Oeuvres*, I, 31.

[77] *Le Pays*, 3 February 1870; *Oeuvres*, I, 80.

[78] "Notre opposition," *Le Pays*, 1 August 1869; *Oeuvres*, I, 53.

[79] Adrien Dansette, "Le rétablissement de l'Empire," *RDM* (15 Sept. 1965), 182.

[80] La Gorce, *Second Empire*, VI (Paris, 1904), 95.

[81] *Le Pays*, 19 April 1870; *Oeuvres*, I, 87.

[82] *Ibid.*

[83] La Gorce, *Second Empire*, VI, 104-5 and 113. See also Jacques Gouault, *Comment la France est devenue républicaine* (Paris, 1954), pp. 25-28, for discussion of the motives that governed the plebiscitary vote.

[84] H. A. L. Fisher, *Bonapartism* (Oxford, 1912), p. 201, expressed doubt that liberalization would have saved the Second Empire; in his opinion, "Bonapartism was a spent force before Count Bismarck changed the Ems telegram." René Rémond, in *La Droite en France: de la première restauration à la Ve République*, 2nd ed. (Paris, 1963), p. 123, estimated that the reconciliation of the liberals, the basis for the parliamentary empire, would not have lasted. Zeldin did not confront this issue directly in either of his books; however, his analysis of how Napoleon III's political system came unstuck in the later 1860s serves to reinforce a pessimistic view.

[85] "Le passé et l'avenir de l'Empire," *Le Pays*, 23 May 1869; *Oeuvres*, I, 40.

[86] Numerous citations from the mid-July 1870 issues of *Le Pays* are quoted in Aimé Dupuy, *1870-1871: la guerre, la commune et la presse* (Paris, 1959), pp. 35-37 and 43. See also Duvall, "Granier de Cassagnac," chapter 7, for details of the Cassagnacs' hawkish journalism.

[87] The War Ministry's written authorization is preserved in the Cassagnac family papers. Paul de Cassagnac had earlier declined a nomination to head the mobile guard unit in Gers so that he might see front-line action in the regular army.

[88] Cassagnac left an amusing account of his experiences on the way to war in a series of newspaper articles, "Souvenirs de 1870," which I found in the Cassagnac papers. I have been unable to account for the place or date of publication of these articles. See also Mitchell's account in Robert Mitchell and Comte [Maurice] Fleury, *Un Demi-siècle de mémoires* (Paris, 1911), chapter 10, and in Mitchell's article in *Le Gaulois*, 6 November 1904.

[89] Cassagnac, "Souvenirs de 1870," 8-18.

[90] See Cassagnac's corrections to the account of Sedan given by Émile Zola in his novel, *La Débâcle*, in *L'Autorité*, 6 September 1892.

[91] Cassagnac, "Souvenirs de 1870," 27-32.

NOTES - CHAPTER III

[1] The classic Right-Left dichotomy, born of the French Revolution and based on conflict over the form of government (Monarchy versus Republic, or as the republicans expressed it after 1879, "reactionary versus republican") gradually disappeared during the Third Republic as the issue of governmental form was superceded by other issues, mostly of a socio-economic nature, and a new generation entered political life. Historians generally agree that the old distinction had little meaning after World War I, although they may disagree on the precise date of its disappearance. Eugen Weber considers 1906 a key date, while Armin Mohler prefers 1917. See the discussion in Weber's two articles, "New Wine in Old Bottles," *FHS*, I (1958), 200-24, and "The Right in France: A Working Hypothesis," *AHR*, LXV (1960), 554-68, and Mohler's book, *Die Französische Rechte: von Kampf um Frankreichs Ideologienpanzer* (Munich, 1958), pp. 15-17. On the revolutionary origins of this dichotomy and its subsequent evolution, see Claude Nicolet, *L'Idée républicaine en France (1789-1924): essai d'histoire critique* (Paris, 1982).

[2] Roger Soltau, *French Political Thought in the 19th Century*, new ed. (New York, 1959), xviii-xxi.

[3] A copy of Cassagnac's electoral manifesto was appended to a police report dated 2 September 1871. A.P.P., B^A 997.

[4] Guy-P. Palmade, "Évolution de l'opinion publique dans le département du Gers de 1848 à 1914" (unpublished D.E.S. mémoire, Faculté des Lettres de Paris, 1949), pp. 26-27. Palmade has pointed to the negative role played by revolutionary tradition in forming the political temperament of Gers and France generally "by contributing to inspire the great fear of the possessors of 1848 before the consequences of the establishment of a democratic republic, judged inevitable by them . . . ."

[5] "Après la guerre," *Le Pays*, 18 October 1871.

[6] *Ibid.*

[7] Paul de Cassagnac, "La République," in *L'Aigle, almanach illustré du suffrage universel* (Paris, 1875), p. 114.

[8] *Le Pays*, 20-21 May 1872.

[9] *Ibid.*

[10] "Le parti Gribouille," *L'Autorité*, 11 February 1892; *Oeuvres*, I, 583. See also *L'Autorité*, 19 August 1888.

[11] See *Le Pays*, 13 January 1877 and 26 January 1878.

[12] See *Le Pays*, 1 January 1879, and *L'Autorité*, 6 June 1886. See also Albert Croquez, *Paul de Cassagnac* (Paris, 1911), p. 32.

[13] Henri Dugué de la Fauconnerie, *Souvenirs d'un vieil homme* (Paris, 1912), p. 72. The original expression appeared in a letter from Voltaire to Saint-Lambert, 7 April 1771, as a comment on Maupeou's abolition of the *parlements*: "I prefer obeying a fine lion, who is born much stronger than I am, to obeying two hundred rats of my own species." The two hundred rats were, of course, the exiled magistrates of Paris. In the Moland edition of Voltaire's *Works*, XLVII, 408.

[14] *Le Pays*, 30 May 1872.

[15] *Le Pays*, 5 November 1873.

[16] Peter Gay, *Voltaire's Politics* (Princeton, 1959), pp. 329-30.

[17] "A propos du scrutin d'arrondissement," *Le Pays*, 15 June 1875; *Oeuvres*, I, 185.

[18] Quoted in *Le Pays*, 8 May 1875.

[19] See *L'Autorité*, 1 and 2 January 1889. Cassagnac's writings and speeches contain no trace of the liberal Christian ethic, of a forgiving God and a self-sacrificing Christ.

[20] *L'Autorité*, 2 January 1889.

[21] *Le Pays*, 1 September 1883; *Oeuvres*, I, 215.

[22] *L'Autorité*, 1 January 1887.

[23] For another expression of the same opinion, by an Orleanist of the Center-Left, see Duc Edme d'Audiffret-Pasquier, "Souvenirs 1871-1873," p. 37; quoted in John Woodall, "The *Ralliement* in France: Origins and Early History, 1876-1894" (unpublished dissertation, Columbia University, 1964), pp. 4-5.

[24] "La Gironde de 1872," *Le Pays*, 21 June 1872.

[25] *J.O. 1889, Ch.D., Débats*, 743. Session of 28 March 1889.

[26] In addition to his *Histoire des causes de la révolution*, and *Histoire des Girondins*, previously cited, Granier de Cassagnac published a *Histoire du Directoire*, 3 vols., new ed. (Paris, 1863). According to his *Souvenirs*, I, 3, the work on the Girondins was intended as a rebuttal to Lamartine's history of the Girondins, while that on the Directory was a reply to Thiers.

[27] See *Le Pays*, 21 June 1872.

[28] "Le radicalisme," *Le Pays*, 13 November 1872.

[29] To Cassagnac, Adolphe Thiers incarnated the Girondin tendency. See his bitter article in *Le Pays*, 6 September 1877. See also his article on E. Vacherot and Jules Simon, the "incorrigible girondins" of 1888, in *L'Autorité*, 9 September 1888. Thiers has finally found his biographer, with J. P. T. Bury and R. P. Tombs, *Thiers 1797-1877: A Political Life* (London, 1986).

[30] It is noteworthy that Paul de Cassagnac never stressed the military guise in which the empire would arrive, although it was an evident part of the Napoleonic tradition. See the program of Cassagnac's departmental paper, *L'Appel au Peuple*, founded in June 1872, and the collection of articles from the

paper's first year by F. Daynaud (with a preface by Paul de Cassagnac), *L'Appel au peuple* (Auch, 1873).

[31] David Thomson, *Democracy in France since 1870*, 4th ed., revised (New York, 1964), pp. 27-35.

[32] *Le Pays*, 26 December 1872; *Oeuvres*, I, 115-16.

[33] *Le Pays*, 16-17 August 1879.

[34] *Le Pays*, 26 February 1878. A characteristic statement of the diametrically opposed liberal view on caesarism can be found in Guido de Ruggiero, *The History of European Liberalism* (Boston, 1959), p. 84: "Caesarism is only a counterfeit democracy, in which the sovereignty of the people conceals their real servitude."

[35] "Qu'est-ce que le Bonapartisme?" *Le Pays*, 20 July 1875; *Oeuvres*, I, 188. See also Paul de Cassagnac, *Empire et royauté* (Paris, 1873), in which the two monarchies are contrasted at length. Cassagnac's view of the rights of the majority was absolute: as he wrote in *Le Pays*, 5 June 1873; *Oeuvres*, I, 125:

> *Nous ne connaissons qu'une base de gouvernement, le nombre, c'est-à-dire la majorité. La majorité a non seulement le droit, mais le devoir de s'imposer à la minorité. Si la France est représentée, par exemple, par le nombre dix, la majorité est six: or, les quatre doivent absolument obéir aux six. Si les quatre sont tranquilles et acceptent la loi du nombre, on les traite avec bienveillance et douceur, mais s'ils se révoltent, on les assomme.*

[36] Cassagnac, *Empire et royauté*, pp. 34-35.

[37] Thomson, *Democracy in France*, pp. 10-13, has noted how "sovereignty of the people" did in fact represent the "essence of the democratic ideal" as put forth by the Revolution of 1789 and "remained the core of the revolutionary tradition." However, Thomson (perhaps in consequence of his British origins) is primarily concerned with its embodiment in an assembly and the working-out of the principle of ministerial responsibility; he never seriously entertains the possibility that "sovereignty of the people" might be equally well represented by the plebiscitary tradition.

[38] *Annales, A.N.*, vols. XX-XXVI inclusive.

[39] Paul de Cassagnac, *Histoire de la Troisième République* (Paris, 1876), p. 1.

[40] *Ibid.*, p. 111.

[41] See Cassagnac's remarks on the campaign of *Paris-Journal* for a legal condemnation, in *Le Pays*, 23 December 1873. Early in 1874 it was rumored that the Bonapartists hoped to precipitate a ministerial crisis by forcing the parliamentary inquiry report to a vote in the Assembly.

[42] *Le Pays*, 2-3 January 1883; *Oeuvres*, V, 22-28.

[43] See the following articles in *Le Pays*: "A Rabagas," 3 March 1872; "Le

menteur," 13 April 1872; "Ce que veut la France," 14 April 1872; "Le Dauphin Rouge," 6 September 1872; and the articles concerning Gambetta's speech at Grenoble in the issues of 1, 2, and 4 October 1872. A new study of Gambetta is J. P. T. Bury, *Gambetta and the Making of the Third Republic* (London, 1973).

[44] "Ave Caesar," *Le Pays*, 24 June 1880; *Oeuvres*, V, 18.

[45] "La réalité," *Le Pays*, 2 October 1872.

[46] See the report dated 31 July 1875 in A.P.P., B[A] 998.

[47] For the text of Gambetta's denunciation, see *Annales, A.N.*, XXXII, 79.

[48] *Le Pays*, 11 June 1874.

[49] *Le Pays*, 12 June 1874.

[50] *Annales, A.N.*, XXXII, 151-56. Session of 9 June 1874. Secondary accounts treating the newspaper suspensions are full of inaccuracies, as for example, Charles Seignobos, *Le Déclin de l'Empire et l'établissement de la IIIe République* (Paris, 1921), p. 383, and Irene Collins, *The Government and the Newspaper Press in France: 1814-1881* (London, 1959), pp. 239-40. Even *L'Année politique--1874* reported erroneously that *La République Française* was one of the suspended papers.

[51] *Journal des Tribunaux*, 2 July 1874.

[52] Cassagnac quoted from Gambetta's speech at Auxerre, printed in *La République Française*, 11 June 1874; from *XIXe Siècle*, 11 and 12 July 1874; and from *Le Rappel* and *Le Patriote Français*.

[53] Sources for the trial of *Le Pays* and its impact on public opinion include *Le Journal des Tribunaux*, 2 July 1874, the article by René de Pont-Just in *Le Gaulois*, 4 July 1874, *Le Pays*, 4 July 1874, and assorted police reports in A.P.P., B[A] 997.

[54] In September 1873 a quiet and ultimately unsuccessful attempt was made to promote Cassagnac's candidacy for a vacant seat from Guadeloupe, where he had family connections through his mother. See *Le Pays*, issues of 9, 11, 16, 18, and 24 September and 17 October 1873. The police agent "Laurent," in a report dated 18 September 1873, commented on the discretion with which the candidacy was being handled, in order to avoid opposition from the Bonapartist party hierarchy. A.P.P., B[A] 997.

[55] "L'anniversaire," *Le Pays*, 3 December 1872; "Les coups d'état," *Le Pays*, 7 January 1874. The latter article, reprinted in Cassagnac's almanac, *L'Aigle*, for 1875, pp. 98-102, provoked the seizure of the entire printing by the police; it was deleted in successive editions.

[56] *Le Pays*, 7 January 1874.

[57] *Le Procès de Belleville: 13 Décembre 1875* (Paris, 1875), pp. 1-20.

[58] Quoted in *Le Pays*, 14 January 1877. Several republican deputies had proposed that prosecution be instigated against the co-authors and accomplices of the *coup* of 2 December. In March 1877, however, the committee of the

Chamber appointed to consider the proposal reluctantly recommended against its being brought to the floor for debate. See their report of 20 March 1877 in *Annales, Sénat et Ch.D., 1877*, vol. II, *Documents*, 523, annex no. 856.

[59] "Bandit et lâche!" *Le Pays*, 28 May 1872.

[60] *Le Pays*, 3 June 1872. On the trial and incarceration of the two journalists, see *Le Temps* and *Le Gaulois* for 4 July 1872, *Le Pays* and *Le Figaro* for 16 July 1872, and *L'Ordre* and *Journal de Paris* for 17 July 1872, and occasional reports in A.P.P., B^A 997.

[61] Among them, A. Granier de Cassagnac (with the collaboration of Napoleon III), *A Chacun sa part dans nos désastres: Sedan, ses causes et ses suites* (Paris, 1871). See also his *Souvenirs du Second Empire*, III, 193-273, where Granier de Cassagnac reprinted the text of this pamphlet, providing also the corrections made in his original text by the emperor.

[62] *Le Pays*, 12 August 1874.

[63] *Le Pays*, 18 August 1874.

[64] Gal E.-F. de Wimpffen, *Sedan* (Paris, 1871) and *Réponse au général Ducrot* (Paris, 1871); Gal A.-A. Ducrot, *La Journée de Sedan* (Paris, 1871). See also the testimony of the two generals before the inquiry committee of the National Assembly, concerning the events of 4 September 1870.

[65] The account of the Sedan trial was published in two popular editions, one featuring a cover photograph of Paul de Cassagnac in the uniform of a *zouave* (see illustration, this chapter, p. 46 above). See *La Journée de Sedan devant la Cour d'Assises de la Seine -- Procès Paul de Cassagnac* (Paris, 1875), and *Le Procès de Sedan* (Paris, 1875).

[66] "Fidus," *Journal*, I, 310.

[67] Granier de Cassagnac had addressed this issue directly in his pamphlet, *A chacun sa part* (see his *Souvenirs*, III, 237-40). He criticized the emperor for abandoning command of the army and voluntarily effacing himself before the desires of the ministry from 27 August on.

[68] "Question personnelle," *Le Pays*, 23 September 1874. Cassagnac's attacks, which appeared originally in *L'Appel au Peuple* (Auch), were directed principally against Victor Luro, who had been one of the most outspoken advocates of the constitution of 1875. In fact Luro was the only one of the six deputies from Gers to vote *for* both the Wallon amendment and the constitutional law of February 1875. Lacave-Laplagne voted against the Wallon amendment and abstained on the law of 25 February, while the other four deputies, Batbie, Dumon, Abbadie de Barrau and Résseguier, voted *against* both proposals. See Jacques Gouault, *Comment la France est devenue républicaine* (Paris, 1954), p. 210.

[69] Reported by "6," 11 September 1875. A.P.P., B^A 998. At the time, the system of election was still the *scrutin de liste*, and the prefect's figures were based on an all-departmental vote.

[70] *Le Pays*, 2-3 January 1876. According to police sources, Cassagnac had wanted to run in the 8th arrondissement of Paris, but Rouher had flatly opposed it. "39," 22 December 1875. A.P.P., B^A 998.

[71] Palmade, "Évolution de l'opinion," 129-31.

[72] A Gers royalist, A. de Thézan, published a reply to Cassagnac's electoral pamphlet, entitled *Réponse à la Revanche de M. P. de Cassagnac. La dynastie napoléonienne et la moralité de ses oeuvres* (Auch, 1875). Thézan was particularly annoyed by Cassagnac's caricature of the royalist as badly educated, sporting a fake title, highly unpopular, and opposed to universal suffrage. He cast opprobrium on the purity of the young imperialist by pointing to past bad behavior of representatives of the Bonaparte dynasty.

[73] Palmade, "Évolution de l'opinion," 128-32. Palmade qualified these results as the "first faithful image of the state of opinion since 1869." The legitimists attracted 9 per cent of the vote. The deputies elected in the other four constituencies of Gers were: for Mirande, Granier de Cassagnac; for Auch, Jules Peyrusse (whose election against Jean David would be invalidated twice); for Lombez, Justin-François Faure, a Center-Right candidate; and for Lectoure, Albert Descamps, the only successful republican.

[74] The figures quoted for Paul de Cassagnac's election are the official tallies, taken from the report of the Chamber election committee. *J. O. 1876, Ch.D., Débats*, 1700. Session of 10 March 1876. Of the 7914 votes cast for Cassagnac's opponents, Lacroix received 6907, and Cugnac 1007.

[75] Condom police commissioner to Prefect (Gers), 24 February 1876. Weekly reports of police commissioners, A.D. Gers, M 2237.

[76] Reports of "6," 22 and 23 February 1876. A.P.P., B^A 998.

[77] *Le Figaro*, 17 March 1876.

[78] See Cassagnac's reply to Clemenceau's seconds, "A MM. Testelin et Schoelcher," *Le Pays*, 13 June 1874. See Chapter VII for further discussion of Clemenceau.

[79] *Le Pays*, 14 May 1876.

[80] Standard electoral studies credit the Bonapartists with 75 deputies in the legislature of 1876-1877. See François Goguel, *Géographie des élections françaises de 1870 à 1951* (Paris, 1951), and A. Bomier-Landowski, "Les groupes parlementaires de l'Assemblée Nationale et de la Chambre des Députés de 1870 à 1940," in François Goguel and Georges Dupeux, eds., *Sociologie électorale* (Paris, 1951).

This was the official membership of the group *Appel au peuple*. However, in scrutinizing the list of voters in the divisive vote of 20 June 1877, where 363 republicans opposed 158 monarchists, it is possible to identify 83 of the 158 as Bonapartists of various nuances. In addition to these 83, four other known Bonapartist deputies did not vote: Janvier de la Motte *père*, Edgard Raoul-Duval, Charles Levert, and Baron René Reille. This number does not, of course, include Prince Napoleon, who voted with the 363. Thus there are 87 identifiable partisans of the empire in this Chamber, as compared with a maximum number of 32 in the National Assembly.

[81] See also the far more hostile description of the newly-elected militants of imperialism by Emmanuel Beau de Loménie, *Les responsabilités des dynasties bourgeoises*, I (Paris, 1943), 286-87.

[82] Gustave Cunéo d'Ornano (1845-1906) was a grandson of a companion-in-arms of Napoleon I, who followed the Bonaparte family into exile in Rome after 1815. Cunéo d'Ornano studied law and was a member of the bar in Paris. After 1870 he pursued a career in journalism, first with Robert Mitchell at *Le Courrier de France*, then with *La Presse*. In 1875, he founded *Le Suffrage universel des Charentes* in Angoulême, and served as a deputy for Charente from 1876 until his death. On his career, see Pierre de Cinglais, *Gustave Cunéo d'Ornano, 1845-1906* (Cognac, 1908).

[83] See the article "Du tapage," *Le Siècle*, 9 July 1876, in which republican deputies were counseled not to respond to the "provocations" of the imperialists. Another writer identified these young imperialists with the young patricians of fifth-century Rome; see Félicien Champsaur and Alfred Le Petit, *Les Contemporains, journal hebdomadaire, no. 26 -- Paul de Cassagnac* (Paris, 1881), 2-3.

[84] *Annales, Sénat et Ch.D., 1876*, III, Ch.D., Débats, 212-13, session of 3 July 1876, and VI, 408, session of 24 November 1874. See also *Le Pays*, 5 July and 26 November 1876.

[85] *Le Pays*, 18 January 1877.

[86] After the June incidents, the editor of *L'Année politique--1877* wrote (pp. 186-87) that "Cassagnac seems to have given himself the mission of rendering debate impossible," and remarked that the fiery young deputy's behavior had even scandalized the Bonapartist notables. See also the vivid resumé of these sessions by Gabriel Hanotaux, *Histoire de la France contemporaine* (Paris, 1903-1908), IV, 28-41, and the reports of police agents "Bonap" and "Grégoire" in A.P.P., B^A 998 and B^A 1257. J.-A. Garnier has left history a striking portrait of these session with his much reproduced painting, "Le voilà, le libérateur du territoire, 16 Juin 1877" (see the illustration, Chapter V, p. 96).

In an effort to end the imperialist disruptions, the republican majority in the subsequent Chamber strengthened house rules on internal discipline, by reinstituting for use by its president the penalties (fines and sanctions) that had been in force during the National Assemblies of 1849-1851 and 1871-1875. See the report of the rules committee, presented to the Chamber on 13 November 1877; see also Cassagnac's remarks to the effect that it was the republicans who provoked disorder by their continual insults to the empire and other former monarchies. He pledged once again to enforce respect of monarchist opinions "by all the means at our disposal!" *J.O. 1877, Ch.D., Débats*, pp. 7375-77. The change was nevertheless enacted, by a vote of 304 to 38, with 182 deputies abstaining.

[87] Cassagnac's nickname was a wordplay on the title of a well-known novel by Théophile Gautier, *Le Capitaine Fracasse*, published originally in 1863, but again serialized in the Bonapartist paper, *L'Ordre*, during late 1875. One police agent reported the rumor that Cassagnac had in fact written the novel. See "4," 28 August 1876, A.P.P., B[A] 998. The imaginative connection between the chevalresque Gascon of the novel and the chevalresque Gascon deputy was certainly not difficult to make. For the anguished objections of the liberal Bonapartist deputy Raoul-Duval (of which more in Chapter IV), see John Rothney, *Bonapartism after Sedan* (Ithaca, N.Y., 1969), p. 246.

[88] From an article, "De l'audace," published in *Les Droits de l'homme*, and reprinted in *Le Pays*, 3 August 1876.

[89] "P," 4 September 1876, in A.P.P., B[A] 998.

[90] See Cassagnac's speech in the Chamber of Deputies, 16 March 1877.

[91] "La vérité," *Le Pays*, 11 May 1875; *Oeuvres*, I, 174-75.

[92] In surveying Cassagnac's many articles in *Le Pays*, I have not found the term *la gueuse* used in print prior to the issue of 19 January 1883. However, the idea of the republic as a woman of easy virtue, the familiar (and sometimes voracious) "Marianne," appeared in earlier articles, as in the issues of 11 May 1875, 14 November 1879, and 25 September 1880. On the imagery of Marianne and the republic, see the studies by Maurice Agulhon, *Marianne into Battle: Republican Imagery and Symbolism in France, 1789-1880*, transl. from the French by Janet Lloyd (London, 1981; originally published in Paris, 1979), and *Marianne au pouvoir: l'imagerie et la symbolique républicaines de 1880 à 1914* (Paris, 1989).

[93] See *Le Pays*, 1 November 1876 and 25 January 1877.

[94] On the state of press legislation between 1871 and 1881, see Henri Avenel, *Histoire de la presse française* (Paris, 1900), pp. 710-14, and Raymond Manévy, *La presse de la IIIe République* (Paris, 1955), pp. 23-27.

[95] Avenel, *Histoire de la presse*, p. 710-11.

[96] *L'Année politique--1875*, p. 327.

[97] *Procès de Belleville*, p. 21.

[98] *Ibid.*, p. 11. Some republicans liked the *procureur*'s speech so well, reported the police agent "Howe," that they were planning to reproduce it for distribution in the provinces. Report dated 13 December 1875, A.P.P., B[A] 998. This dossier also contains a number of other useful reports on Cassagnac's speech and trial.

[99] See the correspondence concerning *Le Pays* between Dufaure, the Minister of Justice and Premier Ministre, and his Minister of the Interior, Marcère, in A.N., F[18] 400.

[100] *Annales, Sénat et Ch.D., 1877*, vol. 1[1], Ch.D., Débats, 227. Session of 5 February 1877.

[101] Letter from the *procureur-général* to the Chamber of Deputies, requesting authorization to prosecute a deputy, dated 21 February 1877. Quoted in *Le Pays*, 28 February 1877.

[102] *J.O. 1877, Ch.D., Débats*, p. 2029. Session of 16 March 1877. See also Cassagnac's previous speeches at Belleville, 29 November 1875, and in the Chamber, 7 July 1876.

[103] *Le Droit, Journal des Tribunaux*, 22 April 1877.

[104] The fine handed down by the Assize Court was 2000 francs. However, Cassagnac's penalty in an earlier trial before the correctional court, 3000 francs, was added to that of Assizes, raising the total to 5000 francs.

[105] "Ma liquidation," *Le Pays*, 27 April 1877.

[106] *Le Pays*, 10 May 1879; *Oeuvres*, IV, 82. See also *Le Pays*, 24 May 1879.

[107] See the second part of Cassagnac's speech of 9 June 1879, and also "Les outrages," *Le Pays*, 27 May 1879.

[108] *Le Temps*, 4 and 5 July 1879; *Le Pays*, 4, 5, and 6 July 1879. I have also consulted the reports on this trial in A.P.P., B[A] 999.

[109] In a letter addressed to Cassagnac by Georges Lachaud and published in *Le Pays*, 2-3 January 1878.

NOTES - CHAPTER IV

[1] The closest any historian has come is the work of John Rothney, *Bonapartism after Sedan* (Ithaca, N.Y., 1969). This study, however, best reflects the perspectives of its two chief characters, Baron Eschasseriaux, a dynastic Bonapartist, and Edgard Raoul-Duval, who was an anomaly in the party. I will take up the case of Raoul-Duval later in this chapter. Pierre Albert has studied the Bonapartist press as part of his *doctorat d'état*, and has been generous in sharing information he has collected. His thesis has since been completed: *Histoire de la presse politique nationale au début de la Troisième République, 1871-1879*, 2 vols., thèse de doctorat, Université de Paris IV, 1977.

Until such time as a comprehensive study of Bonapartist politics has been written, one must rely on these works and on incomplete gleanings from the press and pamphlet literature of the era, the vast collection of dossiers in the archives of the Paris Prefecture of Police, and the several published accounts by contemporaries such as Jules Richard and "Fidus."

[2] As in Gabriel Hanotaux, *Histoire de la France contemporaine*, I (Paris, 1903), I, 531, and III (Paris, 1906), 134, and more recently in René Rémond, *La Droite en France*, 2nd ed. (Paris, 1963), pp. 105-8. However, Rothney in *Bonapartism after Sedan* (pp. 22-35) prefers a multiple classification based on metaphors of the Revolutionary hemicycle, "Mountain," "Plain," and "Coblenz." He has thereby misconstrued Cassagnac as the leader of an ultra-dynastic, neo-legitimist group of Bonapartists of the "Coblence," a designation that fits poorly with the evidence I have assembled.

[3] On the complex nature of the Napoleonic legacy, the legend that grew from it, the various interpretations and representations it has engendered, and the enthusiasms it has inspired, see Albert Guérard, *Reflections on the Napoleonic Legend* (New York, 1924); Jules-Albert Dechamps, *Sur la légende de Napoléon* (Paris, 1931); Pieter Geyl, *Napoleon: For and Against* (New Haven, Conn., 1963); Maurice Descotes, *La Légende de Napoléon et les écrivains français du XIXe siècle* (Paris, 1967); Jean Tulard, *Le Mythe de Napoléon* (Paris, 1971); Frédéric Bluche, *Le Bonapartisme: aux origines de la droite autoritaire, 1800-1850* (Paris, 1980); and Bernard Ménager, *Les Napoléon du peuple* (Paris, 1988).

On the constitutional theory of the empire, see especially Maurice Flory, "L'Appel au peuple napoléonien," *Revue internationale d'histoire politique et constitutionnel*, n.s. II (1952), 215-22; and Marcel Prélot, "La signification constitutionnelle du Second Empire," *Revue française de science politique*, III (1953), 31-56.

[4] See the discussion between Cassagnac and Girardin in *Le Pays*, 3 April and 8 May 1875.

[5] *Le Pays*, 6 May 1875; *Oeuvres*, I, 153.

[6] *Ibid.*

[7] *Le Pays*, 29 July 1872. See also the issue of 26 February 1878.

[8] "Post-scriptum," *Le Pays*, 3 December 1872; *Oeuvres*, I, 111.

[9] "Explications," *Le Pays*, 1 July 1873; *Oeuvres*, I, 133-34.

[10] For example, Baron de Mackau, who had served Prince Napoleon as *chef de cabinet* during the Italian campaigns, qualified him as "*un grossier personnage -- mal élevé -- radical et en même temps autoritaire comme beaucoup de radicaux.*" Mss. memoirs, A.N., 156 API, carton 66. During the decade of the 1870s, the wealthy Maurice Richard appeared to be virtually the only confessed admirer of Prince Napoleon.

[11] Historians of the Third Republic are prone to overrate the importance of Prince Napoleon for Bonapartist politics in the 1870s because of his increased importance following the untimely death of the Prince Imperial in 1879. See, for example, Jacques Chastenet, *Histoire de la Troisième République*, vol. I (Paris, 1952), 337. For Rothney's appreciation of the prince, see *Bonapartism after Sedan*, pp. 270-75.

[12] The well-known remark, "*Le voilà, le César déclassé!*" was made by Edmond About *à propos* a portrait of the prince exhibited in the Salon of 1861. See Paul Lenglé, *Le Neveu de Bonaparte* (Paris, 1893), p. 2.

[13] *Le Pays*, 19 October 1869; *Oeuvres*, I, 64.

[14] *Le Pays*, 1 July 1873.

[15] Daniel Halévy, *La République des ducs* (Paris, 1937), p. 90.

[16] Thiers' prior concern for form over person is discussed by Emmanuel Beau de Loménie, *Les Résponsabilités des dynasties bourgeoises*, I (Paris, 1943), 199.

[17] Cassagnac first replied to Bonapartist accusations on this count in *Le Pays*, 1 July 1873. See also Rémond, *La Droite en France*, p. 152.

[18] See the deposition of the prefect of Nièvre before the electoral inquiry committee of the Assembly. *Annales, A.N.*, XL, 20(annex), 29 January 1875.

[19] *Le Pays*, 2 February 1874.

[20] Eugène Rouher (1814) entered political life after a distinguished career as a provincial attorney. He was a deputy, 1848-1851, minister of justice from 1849-1851 under Louis-Napoleon, and party to plans for the *coup d'état*. During the Second Empire he held various ministries. As minister of agriculture and commerce, he was instrumental in negotiating free-trade treaties with England (1860) and with Belgium and Italy. As minister of State from 1863 to 1869, he defended the emperor's policies, both foreign and domestic,

before the Corps Législatif, earning the sobriquet "vice-emperor" from Émile Ollivier. Following the liberal victory in the elections of 1869, he was named president of the Senate and served in that position until the fall of the regime in 1870. He was elected to the National Assembly in 1872 and to the Chamber of Deputies, where he served until 1881. For an admirable study of Rouher's career, see Robert Schnerb, *Rouher et le Second Empire* (Paris, 1949).

[21] P.-C. Latour du Moulin, *La France et le Septennat* (Paris, 1874), p. 34.

[22] Rémond, *La Droite en France*, p. 152, pointed out the common hostility toward Orleanism shared by legitimists and Bonapartists alike, but in so doing he overlooked the difference in views that separated a Rouher from a Cassagnac.

[23] Schnerb, *Rouher*, p. 311.

[24] See Cassagnac's objections to Rouher's exclusion of the party journalists in "Écrivains et députés," *Le Pays*, 3 August 1873. See also Jules Richard, *Le Bonapartisme sous la République*, 2nd ed. (Paris, 1883), pp. 112-13, for confirmation.

[25] Various police reporters attributed Rouher's animosity toward Cassagnac to an incident that occurred during the 1860s, when Cassagnac was alleged to have seduced Rouher's elder daughter, later Mme Welles de La Valette. See the reports of "Bonap(PM)," 4 April 1877; "Im(PM)," 17 May 1877; and "Lomb," 2 August 1877, all in A.P.P., B[A] 998. Another agent, writing in 1884, reported rumors that Cassagnac had continued relations with Mme Welles de La Valette, citing as proof a suspicious resemblance between the La Valette children and the journalist. See "Wilfred (PM)," 4 July 1884, A.P.P., B[A] 1000.

[26] "La France d'abord," *Le Pays*, 7 December 1873.

[27] *Le Pays*, 7 May 1878.

[28] *Le Pays*, 6 May 1875; *Oeuvres*, I, 160.

[29] *Le Pays*, 11 May 1875; *Oeuvres*, I, 175.

[30] *Le Pays*, 1 July 1873. In addition to those who were chronologically young, Cassagnac designated the following eminent members of the former imperial administration and magistracy, all part of the older generation, as worthy of inclusion among *les jeunes*: Ernest Pinard, Michael Grandperret, Baron de Saint-Paul, Alexandre de Bosredon, Eugène Jolibois, Simon-Maximilien Genteur, the Marquis de La Valette, Colonel Stoffel, and Jean Boffinton. See *Le Pays*, 3 July 1873. Of these men, only two, Pinard and Grandperret, were members of Rouher's advisory committee. The remaining members of this committee (in 1873), were, besides Rouher, the deputies Augustin Gavini, Charles Levert, Baron Eschasseriaux, Prince Joachim Murat, and Alfred Haentjens; the former prefect of police Joanchim Pietri, and Henri Chevreau, the Duc de Padoue (Arrighi de Casanova), General Fleury, the Comte de Casabianca, the Comte de Cambacérès, Jean Forcade-LaRoquette,

and General Palikao. From the deposition of Léon Renault before the parliamentary committee investigating Bonapartist activities, late February 1875. *Annales, A.N.*, XXXVII, 271. As is evident, the central committee was heavily loaded with Corsicans and old Bonaparte family members and friends, to the exclusion of talented servants of the Second Empire.

[31] *Le Pays*, 1 December 1873.

[32] See Suzanne Desternes and Henriette Chandet, *Louis, Prince Imperial* (Paris, 1957), part II, "La douleureuse jeunesse." However, the Prince Imperial's tutor, Augustin Filon, argues that Eugenie effectively stepped aside after the young prince attained his majority in 1874. See his *Souvenirs sur l'Impératrice Eugénie* (Paris, 1920), pp. 297-302.

[33] According to Harold Kurtz, *The Empress Eugenie, 1826-1920* (Boston, 1964), the ultra-clerical image of the empress was the fabrication of Madame Walewska. On Cassagnac's championing of the empress, see Chapter I.

[34] According to the papers seized during the judicial investigation of the Nièvre election (later made public by the parliamentary inquiry committee), only *L'Ordre* and various provincial newspapers were subsidized directly by Rouher's funds. *Annales, A.N.*, XL, section III. Various reports by agent "P" indicate that Cassagnac's *Le Pays* may have received direct subsidies of 10,000 - 12,000 francs yearly from the empress. See the reports dated 7 December 1875, 4 April and 3 June 1876, in A.P.P., B[A] 998, and 16 April 1878, B[A] 999. See also the report of "Brissaud," 17 November 1879, in B[A] 1094.

[35] One of the most damning indictments of Rouher's leadership was the pamphlet signed by "un conservateur," *Le Parti Bonapartiste et ses hommes* (Paris, 1875). From 1873 on, however, the police files are full of reports attesting to dissatisfaction with Rouher's guidance; the reports of "Bonap," who covered the "beat" of the Burgraves, are particularly informative. See A.P.P., B[A] 417 through 419, B[A] 998, and B[A] 1257.

[36] Cassagnac elaborated on the elements of "natural sympathy" that underlay this alliance in *Le Pays*, 8 March 1877. For its earlier expression, see "Fidus," *Journal de dix ans* (Paris, 1886), I, 114, and police reports such as the unsigned report of 4 September 1872, in A.P.P., B[A] 997.

[37] Rémond, *La Droite en France*, pp. 151-52, has pointed to this kinship in ideas. For a closer look at the ideas of the legitimists, see the dissertation by Bobby R. Locke, "The Legitimists: A Study in Social Mentality. The Royalist Right in the French National Assembly of 1871" (unpublished doctoral dissertation, University of California at Los Angeles, 1965), and his subsequent book, Robert R. Locke, *French Legitimists and the Politics of Moral Order in the Early Third Republic* (Princeton, N.J., 1974).

David Pinkney's survey of the actual changes in high government personnel brought about by the "revolution" of 1830 suggests that the essential change effected was the return of the personnel of the First Empire, not the mythic triumph of the liberal bourgeoisie. See David H. Pinkney, "The Myth of the French Revolution of 1830," in *A Festschrift for Frederick B. Artz*, ed. David H. Pinkney and Theodore Ropp (Durham, N.C., 1964), pp. 52-71. Thus, even the personnel underpinnings of the July Monarchy might be considered "imperialist." Pinkney's finding reveals the source, in an earlier period, of the close kinship and empathy that underlay the superficial political division between the moderate royalists (of both nuances) and the imperialists of the 1870s. They agreed on the system, but not on who should head it. It might then be argued that this "conservative alliance" of the 1870s was the final manifestation of the alliance that had backed Guizot and, subsequently, the party of order of 1848-1849.

[38] Pierre de Coubertin, *L'Évolution française sous la Troisième République* (Paris, 1896), xvii-xviii.

[39] According to "Fidus," (*Journal*, I, 32, 140-41, 151-52, 175-82, 184-85), this idea originated with Pope Pius IX who, as the godfather of the Prince Imperial, had suggested it to Chambord as a way of circumventing the house of Orleans. Following the death of Napoleon III, the project gathered considerable support in certain Parisian monarchist circles, but Chambord scotched the idea by refusing to disinherit his cousins.

A complementary version of the story, evidently authoritative, appeared in Comte René Monti de Rezé, *Souvenirs sur le comte de Chambord* (Paris, 1930), pp. 86-88. According to this writer, Isabelle de Bourbon attempted to serve as the intermediary, on behalf of Eugénie and the Prince Imperial. Chambord declined on the grounds that his principles did not allow him to choose his successor (in defiance of lineage).

This aborted adoption project, though neglected in recent studies, nevertheless lends added meaning to the Prince Imperial's subsequent "disinheritance" of Prince Napoleon in favor of his more politically-acceptable son, Prince Victor. See Chapter VI.

[40] Albert de Broglie, "Mémoires," *RDM* (15 October 1929), 810-11. Another excellent statement of Broglie's position is found in his speech of 15 November 1877 before the Chamber. *Annales, Sénat et Ch.D.*, 1877, vol. I², Ch.D., Débats, 153-54. On Broglie, see especially Charles Alan Grubb, "The Politics of Pessimism: A Political biography of Duc Albert de Broglie during the Early Third Republic, 1871-1885," unpublished doctoral dissertation, Columbia University, 1969.

[41] *Le Pays*, 29 April 1883.

[42] This charge provided a useful weapon not only to Thiers, who employed it (unsuccessfully) in attempting to split the majority of 24 May 1873, but especially to the republicans, following the Nièvre election; see Gambetta's accusations, directed at the ministries of Broglie and Buffet, of being "soft" on Bonapartism, in the Assembly during 1874-1875.

[43] See Jacques Droz et al., *Restaurations et révolutions* (Paris, 1953), p. 123.

[44] For example, Dupanloup's *Avertissement à la jeunesse et aux pères de famille* (Paris, 1863); *L'Athéisme et le péril social* (Paris, 1866); and *La Liberté de l'enseignement supérieur* (Paris, 1868).

[45] *Le Pays*, 12 June 1872. Such extravagant language was not uncommon; see the discussion in Martin R. Waldman, "The Revolutionary as Criminal in 19th Century France: A Study of the Communards and Deportés," *Science and Society*, XXXVII (1973), 31-55.

[46] *Ibid.*; *Oeuvres*, I, 293-99. The ensuing quotations are all taken from this article.

[47] See Rothney, *Bonapartism after Sedan*, pp. 115-16. One police agent was certain that a condition of the pact was a promise by the legitimists to support the Bonapartists' call for a plebiscite following the evacuation of Prussian troops. "Brissaud," 12 December 1872, A.P.P., B^A 1257. I have found no evidence that would either support or refute such a claim.

[48] See the reports of "Laurent," dated 13 and 27 December 1872 and 3 January 1873, in A.P.P., B^A 1257 and B^A 997, as well as the several reports on Cassagnac's trip in B^A 997. See also *Le Pays*, 16 December 1872 and 7 January 1873.

[49] "L'alliance conservatrice," *Le Pays*, 23 March 1873.

[50] *Le Pays*, issues of 12 through 21 April 1873; report by "CB" on the conservative gathering, 19 April 1873, in A.P.P., B^A 997. See also the various reports in B^A 1257 on Rouher's displeasure with this "conservative" candidacy, and Richard, *Bonapartisme*, pp. 105-7, who echoed Rouher's opinion that "the party of *Appel au peuple* had lost much of its originality and power" in the episode.

[51] Jacques Gouault, *Comment la France est devenue républicaine* (Paris, 1954), pp. 152-55. Gouault has also pointed out (p. 167) that only *after* the Basrodet-Rémusat contest in April 1873 did the republicans themselves unite behind a single candidate in by-elections. This leads one to ponder how history might have been changed, had the conservatives succeeded in achieving an electoral alliance and consistently enforcing it against the republicans during these years.

[52] "La chute de M. Thiers," *Le Pays*, 26 May 1873; *Oeuvres*, I, 304-5.

[53] "Les deux politiques," *Le Pays*, 5 June 1873; *Oeuvres*, I, 119-27.

[54] *Ibid.*

[55] Duruy's article was reprinted in Cassagnac's *Oeuvres*, I, 122-23. The remaining quotations in this section are all from the article, "Les deux politiques," cited above.

[56] See Emmanuel Beau de Loménie, *La Restauration manquée; l'affaire du drapeau blanc* (Paris, 1932).

[57] *Annales, A.N.*, XXVII, 194-96. Session of 19 November 1873.

[58] *Le Figaro*, 2 June 1873; *Le Pays*, issues of 9, 11, 16, and 18 September 1873.

[59] *Le Pays*, 22 and 30 November 1873.

[60] *Le Pays*, 30 November 1873.

[61] *Ibid.*

[62] *Le Pays*, 28 September and 4 October 1873.

[63] See *Le Pays*, 11 July 1874, where Cassagnac praised the president's message to the Assembly, requesting it to proceed with the organization of public powers. In Bonapartist circles, pessimism began to mount at that point about what aid the president might give to a future imperial restoration. Some, such as Loudun, were pressing for an immediate *coup*. See "Fidus," *Journal*, I, 290-93.

[64] Cited in *Le Pays*, 2 February 1874.

[65] See *Le Pays*, 23 September 1874; *Oeuvres*, I, 147-52.

[66] See the article by Marius Sapin in *La Presse*, reprinted in *Le Pays*, 17 May 1874. Numerous police reports attesting to Cassagnac's low status in the party at that time can be found in A.P.P., B^A 998.

[67] See Ernest Dréolle, *Napoléon IV. 1856-1873. Souvenir de Chislehurst* (Paris, 1873). For a full description of the festivities at the prince's coming-of-age celebration at Chislehurst, see André Martinet, *Le Prince impérial* (Paris, 1895). According to Martinet (p. 223), the empress objected to her son being referred to as Napoleon IV; she insisted that only the French people could confer the crown.

[68] Cassagnac did his best to underscore this point in *Le Pays*, 25-26 May 1874. On this supremely significant election and its aftermath, see Gouault, *Comment la France*, pp. 180-82.

[69] See Chapter III, above.

[70] The charge was possible violation of the association laws. The *procureur-général* concluded in December 1874 that no violation existed and this led the republicans to demand a full-scale investigation by the Assembly. Testimony of various officials before a 15-man committee and the supporting documents were published during the spring and summer of 1875. These provide a valuable repository of information concerning the Bonapartist party in 1874. See *Annales, A.N.*, XXXVII, annex no. 2910, pp. 242-375, and LX, annex no. 3087, pp. 3-386.

[71] *Le Pays*, 7 November 1874.

[72] Latour du Moulin, *France et le Septennat*, p. 34. See also A.P.P., B^A 998, especially the report of "4," 27 November 1874.

[73] *Ibid.*, p. 33.

[74] Léon Gambetta, *Lettres de Gambetta*, ed. Daniel Halévy and Émile Pillias (Paris, 1938), letter no. 193, 26 May 1874.

[75] *Le Pays*, 2 March 1875.

[76] By far the best account of the politics of January-February 1875 is the chapter, "La République fondée," in Hanotaux, *Histoire de la France contemporaine*, III. See also *L'Année politique--1875*, pp. 60-61.

[77] "Enfin!" *Le Pays*, 12 March 1875.

[78] See, for example, "Fidus," *Journal*, I, 238-39 and 293-95. Skeptical about the *Septennat* from the outset, "Fidus" reported that severe disillusionment with Mac-Mahon was already well-developed by the later months of 1874.

[79] *L'Année politique--1875*, p. 77.

[80] Edgard-Raoul Duval, called Raoul-Duval (1832-1887), had been active in the provincial magistracy during the Second Empire, notably at Rouen. He was a deputy in the National Assembly, 1871-1875, and in the Chamber of Deputies, 1876-1766 and 1884-1887. From October 1876 to May 1877, he published *La Nation*, a liberal Bonapartist newspaper. The most complete biography of Raoul-Duval was written by his son and published as an introduction to *Gustave Flaubert. Lettres inédits à Raoul-Duval*, ed. Georges Normandy (Paris, 1950), pp. 1-91. Rothney, *Bonapartism after Sedan*, has drawn on Raoul-Duval's private papers; see especially pp. 232-48. See also J. Valynseele, "Deux personalités protestantes sous la Troisième République: Edgar Raoul-Duval et Léon Say," *Bulletin de la Société de l'histoire du protestantisme français*, CXVII (1971), 214-29.

[81] See the reserved approval of Raoul-Duval's capacities in Richard, *Bonapartisme*, pp. 148-49.

[82] "M. Raoul Duval," *Le Pays*, 16 January 1877.

[83] In a letter to his wife during the summer of 1876. Quoted by Rothney, *Bonapartism after Sedan*, p. 246.

[84] *Le Pays*, 19, 20 and 21 November 1875. Although Cassagnac, like his radical republican antagonists, opposed second chambers in principle (in *Le Pays*, 20 March 1874, he termed the notion "completely baroque") and spoke out against Broglie's Senate proposal in *Le Pays* (17 May 1874), he thought the Bonapartist party would do better to join in the scramble for life senators than to stand aloof on principle.

[85] See Hanotaux, *Histoire de la France contemporaine*, III, 461.

[86] *Le Pays*, 2 December 1875. *Le Figaro* had also been advocating conservative alliance for the elections to the Chamber, but with the inclusion of "moderate" republicans in an alliance against "Thierists, Gambettists, and Intransigents." Raoul-Duval's initiative gave the other conservatives ample excuse not to conclude an alliance with any imperialists: as the columnist "Saint-Genest" wrote in *Le Figaro* in early January 1876, "What guarantee can [Cassagnac] give us that those deputies of his party, newly elected with the government's protection, would support the marshal and won't go off to rejoin

Rouher?" Quoted in *Le Pays*, 8 January 1876.

[87] This argument, used by Raoul-Duval and others, is accepted uncritically by Rothney, *Bonapartism after Sedan*, pp. 201, 228-29, 242, 250, and 263. Consequently, his lengthy interpretation of the 1876 elections reflects an orientation that no conservative imperialist would have accepted. There were, however, Bonapartists who opposed the conservative alliance and, like Raoul-Duval, argued in favor of a legislative plebiscite; see, for example, F. Perron, *Le Reveil de la France* (Paris, 1875), and, subsequently, Georges Lachaud, *Les Bonapartistes et la république* (Paris, 1877), pp. 46-48.

[88] In April 1869, Gambetta himself had publicly advocated ratification of regimes by plebiscite in a speech before the Corps Législatif. In later years, this speech was often singled out by the Bonapartists: see, for example, Jolibois's speech in the Chamber on 30 March 1888, and the brochure by Gustave Cunéo d'Ornano, *Gambetta plébiscitaire* (Paris, 1895).

[89] *Le Pays*, 1 April 1874.

[90] See Cassagnac's much later articles on this point in *L'Autorité*, 27 July and 4 August 1886, which can be contrasted with the arguments employed by *L'Année politique -- 1886*, p. 206.

[91] *Le Pays*, 13 June 1875.

[92] Georges Wormser, *Gambetta dans les tempêtes* (Paris, 1964), pp. 184-86.

[93] "Les deux scrutins," *Le Pays*, 26 April 1874. See also his lengthy debate with Girardin on the subject of voting systems a few weeks earlier. *Le Pays*, issues of 10 through 13 April 1874.

[94] *Le Pays*, 13 June 1875.

[95] Rothney, *Bonapartism after Sedan*, pp. 194-96.

[96] *Le Pays*, issues of 23, 27, and 28 April, 25 and 27 May, 1 and 4 through 15 June 1875. Discussion continued in the issues of 22 and 25 September, 3, 7, through 9, 16 and 18 October, and 11 and 12 November 1875. A.P.P. B^A 998 contains a variety of reports attesting to Cassagnac's bad standing with the Rouherites over the question of the voting system during the summer and autumn months of 1875.

[97] "La victoire," *Le Pays*. 13 November 1875.

[98] Report of "Ancien 5," 24 November 1875. A.P.P., B^A 998.

[99] *Le Pays*, 1 December 1875.

[100] See Rothney, *Bonapartism after Sedan*, pp. 195-96, and his maps, pp. 197, 205, and 208-9. A list of the committee members and their pronouncements can be consulted in *Le Pays*, issues of 25 January, 3 and 28 February, and 4 March 1876.

[101] In a letter dated 12 December 1876. Quoted in Ch. d'Espinay de Briort, ed., "Une correspondance inédite. Le Prince Impérial et E. Lavisse," *RDM* (1 April 1929), 570-71.

[102] For details on Raoul-Duval's role in 1876 and on his newspaper, see Rothney, *Bonapartism after Sedan*, pp. 238-48. "Fidus," *Journal*, II, 47, has recounted the attempt of *La Nation* to achieve a financial merger with the highly successful five-centime *Le Petit Caporal*, which had been founded about the same time. A.P.P., B^A 998 contains a number of reports concerning the difficulties of *La Nation*.

[103] Rothney, *Bonapartism after Sedan*, p. 247.

[104] "M. Raoul-Duval," *Le Pays*, 16 January 1877.

[105] After the republican victory in the legislative elections of 1877 and especially after 1881, acknowledgement of a legislative plebiscite for the republic became a dominant theme in the pleadings of the *ralliés*, and in fact it later became a doctrinal gage demanded of would-be *ralliés* by the republicans themselves.

Notes - Chapter V

[1] For the history of the Catholic campaign for freedom of education and the concurrent republican effort to assert the supremacy of the laic state in education, I have drawn primarily on the following works, listed here in order of publication: Antonin Debidour, *L'Église catholique et l'état sous la Troisième République*, 2 vols. (Paris, 1906-1909); C. S. Phillips, *The Church in France, 1789-1907*. Vol. II (London, 1936); Evelyn M. Acomb, *The French Laic Laws, 1879-1889* (New York, 1941); L. Capéran, *Histoire contemporaine de la laïcité française*, 3 vols. (Paris, 1957-1961); André Latreille and René Rémond, *Histoire du catholicisme en France*, vol. III - *La période contemporaine*, 2nd ed. (Paris, 1962); Mona Ozouf, *L'École, l'église, et la république, 1871-1914* (Paris, 1963); and Adrien Dansette, *Histoire religieuse de la France contemporaine*, new ed. (Paris, 1965). A succinct recent account is John McManners, *Church and State in France, 1870-1914* (London, 1972).

[2] See Capéran, *Laïcité française*, I, 36-38, for a resumé of debate on the Waddington project.

[3] Quoted in *Le Pays*, 3 April 1876. Police reports in A.P.P., B^A 998 ("4," 6 April 1876; "32," 7 April 1876; and "3," 14 April 1876) attest to the annoyance of various Bonapartists, including Rouher, with what they saw as a concerted effort by Cassagnac to force the party into a stand on the clerical question.

[4] *Le Pays*, 22 May 1868; *Oeuvres*, VI, 7-8. See also *Le Pays*, 3 April 1876.

[5] *J.O. 1876, Ch.D., Débats*, 3766. Session of 1 June 1876.

[6] *Ibid.*, 3767.

[7] *Ibid.*, 3764.

[8] *Ibid.*, 3766.

[9] John Rothney, *Bonapartism after Sedan* (Ithaca, N.Y., 1969), pp. 240-41, does not explore the dimensions of the religious question in its impact on the Bonapartist party. Although he alludes to Cassagnac's position during a discussion of Raoul-Duval's efforts to counteract the party's "clerical" image, he seems to accept the latter's distaste for Cassagnac and his tactics, and lets the matter drop there.

[10] On *L'Ordre*, see *Le Pays*, 3, 5, and 9 June 1876.

[11] *Annales, Sénat et Ch.D., 1876*, vol. 2[1], Ch.D., Débats, 335-36. Session of 7 June 1876. Other Bonapartist deputies who abstained included the two Eschasseriaux and three of their colleagues from Charente-Inférieure, Jolibois, Fournier, and Roy de Loulay, and Cunéo d'Ornano from Charente. By

contrast, in 1875, both Rouher and Raoul-Duval had abstained in the critical votes on Article 13 of the law on higher education, although Rouher voted for the full text. *Annales, A.N.*, XXIX, 604-10. Despite the large majority, 357 to 123, for the Waddington project in the Chamber, it was subsequently defeated by the Senate.

[12] From the report of "P," 23 April 1877, A.P.P., B^A 998; *Le Peuple*, 11 July 1877; and the caricature of Cassagnac in *Le Mephisto* (Lyon), 10 March 1878.

[13] See the previous discussion in Chapters III and IV.

[14] Cassagnac made his first statement favoring separation of Church and State in the Chamber. See the *Annales* for 7 March 1882. See also *Le Pays*, 2 October 1882; *Annales, Ch.D., Débats, 1883*, I, p. 426, session of 24 February 1883, and III, p. 849, session of 14 December 1883. From 1886 on, Cassagnac constantly supported Clemenceau's proposals for separation and badgered radical republican ministers for not acting on the question. See *L'Autorité*, issues of 27 September 1886, 31 May 1889, 5 January 1892, as well as his speeches in the Chamber on 5 December 1886 and 11 December 1891. In 1898, however, Cassagnac reversed his position; see *L'Autorité*, 19 April 1898. In face of imminent separation, Cassagnac upheld the Concordat; see Maurice Larkin, *Church and State after the Dreyfus Affair* (London, 1974), p. 149.

[15] This argument first appeared in the 1876 pastoral letter of Mgr. Guilbert, the first "republican" bishop to be named in France. See Dansette, *Histoire religieuse*, p. 391. Subsequently, it was adopted as the official position of the papal nuncio, Mgr. Czacki, who represented Leo XIII in France from 1878 to 1882, and was spelled out in greater detail in the papal encyclicals *Immortale Dei* (1885) and *Sapientiae Christianae* (1890).

[16] See *Le Pays*, issues of 25 February, 27 March and 2 December 1881, and 19 January and 12 June 1882.

[17] See his discussion on this point in *Le Pays*, 8 September 1873, and his article of 27 March 1881, on Albert de Mun's "throne and altar" speech at Vannes; *Oeuvres*, I, 364-71. For a portrait of the legitimist Catholic group whose pretensions Cassagnac so opposed, see Dansette, *Histoire religieuse*, pp. 387-90, and René Rémond, *La Droite en France* (Paris, 1963), pp. 134-37.

[18] See Daniel Halévy, *La République des ducs* (Paris, 1937), p. 24.

[19] "La question de Rome," *Le Pays*, 7 September 1873. See also the subsequent issues of 10 and 12 September 1873, and earlier, the 1861 speech by Granier de Cassagnac on the question of temporal power, in which he argued that France should do no more than defend the status quo, that is, the temporal power of the Pope should be maintained in Rome alone. *Annales, C.L., 1861*, II, 132-40.

[20] *Le Pays*, 26 July 1873.

[21] See the article by Cassagnac's alter-ego, Raymond Cavalier, in *Le Pays*, 26 March 1876.

[22] *Le Pays*, 19 January 1882.

[23] Louis Veuillot (1813-1883) was closely associated with the religious politics of Pope Pius IX, particularly in the campaign for the Syllabus of Errors, whose provisions Veuillot wished to be made articles of faith, and for the doctrine of papal infallibility, which was finally declared by the Vatican Council of 1869-1870. See E. Veuillot, *Louis Veuillot*, 4 vols. (Paris, 1901-1913); Waldemar Gurian, "Louis Veuillot," *Catholic Historical Review*, XXXVI (1951), 385-414; Philip Spencer, *Politics of Belief in Nineteenth-Century France: Lacordaire, Michon, Veuillot* (London, 1954); and Marvin L. Brown, Jr., *Louis Veuillot* (Durham, N.C., 1978).

[24] "Mort de Louis Veuillot," *Le Pays*, 9 April 1883.

[25] Félix-Antoine-Philibert Dupanloup (1802-1878) was named Bishop of Orléans in 1849, following an active career in the Paris diocese. He was elected to the *Académie Française* in 1854, to the National Assembly in 1871, and was named senator for life in 1875. The standard work on Dupanloup is F. Lagrange, *Vie de Monseigneur Dupanloup*, 3 vols. (Paris, 1883-1884). It is complemented by the Veuillotist rebuttal by M.-U. Maynard, *Monseigneur Dupanloup et M. Lagrange son historien* (Paris, 1884). See the remarks on both works by Phillips, *Church in France*, II, 61. See also the profile by Halévy, *République des ducs*, pp. 197-214, 226-40, and 267-70.

My analysis of the similarity between Cassagnac's views and those of Dupanloup was confirmed by that of Jacques Gadille, *La Pensée et l'action politiques des évêques français au début de la IIIe République, 1870-1883*, 2 vols. (Paris, 1967), I, 72-89. Gadille distinguishes four schools of political thought within the French episcopacy, which he identifies with Cardinal Pie, the "Neo-ultramontanes," Dupanloup, and Cardinal Maret, respectively.

[26] Halévy, *République des ducs*, pp. 197 and 267-70, has insisted on the critical though shadowy role played by Dupanloup in urging Mac-Mahon to resistance in 1877. See also "Fidus," *Journal de dix ans*, vol. II (Paris, 1886), 63, and Alan Grubb, "The Duc de Broglie, MacMahon, and the *Seize Mai* Affair of 1877," unpublished paper.

[27] Reported by "Montjoyeux," in an article on Paul de Cassagnac and his new wife in *Le Gaulois*, 14 November 1878.

[28] See Cassagnac's remarks concerning the closeness of his relationship to Dupanloup in his article, "M. de Falloux," *Le Matin Français*, 2 September 1884.

[29] There are only two letters from Dupanloup to Cassagnac in the Cassagnac family papers. See also Dupanloup's letter in *Le Pays*, 23 September 1877. As for police reports, see especially that of "P," 29 October 1877,

A.P.P., B^A 998. See also *La Défense*, issues of 16-17 August 1876 and 6 December 1877. The published version of Dupanloup's personal journal, concerned mostly with his spiritual development, sheds no light whatsoever on this relationship; see *Journal intime de Monseigneur Dupanloup*, ed. L. Branchereau (Paris, 1902).

[30] Anne-Frédéric-Armand, Baron de Mackau (1832_1918) was the scion of a venerable and distinguished monarchist family of Irish origin. His father had been Minister of Marine under Louis-Philippe. Mackau studied law and served in the imperial administration. He was elected to the Corps Législatif in 1869, and to the Chamber of Deputies in 1876, serving the department of Orne until his death. No adequate biography of Mackau has yet been written. The sketches by Adrien Dansette, *Le Boulangisme*, 9th ed. (Paris, 1946), pp. 172-73, and more recently by William D. Irvine, *The Boulanger Affair Reconsidered* (New York, 1989), pp. 42-43, deserve a full supplement.

[31] Baron de Mackau, "Notice sur la situation du parti Bonapartiste, préparée sur la demande du prince impérial," 12 June 1876. In the Mackau papers, A.N., 156 AP I, carton 94.

[32] Letters have been preserved both in the Cassagnac family papers and in the Mackau papers. The details of their political cooperation are outlined in Chapters VI-VIII, below.

[33] On Villemessant (Jean-Hippolyte Cartier, dit de Villemessant, 1812-1879), see the pertinent chapters in Jean Morienval, *Les Créateurs de la grande presse en France* (Paris, 1934), and the remarks in Halévy, *République des ducs*, pp. 292-93.

[34] According to G. Vapereau, ed., *Dictionnaire des contemporains*, 5th ed. (Paris, 1880), p. 845, and reports in A.P.P., B^A 1099. "Mauprat" was the title of a novel by George Sand; the main male character bears an odd resemblance to Granier de Cassagnac.

[35] "M. de Villemessant," *Le Pays*, 14-15 April 1879. According to police agent "Brissaud," 7 July 1876, Cassagnac dined every Thursday at Villemessant's and a project was afoot to marry him to the editor's granddaughter. A.P.P., B^A 998. I have found no further information about their relationship in Villemessant's published memoirs; see Jean-Hippolyte Cartier, dit de Villemessant, *Mémoires d'un journaliste*, 6 vols. (Paris, 1867-1878).

[36] The legislation in question, known as the Mancini bill, would have altered the nature of relations between bishops and the Italian state. The Vatican alleged that the proposal, if enacted, would deform the law of guarantees of 13 May 1871, which regulated the situation of the Pope in Rome. The political impact of the petition has been carefully reconstructed by André Thuillier, "Aux origines du 16 mai 1877: Mgr de Ladoue et Lucien Gueneau," *Revue d'histoire de l'église de France*, LXI (January-June 1975), 37-59.

[37] *J.O. 1877, Ch.D., Débats*, 3283-84. Session of 4 May 1877.

[38] In June 1877, during the height of the anticlerical campaign, J.-J. Weiss, a moderate journalist who criticized the republicans' choice of issues wrote: "Perhaps clericalism will be a danger someday; by talking of the wolf he can be induced to come. Up till now, clericalism is, in our country and in our time, a word devoid of sense." From his article, "La Chambre de 1876," in *Combat constitutionnel* (Paris, 1893), p. 61. In his 1957 work, *Laïcité française* (I, 88), Capéran adopted Weiss's opinion. See also Acomb, *French Laic Laws*, pp. 71-76, 81-82 on the opportunists' use of "clericalism" as a red herring.

[39] Capéran, *Laïcité française*, I, 88 and 93.

[40] *Le Pays*, 20-21 September 1878.

[41] According to the republican spokesman Emmanuel Arène, the specialty of the *cléricals* was "to place the interests of religion above those of their own party and, by extension, above those of the State, when they gain power. Their real chief is the Pope; their capital is Rome . . . ." From *Voltaire*; quoted by Cassagnac in *Le Pays*, 9 June 1881.

[42] Halévy, *République des ducs*, p. 22.

[43] Phillips, *Church in France*, II, 189. An excellent example of republican anticlerical propaganda is provided by the electoral propaganda used against Paul de Cassagnac in Gers during the legislative elections of 1877. The republican press portrayed him as a "feudal type," a clerical and a royalist, and trotted out the war scare issue, insisting that the Right, if victorious, would quickly go to war on behalf of the Papacy. This material was quoted at length by Cassagnac during discussion of his election. See *J.O. 1878, Ch.D., Débats*, 10198. Session of 5 November 1878.

A Gers republican woman who firmly believed in the clerical threat is the subject of an article by Maurice Bordès, "De la Gascogne à Paris: 'La Gazette' de Marie Poirée, militante républicaine des années 80," *BSAG* (1965), 431ff. On the war scare and the aid Bismarck gave to the republicans on this issue, see Halévy, *République des ducs*, pp. 304-10.

[44] See Gabriel Hanotaux, *Histoire de la France contemporaine*, III (Paris, 1906), chap. 9, and Maurice Reclus, *Le Seize Mai* (Paris, 1932). One of the best accounts remains that by Halévy, *République des ducs*, pp. 266-329. For a restatement of this republican perspective, see Fresnette Pisani-Ferry, *Le Coup d'état manqué du 16 mai 1877* (Paris, 1965). But see also the important study by Alan Grubb, "The Politics of Pessimism: A Political Biography of Duc Albert de Broglie during the Early Third Republic, 1871-1885" (unpublished doctoral dissertation, Columbia University), pp. 583-94, in which the author argues that Mac-Mahon's letter to Jules Simon was not the result of a premeditated conspiracy, as his republican opponents insistently alleged.

[45] See *Le Pays*, 27 May 1877; *Oeuvres*, I, 317-22. The last-quoted phrase is from Jules Ferry. *J.O. 1877, Ch.D., Débats*, 4505. Session of 18 June 1877.

[46] *Le Pays*, 24 February 1876.

[47] "Est-ce un coup d'état?"" *Le Pays*, 27 May 1877; *Oeuvres*, I, 317-22. Moderates at the time, such as J.-J. Weiss, and more recently, moderate historians have emphasized that the men of *Seize Mai* did indeed observe the letter of the constitutional laws, if not their spirit. See Weiss, "Chambre de 1876," cited above, in which he insisted on the preponderance of the Senate. See also Jacques Chastenet, *Histoire de la Troisième République* (Paris, 1952), I, 231.

[48] See, for instance, *Le Pays*, issues of 3, 4, 5 June, 4 July, and 12 August 1877.

[49] As in *Le Pays*, 18 September 1877. See also the issues of 16 December 1873 and 4 March 1874, in which Cassagnac advocated the reestablishment of official candidacy. Later commentators on the Right have adopted a modified version of Cassagnac's criticism: see, for instance, Edouard Drumont, *Testament d'un antisemite* (Paris, 1891), p. 400, and Emmanuel Beau de Loménie, *Les Responsabilités des dynasties bourgeoises*, I (Paris, 1943), 313.

[50] *Le Pays*, 20 May 1877.

[51] Reports of "Im(PM)," 19 and 31 May 1877. A.P.P., B^A 998.

[52] Mgr. Dupanloup, Bishop of Orléans, to Paul de Cassagnac, 29 June 1877. Cassagnac family papers.

[53] *Le Pays*, 1 July 1877; *Oeuvres*, I, 325. He repeated this argument a few days later in "Même sujet," *Le Pays*, 3 July 1877; *Oeuvres*, I, 327-31. Police reports indicate that Bonapartists viewed these articles as further proof of Cassagnac's turn toward "Orleanism;" see "Bonap" and "Grégoire," reports of 4 July 1877, A.P.P., B^A 998.

[54] Eugène Jolibois (1819-1896) studied law and served Napoleon III both as *procureur-général* and as prefect of the newly-acquired department of Savoy. From 1876 to 1893 he was deputy for Charente-Inférieure. After 1870 he was prominent as an attorney for his political associates. He was reputed to be one of the best orators of the monarchist minority in the Chamber and, from 1877 on, he presided over the *Appel au peuple* group. In the 1880s he became an active supporter of Prince Victor, and a member of the twelve-man committee that coordinated the "parallel march" with Boulanger.

[55] Ernest-Louis-Henri-Hyacinthe Arrighi de Casanova, duc de Padoue (1814-1888) was the son of General Arrighi, a cousin of Napoleon I. He was first in his class at the École Polytechnique during the 1830s. During the Second Empire he served as a senator and, briefly, as Minister of the Interior. From 1876 to 1881 he was deputy for Corsica, and from 1885 until his death he presided over the Victorist *Comité central impérialiste de l'appel au peuple*.

[56] Information on the electoral committees of the Right is from A.P.P., B^A 581, a dossier on the elections of 1877.

[57] Mackau to Cassagnac, 27 July 1877. Cassagnac family papers.

[58] The agent "Grégoire," reporting that Rouher counted on the election of 120-130 Bonapartists, assessed his maneuvers within the conservative alliance as "very clever." "He began by obtaining . . . all he could reasonably expect; then he set to crying out (in his newspapers) that his party was being sacrificed, thus hoping to obtain a bit more." Report of 31 July 1877, A.P.P., B[A] 1257. For further information on Rouher's complaints, based on his letters to Baron Eschasseriaux, see Rothney, *Bonapartism after Sedan*, pp. 254-58. Unaware of Mackau's letter, Rothney accepts Rouher's complaints at face value.

[59] *Le Pays*, 1 August 1877. According to *Le Pays*, 2 August 1877, Cassagnac received the support of most leading conservative newspapers -- *Le Soir*, *La Défense*, *L'Union*, *La Gazette de France*, *L'Univers*, *Paris-Journal*, *Le Constitutionnel*, and *Le Gaulois*.

[60] Reprinted in *Le Pays*, 3 August 1877.

[61] *Ibid*. According to agent "18," "The event of the day is Paul de Cassagnac's response to M. Rouher. *Everybody*, without exception, in the party, approves this execution, and the Bonapartists whose duty is to blame the deputy of Gers out loud are secretly rejoicing at the brutal frankness of M. Paul de Cassagnac. M. Rouher is profoundly irritated . . . ." Report of 3 August 1877, A.P.P., B[A] 998.

[62] "La mort de M. Thiers," *Le Pays*, 6 September 1877; *Oeuvres*, V, 34-38. Following publication of this article, police agents reported rumors that the radical republicans were planning to converge on Cassagnac's residence following Thiers's funeral. Reports in A.P.P., B[A] 997. Soon thereafter, two posters appeared in Paris, signed by "??? Auteur de la Lanterne d'un Citoyen." The first, entitled "Réponse à M. de Cassagnac au sujet de l'article ordurier publié dans *Le Pays* du 5 Septembre," appeared in 15,000 copies on 7 September; the second, "A nous deux Cassagnac!" in 30,000 copies, appeared on the 12th. Both were bitterly anti-Bonapartist and anti-Cassagnac, and employed a venomous language to denounce the Bonapartists and the conservative alliance. Copies of both are preserved in the Bibliothèque Nationale, Lb[57] 6623 and Lb[57] 6624, and in A.P.P., B[A] 998.

[63] At the chateau d'Argenteins, 18 September 1877. Quoted during discussion of the election of Lectoure in the Chamber, 19 November 1877. *J.O. 1877, Ch.D., Débats*, 7587.

[64] *Le Pays*, 26 September 1877.

[65] Jean David to Louis Tourasse, 24 August 1877. Quoted by Pierre Bayaud, "Luttes électorales dans le Gers en 1876-79," *BSAG*, LX (1959), 349.

[66] Lacroix to Tourasse, 5 October 1877. Quoted by Bayaud, "Luttes électorales," 351-52.

[67] Guy-P. Palmade, "Évolution de l'opinion publique dans le département du Gers de 1848 à 1914" (unpublished *mémoire* submitted for the Diplôme d'Études Supérieures, Faculté de Lettres de Paris, 1949), pp. 136-38.

L'Avenir's remarks earned its publisher a lawsuit, but the jury voted to acquit on 24 October 1877. See the discussion in the Chamber, 19 November 1877, 24 February 1878, and 7 November 1878, in *J.O. 1877, Ch.D., Débats*, 7583-84, and *J.O. 1878, Ch.D., Débats*, 1976 and 10279.

[68] Figures of the Chamber committee examining the election. Cassagnac's electoral notebook gives the figures 10,915 to 6,778.

[69] Lacroix to Tourasse, 16 October 1877. Quoted by Bayaud, "Luttes électorales," 353.

[70] Palmade, "Évolution de l'opinion," p. 138.

[71] These figures, commonly cited (as, for example, by Hanotaux, *Histoire de la France contemporaine*, IV, 187, and by Chastenet, *Histoire de la Troisième République*, I, 258) do not include the results of the 15 seats in *ballotage* or the results of four colonial elections won by the republicans. The total number of seats to be filled in 1877 was 533, of which the republicans ended up with 326 and the Right with 207. The figures provided by *L'Année politique - 1877*, p. 325, do not tally.

[72] *Le Pays*, issues of 6, 7, 8, and 11 November 1877.

[73] *Le Pays*, issues of 3 and 6 December 1877.

[74] *Le Pays*, issues of 11 and 14 December 1877. See the moving account given by Hanotaux, *Histoire de la France contemporaine*, IV, 211-17.

[75] See Cassagnac's remarks in the Chamber on 4 December. *J.O. 1877, Ch.D., Débats*, 8081-82, and *Le Pays*, 9 December 1877.

[76] *Le Pays*, 15 December 1877.

[77] See Cassagnac's debate with "Saint-Genest" (pseudonym of A. Bucheron) of *Le Figaro* on the assignment of responsibility for the failure of *Seize Mai*. In his pamphlet *Quels sont les coupables?* (Paris, 1878), Bucheron blamed the extreme elements in each of the monarchist parties for the failure. See also *Le Pays*, 19 February 1878.

[78] Cassagnac, speaking to the Chamber of Deputies, 5 November 1878. *J.O. 1878, Ch.D., Débats*, 10196.

[79] *Le Pays*, 15 December 1877.

[80] *Le Pays*, 21 December 1877.

[81] The others included the ministers Fourtou, Reille, and Decazes, and the royalists Albert de Mun and the young La Rochejacquelin. For a study of the republicans' extensive use of electoral invalidation against their political enemies in 1877, see Jean-Paul Charnay, *Les Scrutins politiques en France de 1815 à 1962: contestations et invalidations* (Paris, 1964), pp. 81-87.

[82] David to Tourasse, 22 October 1876. Quoted by Bayaud, "Luttes électorales," 349. The report of the inquiry committee on the election of Condom is in *J.O. 1878, Ch.D., Débats*, 6367-68.

[83] *Le Pays*, 25 February 1876.

[84] *J.O. 1878, Ch.D., Débats*, 10198. Session of 4 November 1878.

[85] *Ibid.*, 10271. Session of 7 November 1878.

[86] Figures are those given by the electoral committee of the Chamber. *J.O. 1879, Ch.D., Débats*, 2183-86.

[87] David to Tourasse, 13 and 19 January 1879. Quoted by Bayaud, "Luttes électorales," 356-57.

[88] "La politique de l'Union conservatrice," *Le Pays*, 2 January 1879; *Oeuvres*, I, 346.

[89] Report of "Burg," 2 February 1879. A.P.P., B^A 999.

[90] Victory circular, *Le Pays*, 10 February 1879.

[91] *Le Pays*, 10 May 1879; *Oeuvres*, I, 80.

[92] For background on Ferry's educational ideas, see Louis Legrand, *L'Influence du positivisme dans l'oeuvre scolaire de Jules Ferry* (Paris, 1961). See also the convenient sketch in Ozouf, *L'École, l'église et la République*, p. 280.

[93] See Capéran, *Laïcité française*, I, 95-98.

[94] The third Ferry proposal, suppressing "letters of obedience" as a sufficient credential for cleric-teachers and establishing departmental normal schools, was only introduced in May 1879, and was not enacted for many months.

[95] Cassagnac's letter to Gambetta, reminding the now-president of the Chamber of his desire to speak at the outset of debate on the Ferry laws, has been preserved in the Reinach papers. Letters addressed to L. Gambetta. Bibliothèque Nationale, nouvelles acquisitions françaises 13580, fol. 106.

[96] *Oeuvres*, IV, 117-39. The version of the incidents given in Cassagnac's *Oeuvres*, taken from *Le Figaro*, differs in certain details from that given by the *Journal Officiel* (see *J.O. 1879, Ch.D., Débats*, 5276-77, session of 16 June 1879). Police reports attest to the emotional fever-pitch to which the deputies, particularly the republicans, were aroused during the episode. See, for example, "Howe," 16 June 1879, A.P.P., B^A 999.

[97] *Le Pays*, 18 June 1879. The long text of Cassagnac's intended speech, reprinted from the issue of 19 June 1879, is available in his *Oeuvres*, IV, 142-206.

[98] *Oeuvres*, IV, 143.

[99] *Ibid.*, 152-53.

[100] *Ibid.*, 190-204.

[101] *Ibid.*, 204-206. See also the discussion of this point in Chapter III.

[102] Capéran, *Laïcité française*, I, 167-202, on the debates over Article 7.

NOTES - CHAPTER VI

[1] French archives contain voluminous files of reports and clippings pertaining to the death of the Prince Imperial and its impact on public opinion; see A.P.P. B^A 1203 and A.N. F^7 12429. The fact that the republicans viewed the young prince a serious threat, despite the ramshackle state of his party, can be gauged from the evident relief registered in the republican press following his death. See, for example, the remarks of *L'Année politique -- 1879*, p. 176. See also Suzanne Desternes and Henriette Chandet, *Louis, Prince Imperial* (Paris, 1957), pp. 238-41; and John Rothney, *Bonapartism after Sedan* (Ithaca, N.Y., 1969), pp. 230-31.

[2] Mackau, "Notice sur la situation du parti bonapartiste...." Mackau Papers. A.N., 156 API, carton 94.

[3] *Le Pays*, 21 June 1879; *Oeuvres*, I, 196. Prince Victor's mother, the estranged wife of Prince Napoleon, was Princess Clotilde of Savoy, daughter of Victor-Emmanuel II of Italy and sister of his successor, Humbert I.

[4] *Ibid.*

[5] Jules Amigues (1829-1883) had supported the republic during the Second Empire, and then advocated the empire during the Third Republic. He represented the extreme left wing of Bonapartism and was considered a compromising figure by many Bonapartist notables. A journalist, he published numerous political brochures and edited *L'Espérance nationale*, 1872-1873, *L'Ordre* (along with Jules Richard), 1876-1877, *Le Petit Caporal*, 1878-1881, and *Le Peuple*, 1882-1883. In 1877 he was elected deputy for Cambrai (Nord), but was invalidated and defeated in successive bids in 1878 and 1879. There is, to my knowledge, no extant scholarly study of the colorful Amigues.

[6] *Le Pays*, 1 July 1879. According to Harold Kurtz, *The Empress Eugenie, 1826-1920* (Boston, 1964), p. 312, even the empress had not known about the codicil; it had been the young prince's own addition.

[7] *Le Pays*, 2 July 1879. This article is reprinted in Cassagnac's *Oeuvres*, I, 203, but misdated 7 July 1879. Paul Lenglé, one of Prince Napoleon's closest associates from 1879 on, believed that the notion of "breaking the contract" had originated with Rouher, who, not daring to support it himself, had turned it over to Amigues and Cassagnac to elaborate for him. See Paul Lenglé, *Le Neveu de Bonaparte* (Paris, 1893), p. 44. This book provides an excellent account of Jeromist politics from 1879 to 1893.

[8] Quoted in *Le Pays*, 4 and 11 July 1879.

[9] *Le Pays*, 7 July 1879. "Fidus" interpreted Cassagnac's hedging as a reluctant recognition of Prince Napoleon's legal right of succession. "Fidus"

[E. de Balleyguier, called Loudun], *Journal de Fidus sous la République opportuniste* (Paris, 1888), p. 26. *Pace* "Fidus," Cassagnac never publicly contested the prince's legal rights; it was the moral right he invoked.

[10] *Le Pays*, 9 July 1879. See also Cassagnac's letter to *Le Figaro*, reprinted in *Le Pays*, 26 July 1879.

[11] See *Le Pays*, issues of 21, 22, and 23 July 1879 on the significance of this meeting.

[12] Cassagnac to Mackau, 29 July 1879. Mackau papers, A.N., 156 API, carton Ch-Cy of unclassified correspondence.

[13] *J.O. 1880, Ch.D., Débats*, 3133. Session of 16 March 1880. See *Le Pays*, issues of 18 and 26 March 1880; *Oeuvres*, VI, 21-25.

[14] For the text of the decrees of 29 March, see *L'Année politique -- 1880*, pp. 440-46.

[15] *Le Pays*, 31 March 1880; *Oeuvres*, VI, 29-30. During the interim between the defeat of Article 7 and the issuing of the decrees, anticlerical elements in Paris hosted a series of Good Friday banquets, on the model of that attributed to Prince Napoleon and Sainte-Beuve in the 1860s, in which they ostensibly blasphemed the traditions and rites of the Church. Cassagnac insisted on the solidarity of these men with Ferry in *Le Pays*, 28 March 1880.

[16] *Le Pays*, 1 April 1880; *Oeuvres*, I, 349-51.

[17] Prince Jérôme-Napoléon Bonaparte, "Lettre à un ami." Reprinted in *Le Pays*, 7 April 1880, and in *L'Année politique -- 1880*, pp. 160-61.

[18] *Le Pays*, issues of 7 and 8 April 1880.

[19] The program-manifesto of *Napoléon* is quoted by Lenglé, *Neveu de Bonaparte*, pp. 52-53.

[20] Lenglé, *Neveu de Bonaparte*, p. 52. See also pp. 38-40, where Lenglé tells of his fruitless efforts prior to 1879 to persuade Rouher and the Imperialists to take up the issue of constitutional reform.

[21] *Ibid*, p. 56.

[22] *Ibid.*, p. 53.

[23] *Le Pays*, 4 March 1881.

[24] Lenglé, *Neveu de Bonaparte*, p. 68. See also "Grégoire," 12 June 1881, A.P.P., B^A 594.

[25] Lists of those who signed the manifesto and of the ten additional incumbents who ran as "Napoleonic revisionists" are given in Lenglé, *Neveu de Bonaparte*, p. 75. The list given by *L'Année politique -- 1881*, p. 205, is inaccurate.

[26] Prince Napoléon to Lenglé, 22 August 1881. Quoted in Lenglé, *Neveu*, p. 80. The emphasis appears in the original text.

[27] On Rouher's retirement, see *Le Pays*, 2 August 1881, and "Fidus," *Journal de Fidus*, p. 259. For the lists of Imperialist, Jeromist, and royalist deputies elected in 1881, see *Le Pays*, 7 September 1881. The three new

Imperialists were Daynaud (Gers), Leroux (Vendée), and Pain (Vienne).

[28] Electoral manifesto, published in *Le Pays*, 5 August 1881.

[29] See the account of Cassagnac's speech of August 3rd at Marciac, in *Le Pays*, 13 August 1881. Their electoral competition was climaxed by a duel in November; on this incident, see *Le Pays*, 10 November 1881.

[30] Ferdinand Daynaud (1838-1918) was deputy for Gers from 1881 to 1893. He soon established himself as an authoritative spokesman on political economy and financial questions both in the Chamber and in the press. In later years, he became the business manager for Cassagnac's *L'Autorité*, and was praised by the *Côte de la Presse*, 10 November 1904, as "*peut-être le meilleur des administrateurs de journal que compte, en ce moment, l'industrie parisienne de la presse.*"

"A Messieurs les électeurs de l'arrondissement de Condom," *Le Pays*, 31 August 1881. Cassagnac's political opponents charged that his vote for the *liste* in 1881 and his subsequent change of constituencies were motivated by fears of defeat in Condom. See, for instance, the exchange between Cassagnac and Emmanuel Arène of *Voltaire*, in *Le Pays*, 26 May 1881, and following defeat of the *liste*, the articles in *France*. This charge has been consecrated by *L'Année politique--1881*, p. 207. See also the reports of police agents "R.H." 30 March, 18 April, 24 May 1881, and "303," 5 July 1881, in A.P.P., B^A 594, B^A 604, and B^A 999.

[31] See the polemics between *Napoléon* and *Le Petit Caporal*, as reported in *Le Pays*, issues of 6, 7, 8, 10-11, 12, 19, 20, 24, and 26 April 1882. See also the article by Pierre Giffard on Prince Victor's sojourn in Heidelberg in *Le Figaro*, 24 April 1882; reprinted in *Le Pays*, 25 April 1882.

[32] Henri-Alexis Dichard (also known as Chapoulard and Dey), (1845-1897), was reputed to be the son of an unmarried woman who had been in the domestic service of Napoleon III. He was legally recognized by his father at the age of 22. In late 1881 he joined the staff of *Le Petit Caporal*, and became editor in March 1882. In September 1882, he killed his rival Massis, the editor of *Combat*, in a duel, but was acquitted of wrongdoing in the subsequent trial. From late 1882 until May 1884, Dichard waged a losing battle against the impending bankruptcy of *Le Petit Caporal*, which was then sold. He fell from credit with the Imperialists from 1885 on because of his opposition to the conservative alliance, and then published two polemical brochures, of importance for the history of Victorisme -- *Le Victorisme et le parti Bonapartiste* (Paris, 1885), and *La Fin d'un prince* (Paris, 1886). The above biographical information was pieced together from materials in Dichard's police file, B^A 1038, in the archives of the Prefecture of Police.

[33] Their speeches were reprinted in *Le Pays*, 16-17 August 1882. On the prince's birthday, see *Le Pays*, 27 July 1882.

[34] Lenglé, *Neveu de Bonaparte*, p. 109. Victor's princely consciousness was exemplified by his reported refusal to marry a commoner, even for the sake of a substantial dowry. ["Alexandre," 30 April 1893, A.P.P. B^A 70]. In November 1910, at the age of 47, he finally married Princess Clémentine of Belgium.

[35] Reported by "Grégoire," 23 January 1882, A.P.P., B^A 69. Police reports indicate that Pugliesi-Conti acted as intermediary between Amigues and Prince Victor, then between Cassagnac and Prince Victor: see the reports of "Grégoire," 15 May 1884, and "16(PM)," 20 September 1885, both in A.P.P., B^A 69.

[36] In *Le Pays*, 25 and 27 January 1873, 24 July and 16-17 August 1875. But see Cassagnac's defense of Amigues in *Le Pays*, 28 November 1879. Lenglé, *Neveu de Bonaparte*, p. 43, also attested to their hostility.

[37] *Le Pays*, 1 and 4 May 1883. See also the several reports relative to the funeral in A.P.P., B^A 865.

[38] The police did not consider Amigues' committees to be a threat to the republic, since they lacked centralization and no other leading political figures were involved. Report of "Contrôle Général," 18 October 1882, A.P.P., B^A 62. Following Cassagnac's entrée, however, the police kept close watch over the reorganized committees. Various reports in B^A 62 and B^A 1000 trace their development.

[39] Victor's letter was published in *Le Pays*, 29 November 1883. It is also reprinted in Dichard, *Fin d'un prince*, p. 23.

[40] *Le Pays*, 3 December 1883. See also *Le Pays*, 5 and 7 December 1883.

[41] Prince Victor to Prince Napoleon, 16 December 1883. Reprinted from *Le Figaro* by *Le Pays*, 19 December 1883, and in Dichard, *Fin d'un prince*, pp. 24-25.

[42] *Le Pays*, 19 December 1883.

[43] *Le Pays*, 28 December 1883. The mss. draft of the note, slightly less amplified than the published statement, is in the Cassagnac family papers.

[44] Prince Victor to Prince Napoleon, 21 December 1883. Quoted in the letter of Baron Brunet to *Le Figaro*, and reprinted in *Le Pays*, 30 December 1883, and in Dichard, *Fin d'un prince*, p. 25.

[45] Quoted in *Le Pays*, 30 December 1883. In the meantime Cassagnac had evidently written a blistering letter to Victor's tutor, Pugliesi-Conti, concerning Victor's responses, for he soon received a personal reply from Victor, dated 30 December 1883, which has lain unpublished until this moment in the Cassagnac family papers.

> . . . *Je maintiens que l'autorisation de pubier une note que j'avais vue et corrigée n'est pas un mandat; mais je regrette de voir ainsi interpreter mes sentiments à votre égard.*

> *On vous a montré une lettre que j'ai écrite à mon Père,*
> *j'avoue franchement avoir été de bonne foi en lui disant que*
> *les corrections n'étaient pas de ma main, je lui ai écris*
> *d'ailleurs que peu importait qu'elles fussent de ma main ou*
> *non puisque je les avais faites.*
>
> *Je n'ai jamais "laché" personne en aucune*
> *circonstance, c'est vous dire assez, que je comptes toujours*
> *sur votre dévouement, et que je place mon honneur trop haut*
> *pour le faire intervenir dans des discussions de presse.*
>
> *Je vous écris cette lettre pour vous faire connaître mes*
> *véritables sentiments et vous dire que je n'ai jamais douté de*
> *votres, elle vous est d'ailleurs toute personnelle.*

In a telegram addressed to his father dated 29 December 1883, Victor had indeed acknowledged his part in making the corrections, but this communication was not made public until much later. The text is given in Dichard, *Fin d'un prince*, p. 25.

[46] *Le Pays*, 30 December 1883.

[47] From *Paris*; quoted in *Le Pays*, 1 January 1884.

[48] The resolution of the imperialist committees was published in *Le Pays*, 19 January 1884, along with the text of Cassagnac's letter to the prince and the latter's reply.

[49] Cassagnac did not publicly acknowledge making a personal visit to Victor until the summer of 1884. See his speech of 21 June 1884.

[50] From *Le Figaro*; reprinted in *Le Pays*, 19 January 1884. A second letter, addressed to Cassagnac personally and never published, reiterated Victor's desire to "dot the i's" on what he had said earlier and to put an end to the polemics.

[51] "Grégoire," 22 and 26 January 1884, A.P.P., B^A 1201. See also *Le Pays*, 2 and 3 February 1884. According to Dichard, during this visit Prince Victor turned over to his father the papers (probably correspondence) that established the entente between the young prince and the Imperialists. See Dichard, *Victorisme*, p. 3, and *Fin d'un prince*, p. 26.

[52] Prince Victor to Prince Napoleon, 27 January 1884. This letter was later published in *Le Peuple*, 27 June 1884, and also in Dichard, *Fin d'un prince*, p. 25, and Lenglé, *Neveu de Bonaparte*, p. 117.

[53] A hint may have been provided by Victor to Cassagnac in another letter dated 2 February 1884, in which Victor insisted on the impossibility of any further action at that time. On Imperialist activities, see *Le Pays*, issues of 6 and 16 February 1884.

[54] On the Jeromist reunion, see *Le Pays*, 19 February 1884; *Le Figaro*, 23 February 1884; Lenglé, *Neveu de Bonaparte*, pp. 101-105; and Dichard, *Fin d'un prince*, pp. 26-27.

[55] See *Le Pays*, 8 February 1884, where Cassagnac discussed the story circulated in the *New York Herald* of 21 January, which had been picked up by *L'Intransigéant*.

[56] The Auban-Moët story broke in *L'Evènement*; see the denial published in *Le Pays*, 30 May 1884. Monsieur Auban issued a formal denial of participation in the fund (*Le Pays*, 26 May 1884), but subsequent police reports maintain that a sum was indeed given to Prince Victor in accordance with the will of Madame Auban-Moët ("Clovis," 13 September 1889, A.P.P., B^A 70). Speculation on the sources of Victor's funds continued to occupy the Jeromists well into 1885. According to a report by agent "15" from July of that year, the Jeromists then suspected Béhic, Levert, Padoue, and LaValette, of being Victor's principal benefactors. A.P.P., B^A 69.

[57] A long report by agent "Howe," 5 May 1884, A.P.P. B^A 69, described the confrontations between Prince Napoleon and his son, then between Prince Napoleon and Jolibois. A second lengthy report by "Wilfrid," 30 May 1884, in B^A 69, told the story from the perspective of Ernest Pascal. Of particular interest is the article signed "Mermeix," "Le Prince Napoléon et le Prince Victor," in *Le Gaulois*, 8 May 1884, in which Cassagnac and Frédéric Masson, the latter a partisan of Prince Napoleon, were interviewed. See also *Le Pays*, 9 May 1884.

[58] Lenglé, *Neveu de Bonaparte*, pp. 110-11, and his article "Deux politiques," *Le Matin*, 10 May 1884.

[59] On Prince Victor's departure from his father's household, see *Le Pays*, 22, 23, and 24 May 1884, and *Le Matin*, 22 May and 1 and 3 June 1884.

[60] This letter was only published several weeks later in *Le Peuple*, 27 June 1884.

[61] See the account of the meeting by Cassagnac in *Le Matin*, 22 June 1884. See also Lenglé, *Neveu de Bonaparte*, p. 116, and reports in A.P.P., B^A 1000.

[62] *Ibid.* See *Le Pays*, 27 April 1884, for Prince Napoleon's manifesto and Cassagnac's commentary. Lenglé later claimed that Prince Victor had demanded the substitution of the word "radical" in place of "republican" in his father's manifesto. *Neveu de Bonaparte*, p. 109.

[63] *Ibid.*

[64] See endnotes 52 and 60 above.

[65] *Le Pays*, 28 June 1884; Dichard, *Fin d'un prince*, p. 28.

[66] From the account of the meeting in *Le Matin*, 3 July 1884. See also Lenglé, *Neveu de Bonaparte*, p. 123.

[67] Lenglé, *Neveu de Bonaparte*, pp. 116-17.

[68] There are many reports on the difficulties of *Le Petit Caporal* in A.P.P., B^A 1038.

[69] Lenglé had been charged with the negotiations for acquisition of *Le Petit Caporal*. In retrospect, he blamed his failure directly on Prince Victor, saying

that the prince had heard from him that the bankruptcy had been approved by the court, and had then quickly informed the Imperialists, in order to clinch acquisition of the paper for his own cause. *Neveu de Bonaparte*, pp. 106-7.

As for the connection with the Orleanists, a later report by agent "32," 7 August 1886, A.P.P., B^A 1000, quoted one Jeromist's allegation that Cassagnac had received 35,000 f. from the Duc d'Aumale, by intermediary of the Marquis de Beauvoir, with which to purchase *Le Petit Caporal*, and that the Comte de Paris retained the receipt which would prove this. I have not succeeded in locating any archival evidence which would either prove or disprove this allegation.

[70] Lenglé edited *Le Peuple* until April 1885, at which time he was replaced by an editor he considered far more conservative than himself. *Neveu de Bonaparte*, p. 124-26. In July 1885, the disillusioned Victorist Dichard took over *Le Peuple*, but the paper petered out in mid-September of that year.

[71] The account of the gathering appeared in *Le Matin*, 10 July 1884.

[72] Jules-Victor Delafosse (1843-1916) was deputy for Calvados from 1877 to 1898 and from 1902 to 1916. Trained in the law, he became a journalist in Paris, where he wrote for *Journal de Paris, Paris-Journal, La Nation*, and then in Caen, where he edited *L'Ami de l'Ordre*. Delafosse gained a reputation as an orator on foreign policy questions, and was a bitter critic of the Near Eastern and Far Eastern policies of Ferry and Freycinet. In 1886 he succeeded Cassagnac as the Imperialist columnist at *Le Matin*. Delafosse awaits his biographer.

[73] Recounted in *Le Pays*, issues of 7 and 8 December 1880, 29, 30, and 31 March, and 1 and 2 April 1881. See also the reports of "Grégoire" and "R.H." during that time in A.P.P., B^A 999.

[74] The reports of agent "P" are scattered through dossiers in A.P.P., B^A 998, 999, and 1000, as well as through others, beginning in the spring of 1876. His reports on men other than Cassagnac make it apparent that "P" believed money provided the unique motive for political allegiance; in his perception, every political personality could be "bought". This bias on his part lessens the import of the charges he made against Cassagnac.

[75] Cassagnac to Mayol de Lupé, editor of *L'Union*, in *Le Pays*, 16 March 1872.

[76] *Le Pays*, 1 July 1873; *Oeuvres*, I, 132.

[77] *Le Pays*, 2 August 1879. See also the remarks of "Fidus" on the Chambord letter in *Journal de Fidus*, pp. 81-82. In two reports, for 4 and 5 August 1879, the agent "Bonap" reported the rumor that Cassagnac was about to abandon the Bonapartist party for the legitimists and, moreover, aspired to the literary-political succession of the ailing Louis Veuillot. A.P.P., B^A 999.

[78] In reply to the editor of *La Défense*, quoted in *Le Pays*, 8 August 1879. See also *Le Pays*, issues of 1 October 1879, 26 May and 5 November 1880, for

additional disclaimers.

[79] Chambord's representative in France was optimistic about the possibility of recruiting Bonapartists. See Marquis de Dreux-Brézé, *Notes et souvenirs pour servir à l'histoire du parti royaliste, 1872-1883* (Paris, 1899), pp. 55-56.

[80] "Fidus," *Journal de Fidus*, p. 117.

[81] "Bonap," 16 April 1880, A.P.P., B^A 999.

[82] Report of 19 July 1884, A.P.P., B^A 1201

[83] The reports of agent "L.T." (Léo Tholl) from 1890 to 1896 provide the most precise detail of this alleged event. According to his report of 31 July 1890 (B^A 1000), based on an account of the events of May 1884, an account the Victorists planned to use against Cassagnac, the latter was desperately in need of 100,000 francs and had told Lacave-Laplagne of this. The senator from Gers then arranged a meeting with the Prince de Joinville and the Prince de Nemours, uncles of the Comte de Paris, under the pretext of a dinner. At that time it was reportedly agreed that in exchange for 100,000 f. in cash, Cassagnac would precipitate Prince Victor's departure from his father's house, thus splitting the Bonapartist party and combatting Prince Napoleon, whom the Orleans faction considered a great threat. In another report, dated 14 May 1895 (in B^A 70), "L.T." cited Lacave-Laplagne's domestic servant as his source for a similar account, with the significant difference that the sum reported had risen from 100,000 to one million francs. See also the reports of "L.T." for 31 Jay, 21 and 27 July, 8 September, 7 and 16 December 1895, and 24 May 1896 (all in B^A 1000), an unsigned report dated 12 March 1901 (B^A 1001), and the reports of "Chatenet," who was also informing on the Victorists during 1900-1904 (all in B^A 1000 and 1001).

[84] After Robert Mitchell, varous persons in the Jeromist and later in the Victorist camps undertook to "expose" Cassagnac's alleged dealings with the Orleanists. One such campaign was instigated in early 1886 by Baron Dufour, Jeromist deputy from Indre, in *Voltaire* (see *L'Autorité*, issues of 9, 13, and 16 March 1886). Others were threatened -- as in 1889 (unsigned report, 28 February 1889, B^A 1000), and again in 1904, when Marquis Albert de Dion began a campaign to wrest control of the Imperialist committees from Cassagnac.

[85] Agent "19," 11 January 1878, reported a conversation in which the local tax director estimated Cassagnac's debts at 260,000 francs. "P." 12 March 1878, reported that Cassagnac's salary as editor of *Le Pays* had been attached by his creditors, while "Ponce," 13 June 1878, remarked that Cassagnac's financial difficulties were no mystery to anyone. All these reports are in A.P.P. B^A 999.

[86] Cassagnac's affinity for *tout Paris* were criticized by his Bonapartist colleagues such as Jules Richard, who remarked that "in the urn of universal suffrage, the Faubourg Saint-Germain occupies very little space." See Jules

Richard, *Le Bonapartisme sous la République*, 2nd ed. (Paris, 1883), p. 54. Cassagnac was a frequent guest at the most elegant affairs, such as the gatherings at Arsène Houssaye's [See Arthur Meyer, *Ce que je peux dire* (Paris, 1912), pp. 184-90], the millionaires' fencing matches [as recounted by the Paris correspondent of the New York *Sun* in December 1882; quoted by Ben C. Truman, *The Field of Honor* (New York, 1884), pp. 26-27], and balls such as the splendid event thrown in 1888 by the La Rochefoucaulds [*L'Autorité*, 10 May 1888].

[87] On Cassagnac's marriage, see Chapter I.

[88] From *Le Figaro*, as confirmed in *Le Pays*, 13 November 1878. For further information concerning Victor Julien's involvement in the Raffinerie de Saint-Louis, see Jacques Fierain, *Les Raffineries de sucre des ports en France, XIXe - début du XXe siècles* (New York, 1977), pp. 439-48.

[89] Julien to Cassagnac, 3 April 1881. Reprinted in *Le Pays*, 7 April 1881.

[90] See Cassagnac's letter to *Le Figaro*, reprinted in *Le Matin*, 27 October 1884, correcting misrepresentations made by the press concerning Julien's legacy.

[91] *Le Gaulois*, 1 September 1880.

[92] Reports of "Wilfrid," 8 May and 10 July 1884. A.P.P., B^A 1000. In the latter report, Wilfrid reported Cassagnac's annual income at 36,000 francs, comprised of 15,000 from *Le Matin*, 12,000 from *Le Petit Caporal*, and 9,000 as a deputy. In addition, Madame de Cassagnac was alleged to receive some 24,000 francs yearly in *rentes*.

[93] My only source of information on the estate is "Grégoire," reports of 12, 16, and 20 June 1883. A.P.P., B^A 1000. I found nothing concerning this matter in the Cassagnac family papers.

[94] Adrien Maggiolo in *La France nouvelle*, 2 April 1881; reprinted in *Le Pays*, 3 April 1881.

[95] *L'Autorité*, 4 February 1897.

[96] Comte de Paris to Paul de Cassagnac, 9 January 1887. Unpublished letter in the Cassagnac family papers.

[97] Comte de Paris to Cassagnac, 10 January 1892. Cassagnac family papers.

[98] From the 1877 poster, "A Nous deux Cassagnac," by "??? Auteur de la Lanterne d'un Citoyen." Bibliothèque Nationale, Lb^{57} 6624.

[99] See, for example, the *Gazette de France*, and much of the contemporary republican press, including *Le Temps*.

[100] Dichard in *Le Peuple*, 2 August 1885.

[101] Eugène de Mirecourt, *Histoire contemporaine. Portraits et silhouettes au XIXe siècle. No. 93 -- Paul de Cassagnac* (Paris, 1870), pp. 53-54.

NOTES - CHAPTER VII

[1] The royalist committee of Gers endorsed the Bonapartist candidates in a letter published in *Le Conservateur*, 6 August 1881, and reprinted in *Le Pays*, 10 August 1881. See *Le Pays*, 12 March 1882, for remarks on the uniqueness of the conservative alliance in Gers; *Oeuvres*, I, 377-81.

[2] This election analysis, based on reports from the Havas news agency (and which does not include the results of 10 elections in the colonies), appeared in *Le Pays*, 6 September 1881. The monarchist parties had no candidates in 120 constituencies. They nevertheless obtained 25 per cent of the popular vote, if only 17.7 per cent of the seats, an indication of their heavily localized concentrations of strength.

[3] Most accounts of the elections of 1881 gloss over the effort of the republican administration to "make" the elections. See, for example, Jacques Chastenet, *Histoire de la Troisième République* (Paris, 1954), II, 77. Adrien Dansette, who has explored the career of Constans, has remarked without further elaboration that "les élections auxquelles il présida furent le meilleures de la République." *Le Boulangisme* (Paris, 1946), p. 267. On Constans, see L. Bruce Fulton, "The Political Ascent of Ernest Constans: A Study in the Management of Republican Power" (unpublished doctoral dissertation, University of Toronto, 1971).

[4] *Le Pays*, 21 May 1881.

[5] See Cassagnac's call for a conservative alliance based on religious defense in *Le Pays*, 2 and 26 May 1880. Formation of the group in the Chamber, although not yet announced publicly, was alluded to by "P," 7 January 1882, A.P.P., B^A 404.

[6] See Cassagnac's earlier (1880) qualification of the conservative alliance as "a mutual aid society in time of elections and nothing more." *Le Pays*, 11 April 1880; *Oeuvres*, I, 351-53.

[7] "Protestation des Députés contre la loi de l'enseignement," published in *Le Pays*, 3 April 1882. The protest carried the signatures of 50 deputies and Cassagnac remarked that there would have been more, had the Chamber not adjourned for vacation on the lst; *Le Pays*, 5 and 6 April 1882.

[8] Preamble to mss. memoirs of Baron de Mackau. A.N., 156 AP I, carton 66.

[9] I have found no discussion of the effects of this sense of decadence among men in political life. There is, however, an interesting treatment of its significance among men of letters in K. W. Swart, *The Sense of Decadence in Nineteenth-Century France* (The Hague, 1964). That the feeling of *malaise* was

well-developed in monarchist circles is indicated by "Fidus," *Journal de Fidus sous la République opportuniste* (Paris, 1888), pp. 338-339. Even the staunchly republican newspaper, *La République Française*, was speaking in 1882 in terms of the avachissement of France; quoted in *Le Pays*, 21 June 1882.

[10] *Le Pays*, 17 February 1883.

[11] *Le Pays*, 20 March 1883. See also Cassagnac's remarks in the Chamber concerning the demonstrations of 9 March, "*la cri de la faim et de la misère.*"

[12] As for instance in *L'Autorite*, 8 March 1889; *Oeuvres*, VI, 135-38, and in the article "La mère la ruine," *L'Autorité*, 4 April 1893 (in *Almanach de l'Autorité--1894*), from which the following excerpt is taken:

> *Ce peuple n'a plus la foi, n'a plus de dévouement, n'a plus la chevalerie d'autrefois.*
>
> *Il n'a plus rien, sinon le souci de ses intérêts matériels, de son repos ignominieux, et la satisfaction ignoble de ses appetits.*
>
> *Aussi nous rejoissons-nous de voir que c'est à son porte-monnaie, qui lui tient lieu de politique et de religion, que la république va frapper encore.*
>
> *C'est le seul point sensible encore chez lui: L'intérêt !*
>
> *C'est de sa révolte, quand on lui aura pris son dernier écu, qu'il faut attendre une réaction salutaire.*
>
> *Monarchie, Religion, Famille, il a tout livré -- sans murmurer.*

[13] *Le Pays*, 6 March 1882. See also *Le Pays*, 12 November 1883.

[14] On the committee system in the Chamber and its evolution, see Robert K. Gooch, *The French Parliamentary Committee System* (New York, 1935), and Guy Chapman, *The Third Republic of France*, I (London, 1962), appendix VII on parliamentary procedure.

[15] *Annales, Ch.D., 1882*, III, p. 484. Session of 8 December 1882. See also *Le Pays*, 8 December 1882. A total of 44 deputies of the Right voted against the budget.

[16] In 1884 some of the monarchist deputies submitted an extensive proposal for budget reform, *proposition de loi* no. 3035, "Sur les réformes à introduire dans le budget de l'état et dans la comptabilité publique." See remarks in *L'Autorite*, 9 April 1887.

[17] *Le Pays*, 20 and 21 January 1881.

[18] In 1881 twelve monarchists had their elections contested. Nine were finally invalidated, and only three returned to the Chamber.

[19] For Cassagnac's earlier comments on the "republicanization" of mayors and prefects, in Gers and elsewhere, see *J.O. 1876, Ch.D., Débats*, pp. 4946 and 5463, sessions of 7 and 22 July 1876, and *Le Pays*, 7 January 1877 and 7 October 1878.

[20] As, for example, in *Le Pays*, 14 March and 22 October 1876, and 11 May 1879. See also (on the army) *Le Pays*, 12 January 1878, 19 November 1880, 21 and 27 December 1881, and his remarks in the Chamber on 4 December 1879 and 24 February 1883. For insight into Gambetta's plans for republicanizing the army, see François Bédarida, "L'Armée et la république: les opinions politiques des officiers français en 1876-78," *Revue Historique*, CCXXXII (1964), 119-64. On the magistracy, see *Le Pays*, 29 July and 19 October 1878, 15, 17, and 24 November 1880, and 13 June and 3 July 1882, concerning the republican proposal to repeal life tenure of magistrates, and the 1880 series, "Livre d'Or de la Magistrature," honoring the magistrates who resigned their posts rather than enforce the March decrees against the religious congregations.

[21] *Le Pays*, 31 August and 17 November 1878. Cassagnac was by no means the only one to be concerned with republican appetites. See also the *Souvenirs* of Maxime Du Camp (Paris, 1949), II, 320, in which he remarked on the incitement to ambition provided by the 1879 election of Jules Grévy to the presidency of the republic: "*elle a ouvert la porte des fonctions publiques aux déclassés, aux fruits secs, aux ratés de toutes les professions . . . .*"

[22] *Le Pays*, 5 January 1881.

[23] *Le Pays*, 20 May 1876.

[24] *Le Pays*, 11 October 1879, and *J.O. 1880, Ch.D., Débats*,.p. 6837, session of 21 June 1880. Cassagnac supported the return of the legislature to Paris from Versailles for similar reasons. See *Le Pays*, 25 March and 16 June 1879. For a full discussion of the politics leading to the amnesties, see Jean T. Joughin, *The Paris Commune in French Politics, 1871-1880*, 2 vols. (Baltimore, 1956).

[25] "Comment l'Empire reviendra," *Le Pays*, 2 August 1872.

[26] Cassagnac's proximity to the radical republicans and distance from the opportunists is underscored by a quantitative study of votes in the Chamber of Deputies. See Antoine Prost and Christian Rosensveig, "La Chambre des députés (1881-1885), analyse factorielle des scrutins," *Revue Française de Science Politique*, XXI (1971), 5-50.

[27] *Le Pays*, 29 August 1880. See also his remarks in the Chamber, sessions of 16 March 1877 and 24 February 1883 [*J.O. 1877, Ch.D., Débats*, p. 2026, and *Annales, Ch.D. 1883*, I, 433], and the article "Si j'étais républicain...," *L'Autorité*, 15 May 1898.

[28] For Cassagnac's distinction between *politique honnête* and *politique habile*, see *Le Pays*, 30 November 1873. See also Georges Lachaud, *Nos politiciens: voyage au pays des blagueurs* (Paris, 1879), for further elucidation on the political morés of the age.

[29] *Le Pays*, 28 August 1880.

[30] *Le Pays*, 29 September 1880, 10 November 1883, and 6 March 1884.

[31] Their respect seems to have been reciprocal. See Clemenceau's farewell tribute to his "most distinguished colleague and enemy" in *L'Aurore*, 6 November 1904. In 1918, when he was *président du conseil*, Clemenceau called on Cassagnac's surviving son and namesake, Paul-Julien, to head the press mission attached to the army's general staff, an appointment which the younger Cassagnac always pointed to with pride. An important new biography of Clemenceau is Jean-Baptiste Duroselle, *Clemenceau* (Paris, 1988).

[32] See the analysis of the radical position by Jacques Kayser, "Le radicalisme des radicaux," in *Tendances politiques dans la vie française depuis 1789* (Paris, 1960), pp. 65-88, and Kayser's book, *Les Grandes batailles du radicalisme* (Paris, 1962), pp. 82-86.

[33] See, for instance, *L'Autorité*, 29 September 1886, 7 November 1888, and 21 May 1894.

[34] Discussion of this point centered on proposals for state monopolies of trade industries. See the articles in *L'Autorité* concerning the pharmaceutical trade (13 January 1890); state-subsidized workers' pensions (7 June 1891); fire insurance (10 August 1894); alcohol trade (22 September 1896); grain trade (9 March 1900); and ownership of railroads (23 January 1904).

[35] See, for example, *L'Autorité*, 12 October 1892 and 29 March 1893.

[36] *Le Pays*, 11 November 1881. See also *Le Pays*, 22 April 1882.

[37] *J.O. 1882, Ch.D., Débats*, p. 2193. Session of 26 December 1882.

[38] *Le Pays*, 28 January 1882. See also the earlier issue of 25 September 1880, where Cassagnac characterized Marianne as a man-eater ("*mangeuse d'hommes*").

[39] On the manifesto, see the voluminous dossiers in A.N., F[7] 12429-12430; Paul Lenglé, *Le Neveu de Bonaparte* (Paris, 1893), p, 88; and *Le Pays*, 18 and 19 January 1883.

[40] *Annales, Ch.D., 1883*, I, 259. Session of 1 February 1883. See also *Le Pays*, 4 February 1883, and Cassagnac's subsequent speech of 24 February 1883 in the Chamber, reprinted in *Oeuvres*, IV, 231-66.

[41] See the interpellation of 24 February 1883 and Cassagnac's speech.

[42] See his speech on conversion of the *rente*, *Annales, Ch.D., Débats, 1883*, II, 43-51, session of 23 April, and his interpellation on the *caisses d'épargne, ibid.*, II, 705-14, session of 14 June.

[43] See his speech during the interpellation on colonial policy, *ibid.*, II, 1153-58, session of 10 July 1883. On Ferry's expeditions to Tunisia and Tonkin, see the resumé by Chastenet, *Troisième République*, II, 78-89 and 141-68, and the fuller treatments by Thomas F. Power, *Jules Ferry and the Renaissance of French Imperialism*, new ed. (New York, 1966), and Fresnette Pisani-Ferry, *Jules Ferry et le partage du monde* (Paris, 1962), especially chapter IV.

[44] *Le Pays*, 20 July 1878.

[45] See *Le Pays*, 18-19, 21, 22, 25 April, 14, 15, 16, 18 May 1881. See also Cassagnac's electoral manifesto, in *Le Pays*, 5 August 1881, and Guy-P. Palmade, "Évolution de l'opinion dans le département du Gers de 1848 à 1914" (Paris, 1949), pp. 141-42, on the use of the war scare in Tunisia as a campaign issue in Gers in 1881. The Chamber committee examining Cassagnac's election denounced his use of the war threat, although they recommended validation of his election. *J.O. 1881, Ch.D., Débats*, p. 2079, session of 24 November.

[46] As in *Le Pays*, 21 April 1881, 10 November 1881, and in the Chamber, 10 July 1883.

[47] *Le Pays*, 1 July 1883.

[48] *Ibid.* Moderate republican supporters of Ferry's policies, such as the editor of *L'Année politique*, continually accused the Right of undermining colonial efforts. See, for example, *L'Année politique -- 1884*, vi-viii.

[49] *Le Pays*, 23 July 1884.

[50] *L'Autorité*, 26 February 1886.

[51] *Ibid.* In 1884, when an epidemic of cholera swept southern France, Cassagnac blamed it on the republicans, holding them responsible for its importation from Tonkin. See his article, "Cholera," in *Le Matin*, 15 July 1884. In April 1885, the Gers *conseil-général* voted the following resolution, submitted by Cassagnac:

> *Les soussignés, considérant que s'il est toujours hasardeux de tenter la colonisation d'un pays, même riche et salubre, il est absolument téméraire d'essayer celle d'une contrée dont l'insalubrité est notoire et la richesse plus que problematique.*
>
> *Emettent le voeu que l'expédition du Tonkin prenne fin au plus tôt par le retrait de l'armée et la cessation des énormes dépenses engagées dans cette entreprise aventureuse et profondément impopulaire.*

[52] For details, see Chastenet, *Troisième République*, II, 144-45 and 151-68.

[53] *Le Pays*, 29 March 1883. China was then receiving military training assistance from both Germany and England.

[54] See Chastenet, *Troisième République*, II, 147.

[55] Rochefort had just been tried and acquitted for his remarks on the financial dealings of the republicans. As to the opportunists' motivation, Chastenet, *Troisième République*, II, 157-58, argues that prestige was a stronger motive than financial interests, though he does not discount the latter.

[56] *Annales, Ch.D., 1883*, II, 1154-58, session of 10 July 1883. The *Journal Officiel* refused to print Cassagnac's insult to Ferry, but both the conservative and radical press circulated it widely. See the resumé of their remarks in *Le Pays*, 14 July 1883. Rochefort himself subsequently embroidered on Cassagnac's insult; following Ferry's duel with General Boulanger in 1887,

he wrote: "*Depuis hier, Ferry a monté en grade: il était le dernier, il est maintenant le premier des lâches.*" Quoted by Dansette, *Boulangisme*, p. 105.

[57] *Le Pays*, 23 August 1884. See also the issues of 30 and 31 August 1884.

[58] *Le Pays*, 4 September 1884.

[59] *Le Pays*, 9, 12, 27, 28 and 30 November 1884; 5 and 17 February, 11, 12, 15, 17, 28 and 30 March 1885.

[60] *Le Pays*, 1 and 2 April 1885.

[61] See *Le Pays*, 12 May 1885. Jules Ferry never recovered politically from the discredit he suffered over Tonkin. Only in the 1890s did he begin to emerge from the ostracism to which he had been subjected, but his death in 1893 cut short any possible comeback. His generation never forgave him for these unpopular colonial ventures, and his rehabilitation came only at the hands of later historians, for whom Ferry's immense accomplishment in providing France a colonial empire overshadowed the intense opposition directed against his policies and methods by contemporaries. See, among others, the sympathetic assessments of Chastenet, *Troisième République*, II, 166-68, and Pisani-Ferry, *Jules Ferry*, pp. 21-37. A recent reevaluation is Charles-Robert Ageron, "Jules Ferry et la colonisation," in *Jules Ferry, fondateur de la République*, ed. François Furet (Paris, 1985), 191-206. See also Jean-Michel Gaillard, *Jules Ferry* (Paris, 1989).

[62] *L'Autorité*, 10 September 1894; *Oeuvres*, II, 130-31.

[63] The Comtesse de Paris was the daughter of the Duc de Montpensier, her husband's uncle, and of the younger sister of Isabelle de Bourbon. See Chapter I on the friendship between Paul de Cassagnac and Isabelle de Bourbon. The Cassagnac family papers contain a sizeable collection of letters from Isabelle to various family members, dating from 1878 to 1902. In 1878 Isabelle's son, Alphonso XII, the restored king of Spain, awarded Cassagnac the decoration of the order of Isabelle the Catholic. In 1881 Isabelle stood as godmother to the Cassagnac's first child. Paul de Cassagnac made a public tribute to Isabelle, following the death of her son; see *Le Pays*, 27 November 1885.

[64] Comte de Paris to Cassagnac, dated Cannes, 16 April 1882. Cassagnac family papers.

[65] Comte de Paris to Cassagnac, 8 January 1883. Cassagnac family papers.

[66] Quoted by *Le Pays*, 24 January 1880, from an article "La politique à Chantilly," in *Le Figaro*. For similar citations from the Comte de Paris, see Gabriel Hanotaux, *Histoire de la France contemporaine*, III (Paris, 1906), 168, and 199-200.

[67] *Le Pays*, 24 January 1880.

[68] *Le Pays*, 5 July 1883. At the time, Prince Victor had not yet consummated the break with his father, which was discussed in Chapter VI.

[69] *Le Pays*, 29 August 1883. See also the issue of 1 September 1883.

[70] *Le Pays*, 7 July 1883. This dinner antedated the one discussed in Chapter VI, during which Prince Victor's departure from his father's house was allegedly arranged.

[71] *Le Pays*, 2 September 1883.

[72] Charlotte Muret, *French Royalist Doctrines since the Revolution* (New York, 1933), pp. 134-38, has remarked that "The Second Empire was, as a matter of fact, founded on exactly the theory of monarchy exposed by La Rochejacquelein, and the latter was quite consistent when he rallied to it, and in 1856 accepted a seat as senator." For the background of the Wiesbaden circular, see M. R. Cox, "The Liberal Legitimists and the Party of Order under the Second French Republic," *FHS*, V (1968), 446-64.

[73] In "Les deux droits," *Le Matin Français*, 16 September 1884.

[74] Cornély's overtures were dutifully reported by agent "P," 9 and 17 February 1884, A.P.P., B[A] 1000. "P" continually quoted Cassagnac as insisting that "I must remain what I am -- but when I rally, the entire party will follow me." On Cornély, see Félicien Champsaur and Alfred Le Petit, *Les Contemporains, journal hebdomadaire -- Jean Cornély* (Paris, 1881), and his dossier in A.P.P., B[A] 909.

[75] For the diplomatic repercussions of this act, see L. Capéran, *Histoire contemporaine de la laïcité française*, III (1961), 51-66 and 76-77.

[76] See "Lettre du Papa à M. Grévy," *Le Pays*, 23 June 1883. See also Capéran, *Laïcité française*, III, 66-73, and Adrien Dansette, *Histoire religieuse de la France contemporaine*, new ed. (Paris, 1965), pp. 437-38.

[77] *Annales, Ch.D., 1883*, III, 849-50, session of 14 December 1883.

[78] Capéran, *Laïcité française*, III, 81-84.

[79] *Ibid.*, 128-33.

[80] See Chapter V for a sketch of Cassagnac's position on the church-state relationship. See also Capéran, *Laïcité française*, III, 52-53.

[81] Earlier historians, such as Capéran, were more interested in the Ralliement than in the royalists. Their studies have relied heavily on the diplomatic correspondence between the French government and the Vatican. The same can be said of John Woodall, "The Ralliement in France: Origins and Early History, 1876-1894" (unpublished doctoral dissertation, Columbia University, 1964) who studied documentation from the Ministry of Cults (A. N., sub-series F[19]).

[82] Comte de Paris to Mackau, 3 November 1888. Mackau papers, A.N. 156 AP 1. The pretender was criticizing a recent speech by General Charette, one of the most outspoken of the old legitimists. A police agent suggested that the attitude of the Comte de Paris on the subject of "throne and altar" was greatly influenced by his uncle and father-in-law, the Duc de Montpensier, who believed that exaggerated clericalism had killed the monarchy in France and would kill it in Spain as well. Report of "P," 10 July 1884. A.P.P., B[A] 405.

[83] On the press controversy and d'Hulst's visit to Rome, see Capéran, *Laïcité française*, III, 151-53. Mackau left an account of his trip and of his interview with the Pope in his memoirs. Mss., A.N., 156 AP I.

[84] Leo XIII to Mgr. di Rende, 4 November 1884; quoted by Dansette, *Histoire religieuse*, pp. 438-39. See also Cassagnac's comments in *Le Pays*, 18 November 1884, and Capéran, *Laïcité française*, III, 151.

[85] Freppel's overt monarchism and his unwillingness to cooperate with the *Union des Droites* in opposing Ferry's colonial policies led Cardinal Guibert to remark in 1884, "There are too many bishops in the Chamber." Quoted by Dansette, *Histoire religieuse*, p. 390. Freppel was, of course, the sole bishop in the Chamber at the time. On his career, see Étienne Cornut, *Monseigneur Freppel* (Paris, 1893), and Eugène Terrien, *Monseigneur Freppel, sa vie ses ouvrages, ses oeuvres, son influence et son temps*, 2 vols. (Paris and Angers, 1931-1932).

[86] Adrien-Albert-Marie, Comte de Mun (1841-1914) was deputy for Morbihan, 1876-1878 and 1881-1893, and for Finistère, 1894-1914. On his mother's side, he was the great-grandson of the philosophe Helvétius. He was a graduate of Saint-Cyr, and an officer in the army until his resignation in 1875. Known principally for his work in social Catholicism, he was also one of the principal orators of the monarchist Right. The biography of Mun by Jacques Piou, *Le Comte Albert de Mun: sa vie publique* (Paris, 1919) virtually ignored Mun's political career. His advocacy of a Catholic party has been discussed by Henri Rollet, *Albert de Mun et le parti catholique* (Paris, 1947), and Capéran, *Laïcité française*, III, 170-71. A fine recent study is Benjamin F. Martin, *Count Albert du Mun, Paladin of the Third Republic* (Chapel Hill, N. C., 1978). See also the study by Philippe Levillain.

The Vatican intervened directly to oppose Mun's plan in November 1885. Both Mackau and Cassagnac were critical of Mun's initiative: see *Le Pays*, 11 November 1885, and Mackau's memoirs, where he detailed his part in opposing Mun's plan. See also *Le Matin*, 17 June, 23 September and 7 October 1884, where Cassagnac considered the factors that prohibited formation of a confessional party in France.

[87] Mackau memoirs, A.N., 156 AP I. For the text of the encyclical, see Leo XIII, *The Great Encyclical Letters of Leo XIII* (New York, 1903), "Immortale Dei," 1 November 1885. See also Capéran, *Laïcité française*, III, 173-174, and for a considered discussion of the encyclical's significance, the articles by John Courtney Murray on Church and State in the thinking of Leo XIII in *Theological Studies*, 1953-1954.

[88] "L'accord," *Le Matin*, 13 May 1884.

[89] See the discussion of this proposal in *Le Pays*, 18 and 19 May and 13 June 1884. See also the comments by Arène in *Le Matin*, 26 May 1884, and the reports of "P," 15, 17, 24 May and 12 June 1884, A.P.P., B^A1000 and B^A405.

[90] For the latter terms, see "Les n'importequistes," in *La Gazette de France*, 13 January 1886; *L'Année politique -- 1886*, p. 166; and the article by Charles Laurent in Paris, 11 September 1887, in which he attributed the term "bimonarchisme" to J.-J. Weiss.

[91] "N'importe qui!" *Le Matin*, 4 March 1884.

[92] "Le courant," *Le Matin*, 1 April 1884.

[93] *Le Pays*, 8 April 1884.

[94] From Richard's speech at a Jeromist meeting, 19 June 1885; quoted by Lenglé, *Neveu de Bonaparte*, p. 132.

[95] This anti-Orleanist school of thought was well-expressed in the brochure by Fernand Giraudeau, *L'Empire* (Paris, 1884). See Cassagnac's critique of this tract in *Le Matin Français*, 21 October 1884. The various pamphlets by Dichard also expound this anti-Orleanist thesis. On Dichard and his deteriorating relationship with Cassagnac during mid-1884, see the reports of "Wilfrid," 30 May, 21 June, and 13 July 1884, A.P.P., B^A 69 and B^A 1038.

[96] Mitchell had returned to Bonapartism following an active flirtation with Gambettist republicanism prior to the elections of 1881. His first article for *Le Matin* appeared 28 June 1884. In 1883, Isabelle de Bourbon had unsuccessfully attempted to effect a reconciliation between Cassagnac and Mitchell; correspondence concerning her efforts is in the Cassagnac family papers.

[97] Reports of "Bonap" and "Grégoire", July through December 1884. A.P.P., B^A 1000.

[98] "L'Empire," *Le Matin Français*, 21 October 1884.

[99] *Le Pays*, 7 August 1884. Cassagnac qualified Prince Napoleon's manifesto to the National Assembly as a "last gasp."

[100] "A Versailles," *Le Matin Français*, 3 August 1884.

[101] *Ibid.*

[102] *Le Pays*, 13 June 1884.

[103] This oft-repeated charge was consecrated by *L'Année politique -- 1885*, p. 224, and has led to another frequently reiterated assertion, that the "real" conservatives in 1884-1885 were the opportunist republicans, their opponents on the Right being "reactionaries." Strictly speaking, this is true; however, the conservatism of the monarchists concerned the broader social order, not the immediate political order.

[104] "Mon but," *Le Matin*, 17 May 1884.

[105] See "Garde à nous," *Le Matin*, 14 October 1884, and *Le Pays*, issues of 31 January, 3, 8, and 14 February, 19, 21, 23, 25, 26, and 27 March 1885. See also Cassagnac's interview in *Le Gaulois*, 22 October 1885; reprinted in *Oeuvres*, I, 396.

[106] Marie-Charles-Gabriel-Sosthène de La Rochefoucauld, Duc de Bisaccia, and subsequently Duc de Doudeauville (1825-1908), was a member of one of the most distinguished families of the French aristocracy. Deputy for Sarthe,

1871-1898. He promoted "fusion" of the Bourbon and Orleans families in 1871-1872. In 1873-1874, he served as French ambassador to England, but was forced to resign after submitting a proposal to restore the monarchy. La Rochefoucauld was president of the prestigious Jockey Club in Paris.

[107] From the report of "23," 17 July 1885, A.P.P., B[A] 611. See also the reports in B[A] 614, and the articles in *Le Figaro*, 7 August 1885, and *Le Gaulois*, 17 August 1885. It is clear that no conservative alliance would have been realized without the consent and cooperation of the Comte de Paris, but it is equally clear that the alliance was not his idea and that he should not be credited for it, despite the claims of Louis Teste, *Les Monarchistes sous la IIIe République* (Paris, 1891), pp. 87-88 and 92. Teste has been taken at his word by later authors such as Samuel Osgood, *French Royalism under the Third and Fourth Republics* (The Hague, 1960), p. 40. In fact, Cassagnac publicly contested Teste's position in 1887; see *L'Autorité*, 5 and 6 September 1887.

[108] By Paul Bosq, "Les comités conservateurs," *Le Gaulois*, 17 August 1885.

[109] On the imperialist central committee, see *Le Pays*, 8 January and 6 February 1885, and the dossier on imperialist activities in A.P.P., B[A] 611.

[110] For the text of the manifesto, see *Le Pays*, 11 June 1885. See also the report of "17," 10 June 1885, in A.P.P., B[A] 614, and the cluster of reports concerning the manifesto in B[A] 611.

[111] Basses-Alpes, Hautes-Alpes, Alpes-Maritimes, Cantal.

[112] Mitchell, "A la Gazette de France," *Le Pays*, 5 December 1885. For the public debate over the list for the department of the Nord, see *Le Figaro*, 1, 2, and 6 August 1885; *Le Pays*, 2 August 1885; and the commentary by Dichard, "Le triomphe de M. de Cassagnac," in *Le Peuple*, 2 August 1885. See also the angry letter from Mitchell to Dichard, in *Le Peuple*, 20 August 1885, in which he lashed out at Cassagnac.

[113] Cassagnac purportedly ruled the Seine imperialist committees with an iron hand, arguing that "the chiefs must command and the soldiers must obey." *Le Pays*, 22 March 1885. Nevertheless, incipient revolt was always a threat. In August 1885 Cassagnac reasserted his authority over the committees by engineering the replacement of Georges Amigues by Marius Martin as vice-president, and achieving reconfirmation in his own presidency with full powers to negotiate the list. See *Le Pays*, 10 August 1885, and Dichard's article on "the elimination of dissent from the committees of the Seine" in *Le Peuple*, 14-15 September 1885.

[114] See the reports of "15," "23," and others during August and September 1885 in A.P.P., B[A] 611 and B[A] 615, and *Le Pays*, 11 August and 12 September 1885. The full list was published in most newspapers. B[A] 611 contains a dossier on the gathering of 16 September. The election of 1885 marks the only occasion on which Cassagnac was a candidate for the Chamber in Paris,

although since 1876 he had been seriously mentioned as a candidate in the 8th arrondissement.

[115] Jean Rossi, president of the *Comité de la Jeunesse Corse*, in *Le Peuple*, 13 September 1885.

[116] In a series of Victorist meetings during late September, the officers of the imperialist committees pleaded -- in vain -- for maintenance of the conservative alliance in Paris. See reports of "(2e Brig. Recherches)," 21 and 24 September 1885, and other reports on the meeting of 2 October, A.P.P., B^A 615 and B^A 616. The imperialist central committee (rue d'Anjou) in turn disavowed the Victorist list; see *Le Soleil*, 4 October 1885, clipping in B^A 613.

[117] Padoue to the editor of *La Patrie*; reprinted in *Le Pays*, 26 September 1885. One department in which the rue d'Anjou had settled for satisfaction in principle was Indre, where the choice of the local Bonapartist committee, d'Aussigny, was replaced by a royalist; see the discussion of this decision in *Le Temps*, 19 March 1886.

[118] There were some notable Bonapartist and royalist names missing from the manifesto, as Dichard pointed out in *Le Peuple*, 4 September 1885.

[119] "Déclaration des Droites," in *Le Pays*, 3 September 1885. Copies can also be consulted in A.P.P., B^A 611 and in the Mackau papers. In his memoirs, Mackau remarked that the declaration had been submitted to the Vatican in June 1885, prior to its publication; he also commented on the great effect produced by the manifesto. Mss., A.N., 156 AP I. The republican historian Charles Seignobos, in *L'Évolution de la IIIe République, 1875-1914*, p. 115, characterized the program of the *Déclaration des Droites* as "negative;" it should be noted, however, that the republicans did not offer a more positive program.

[120] "17," 5 August 1885, A.P.P., B^A 614. A more specific report by "Durantaud," 15 October 1885, B^A 611, indicated that the Comte de Paris personally contributed 500,000 francs to the electoral fund to insure the presence of the imperialists on the conservative list in Paris; according to this reporter, the royalists had budgeted 3,000,000 francs for the election in the Seine alone.

[121] Alfred Verly, *Le Général Boulanger et la conspiration monarchique* (Paris, 1893), p. 236.

[122] Aveyron, Calvados, Eure, Finistère, Indre, Nord, Pas-de-Calais, Hautes-Pyrénées, Basses-Pyrénées, Somme, and Tarn-et-Garonne. Election figures from *L'Année politique -- 1885*, p. 218.

[123] For the electoral manifesto of the Gers conservatives, see *Le Pays*, 23 September 1885. The Conservative Union in Gers was consecrated in August during an amiable banquet in Plaisance held to honor Cassagnac; see the account in *Le Pays*, 28 August 1885. On the election and the problems of the Gers republicans, see Palmade, "Évolution de l'opinion," pp. 145-47; *Le Pays*,

19 July 1885; *L'Autorité*, 9 March 1886; and the departmental press of the period.

[124] See Cassagnac's article, "Un simple mot," *Le Pays*, 7 October 1885; *Oeuvres*, I, 389-91.

[125] See the criticism by *Le Figaro* and Cassagnac's defense in *Le Pays*, 13 October 1885. In addition, numerous reports in A.P.P., B[A] 1000 and B[A] 611, suggest the breadth of the controversy concerning the Conservative Union's ultimate intentions, which "Le Balai" stirred up.

[126] *Le Temps*, 10 October 1885. See also the following articles, which reveal the use to which Cassagnac's editorial was put by the republican press: "Révolution," *Le Petit Parisien*, 4 November 1885; "Les révolutionnaires de droite," *Paris*, 5 November-1885; A. Vacquerie, "Masques et visages," *Le Rappel*, 7 November 1885. See also the subsequent commentaries on this article by H. de Gallier, "Deux polémistes," *Le Carnet*, VI (1903), 109, and Charles Laurent, in *Le Matin*, 6 November 1904.

[127] Unsigned report, 17 October 1885. A.P.P., B[A] 611.

[128] *L'Année politique -- 1885*, p. 226.

[129] *Le Pays*, 21 October 1885; interview with Cassagnac in *Le Gaulois*, reprinted in *Le Pays*, 22 October 1885; *Oeuvres*, I, 394-98.

[130] Altogether twenty-two deputies, comprising the lists for Ardèche, Corsica, Landes, Lozère, and Tarn-et-Garonne, were invalidated; the four from Tarn-et-Garonne were, however, re-elected.

NOTES - CHAPTER VIII

[1] See the post-election statement of the Right, which is reproduced in *L'Année politique -- 1885*, p. 234.

[2] Cassagnac was furious with his colleagues for breaking the alliance; see his article, "La leçon," in *Le Matin*, 16 February 1886.

[3] *Le Temps*, 25 and 27 February 1886.

[4] Jacques Piou (1838-1932) was deputy for Haute-Garonne, 1885-1893, 1898-1902, and 1906-1919. He was trained in law and was a member of the bar in Toulouse. He was a liberal and a Catholic of monarchist opinions. See the biography by J. Denais, *Un Apôtre de la liberté: Jacques Piou, 1838-1932* (Paris, 1959).

[5] Paul Lenglé, *Le Neveu de Bonaparte* (Paris, 1893), p. 173.

[6] See Mitchell's article, "Ave César," from *Le Pays* (reprinted in *La Gazette de France*, 13 January 1886) in praise of Prince Victor's new program. A private letter (in the Cassagnac family papers) from Prince Victor to Cassagnac, dated 14 January 1886, invited Cassagnac to visit him in order to straighten out "misunderstandings." Meanwhile, Cassagnac addressed an open letter to the committees of the Seine, which was published in *Le Figaro*, 15 January 1886.

[7] Henri Dichard, *La Fin d'un prince* (Paris, 1886), p. 29.

[8] Dufour's first letter was quoted in *Le Temps*, 28 February 1886; see also *Le Temps*, 27 February 1886, and the unsigned police report dated 2 March 1886, in A.P.P., B^A 1000. First *Gironde*, then *Voltaire* published the letters of Baron Dufour; Cassagnac's *L'Autorité* maintained total silence in this matter.

[9] For the moderate republican responses, see *Le Temps*, 20 February (on the Dichard pamphlet) and 28 February 1886, and the article by Emmanuel Arène, "La fin d'un parti," in *Le Matin*, 1 March 1886.

[10] As attested to by a series of unsigned police reports for 8 March 1886, 25 March, 28 April, 4 and 5 May 1886, in A.P.P., B^A 70 and B^A 1000.

[11] In a letter to *Le Figaro*, 25 June 1886, Cassagnac explained his absence at the Gare du Nord as deference to the advice of Prince Victor's secretary. However, an unsigned police report dated 25 June 1886 (A.P.P., B^A 1000) suggests that Cassagnac was miffed at Victor's refusal of the journalist's offer, made during an earlier visit, to arrange a demonstration in his favor. Only during the summer of 1895 did Cassagnac see Victor once again, at Spa in Belgium; see the reports of "Noir," in B^A 1000.

[12] Polemic and sniping which was at once anti-Cassagnac and anti-conservative-alliance characterized several Bonapartist newspapers during the

summer and autumn of 1886. Both *Le Pays* (edited by Robert Mitchell from November 1885 on) and *Souverainété* (founded on 25 October 1886, and also edited by Mitchell), the latter intended to rival *Le Petit Caporal* for the 5-centime audience, were in this category, as was *Jeune Garde* (which published articles by Dichard). A police report, "Au sujet du Prince Victor et de M. Paul de Cassagnac," 30 August 1886, (A.P.P., B^A 1000), suggested that Victor was trying to attract Cassagnac back to the party, although he feared that the latter did have obligations toward the Orleans princes. Cassagnac's public break with Victor was precipitated by a series of incidents, the last of which was the prince's intervention in September in a press quarrel in the Dordogne, at which time he made public his hostility to the conservative alliance. *L'Autorité*, 7 September 1886. See also "15," 11 September 1886, B^A 69 and the caricature in *Don Quichotte* (Bordeaux), 11 September 1886.

[13] Quoted in *L'Autorité*, 4 November 1886. See also the issue of 6 November for the text of Cassagnac's letter of resignation. The commentaries of Charles Laurent in *Paris* ("Grandeur et décadence de l'Union conservatrice," and "Impérialisme et Bonapartisme") of 4-5 and 6 November 1886 are of particular interest. Laurent, a rarity among republican commentators, fairly represented Cassagnac's position and did not distort the imperialist's distinctions.

[14] "17," 4 November 1886. A.P.P., B^A 1000. Cassagnac never broke irrevocably with the Bonapartist party, however. The popular image he enjoyed, particularly in the provinces but also in Paris, as head of the imperialists seems to have made it essential for the party to preserve its relationship with him. From time to time, the presidents of the central committee (first Padoue, then General du Barail) tried to attract Cassagnac back into the party leadership; likewise, the presidents of the Seine committees never accepted Cassagnac's resignation as their head. In July 1887, following considerable internal strife within the committees over the question of conservative alliance, Prince Victor took personal charge of the committees. (See *Le Petit Caporal*, 10 July 1887; *Souverainété*, 13 July 1887; and the article, "Les comités impérialistes et M. Paul de Cassagnac," in *Le Figaro*, 24 July 1887.) The following year, Victor sent his personal representative, Baron Jules Legoux, to preside over the committees in order to check any action by Cassagnac, who was still looked to for leadership.

[15] As Mackau himself acknowledged in a letter to the Comte de Paris, 26 July 1889. A.N., 156 AP I.

[16] The secretariat was headed by two secretary-generals, the Marquis d'Auray and Comte Hélion de Luçay. By 1889 there were six staff assistants. (*L'Autorité*, 27 June 1889). This office published yearly reports on the work of the Right, as well as a variety of tracts. See Comte H. de Luçay. Secrétariat général des Droites de la Chambre. *Rapport sur les travaux du Comité d'études*

parlementaires. Novembre 1885 - Decembre 1886 (Paris, 1887); *Pendant l'année 1887* (Paris, 1888); *Pendant l'année 1888* (Paris, 1889); *L'Oeuvre parlementaire de novembre 1885 à Decembre 1888. 4e rapport annuel sur les travaux du comité, de janvier à juillet 1889* (Paris, 1889). A committee of legal advisors (*Comité des juriconsultes*) was likewise affiliated with the secretariat, giving advice on various issues, including electoral questions. See, for instance, their publication by T. de Croissy, *Droits et devoirs des électeurs* (Paris, 1889).

[17] Mackau to the Comte de Paris, 26 July 1889. A.N., 156 AP I.

[18] See *L'Année politique -- 1886*, pp. 102-106, for a resume of the affair of the expulsion of the princes.

[19] *L'Autorité*, 31 May and 10 June 1886, and Delafosse's article, "L'affolement," 20 June 1886; reprinted in his collection *A travers la politique* (Paris, 1889), p. 133. Despite the fact that Cassagnac expected good results from the expulsion, he was extremely harsh with the republicans, particularly with Camille Pelletan, editor of *La Justice* and reporter of the expulsion bill. See *L'Autorité*, 10 and 26 June 1886. He was also harsh with his colleagues on the Right, who broke ranks on the Right's projected strategy to vote against the measure. *L'Autorité*, 13 June 1886.

[20] *L'Autorité*, 27 June 1886. See also *L'Année politique -- 1886*, pp. 166-67.

[21] *Le Temps*, 22 March 1888.

[22] The *Société des Journaux-Réunis* had been dissolved and recapitalized in 1876 as the *Compagnie des Journaux-Réunis*. During the summer of 1885, the shareholders of the company voted to dissolve the group and liquidate the two newspapers. See *Le Pays*, 26 June and 21 September 1885, and the assorted reports in A.P.P., B^A 1000, particularly those concerning Loqueyssie's intentions.

[23] Circumstances surrounding Cassagnac's departure and the staff letter of solidarity, signed by A. Rogat, P. de Léoni, de Beauvallon, A. Deflou and H. Pellerin, and dated 29 November 1885, were published in the *Annuaire de la Presse 1886*, pp. 111-12.

[24] *Le Pays*, 2 and 5 December 1885. Mitchell edited *Le Pays* until early 1889, when it was acquired (along with *Souveraineté*) by Paul Lenglé, apparently with funds procured from Boulanger's campaign manager, Comte Dillon. See Lenglé, *Neveu de Bonaparte*, pp. 263-69, and Dansette, *Boulangisme*, p. 232.

[25] After Cassagnac's death in 1904, *L'Autorité* continued under the editorship of his two sons, Paul-Julien and Guy. Although they retained the essentials of their father's political and religious orientation, the two sons transformed *L'Autorité* into a "modern" newspaper, according to Arthur Meyer, *Ce que mes yeux ont vu* (Paris, 1912), p. 387.

[26] The press runs quoted here were drawn from an article on Cassagnac in

Côte de la Presse, 10 November 1904. Within three months of its founding, *L'Autorité* was printing 12,600 copies per day, boasted 4000 regular subscribers, and had maintained its capital intact. *L'Autorité*, 28 May 1886. When the paper, originally priced at 15 centimes per copy, became a 5-centime paper in early 1889, its print run rose to over 100,000 copies per day. In 1901, it was still printing 65,000 copies daily, although the figures began to drop about this time. Reports by "Chatenet," 13 August 1901, 3 July 1903, and 25 April 1904, in A.P.P., B^A 1001, record the falling interest in the newspaper.

[27] On the audience of *L'Autorité*, see Cassagnac's articles, "Notre oeuvre," *L'Autorité*, 2 January 1891, and "L'égalite sous la R. F.," *L'Autorité*, 25 ˜lay 1891.

[28] From Cassagnac's circular letter introducing *L'Autorité*; published in *L'Univers*, 21 February 1886.

[29] *Ibid.*

[30] Cassagnac to Magnard of *Le Figaro*; *L'Autorité*, 14 July 1886; *Oeuvres*, IV, 321.

[31] "Discours d'Armentières," 11 July 1886; *Oeuvres*, IV, 325.

[32] *Ibid.*, 333.

[33] *Ibid.*, 336. Compare Cassagnac's speech in the Chamber, 26 June 1886, in *J.O. 1886, Ch.D., Débats*, p. 1206.

[34] *Ibid.*, 338-39.

[35] *Ibid.*, 327. See *L'Autorité*, 1 September 1886, for analagous remarks.

[36] Compare Cassagnac's language on the occasion of his speech at Armentières with the language he employed in 1880, when the editor of *Le Figaro* broached the possibility of reforming the conservative party within the republican framework. From *Le Pays*, 5 August 1880:

> Combat and combat always! Combat in implacable fashion this government of the republic to which we owe the crumbling of all the social principles that have been the honor and the power of our country!
>
> To rally to it in order to obtain a minimum of guarantee and of security, so that nobody takes either our wallet or our head, and be thankful to it for that relative reserve, would be cowardly and infamous.
>
> We have nothing to accord to it; we should pass on nothing to it, for we are the intransigents of monarchic and religious France.
>
> We have a mission, in the midst of the general alarm and during the momentary triumph of ignoble passions, to guard as precious the sacred depot of all that is attacked, all that is destroyed, all that is outraged in the name of the Republic.

[37] See Cassagnac's article, "Le rôle de la Droite," *L'Autorité*, 17 August 1886.

[38] A letter from the Comte de Paris to one of his aides, dated early September 1886, was leaked to the *London Times* and published there in December. The text was published in *L'Autorité*, 17 December 1886.

[39] The text of Le Poutre's letter to *Le Temps*, along with the commentary by Rogat, appeared in *L'Autorité*, 24 August 1886. An early letter from Raoul-Duval, arguing for the formation of a constitutional Right appeared in *Le Petit Stephanois* (Saint-Etienne), 29 August 1886: this information was provided by John Woodall, who discusses this movement at length in his unpublished doctoral dissertation "The Ralliement in France: Origins and Early History, 1876-1894" (Columbia University, 1964).

[40] "Lettres du Gers -- Les appelants," *L'Autorité*, 28 August 1886.

[41] In *Le Pays*, 8 December 1880, Cassagnac had remarked that Raoul-Duval "wants to improve the Republic; we ourselves want to suppress it."

He wants to keep it; we ourselves want to overthrow it.

He wants to constitute a liberal party within the Republic; we ourselves want to constitute an authoritarian party against the Republic.

[42] For Cassagnac's remarks on the school law of 1886, see *J.O. 1886, Ch.D., Débats*, pp. 1630-31 and 1636-37, session of 25 October 1886, and *L'Autorité*, issues of 24, 27, 28, and 29 October and 10 November 1886.

[43] "La chute d'un homme," *L'Autorité*, 9 November 1886. Raoul-Duval stood alone in advocating a republican Right until his untimely death only three months later. See Cassagnac's article of 20 February 1887, in which he celebrated the shattering of the republican Right.

[44] *L'Autorité*, 8 December 1886; *Oeuvres*, I, 408.

[45] A recapitulation of the press discussion concerning the "Declaration des Droites" appeared in *L'Autorité*, 18 December 1886; *Oeuvres*, I, 409-13.

[46] A second letter from the Comte de Paris, dated 27 December 1886, appeared soon thereafter. Once again, the prince underscored his reliance on winning the country over to the monarchy by legal means. Such commentators as Louis Teste of *Le Gaulois* insisted that the Right's conciliatory attitude was achieved only in the aftermath of these letters. Cassagnac was, however, always quick to deny any direct connection. See *L'Autorité*, 5 September 1887.

[47] For Cassagnac's remarks on Mackau's speech, see *L'Autorité*, 17 January 1887; *Oeuvres*, I, 414-17.

[48] Memoirs of Baron de Mackau, mss., A.N., 156 AP I.

[49] *L'Année politique -- 1886*, vi. Even Cassagnac hinted at the idea that such support might be possible in *L'Autorité*, 10 December 1886.

[50] See Cassagnac's article "Anticonstitutionnelle?" in *L'Autorité*, 20 December 1886.

[51] For instance, in the Chamber, Cassagnac interpreted an appeal by Goblet for a vote of confidence on a budget vote, in the name of the republic, as an invitation to treason for the Right. The appeal should have been issued, Cassagnac argued, on behalf of the cabinet, not on behalf of the republic. *J.O. 1887, Ch.D., Débats,* pp. 892-93. Session of 30 March 1887. Of such fine distinctions was political controversy made.

[52] "Un danger public," *L'Autorité,* 22 January 1887. Mackau left an account of his meeting with Grévy during the war scare in February 1887. See his memoirs, mss., A.N., 156 AP I.

[53] Following its exclusion from the Budget Committee in 1886, the Right had published a protest against the direction of finances by the republicans; see *L'Autorité,* 26 March 1886. When the budget came to a vote later that year, however, a majority of the deputies of the Right supported it; Cassagnac and twenty-three others voted against it. See the article by Fernand Daynaud in *L'Autorité,* 15 February 1887.

[54] *L'Autorité,* 4 April 1887.

[55] *L'Autorité,* 20 May 1887. Comte Munster, Bismarck's ambassador in Paris, took note of Cassagnac's remarks on the cabinet defeat. See *Grosse Politik,* VI, 191.

[56] *L'Autorité,* 20 May 1887. See also Cassagnac's commentary on the Right's second declaration in *L'Autorité,* 21 May 1887; *Oeuvres,* I, 417-20.

[57] *L'Autorité,* 23 May 1887.

[58] *L'Autorité,* 24 May 1887. Neither did Grévy consult with Clemenceau, leader of the radical republicans.

[59] See *Le Temps,* 22 June 1887, for the official communiqué on this matter.

[60] Mss., A.N., 156 AP I.

[61] *Ibid.*

[62] Police report, 25 May 1887, A.P.P., B^A 1000.

[63] The conditions on which the cabinet agreement rested were unknown to the public for a number of years. Only during 1892-1893 did the details begin to leak out. In 1892 Cassagnac responded to an article on the Rouvier ministry in *Le Figaro* with the claim that there had been four points of agreement. "The day they become known, M. Rouvier will have ended his political career," Cassagnac affirmed. "Le pacte," *L'Autorité,* 28 February 1892. See also *L'Autorité,* issues of 9, 11, 12, 14, and 17 May 1893 when, in discussion with Mackau, Cassagnac revealed the existence of minutes of the meetings with President Grévy, documenting the points of agreement, and called for their publication. See also *L'Autorité,* 5 May 1896, for further remarks on this subject.

[64] *L'Autorité,* 5 September 1887.

[65] *L'Autorité,* 18 September 1887.

[66] *L'Autorité,* 31 May 1887.

[67] Comte de Paris to Mackau, 16 June 1887. A.N., 156 AP I.

[68] Dansette, *Boulangisme*, p. 84.

[69] In *Le Matin*; quoted in *L'Autorité*, 19 June 1887.

[70] The leaders of the Right met with Rouvier on this question on 23 June 1887. The manuscript account of the meeting is in the Mackau papers, A.N., 156 AP I. There is a good, extended summary of discussion on the military law in *L'Année politique -- 1887*, pp. 164-76.

[71] *J.O. 1887, Ch.D., Débats*, pp. 1655 and 1661. Session of 11 July 1887. This interpellation and other radical provocations were roundly criticized by the moderate republican *L'Année politique -- 1887*, pp. 150-151.

[72] *L'Année politique -- 1887*, pp. 155-156.

[73] *L'Autorité*, 6 September 1887; *Oeuvres*, I, 427.

[74] Mackau, Memorandum on the fall of the Rouvier ministry, dated 10 May 1893, ms., A.N., 156 AP I, carton no. 101.

[75] Mackau to Cassagnac, 14 August 1887. Cassagnac family papers. The letter provides a detailed account of Mackau's trip to Paris to visit with the ministers.

[76] *L'Autorité*, 19 August 1887. Long after the fall of the Rouvier ministry, Cassagnac reproached the ministers for lacking sufficient courage to stand up to the radicals. See, for example, the following articles in *L'Autorité*: "Le parti républicain et la droite," 20 May 1888; "Regard en arrière," 13 August 1888; and "Simples souvenirs," 17 August 1888.

[77] *L'Autorité*, 4 September 1887. See also "Jusqu'au bout," in the issue of 18 September 1887; *Oeuvres*, I, 429-33. Cassagnac did, however, toy with a change of attitude in his article, "Assez!" in the issue of 6 October 1887. Critics of the Right's continued support of the ministry included Teste and Dugué de la Fauconnerie in *Le Gaulois*, and Audiffret-Pasquier and Hervé in *Le Soleil*. Their various letters and articles, manifesting their discontent, are quoted in *L'Année politique -- 1887*, pp. 199-202.

[78] Mackau, Memorandum on the fall of the Rouvier ministry, dated 10 May 1893, ms., A.N., 156 AP I.

[79] Wilson's scandalous activities had been in the wind since 1884; see *L'Autorité*, 30 January 1884. See Dansette, *Boulangisme*, p. 101, for an appreciation of the scandal's impact. The details of the scandal have been recounted by Dansette in an earlier work, *L'Affaire Wilson et la chute du Président Grévy* (Paris, 1936).

[80] Mackau, Memorandum on the fall of the Rouvier ministry. See also *L'Autorité*, 5 November 1887.

[81] Comte de Paris to Mackau, 3 November 1887. A.N., 156 AP I.

[82] Quoted in *L'Autorité*, 6 November 1887; *Oeuvres*, V, 80.

[83] "En famille," *L'Autorité*, 6 November 1887; *Oeuvres*, I, 80-81. According to Dansette, *L'Affaire Wilson*, pp. 73-74, the reference to the

Dreyfus guano alluded to an earlier shady matter in which Daniel Wilson had been involved.

[84] "C'est du propre, " L'Autorité, 13 November 1887; Oeuvres, I, 85. See also L'Autorité, 1 January 1888.

[85] "Dehors!" L'Autorité, 15 November 1887.

[86] Dansette, L'Affaire Wilson, pp. 118-24.

[87] "La chute du cabinet," L'Autorité, 21 November 1887.

[88] Comte de Paris to Mackau, 22 November 1887. A.N., 156 AP I.

[89] Dansette, L'Affaire Wilson, p. 127.

[90] The arguments presented by various speakers in the meeting of the Right that preceded the vote of 19 November are recorded in Mackau's memorandum. In the final vote of the Chamber, 148 deputies of the Right voted with the radicals against the cabinet; 7 voted with the cabinet, according to Dansette, L'Affaire Wilson, p. 127. In letters to Mackau dated 3 and 22 November 1887, the Comte de Paris bemoaned his lack of influence over the two newspapers that had argued for tumbling the Rouvier ministry. The Gazette's hostility toward the conciliatory politics of the Right continued throughout 1888.

[91] "La faute," L'Autorité, 7 December 1887. The intricate series of political convolutions engaged in by all factions during the presidential crisis, not immediately relevant to this study, is amply recounted by Dansette, L'Affaire Wilson, chapters 5 and 6. See also André Siegfried, "Une crise ministérielle en 1887, d'après le journal de mon père [Jules Siegfried]," Hommes et mondes, no. 45 (1950), 477-500.

[92] Comte de Paris to Fezensac, 8 December 1887. Cassagnac family papers. This letter was evidently forwarded to Cassagnac by its recipient.

[93] Comte de Paris to Cassagnac, 12 January 1888. Cassagnac family papers.

[94] L'Autorité, 17 December 1887. See also L'Autorité, 24 January 1888.

[95] See Mackau's speech to the Union des Droites, following his re-election. L'Autorité, 28 January 1888.

[96] At least this was Cassagnac's interpretation of a recent speech by Floquet. L'Autorité, 16 January 1888. As late as November 1887, the Comte de Paris considered the prospect of dissolution as "adventure," although he thought that the Right should risk it if conditions seemed more advantageous than what could be expected in 1889. Comte de Paris to Mackau, 22 November 1887. A.N., 156 AP I. According to Dansette (L'Affaire Wilson, p. 147), however, it was doubtful that the Senate would have seconded dissolution at the time, even if Grévy had requested it.

[97] See the Right's interpellation of the Minister of Justice, Fallières, on his handling of the Wilson case. J.O. 1888, Ch.D., Débats, p. 262-63, session of 3 February 1888.

[98] Comte de Chambord, Comte de Paris, Duc d'Orléans, *La Monarchie française: lettres et documents politiques (1844-1907)* (Paris, 1907), p. 157. See also *L'Autorité*, 16 September 1887. A good analysis of the "Instructions" is available in Samuel Osgood, *French Royalism under the Third and Fourth Republics* (The Hague, 1960), pp. 43-44.

[99] Comte de Paris to Cassagnac, (undated, but from context it is clearly from late 1887). Cassagnac family papers.

[100] *Ibid.*

[101] *L'Autorité*, 16 September 1887. See also Cassagnac's remarks in a letter to Mackau (undated, but from context April 1888). A.N., 156 AP I.

> *M. le comte de Paris, avec un flair admirable, a compris que si pour lui, que si pour ses amis, le plébiscite ne saurait créer un droit qui est antérieur à tout et que la designation des siècles a confirmé, il y avait lieu néanmoins et après tous les evènements qui ont brisé la chaîne héréditaire, de faire sanctionner ce droit par le peuple.*
>
> *On ne saurait, en effet, soutenir un pays comme le nôtre, qu'avec la volonté clairement manifestée, qu'avec l'assentiment de la majorité.*
>
> *Dans cet assentiment seul, on trouverait la force, l'autorité necessaires afin de prendre toutes les mesures que commande la renovation de nos institutions et leur consolidation sans conteste.*
>
> *L'heure et la forme du plébiscite importent peu. Mais le principe est tout.*
>
> *C'est cette acceptation loyale, spontanée du plébiscite, qui nous a tous rapproché de M. le comte de Paris, à tel point qu'aucune barrière ne subsiste plus entre nous. Il y a donné, pour ainsi dire, rendezvous aux générations nouvelles, se faisant à la fois, le souverain de la tradition et le souverain de la démocratie moderne.*

[102] Bonapartist dissension over the "Instructions" was compounded by an interview given by Robert Mitchell, which drew criticism from Prince Victor. See "Le manifeste de Mgr. le comte de Paris jugé par le Prince Victor," *Le Gaulois*, 5 October 1887; a denial of Mitchell's interpretation in *Le Figaro*, 7 October 1887; and Prince Victor's public letter to Jolibois on the subject later in the month, in *L'Autorité*, 27 October 1887.

[103] *L'Année politique -- 1887*, p. 203. This point of view on the "Instructions" predominates in secondary works. See, for example, Osgood, *French Royalism*, p. 52. A comprehensive review of press reactions to the "Instructions" appeared in *Le Temps*, 19 September 1887.

[104] Charles Maurras, *Enquête sur la monarchie*. 3rd ed. (Paris, 1909), p. 9.

[105] Jacques Néré, *Le Boulangisme et la presse* (Paris, 1964), p. 77.

[106] The articles in *Le Matin* during the later months of 1884 are particularly instructive in this regard: both the radical republicans Louis Andrieux and Georges Laguerre and the monarchist Joseph Cornély were writing in an antiparliamentary vein. Néré, *Boulangisme*, pp. 77-121, quotes extensively from the press of the antiparliamentary Left (radicals and socialists) during 1886-1888. See also Dansette, *Boulangisme*, pp. 144-45.

In his study, *Emile Ollivier and the Liberal Empire of Napoleon III* (Oxford, 1963), Theodore Zeldin has made the point (p. 67) that 19th century French republicans were traditionally antagonistic to parliamentary government; only during the later years of the Second Empire did their views begin to shift. And only after the triumph of the opportunist republicans in 1877, did they defend parliamentary government with fervor, while their colleagues further to the left grew restive at their exclusion.

In the early 1880's even the partisans of parliamentary government began to recognize its inadequacies in practice. See, for example, E. de Lavelaye, "La démocratie et le régime parlementaire," *RDM* (15 December 1882), 824-50. Lavelaye was concerned with the extreme centralization of French government and with the relative underdevelopment of French political parties, both of which seemed to him to be liabilities for the practice of sound parliamentary government. See also the remarks of another enthusiast in *L'Année politique -- 1884*, iii.

[107] Judging from the range of the critiques of parliamentary government during the 1880's, it is simply inaccurate to make the blanket statement that "in 1887, French Monarchists and Republicans both accepted parliamentary government as an article of faith." See Edward M. Fox, "An Estimate of the Character and Extent of Antiparliamentary Thought in France, 1887-1914" (unpublished doctoral dissertation, Harvard University, 1942), p. 1. This author's judgment might be excused, however, by the fact that, due to the European war, his only sources for the early years of his study (as well as for the later ones) were published books and selected periodicals: had he had the opportunity to sample the daily press and pamphlet literature of the time, his conclusions might have differed significantly.

Other historians of Anglo-Saxon background can be excused less easily for their propensity either to overlook the antiparliamentary currents in French political life, to dismiss them out of hand, or otherwise to underrate their importance. This tendency is due in part, no doubt, to an uncritical acceptance of the "republican" view of the Third Republic, which so long dominated French historiography. It can also be attributed, however, to the Anglo-Saxon's instinctive (and uncritical) belief in the superiority of his (and her) own political heritage, which has been thrown into relief by his antipathy toward the movements of antiparliamentary character that have dominated Europe in the twentieth century. It is a rare historian whose appreciation of the nature and extent of antiparliamentary sentiment in France is not colored by his own preconceptions. The American, for instance, finds himself sympathizing implicitly with republicans against monarchists and with governments he considers more "representative" against those he finds less so; his English counterpart finds himself attracted to practitioners of the parliamentary mode of government, be it embodied in monarchical or republican form, against the advocates of any sort of authoritarian, antiparliamentary, or plebiscitary regime. For pertinent examples, see R. W. Hale, *Democratic France: The Third Republic from Sedan to Vichy* (New York, 1941), and J. A. Scott, *Republican Ideas and the Liberal Tradition in France: 1870-1914* (New York, 1951), among the Americans, and D. W. Brogan, *The Development of Modern France*. New ed. (London, 1963), and David Thomson, *Democracy in France Since 1870*, 4th ed., revised (New York, 1964), among the English.

[108] See Cassagnac's remarks on the nature of parliamentary government under the constitutional laws of 1875 in *Le Pays*, 4 and 16 September 1875. In 1880, following the Senate's rejection of the full amnesty, Cassagnac threatened to interpellate the ministry on its "understanding of the principle of ministerial responsibility." See *J.O. 1880, Ch.D., Débats*, p. 7651, session of 5 July 1880, and pp. 7755-56, session of 7 July 1880.

[109] *Le Pays*, 14 March and 23 September 1881.

[110] In view of the many links between the Comte de Paris and the English aristocracy, it could be worthwhile to investigate the extent to which his "Instructions" may have also been influenced by the discussion on parliamentary government vs. democracy in England.

[111] Letter from Ollivier to A. Darimon, published in *Le Figaro*; reprinted in *Le Pays*, 10 January 1885.

[112] See Jacques Chastenet, *Histoire de la Troisième République*, II, 208; Dansette, *Boulangisme*, p. 151. For recent historiographical restatements of such charges, see the studies by Sanford Elwitt, *The Making of the Third Republic: Class and Politics in France, 1868-1884* (Baton Rouge, La., 1975), and *The Third Republic Defended: Bourgeois Reform in France, 1880-1914* (Baton Rouge, La, 1986).

NOTES - CHAPTER IX

[1] Adrien Dansette, *Le Boulangisme*, 9th ed. (Paris, 1946; originally published in 1938), p. 371.

[2] The Boulanger phenomenon has proved to be the most convenient focus for historical discussion of the 1880s, and continues to provide something for everyone. The account by Dansette, which described *Boulangisme* as a multi-phased movement and interpreted the swell of support for the general as frankly authoritarian in character, remains not only the best-rounded but the most readable.

Jacques Néré has probed the economic background of Boulangism, only to conclude that economic discontent does not appear to have been primarily responsible for the surge of support given to the general. Although Néré's doctoral theses remain unpublished, his views are summarized in a shorter work, *Le Boulangisme et la presse* (Paris, 1964). By employing extensive quotation of newspaper sources contemporary to the events, he has recreated the Boulangist experience as it was seen by contemporaries, thus making available an interpretation less susceptible than many to the distortions of hindsight.

Since my dissertation was completed in 1970, a fine study in English by the Canadian historian William D. Irvine, *The Boulanger Affair Reconsidered* (New York and Oxford, 1989) has reasserted the importance of the monarchist Right in the politics of Boulangism, based on extensive research in the Mackau papers and in the newly-available Archives of the House of France (now deposited in the Bibliothèque Nationale, Paris). This work supercedes that of Frederic Seager, *The Boulanger Affair* (Ithaca, 1969), which restricted its appreciation of the movement to its quality as a republican "revisionist" political campaign, redefining Boulangism as simply "the composite political philosophy of the leading Boulangists," a definition that provided little explanatory power.

Additional insight into the particulars of Boulangism has been provided by the scholarship of Benjamin F. Martin, *Count Albert de Mun: Paladin of the French Third Republic* (Chapel Hill, N.C., 1978); Patrick H. Hutton, "The Boulangist Movement in Bordeaux Politics" (unpublished doctoral dissertation, University of Wisconsin, 1969), the major themes of which are incorporated into his book, *The Cult of the Revolutionary Tradition: The Blanquistes in French Politics, 1864-1893* (Berkeley, Calif., 1981); Zeev Sternhell, *La Droite révolutionnaire, 1885-1914* (Paris, 1978); Steven Englund, "The Origin of Oppositional Nationalism in France, 1881-1889" (unpublished doctoral dissertation, Princeton University, 1981); Philippe Levillain, *Boulanger, fossoyeur de la monarchie* (Paris, 1982); Michael Burns, *Rural Society and*

French Politics: Boulangism and the Dreyfus Affair, 1886-1890 (Princeton, N.J., 1984); and Philip G. Nord, Paris Shopkeepers and the Politics of Resentment (Princeton, N.J., 1986). See the "Introduction" to Irvine, Boulanger Affair Reconsidered, for a good review of the recent historiography, which continues to focus obsessively on the question, emanating from the "problem of attributing fascism," of whether Boulangism was a phenonemon of the political Right or the Left.

[3] L'Année politique -- 1888, p. 50.

[4] L'Autorité, 29 February 1888.

[5] L'Autorité, 1 March 1888.

[6] Quoted in L'Autorité, 23 March 1888.

[7] The Bonapartists, both Jeromists and Victorists, were quick to recognize the authoritarian overtones of Boulanger's successes. Boulanger's first campaign manager, Georges Thiébaud, was a former Jeromist. Prince Napoléon himself endorsed Boulangism, which he considered compatible with this own brand of Bonapartism but incompatible with Victorism; in a letter dated 12 April 1888, to Paul Lenglé, he insisted that the imperialists only wanted to compromise Boulanger. Quoted by Lenglé in Le Neveu de Bonaparte (Paris, 1893), p. 210. The imperialist Delafosse similarly characterized Boulangism (in retrospect) as "only a de-baptized Bonapartism." See Jules Delafosse, "Le Bonapartisme," Revue Hebdomadaire (19 February 1910), 331.

[8] L'Autorité, issues of 29 April, 2, 3, 19 and 21 July, and 17 November 1886; 18 and 20 March, 19 April, and 11 July 1887. See also the issues of 3 and 5 November 1888.

[9] "Caveant," L'Autorité, 2 July 1886.

[10] "L'Autorité, 17 March 1888.

[11] J.O. 1888, Ch.D., Débats, pp. 1092-1095, session of 20 March 1888.

[12] Dansette, Boulangisme, p. 134.

[13] L'Année politique -- 1888, p. 70.

[14] L'Autorité, 3 and 4 April 1888.

[15] See L'Autorité, 9 August 1888, and Cassagnac's criticism of the ministry's position on the Budget of Cults, in the Chamber, 5 December 1888. J.O., 1888, Ch.D. Débats, p. 2815.

[16] "Le peril Boulanger," L'Autorité, 12 April 1888. See also Dansette, Boulangisme, p. 144.

[17] "Après," L'Autorité, 18 April 1888.

[18] "Le mouvement," L'Autorité, 19 April 1888.

[19] "Le parti républicain et la Droite," L'Autorité, 20 May 1888.

[20] The details of these meetings were first related by Dansette, Boulangisme, pp. 115-17 and 121. His source and mine was the minutes of each meeting kept in the papers of Baron de Mackau, now in the Archives Nationales, 156 AP I. In July 1887, Francis Laur, writing in La France,

charged the Right with sending a delegation to see Boulanger in April 1887, insinuating that ninety-four generals and a group of deputies were contemplating a coup. Cassagnac promptly engaged Laur in a bitter polemic that led to court cases and nearly to a duel. See *L'Autorité*, 28, 30 and 31 July, 1-3 and 22 August 1887, and *L'Année politique, 1887*, pp. 145-46.

[21] For details, see the published excerpts from the memoirs of the Marquis de Breteuil, "Les coulisses du Boulangisme," *Revue des Deux Mondes* (1 June 1969), 467-70. These memoirs have since been published as *La Haute société: Journal secret 1886-1889* (Paris, 1979). Breteuil did not think much of Paul de Cassagnac (see pp. 241-42).

[22] Henry-Charles-Joseph Le Tonnelier, Comte de Breteuil (1848-1916) was deputy for Hautes-Pyrénées, 1877-1881 and 1885-1892. He was a graduate of Saint-Cyr. On his mother's side, he was a grandson of the financier Fould and, thus he incarnated the new merger between the old aristocracy and the new plutocracy in French society. He was closely associated with the Comte de Paris and with leading members of the English aristocracy, including Lord Randolph Churchill and the then Prince of Wales, later George V.

[23] Edmond-Louis-Marie, Comte de Martimprey (1849-1892) was deputy for the Nord, 1885-1889. He was the son of General de Martimprey, a senator under the Second Empire. Like Breteuil and Mun, he was a graduate of Saint-Cyr. He served in the cavalry during the war of 1870, but resigned from the army in 1875 and entered business with his father-in-law in Cambrai. For details of his role in the "parallel march," see the memoirs of Breteuil, cited in note 21 above.

[24] The existence of the "Six" was not known until after the publication of the revelations of "X" (Gabriel Terrail), "Les coulisses du Boulangisme," in serial form in *Le Figaro* during the autumn of 1890 [in book form under the same title (Paris, 1890), pp. 111, 128]. Only in 1892 did their activities become a subject of public discussion and even then their identities were not definitely known to public authorities. The Paris police forthwith scurried to reconstruct a list of members; see the report of "Leo Tholl," 28 August 1892 in Cassagnac's dossier, Archives of the Prefecture of Police, B[A] 1000. See *L'Autorité*, issues of 15, 16, 24, and 28 August 1892. Besides Breteuil, only one other member of the Six left a published account of his role in the "parallel march;" see Jacques Piou, "Le Boulangisme," *Revue de Paris* (15 March 1932), 301-20. Following the publications of "X", however, some of the others spoke out in the press. Mun, Martimprey, and Breteuil concerned themselves primarily with finances, while Mackau handled electoral negotiations; see Dansette, *Boulangisme*, pp. 181-84.

[25] See Arthur Meyer's chapter on Boulangism in his memoirs, *Ce que mes yeux ont vu* (Paris, 1912). See also Breteuil, "Coulisses," 493.

[26] According to the correspondence between Beauvoir and Mackau on arrangements for the meetings, Cassagnac was scheduled to accompany the delegation to England, but did not go. See also the letter from the Comte de Paris to Mackau, 21 April 1888. All in A.N., 156 AP I. See also Breteuil, "Coulisses," 482-84.

[27] Cassagnac to Mackau (undated, but the context suggests that the letter was written prior to 25 April 1888). A.N., 156 AP I. On 25 April the Comte de Paris issued a note that paraphrased Cassagnac's arguments, albeit with dynastic overtones. In this note (which he issued over the objections of Breteuil and others) he described the Boulanger elections as "the cry of France, weary of such a regime and aspiring to deliverance." He called for dissolution and revision, warning however that no name alone could provide a solution to the nation's problems; the only solution lay in constitutional revision, based on consultation of the nation, which would designate the monarchy as proposed by the prince in his 1887 "Instructions". For the text, see *Le Temps*, 26 April 1888; for Cassagnac's comments, see *L'Autorité*, 26 and 27 April 1888. See also Dansette, *Boulangisme*, p. 184.

[28] Outlined in the letter from Cassagnac to Mackau cited in note 27.

[29] Draft letter in Cassagnac's hand, dated 16 May 1888, requesting the prince's approval of the project. Mackau papers, A.N., 156 AP I.

[30] *L'Autorité*, 20 May 1888.

[31] Police report on the *Ligue de la Consultation Nationale*, written sometime after 8 November 1888. A.P.P., B[A] 1496. See also Cassagnac's article, "Faisons comme eux," *L'Autorité*, 27 May 1888.

[32] By 1888 the Victorist central committee was dominated by men who, for the most part, opposed Cassagnac's "solutionism" and remained extremely suspicious of the Orleanists. In April this group had decided publicly to support Boulanger in all circumstances, but not within any framework provided by the royalists. [See the interview given by Clement de Royer in *Le Matin*, 8 April 1888, and police agents' minutes of the central committee's monthly meetings in A.P.P. B[A] 62 and B[A] 70.] In June, to counter Cassagnac's efforts to enroll the Paris imperialist committees in the *Ligue*, Prince Victor formally instructed the groups to avoid adhering to any "unauthorized associations" without his explicit permission. [See the report by "16," 21 June 1888, B[A] 62.] But shortly thereafter, Victor changed his mind, leaving the matter once again in the hands of the central committee. In early July the new president of the central committee, General du Barail, publicly adhered to the Ligue. [See the report dated 28 June 1888, B[A] 70, on Prince Victor's meeting with his advisors, and *L'Autorité*, 11 July 1888, for Barail's letter of adhesion.]

Once within the *Ligue*, the Victorists created more dissension. In later 1888 Robert Mitchell called for the formation of a counter-organization, a *Ligue*

de la Consultation Plébiscitaire, by the imperialists who disliked "solutionism."
[Report of "32," 20 October 1888, B^A 62.] And in early December the
imperialist central committee called for a plebiscite as the preliminary condition
for any constitutional revision. Cassagnac criticized this declaration for creating
a "regrettable element of discord in the conservative party," and lectured the
committee on the exigencies of practical politics. [*L'Autorité*, 7 and 8
December 1888.] A press debate between Delafosse and Cassagnac, writing in
Le Matin and *L'Autorité* respectively ensued. [An unsigned police report dated
13 December 1888, B^A 1000, reported at the two journalists had met for a long
explanation of their differences.]

Certain royalists were also causing problems for the *Ligue*. Mackau's
correspondence revealed that some royalists feared that the *Ligue* would absorb
existing royalist committees and funds; Mackau demanded a vote of confidence
from the Comte de Paris to dispell their doubts and ensure their cooperation.
["Minute" of Mackau to Dufeuille, 24 June 1888, A.N., 156 AP I.] In
September the columnist Grandlieu, writing in *Le Figaro*, voiced the anxieties
of some royalists, claiming that the *Ligue* was dominated by imperialists ["Où
en est le Bonapartisme?" *Le Figaro*, 15 Sept. 1888.] Cassagnac refuted the
charges publicly in *L'Autorité*, 18 and 22 September 1888.

[33] Statutes of the *Ligue*. *L'Autorité*, 10 June 1888.

[34] According to the police report on the *Ligue* cited in footnote 31,
members were recruited by distribution of a packet containing the statutes of the
organization, a cover letter, and a membership form to be returned with
minimum dues of one franc per month, for printing and mailing costs.
According to police files, the packets were sent throughout France "to Catholic
cercles, religious *oeuvres*, associations, and communities, to conservative
electoral committees, to charitable societies, orphanages, employers'
associations, to all the high clergy and to all the subscribers of *Le Figaro* and *Le
Gaulois*." A.P.P., B^A 1496.

[35] The *Ligue* sponsored conferences in Montauban (Tarn-et-Garonne) in
August, in Sens (Yonne) in September, and in Sedan and Charleville (Ardennes)
in November. The *Ligue* also held a public meeting in Paris in November,
which was broken up by delegations described by the police as "possibilistes"
and "anarchistes." *L'Autorité*, 30 August 1888, and report on the *Ligue* cited in
the previous note.

[36] *L'Autorité*, 27 May 1888.

[37] Jules-Augustin Auffray (1852-1916) had earned his doctorate in law and
was a past-president of the *Conférence Molé*. He had been first in the
examinations for auditor of the *Conseil d'état*, where he served from 1878 to
1880, leaving to defend Catholic interests threatened by laic legislation. He
subsequently served as deputy for Paris, 1902-1906. Biographical material is
from Jolly, *Dictionnaire des parlementaires français (1889-1940)*, I, 414-15,

and a pamphlet, *La Future Chambre 1889*, found in the Mackau papers, A.N., 156 AP I.

[38] The term is from Albert Verly, *Le Général Boulanger et la conspiration monarchique* (Paris, 1893), p. 233.

[39] Dansette, *Boulangisme*, pp. 200-1. Dansette's analysis of the elections confirms the Right's conviction that the general's patronage of another candidate was not nearly as effective as his own candidacy in changing the voting pattern. "When Boulanger is the candidate, the division of votes operates according to temperament. When a Boulangist is the candidate, it operates according to the habitual party divisions without Boulanger's patronage exercising a determining influence." *Boulangisme*, appendix II, p. 395.

[40] Breteuil likewise judged the Boulanger venture to be a calculated risk. "Coulisses," 470, 480, 482, and *Haute Société, passim*.

[41] The Right had nothing good to say about Boulanger's committee members either. See, for example, Cassagnac's vitriolic articles on Boulanger's "Comité national" in *L'Autorité*, 23 June 1888 and 24 April 1889.

[42] "République et liberté," *L'Autorité*, 19 August 1888; *Oeuvres*, I, 434.

[43] In *L'Autorité*, 21 August 1888. See also the issue of 25 August 1888.

[44] Jules Ferry, *Lettres de Jules Ferry* (Paris, 1914), p. 486.

[45] Dansette, *Boulangisme*, pp. 231-32.

[46] *Ibid.*, pp. 228-29.

[47] Comte de Paris to Mackau, 9 December 1888. A.N., 156 AP I; Dansette, *Boulangisme*, pp. 230-31.

[48] Comte de Paris to Mackau, 25 December 1888. A.N., 156 AP I.

[49] *L'Autorité*, 2 January 1889; *Oeuvres*, I, 440. The Comte de Paris expressed a similar sentiment to Cassagnac in an unpublished letter, dated 12 January 1889, in the Cassagnac family papers.

[50] Details of Victorist support are provided by various police reports in A.P.P., B^A 70 and in the dossier on General du Barail in B^A 909.

[51] See Cassagnac's articles, "Autour d'un comité," and "Un faux comité" in *L'Autorité*, issues of 7 and 15 January 1889; the report of "Stephenson," 9 January 1889, A.P.P., B^A 1000; and Néré, *Boulangisme*, pp. 177-80.

[52] *L'Autorité*, 4 January 1889.

[53] A dramatic account of the "night of 27 January" is given by Dansette, *Boulangisme*, pp. 239-54. For demolition of this legend of the *coup manqué*, see Seager, *Boulanger Affair*, pp. 202-10. In fact, the general's disinterest in attempting a coup should have been clear from his remarks in a speech at Clichy, concerning Louis-Napoleon, on the symbolic date of 2 December 1888; see Dansette, *Boulangisme*, p. 228.

[54] Indeed, in early January when *Le Soleil* asked whether the Right, in exchange for its support, should demand certain guarantees from Boulanger in the event of a coup, Cassagnac archly dismissed the idea, replying that "you

don't negotiate with a battering ram or a catapult." To the leaders of the "parallel march," Boulanger remained a tool, never a threat in his own right. The only sort of *coup* that appeared to concern them was on the part of the ministry. In late November 1888, *L'Autorité* and several other "Boulangist" newspapers revealed an ostensible plan by the Floquet ministry to mount a *coup* against the leaders of the coalition, following the vote of the budget. According to this plan, conservative and Boulangist deputies were to be arrested in session; freedom of the press and of assembly would be suppressed. See *L'Autorité*, 24 November 1888. It is apparent from a letter written by the Comte de Paris to Mackau, dated 21 November 1888 [A.N., 156, AP I] that both knew of the information that had been furnished to Cassagnac concerning the prospective *coup*, but it is not clear where the information came from. Dansette makes no reference to this incident, but see Levillain, *Boulanger*, p. 132.

[55] *J.O. 1889, Ch.D., Débats*, pp. 253-55. Session of 31 January 1889.

[56] *Ibid.*

[57] Cassagnac had announced his intention to vote against the Floquet project for constitutional reform in "La révision," *L'Autorité*, 14 February 1889.

[58] On Constans, see Chapter VII (above). See also Adrien Dansette, "Ernest Constans et le Boulangisme," *La Revue universelle*, 71, no. 13 (1 Oct. 1937), 14-32.

[59] Boulanger's flight has long been portrayed as the beginning of the end of Boulangism. The standard account, once again, is that of Dansette, *Boulangisme*, pp. 276-88 and 292-95. This interpretation has been challenged by Jacques Néré, who based on his sampling of the contemporary press, has argued that neither the general's flight nor his trial *in absentia* had any determinant effect on the destiny of Boulangism. See his *Boulangisme et la presse*, p. 203. According to Néré, the comments evoked in the press by the general's departure were "in conformity with well-established political positions."

> Boulanger's adversaries saw it as both proof of his cowardice and as an avowal of his guilt. On the other side, those who supported him congratulated him for having played a good trick on the government and for putting himself beyond range of any attempt at assassination. If certain Boulangists considered his flight to have had a deplorable moral effect, they generally kept their opinions to themselves . . . . (pp. 164-66)

The material I have found on Cassagnac's role in the Boulangist effort lends support to Néré's position. The Right seemed happy to have the general out of the way and its only concern was to get him back just before the elections, a point which will be discussed below.

[60] In the articles, "Il a bien fait!" and "La lachêté," *L'Autorité*, issues of 5 and 6 April 1889.

[61] Cassagnac was the sole dissenting member of both committees elected by the Chamber to consider the requests for permission to prosecute the deputies. See his speeches in the Chamber, 14 March 1889 and 4 April 1889. *J.O. 1889, Ch.D., Débats*, pp. 573 and 828-30.

[62] For example, Néré, *Boulangisme*, p. 203. According to Dansette, "Constans," 18, even Constans thought the trials would appear ridiculous unless Boulanger could be induced to flee the country.

[63] Quoted in *L'Autorité*, 6 April 1889.

[64] *L'Autorité*, 15 April 1889.

[65] *L'Autorité*, issues of 9 and 16 April and 14 August 1889.

[66] *J.O. 1889, Ch.D., Débats*, p. 1172, session of 28 May 1889.

[67] "Mon expulsion," *L'Autorité*, 1 July 1889. See also *J.O. 1889, Ch.D., Débats*, p. 1656. Session of 29 June 1889.

[68] See *L'Autorité*, issues of 11 April and 2, 5, and 8 May 1888. In August 1888 the parliamentary republicans introduced resolutions favoring the *scrutin d'arrondissement* at the meetings of the *conseils-généraux*; see *L'Autorité*, 29 August 1888.

[69] "L'amende honorable," *L'Autorité*, 12 February 1889.

[70] The conditions for forming joint lists with the Boulangists, in which the monarchists authorized the candidacy of Boulanger in conjunction with their own in a choice of 30 out of 32 designated departments, had been set down by the Comte de Paris in a letter to Mackau, dated 10 November 1888. A.N. 156 AP I. In *L'Autorité*, 21 December 1888, Cassagnac alluded to problems in achieving agreement on the lists, remarking that where a third political element was in evidence, *scrutin d'arrondissement* would be preferable. A letter from the Comte de Paris to Mackau, 12 September 1889, A.N., 156 AP I, attested to the relief of the monarchists over this change.

[71] *J.O. 1889, Ch.D., Débats*, p. 438. Session of 26 February 1889.

[72] "L'agonie du requin," *L'Autorité*, 28 February 1889.

[73] "Ça va mal," *L'Autorité*, 7 July 1889. This time the measure was characterized as "an insult to universal suffrage, an outrage to the nations, and a crime of popular *lèse-majesté*."

[74] Paul de Cassagnac had planned to run in Paris and in Gers. Three prominent Parisian conservatives, Hervé, Marius Martin, and Maurice Binder, had all withdrawn their candidacies in the 8th arrondissement in favor of Cassagnac. With the passage of the amended electoral law and Cassagnac's option for Gers, all three men re-entered the race. Martin was elected. See *L'Autorité*, 12 August 1889.

[75] Dansette, *Boulangisme*, pp. 312-13. See also Cassagnac's articles directed against Constans' administrative pressures, "Les fonctionnaires," et

"La dernière cartouche," in *L'Autorité*, issues of 28 and 29 July 1889. In an unpublished letter to Mackau prior to the elections of 28 July, Cassagnac described the viciousness of the republican campaign against him in his own canton of Plaisance. Mackau papers, A.N., 156 AP I.

[76] According to Dansette, the royalist electoral fund amounted to four million francs, of which 1.3 million went to the Boulangists. This sum did not include the original three million francs contributed by the Duchesse d'Uzès, most of which had been spent long before the general elections. *Boulangisme*, pp. 317-19.

[77] According to the correspondence between Mackau and the Comte de Paris (A.N., 156 AP I), the monarchists' conditions had been set forth in early May 1889, when Mackau met with Boulanger and Dillon in England. The royalist pretender was continually preoccupied by the fear of treachery on the part of the Boulangists in the matter of candidates [indicated in his unpublished letters to Mackau dated 24 May and 12 September 1889]. On the weakness of Boulanger's own organization, see Verly, *Boulanger*, pp. 137, 181-2, and 195-200, and Dansette, *Boulangisme*, pp. 322-24.

[78] "Mesure urgente," *L'Autorité*, 15 June 1889. Reports in A.P.P., B^A 1000, describe the Boulangists' angry reaction to this development.

[79] Verly, *Boulanger*, pp. 291-320. See also Dansette, *Boulangisme*, pp. 322-26.

[80] Dansette, *Boulangisme*, pp. 319-20. See also Chapter VIII, above.

[81] This material was listed by the Comte de Luçay for the Secrétariat général des Droites de la Chambre, *Répertoire contenant l'indication des brochures et tracts de propagande, des ouvrages à consulter et des sources de renseignements fournis par les documents parlementaires à l'usage des candidats et des conférenciers* (Paris, 1889). A copy can be found in the Mackau papers, A.N., 156 AP I. The program of reforms was outlined by the Marquis de Castellane, *La politique conservatrice en 1889* (Paris, 1889); it called for tax equalization, religious pacification, emancipation of workers, "*déniaisement administratif*, and the suppression of *parlementarisme* so as to liberate the executive power and return the legislature to the position of a controlling, rather than a governing body.

[82] For the statements of the pretenders, see *L'Année politique -- 1889*, pp. 173-76.

[83] Text in *L'Autorité*, 5 September 1889, and in *L'Année politique -- 1889*, pp. 177-78.

[84] Dansette, *Boulangisme*, pp. 330-32; Verly, *Boulanger*, pp. 108-13.

[85] "La fin d'un homme," *L'Autorité*, 7 May 1890.

[86] "Les responsabilités," *L'Autorité*, 15 October 1889; "Rendons-leur justice," 29 October 1889; and "A propos d'un suicide," 4 October 1891.

[87] See Cassagnac's articles, "Silence aux menteurs," *L'Autorité*, 25 September 1889, and "Les ballotages," issue of 8 October 1889. According to Mackau (in an unpublished letter to the Comte de Paris, 8 Dec. 1889), the republicans won 87 seats with a majority of less than 1000 votes, while the conservatives racked up all the large majorities. A.N., 156 AP I.

[88] "Les ballotages," *L'Autorité*, 8 October 1889. Only later did the Boulangists and Jeromists hostile to the coalition insist that Boulanger's cause did less well than anticipated because the electorate disapproved of his alliance with the monarchists. See, in particular, Lenglé, *Neveu de Bonaparte*, p. 282, and "X," *Coulisses*, p. 316. During the campaign, the governmental republicans exploited anti-Bonapartist and anti-royalist sentiments as part of their campaign against Boulangism. See, for example, the pamphlet by P. Cordier, *Boulangisme et bonapartisme, ou la réaction masquée* (Paris, 1889), the theme of which was that Boulangism was a "gross counterfeit of Bonapartism, which itself is nothing but a bastard royalism." Cordier also asserted that parliamentary government was essential to the very notion of a republic.

[89] Peter Campbell, *French Electoral Systems and Elections Since 1789*, 2nd ed. (Hamden, Conn., 1965), p. 81.

[90] "Je demande la parole," *L'Autorité*, 18 September 1889.

[91] Guy-P. Palmade, "Évolution de l'opinion publique dans le département du Gers de 1848 à 1914" (unpublished D.E.S. mémoire, Faculté des Lettres de Paris, 1949), pp. 150-51. In his study of *Rural Society and French Politics*, pp. 38, 101-5, Michael Burns seriously misapprehends the character of political life in the Gers; the fact was that Paul de Cassagnac and his colleagues had no need of Boulanger or *Boulangisme* to win their elections in 1889. Cassagnac's politics in his home base continued to be populist authoritarian, not "conservative."

[92] Mackau to the Comte de Paris, 24 September 1889. A.N., 156 AP I.

[93] Influential post-mortem accounts by royalist critics of the "parallel march" include: Comte d'Haussonville, "Le Comte de Paris -- Souvenirs personnels," *RDM*, 335 (1 Sept. 1895), 5-38; and Louis Teste (of *Le Gaulois*), *Les Monarchistes sous la IIIe République* (Paris, 1891). Such views have colored all subsequent historical discussions of royalism, including Samuel Osgood, *French Royalism under the Third and Fourth Republics* (The Hague, 1960), and P. Du Puy de Clinchamps, *Le Royalisme* (Paris, 1967). Even Dansette seemed disposed to accept their critiques at face value.

[94] "Que risquons-nous?" *L'Autorité*, 30 April 1889.

[95] "Avant la victoire," *L'Autorité*, 20 April 1889. See Dansette, *Boulangisme*, p. 266, and Néré, *Boulangisme*, pp. 180-92, for further press responses to Boulanger's republican declarations at Tours.

[96] Edouard Drumont, *La Fin d'un monde* (Paris, 1889), p. 343.

[97] Mackau to the Comte de Paris, 24 Sept. 1889. A.N., 156 AP I. See Cassagnac's earlier remarks on the conservatives' "lack of guts" ("*manque d'estomac*") in *L'Autorité*, 11 November 1886.

[98] "Platonisme royaliste," *L'Autorité*, 22 September 1890. Analagous considerations were expressed by Breteuil, "Coulisses," 470, 480, 482.

[99] Mackau to the Comte de Paris, 24 Sept. 1889. A.N., 156 AP I.

[100] "X," *Coulisses du Boulangisme*, p. 107.

[101] Dansette, *Boulangisme*, pp. 180-84. Leading churchmen, such as Mgr d'Hulst, rector of the *Institut Catholique* and a close friend of the Comte de Paris, also opposed the "parallel march." Most high-ranking clergy in the state-associated Catholic Church remained committed to working with the opportunist republicans. See E. Lecanuet, *L'Église de France sous la Troisième République*, II (Paris, 1910), 359.

[102] Comte de Paris to Cassagnac, 6 January 1891. Cassagnac family papers.

[103] Dansette, *Boulangisme*, p. 333.

[104] In his articles, "A bas la loi!" *Le Matin*, 24 March 1884; "Les deux droits," *Le Matin français*, 16 Sept. 1884; "Pas de révolution?" *L'Autorité*, 21 December 1886; and "La mort de Monseigneur le comte de Paris," *L'Autorité*, 10 September 1894. But see also his post-election article, "Les responsabilités," *L'Autorité*, 15 October 1889, in which he severely criticized Boulanger for remaining within the framework of legality.

[105] *J.O. 1889, Ch.D., Débats*, p. 575, session of 14 March. Cassagnac called for suppression of the anti-revision article so that the monarchists could "raise their flags."

[106] *J.O. 1886, Ch.D., Débats*, p. 1203, session of 26 June.

[107] *Ibid.*, p. 1206.

[108] *J.O. 1889, Ch.D., Débats*, p. 263, session of 31 January.

[109] "Notre droit," *L'Autorité*, 9 August 1889. This article constituted a rebuttal to *Le Temps*, 5 August 1889.

[110] "Manifeste de la Délégation des Droites," *Le Figaro*, 22 June 1889. Judging from the style and tone, it is likely that Cassagnac drafted this manifesto. For the endorsement of Prince Victor, see *L'Autorité*, 26 June 1889. The principal points of the manifesto were echoed by Baron de Mackau in his end-of-session speech before the assembled deputies of the *Union des Droites*, 12 July 1889.

[111] "Le parti national," *L'Autorité*, 12 August 1887; *Oeuvres*, I, 421. See also Cassagnac's speech in the Chamber, 31 January 1889 [*J.O. 1889, Ch.D., Débats*, p. 255].

[112] "Verte réplique," *L'Autorité*, 26 July 1889. See also his speech in the Chamber, 14 March 1889, and the articles, "Leur personnel" and "Contre qui?

in *L'Autorité*, issues of 8 July and 20 Sept. 1889.

[113] "Leur personnel," *L'Autorité*, 8 July 1889. In late July 1889, Mackau counseled the Comte de Paris to make no move that could be interpreted as specifically royalist. No properly "political" currents, monarchist or republican, were in evidence, he wrote; even *Boulangisme*, "however intense as a state of opinion, avowed or latent, is not a political current . . . . It does not correspond to a special form of government." Letter of 26 July 1889. A.N., 156 AP I.

[114] In a series of articles in *L'Autorité*, 20, 21, and 22 April 1889; reprinted in pamphlet form as "Les trois étapes."

[115] "Après la victoire," *L'Autorité*, 21 April 1889.

[116] "La prise de pouvoir," *L'Autorité*, 22 April 1889.

[117] "Sans révolution" *L'Autorité*, 12 May 1889. See also "Pas de révolution," *L'Autorité*, 21 September 1889.

[118] *L'Autorité*, 30 April 1889.

[119] Edouard Drumont, *La Dernière bataille* (Paris, 1890), p. 186.

NOTES - CHAPTER X

[1] S. William Halperin, "Leo XIII and the Roman Question," in Edward T. Gargan, ed., *Leo XIII and the Modern World* (New York, 1961), pp. 114-17. Quotation, p. 116.

[2] *Ibid.*, footnote 43, pp. 123-24.

[3] Eduardo Soderini, *Leo XIII, Italy and France*, tr. from the Italian by Barbara B. Carter (London, 1935), p. 199. Soderini was an intimate of the papal household and had access to materials in the Vatican archives that were, at that time, unavailable to the public.

[4] For Cassagnac's criticism, see *L'Autorité*, issues of 16 November 1890, 28 December 1891, and 24 February 1892. See also the letter addressed by Keller to Leo XIII, 7 February 1891, published by Xavier de Montclos, *Le Toast d'Alger: Documents 1890-1891* (Paris, 1966), pp. 316-22, and the arguments advanced by Hulst to various colleagues, which were incorporated into Freppel's memo of 13 February 1891, quoted by Alfred Baudrillart, *Vie de Monseigneur d'Hulst*, II (Paris, 1914), 308-14.

[5] That the Vatican was sensitive to such charges and sought to counter them early in the discussion is clear from the perceptive analysis of the Roman question by Montclos, *Toast d'Alger*, pp. 28-30. Leo XIII firmly believed that separation of Church and State in France, which would result from any rupture of the Concordat, would not lead to freedom for the Church but to a diminuition of its strength and influence. See Soderini, *Leo XIII*, pp. 201-2. Recently, however, a scholar who has carefully examined the functioning of the Concordatory regime between 1891 and 1902 has criticized it for its "discouragement of any Catholic initiative outside the traditional pattern." See Maurice J. M. Larkin, "The Church and the French Concordat, 1891 to 1902," *English Historical Review*, LXXXI(1966), 739.

[6] According to Soderini, *Leo XIII*, pp. 183-84. However, according to Baudrillart, *Mgr d'Hulst*, II, 270-73, the seeds of the ralliement had been planted in Rome in 1880 by Cardinal Lavigerie.

[7] Among the principal sources and studies that reflect a pro-ralliement point of view, the most important are the statements of Cardinal Lavigerie himself, available in Jules Tournier, *Le Cardinal Lavigerie et son action politique (1863-1892), d'après des documents nouveaux et inédits* (Paris, 1913); of Cardinal Ferrata, papal nuncio in France from July 1891 to October 1896, in his *"Mémoires," ma nonciature en France* (Paris, 1922); and of Jacques Piou, *Le Ralliement, son histoire* (Paris, 1928). These arguments are likewise enshrined in the valuable series of volumes published by the Oratorian scholar, Edouard

Lecanuet, under the general title of *L'Église de France sous la Troisième République* (Paris, 1910-1931), and predominate in a number of the more general works including C. S. Phillips, *The Church in France, 1789-1907*, II (London, 1936), and Adrien Dansette, *Histoire religieuse de la France contemporaine* (Paris, 1965). Recent monographs that reflect the pro-ralliement point of view include the dissertation by John Woodall; the study of the politics of the Right in the Chamber from 1898 to 1898 by David Shapiro, "The Ralliement in the Politics of the 1890's," in David Shapiro, ed., *The Right in France 1890-1919* (London, 1962); and the study of Étienne Lamy, one of the rare Catholic republicans, by Alexander Sedgwick, entitled *The Ralliement in French Politics, 1890-1898* (Cambridge, Mass., 1965). For an excellent summary of the historiography of the Algiers toast (as well as of subsequent steps in *ralliement*, see Montclos, *Toast d'Alger*, pp. 3-24. See also the overview by John McManners, *Church and State in France, 1870-1914* (London, 1972).

[8] As, for instance, in Raymond H. Schmandt, "The Life and Work of Leo XIII," in Gargan, ed., *Leo XIII and the Modern World*, pp. 31-32.

[9] This argument was publicly articulated by Comte Othénin d'Haussonville in a speech to a royalist group in Nîmes, 8 February 1891. The Comte de Paris drew constantly on this argument, as is clear from his letters to various sympathizers during 1891 and 1892; for examples, see those quoted in *La Monarchie française*, pp. 178-89, and in Baudrillart, *Mgr d'Hulst*, II, 302 and 332-334. Following Haussonville's speech, Lavigerie drew up a memo in which, adopting the viewpoint of an ultramontane priest, he denounced dissenters from the *ralliement* instructions as Gallicans and, therefore, heretics by the definition of the Vatican Council of 1870. This document, never published in its day, is quoted by Montclos, *Toast d'Alger*, pp. 283-87.

[10] Fernand Laudet, *Soixante ans de souvenirs* (Paris, 1934), p. 116. Fernand Laudet (1860-1933) was a diplomat and writer He was trained in law and served in the diplomatic service in Berlin and at the Vatican (in the latter post from 1899 to 1904). In 1893 he ran against Paul de Cassagnac for the Chamber as a *rallié*. He was a member of the Gers *conseil-général* from 1892 to 1898. Later he wrote in the conservative press and published a number of books, many of which dealt with Gascony. He was director of the *Revue hebdomadaire* until 1919 and, from 1920 until his death, of the *Revue de la semaine*. He was elected to the *Académie des sciences morales et politiques* in 1919.

[11] See the letters quoted by Montclos: Lavigerie to Leo XIII, 22 November 1890, 14 December 1890; Lavigerie to Cardinal Ferrata, 2 January 1891. *Toast d'Alger*, pp. 94, 114, and 292-93. See also the minute of a note destined for *L'Univers*, from Lavigerie, undated, *ibid.*, esp. pp. 271-72.

[12] As, for example, that of Dansette, *Histoire religieuse*, pp. 479-80.

[13] On this subject, see Lavigerie's memo to Mgr d'Hulst in 1885; quoted by Baudrillart, *Mgr d'Hulst*, II, 289.

[14] In 1906 Cassagnac's two sons, Paul-Julien and Guy, in the company of the deputy Jules Delahaye, founded an organization for political action which they called the *Ligue de Résistance des Catholiques Français*. After encountering considerable initial popular success, the young Cassagnacs met serious opposition from the French episcopacy which, in line with the above-stated principle, effectively forbade participation, either by clerics or by members of other Catholic lay organizations, in this *Ligue*. At that time, the only French Catholic political organization which had the approval of the hierarchy and Rome was Piou's *Action libérale*. For the details of this situation, see the account by Emmanuel Barbier, *Histoire du catholicisme libéral et du catholicisme social en France du Concile du Vatican à l'avènement de S.S. Benoît XI (1870-1914)* (Bordeaux, 1924), IV, 128-33.

[15] A sample: from *L'Osservatore Romano*, reprinted in *L'Avenir du Gers*, 5 January 1892, more than a month before the *ralliement* encyclical:

> *En vérité, on ne peut considérer comme un vrai zèle celui qui pousse un homme qui veut prendre l'attitude de défenseur de la foi et de l'Église à faire une amère censure de la conduite du Saint-Siège et de ses représentants en ce qui regarde les intérêts religieux, à jeter des injures et du discrédit sur les prélats respectables qui ne font pas tout ce que voudrait le journaliste et à pousser les fidèles à la révolte contre la légitime autorité ecclésiastique. M. de Cassagnac devrait se rappeler que ceux qui veulent défendre, avec l'esprit du catholique sincère, la religion, ne peuvent ni ne doivent mêler les intérêts religieux avec ceux de leurs partis.*

Quoted by Maurice Bordès, "La presse gersoise et le ralliement," *Congrès de Rodez des Fédérations des Sociétés Savantes Languedoc-Méditerranéen et du Languedoc-Pyrénées. Juin 1958* (Rodez, 1958), 354-55.

[16] In the diocese of Digne, October 1892, and in the diocese of Nantes, September 1894; see *L'Autorité*, 3 October 1892 and 22 September 1894. Cassagnac's paper usually shared the blacklist with Drumont's *La Libre Parole*.

[17] "Un vrai!" and "Nos évêques," *L'Autorité*, 1 and 5 September 1891.

[18] The Comte de Paris referred to this in his reply to Mackau, 31 January 1889; see also Mackau to the prince, 17 October 1889. A.N., 156 AP I.

[19] "Les avances," *L'Autorité*, 7 October 1889; "L'opposition systématique," *L'Autorité*, 21 October 1889. Both in *Oeuvres*, I, 450-53 and 459.

[20] "A Droite," *L'Autorité*, 15 November 1889. See also *L'Année politique -- 1889*, pp. 204 and 211-12.

[21] "Les groupes de Droite," *L'Autorité*, 22 December 1889.

[22] "L'union de la Droite," *L'Autorité*, 25 January 1890.

[23] *L'Autorité*, 26 January 1890; *Oeuvres*, I, 459-63.

[24] It was Paul de Cassagnac who moved Méline's election as president, stressing the Right's intention to place the spirit of duty before the spirit of party in the national interest. On the formation of this group, see *L'Autorité*, 1 and 4 December 1889, and on the organizational meeting of 5 December, see the account in E. O. Golob, *The Meline Tariff* (New York, 1944), pp. 170-72.

[25] *L'Autorité*, 30 January 1890.

[26] *L'Autorité*, 13 March 1890.

[27] *L'Autorité*, 24 and 27 March, 2 and 3 April 1890; *Oeuvres*, I, 463-69.

[28] Mackau to the Comte de Paris, 20 May 1890. A.N., 156 AP I.

[29] See his remarks on the adoption of an anti-republican slogan by a newspaper in western France, in *L'Autorité*, 23 June 1890; *Oeuvres*, I, 469-73.

[30] From an extensive report on the *Ligue*, signed "Pepin," 3 July 1890, A.P.P., B^A 1000. I have found no mention of this organization in *L'Autorité* and no further record of its development. Cassagnac may have been inspired by the publication by a provincial conservative newspaper of a list of freemasons, with the suggestion that commerce with them be avoided; he remarked at that time that such a thing should be done all over France. *L'Autorité*, 11 September 1886.

[31] "L'affaissement," *L'Autorité*, 6 November 1890.

[32] "Ma République," *L'Autorité*, 14 November 1890; *Oeuvres*, I, 477-81.

[33] "Adhésion-résignation," *L'Autorité*, 16 November 1890; *Oeuvres*, I, 482-86.

[34] "Ce qu'est la République," *L'Autorité*, 22 November 1890; *Oeuvres*, I, 486-90. See Montclos, *Toast d'Alger*, p. 4, for prior uses of this argument.

[35] "La question des évêques," *L'Autorité*, 26 November 1890; *Oeuvres*, I, 490-95. See also *L'Autorité*, 22 September 1894 and 27 May 1896.

[36] *Ibid*.

[37] In the Chamber, 10 December 1890. *Oeuvres*, IV, esp. 430-38. See also the articles "Ma contrition," and "L'attitude du parti conservateur," *L'Autorité*, issues of 13 and 15 December 1890.

[38] Quoted in *L'Autorité*, 15 December 1890.

[39] "Entre deux selles," *L'Autorité*, 11 February 1891.

[40] "La réponse de M. Piou," *L'Autorité*, 13 February 1891.

[41] "Leur évolution," *L'Autorité*, 14 February 1891.

[42] The text of Freppel's note submitted to Leo XIII on 13 February 1890 is reproduced in Montclos, *Toast d'Alger*, pp. 328-31. Barbier, *Histoire du catholicisme libéral*, II, 298-300, provides considerable information on Freppel's visit as well as the text of the note from the deputies referred to above. For Cassagnac's comments, see *L'Autorité*, 28 December 1891.

[43] See Cassagnac's remarks in "La vraie formule," *L'Autorité*, 7 March 1891; *Oeuvres*, I, 521-24. See also Dansette, *Histoire religieuse*, p. 455.

[44] Dansette, *Histoire religieuse*, p. 455. This group was dissolved the following year.

[45] On Lavigerie and Fava, see *L'Autorité*, 25 July 1891; on Fould, *L'Autorité*, 21 and 31 August and 4 September 1891.

[46] "Drapeau au vent!" *L'Autorité*, 10 September 1891.

[47] For details, see Dansette, *Histoire religieuse*, pp. 457-58.

[48] In the Chamber, 11 December 1891. Cassagnac's speech is reprinted in *Oeuvres*, IV, 439-68. See his additional remarks concerning this speech in *L'Autorité*, 5 and 10 January 1892. For discussion of Cassagnac's earlier statements on separation of Church and State, see Chapter V.

[49] "A M. Francis Magnard, directeur du *Figaro*," *L'Autorité*, 14 January 1892.

[50] The text of the cardinals' declaration, complemented by an unsympathetic *explication de texte*, is given by R. Schnir, "Une épisode du ralliement: contribution à l'étude des rapports de l'église et de l'état sous la Troisième République," *Revue d'histoire moderne*, IX (1934), 193-226 and 317-39.

[51] Mgr d'Hulst to Abbe Pisani, 24 January 1892; quoted by Baudrillart, *Mgr d'Hulst*, II, 332. See also pp. 327-30 on Hulst's part in drafting the declaration.

[52] "Les cinq," *L'Autorité*, 24 January 1892.

[53] Dansette, *Histoire religieuse*, pp. 458-59.

[54] "Le dernier crapaud," *L'Autorité*, 15 February 1892; *Oeuvres*, VI, 248-52.

[55] The text of the encyclical is reproduced, among many other places, in Débidour, *L'Église catholique*, II, appendix III. In English, see *The Great Encyclical Letters of Leo XIII* (New York, 1903). For a discussion of its content and its implications, see Dansette, *Histoire religieuse*, pp. 460-61.

[56] "La grande parole," *L'Autorité*, 22 February 1892; *Oeuvres*, I, 586-87.

[57] *Ibid.*, 589.

[58] "L'interprétation et les conséquences," *L'Autorité*, 24 February 1892; *Oeuvres*, I, 591.

[59] *Ibid.*, 594.

[60] See, for instance, the harsh appreciation of Cassagnac's articles concerning the encyclical, quoted from Ferrata's *Mémoires* by Marcel Prélot in his collection, *Le Libéralisme catholique* (Paris, 1969), p. 307.

[61] On these letters, see Dansette, *Histoire religieuse*, pp. 461-62. See also *L'Autorité*, 8 and 10 May 1892.

[62] As attested by the Comte de Paris in a private letter to Cassagnac, 26 June 1892. Cassagnac family papers.

[63] From *L'Autorité*, 11 June 1892; , II, 7-8.

[64] Soderini, *Leo XIII*, p. 229.

[65] *Ibid.*, pp. 229-30.

[66] *L'Autorité*, 24 March and 10 June 1892.

[67] Text in *L'Autorité*, 14 October 1892.

[68] "Bonne chance!" *L'Autorité*, 16 October 1892; *Oeuvres*, II, 30-34.

[69] Cassagnac to Mackau, undated (but context dates it as October 1892). Mackau papers, A.N., 156 AP I.

[70] *L'Autorité*. 22 October 1892.

[71] *L'Autorité*, 4 June and 22 September 1892.

[72] *L'Osservatore Romano*, 5 June 1892. Quoted in *L'Autorité*, 11 June 1892.

[73] Edouard-Adolphe Drumont (1844-1917). A good summary of Drumont's career is provided in Emmanuel Beau de Loménie, *Edouard Drumont, ou l'anticapitalisme national* (Paris, 1968), an anthology of Drumont's work prefaced by an introductory essay. See also Georges Bernanos, *La Grande peur des bien-pensants, Edouard Drumont* (Paris, 1931), and Michel Winock, *Edouard Drumont et Cie: antisémitisme et fascisme en France* (Paris, 1982).

[74] *L'Autorité*, 5 May 1886. See also the issues of 22 April 1887 and 26 October 1889.

[75] "Le nouveau livre de Drumont," *L'Autorité*, 20 March 1891.

[76] "La question juive," *L'Autorité*, 18 November 1891; *Oeuvres*, VIII, 219-22.

[77] On antisemitism among the Catholics, see Chapter V of Robert F. Byrnes, *Antisemitism in Modern France* (New Brunswick, N.J.), 1950), pp. 179-224. In *The Dreyfus Case: A Reassessment* (London, 1955), Guy Chapman has also commented on Cassagnac's distinctive position (pp. 79, 85, 127, 267).

[78] See *L'Autorité*, issues of 9 and 14 December 1894, 14 September 1896, and 14 November 1897. The above-listed articles have been quoted by Patrice Boussel, *L'Affaire Dreyfus et la presse* (Paris, 1960), pp. 56, 58, 93-94, and 122.

[79] *L'Autorité*, 14 November 1897.

[80] See the prior discussion on this point in Chapter VI.

[81] Edouard Drumont, *Testament d'un antisémite* (Paris, 1891), pp. 4-6.

[82] See the account by Adrien Dansette, *Les Affaires du Panama* (Paris, 1934).

[83] *L'Autorité*, 18 May 1889. In a later article (23 December 1892), Cassagnac remarked that he had written fifty articles and had made three speeches on behalf of the victims of Panama.

[84] *L'Autorité*, issues of 23 November and 23 December 1892, and "Lettre à M. Brisson, président de la commission d'enquête," *L'Autorité*, 17 January 1893.

[85] "Devant la commission d'enquête," *L'Autorité*, 19 January 1893.

[86] See *L'Autorité*, 20 May and 7 August 1892.

[87] *L'Autorité*, 12 August 1893.

[88] *L'Autorité*, 7 August 1892.

[89] Bordès, who has studied the question most closely, has concluded (and in this he concurs with Cassagnac) that the republicans achieved victory in Gers in 1893 primarily because of the way conservative opinion was disoriented by *ralliement*. "La presse gersoise," 359.

[90] *L'Autorité*, 9 June 1893. On Laudet, see the biographical sketch in the notes earlier in this chapter (n. 10).

[91] "La parfait 'honnête homme' et catholique pratiquant," *L'Autorité*, 8 August 1892. For Laudet's versions of the election, see his *Souvenirs*, pp. 136-37. Laudet insisted that Cassagnac initially encouraged his candidacy, then turned against him.

[92] "Par file a Gauche!" *L'Autorité*, 9 June 1893; *Oeuvres*, II, 64-67.

[93] Bordès, "La presse gersoise," 358. See also Maurice Bordès, "Contribution à l'étude de la presse dans le département du Gers, sous la IIIe République," *Recueil des Actes du XIIe Congrès d'Études de la Fédération des Sociétés Académiques et Savantes Languedoc, Pyrénées, Gascogne. Toulouse, 21-23 Avril 1956* (Albi, 1958), 117-18.

[94] "En pleine bataille," *L'Autorité*, 16 June 1893.

[95] "Non et jamais!" *L'Autorité*, 5 November 1892; *Oeuvres*, II, 39-43. See also Laudet's letter to the *Journal des Débats* and Cassagnac's reply, in *L'Autorité*, 16 August 1893 (Laudet did not mention any of these incidents in his *Souvenirs*), and *L'Autorité*, 12 August 1893.

[96] "A MM. les électeurs de l'arrondissement de Mirande," *L'Autorité*, 6 August 1893.

[97] He spelled out the details in "Le vol," *L'Autorité*, 30 August 1893; *Oeuvres*, II, 76-79. The Comte de Paris offered Cassagnac the services of a royalist deputy to protest the administrative tampering in the Chamber, but Cassagnac declined. Letters of the Comte de Paris to Cassagnac, 4 September 1893 and 5 January 1894. Cassagnac family papers.

[98] *L'Autorité*, 23 and 24 August 1893.

[99] "A mes amis," *L'Autorité*, 6 September 1893; *Oeuvres*, II, 79.

[100] *Ibid.*, 81-83.

[101] *Ibid.*, 80.

[102] Albert Guerard, *French Prophets of Yesterday* (New York, 1920), p. 182.

[103] *Le Figaro*, 8 March 1889; quoted by Jacques Néré, *Le Boulangisme et la presse* (Paris, 1964), p. 182.

[104] See the remarks of David Shapiro, "Ralliement," in Shapiro, ed., *The Right in France*, p. 44.

[105] See Eugen Weber's remarks on the Vatican campaign against the *Action Française* in his book of the same name (Stanford, Calif., 1962), pp. 236-39.

[106] Schmandt, "Life and Work of Leo XIII," p. 32.

[107] *Ibid.*

[108] Weber, *Action Française*, pp. 219-55.

[109] Dugué de la Fauconnerie, in a speech before the Chamber, 2 December 1886. Quoted in *L'Autorité*, 4 December 1886.

[110] See Delafosse's article, "En vacances," 18 May 1886. Quoted in his collection, *A travers la politique* (Paris, 1889), pp. 94-95.

[111] In one article, "La charité sous la R.F.," *L'Autorité*, 3 January 1890, Cassagnac cited the example of the Bureau de bienfaisance in Besançon, which had refused charity to the child of a poor family because he attended a parochial school rather than the communal school.

[112] In the article "Trop tard," *L'Autorité*, 1 September 1886. See also "La république et les catholiques," *L'Autorité*, 21 March 1889; *Oeuvres*, I, 441-44.

[113] In 1897 Cassagnac was elected vice-president of the *Syndicat de la presse parisienne*, and served as its acting president during the Waldeck-Rousseau ministry, at which time the titular president, Jean Dupuy, was a minister. See "M. Paul de Cassagnac, " *La Croix*, 6 November 1904.

[114] "Les gages," *L'Autorité*, 5 May 1896; *Oeuvres*, II, 218.

[115] "Chrétiens et chrétiens," *L'Autorité*, 15 May 1896; *Oeuvres*, II, 220-25.

[116] See his letter to his constituents, *L'Autorité*, 6 April 1898; *Oeuvres*, II, 309-10.

[117] This photograph, a copy of which is in my possession, was partially reproduced in 1904 in *La France contemporaine, album illustrée, biographique,* 5 vols., III (Paris, 1904), accompanied by a sketch by Edouard Drumont. Unpaginated. See the illustration following this chapter.

[118] "Lettre de Paris," in the *Journal de Génève*, 6 November 1904. See also the remarks by H. Harduin, "Propos d'un Parisien," *Le Matin*, 7 November 1904. Both articles were found in a collection of obituary clippings in the Cassagnac family papers.

[119] Drumont in *La Libre Parole*, 8 November 1904.

[120] *Ibid.*

[121] H. de Gallier, "Deux polemistes," *Le Carnet*, VI (1903), 110. The epitaph translates roughly as follows:

> The bugle can still be heard, but there are anguished notes.
> It is the horn of Roland that sounds. But Charlemagne has
> not appeared, alas! nor has his army. . . .

NOTES - CHAPTER XI

[1] See, for example, the study by Michael Curtis, *Three against the Third Republic: Sorel, Barrès, and Maurras* (Princeton, N.J., 1959).

[2] See René Rémond, *La Droite en France: de la première restauration à la Ve République*, 2nd ed., rev. (Paris, 1963), pp. 157-77, for his elaboration of this view.

[3] *Ibid.*, p. 171.

[4] *Ibid.*, p. 165.

[5] As, for example, in the articles of Raoul Girardet, "Pour une introduction à l'histoire du nationalisme français," *Revue Française de Science Politique*, VIII (1958), 505-28, and D. R. Watson, "The Nationalist Movement in Paris, 1900-1906," in David Shapiro, ed. *The Right in France 1890-1919: Three Studies* (London, 1962), pp. 49-84.

See also Zeev Sternhell, "Paul Déroulède and the Origins of Modern French Nationalism" *Journal of Contemporary History*, VI (1971), 46-70; Sternhell seems unaware of the Bonapartist sources of Déroulède's plebiscitary nationalism. More recently, the earlier tendency to discuss nationalism in terms of a shift from Left to Right without examining the deeper implications of those terms is evidenced in an otherwise enlightening study by Peter M. Rutkoff, "The Ligue des Patriotes: The Nature of the Radical Right and the Dreyfus Affair," *French Historical Studies*, VIII (Fall 1974), 585-603. Rutkoff attempts to steer for safer shores in the "Conclusion" to his book, *Revanche and Revision: The Ligue des Patriotes and the Origins of the Radical Right in France, 1882-1900* (Athens, Ohio, 1981). An additional important contribution is Steven Englund, "The Origins of Oppositional Nationalism in France, 1881-1889" (unpublished doctoral dissertation, Princeton University, 1981)

[6] In a tribute to Cassagnac in *La Libre Parole*, 8 November 1904. Indeed, Cassagnac himself had insisted on this similarity. In early 1900 he remarked that, electorally speaking, the new *ligues* "ne sont que des copies, que des imitations de 'l'Union Conservatrice,' et des imitations incomplètes et maladroites, condamnées à être stériles. . . ." because they demanded support of the republic. *L'Autorité*, 17 February 1900; *Oeuvres*, II, 386-90. See also his article calling for a *Union Nationale* in *L'Autorité*, 14 May 1900; *Oeuvres*, II, 416-21.

[7] "Lettre ouverte à M. Jules Lemaître," *L'Autorité*, 15 February 1900; *Oeuvres*, II, 382-85. At the time of its founding, Cassagnac characterized this *Ligue* as "La Ligue de la chèvre et du chou." *L'Autorité*, 5 January 1899; *Oeuvres*, II, 329.

On the *Ligue de la Patrie Française*, see V. Cleve Alexander, "Jules Lemaître and the *Ligue de la Patrie Française*" (unpublished doctoral dissertation, Indiana University, Bloomington, 1975), and Jean-Pierre Rioux, *Nationalisme et conservatisme: la Ligue de la Patrie Française, 1899-1904* (Paris, 1977).

[8] Gustave Cunéo d'Ornano provided the handbook for revisionist republican Victorism with his book, *La République de Napoléon* (Paris, 1894).

[9] "Le plébiscite intégral," *L'Autorité*, 20 August 1900. See also Cassagnac's earlier polemic with Cunéo d'Ornano on this subject in *L'Autorité*: "Empire ou République," 7 July 1895; "Affaire des gouts!", 25 May 1896; and "D'Orléans et Napoléon," 28 May 1896. All reproduced in *Oeuvres*, I, 236-56. During the polemic, Cunéo d'Ornano wrote to Mme de Cassagnac, asking for her advice as he feared the dispute might endanger his lifelong friendship with Cassagnac. His letters, dated 28 May and 3 June 1896, are preserved in the Cassagnac family papers. There are also police reports concerning this polemic in A.P.P., B[A] 1000.

[10] "Le patriotisme," *L'Autorité*, 1 June 1899; *Oeuvres*, II, 338-42. This article is misdated in the *Oeuvres* as 1 June 1900. See also "Le vrai nationalisme," *L'Autorité*, 29 July 1900; *Oeuvres*, II, 446-50.

[11] See the report by "Moineau," 22 December 1899. A.P.P., B[A] 1000.

[12] See the "imperialist" resolution voted in 1900 by the plebiscitary Bonapartist committees of the Seine at their annual 15 August banquet, and Cassagnac's exultant comments thereon, in *L'Autorité*, 20, 23, and 27 August 1900. The Paris police closely followed this struggle for capture of the Paris committees, as frequent reports in A.P.P. B[A] 1000 and B[A] 1001 attest.

[13] Cassagnac's police dossier B[A] 1001 contains a variety of press clippings and reports concerning this duel.

[14] "Le nationalisme," *L'Autorité*, 17 May 1900; *Oeuvres*, II, 425.

[15] "Religion et patrie," *L'Autorité*, 26 January 1887; *Oeuvres*, VI, 127-29. See also his article, "Dieu et la république," *L'Autorité*, 17 September 1900; *Oeuvres*, II, 454-57.

[16] Cassagnac's earliest complaints on this subject appeared in *Le Pays*, 5 October 1883. His thoughts found continuation in a book written by his elder son, Paul-Julien de Cassagnac, *Pour la tradition: Le Solutionnisme* (Paris, 1910). On p. 24, the young Cassagnac distinguished five elements that in his estimation comprised French tradition -- Catholic religion, monarchy, *patrie*, the [male-headed] family, and individual property -- which he juxtaposed with five "revolutionary" opposites -- atheism, republican parliamentarism, international society, the individual, and collectivist property.

[17] In T. W. Adorno et al., *The Authoritarian Personality* (New York, 1950). See also R. Christie and M. Jahoda, eds., *Studies in the Scope and Method of "The Authoritarian Personality"* (Glencoe, Ill, 1954). Christie

remarked in his study, "Authoritarianism Re-examined," in the latter book (p. 126), that the term "authoritarian" is used by Adorno and his associates in the sense of "potential fascist," but (pp. 130-33) in fact their F-scale does not discriminate between fascistic and non-fascistic authoritarians, just as it does not screen out authoritarians of the political Left from those of the political Right. It seems unlikely, knowing what we do of Paul de Cassagnac's political and cultural beliefs, and even taking cultural differences into account, that he would have scored high on the F-scale test.

In *La Droite en France* (2nd ed., pp. 212-15), Rémond has tackled the question of what is properly "authoritarian tradition" and what is "fascism" in France. He posits, on the experience both of Bonapartism and of the *ligues* gravitating to the Right, that an "authentic fascism," with its anti-traditionalism and its insistence on being a unique party, could never acclimate itself in France. See also the discussion of this question by Raoul Girardet, "Notes sur l'esprit d'un fascisme français, 1934-1939," *Revue Française de Science Politique*, V (1955), 529-46, which supports Rémond's conclusions.

[18] Rémond, *La Droite en France*, p. 171.

[19] David Thomson, *Democracy in France since 1870*, 4th ed., revised (New York, 1964) p. 34.

[20] For attempts by a team of German and French historians and social scientists to sort out this confusion, see Karl Hammer and Peter Claus Hartmann, eds., *Le Bonapartisme/Der Bonapartismus: phénomène historique et mythe politique* (Munich, 1977).

[21] The confusion appears to have been consecrated by the late André Siegfried who, in his *Tableau politique de la France* , underscored the Caesarian aspects of neo-royalist nationalism incarnated by the *Action Française*; quoted by Robert K. Gooch, "The Antiparliamentary Movement in France," *American Political Science Review*, XXI(1927), 552, note 32. More recently, see the reevaluation by Paul Mazgaj, *The Action Française and Revolutionary Syndicalism* (Chapel Hill, N.C., 1979).

[22] See Eugen Weber, *Action Française* (Stanford, Calif., 1962), and Ernst Nolte, *Three Faces of Fascism: Action Française, Italian Fascism, National Socialism* (New York, 1966; originally published in German, 1963).

[23] It was Gooch (*ibid.*, 356) who emphasized the point that all those who favored direct action were antiparliamentary. This may have been true in the 1920s but the claim ought not be projected backward.

[24] Jean-Marie Mayeur, *La Séparation de l'Eglise et de l'Etat* (Paris, 1966), and Benjamin F. Martin, *Count Albert de Mun* (Chapel Hill, 1978).

See also Maurice Larkin, *Church and State after the Dreyfus Affair: The Separation Issue in France* (London, 1974); and Malcolm O. Partin, *Waldeck-Rousseau, Combes, and the Church, 1899-1905: The Politics of Anticlericalism* (Durham, N.C., 1974). New studies on the thought and politics of Maurras are: Colette Capitan, *Charles Maurras et l'idéologie de l'Action française: Etude sociologique d'une pensée de droite* (Paris, 1972); and Michael Sutton, *Nationalism, Positivism, and Catholicism: The Politics of Charles Maurras and French Catholics, 1890-1914* (New York and Cambridge, 1983).

[25] The Cassagnac family papers contain many clippings, photographs, and documents pertaining to this duel, which took place on 26 February 1912.

[26] Mss. "Souvenirs de trois générations," p. 178. Cassagnac family papers.

[27] See especially Alphonse V. Roche, *Les Idées traditionalistes en France de Rivarol à Charles Maurras* (Paris, 1937), pp. 34-109.

[28] Charles Maurras, *Enquête sur la monarchie*, 3rd ed. (Paris, 1909), p. 9. Maurras apparently did not interview Cassagnac during his original inquiry. This surprising absence might be explained by the long-standing hostility that existed between Cassagnac and "legitimist" *La Gazette de France*, for which Maurras was writing at the time.

[29] Teste, *Les Monarchistes sous la IIIe République*, pp. 172-73.

[30] Quoted by Samuel Osgood, *French Royalism under the Third and Fourth Republics* (The Hague, 1960), p. 60, from the *Dictionnaire politique et critique*, II, 76.

[31] Georges Hoog, *Les Conservateurs et la IIIe République: notes d'histoire* (Paris, 1910), p. 118. Hoog was a leading figure in *Le Sillon*.

BIBLIOGRAPHY

1. Manuscript sources

Unpublished materials in private collections

Cassagnac Family Papers

Family papers preserved by Xavier de Cassagnac, Graulhet (Tarn); formerly at the Chateau de Couloumé, near Plaisance (Gers). These papers comprise part of a larger family archive which is described (although some of the materials described can no longer be located and are presumed destroyed) in an article by Émile Houth, "Note sur trois fonds d'archives privées du département du Gers," *Bulletin philologique et historique du Comité des Travaux historiques et scientifiques, 1958* (Paris, 1959).

Papers concerning Paul-Adolphe-Marie-Prosper Granier de Cassagnac include a collection of correspondence, scrapbooks, electoral notebooks and newspaper clippings, photographs and caricatures. Of particular interest for this study is Cassagnac's correspondence with the Prince Imperial, with Prince Victor-Napoléon, with Philippe d'Orléans (the Comte de Paris), and with Isabelle de Bourbon, former queen of Spain and godmother to Cassagnac's elder son. Also of interest are several letters from Baron de Mackau and Mgr. Dupanloup.

Unpublished materials in public depositories

ARCHIVES NATIONALES (A.N.), Paris

Mackau Papers, 156 AP I

Papers of Anne-Frédéric-Armand, Baron de Mackau. Formerly preserved at the Chateau de Vimer (Orne). Deposited at the Archives Nationales by his granddaughter, the Vicomtesse de Bonneval. A published inventory is now available.

Of particular importance for this study are Mackau's manuscript memoirs, which illuminate his role in the *Seize Mai*, his mission to the Vatican in 1884, and his part in the Rouvier ministry in 1887. Also important is his extensive correspondence with the Comte de Paris during the 1880s.

Of general importance are the vast files concerning Mackau's legislative career. These contain a number of confidential reports and press clippings concerning Bonapartist party activities and the alliance of the Right with Boulanger, as well as correspondence pertaining to the electoral campaigns of 1889. These files contain a number of letters from Paul de Cassagnac and other leading figures of the monarchist right.

Jules Simon Papers, 87 AP 17

Dossier 11: Correspondence with Lissagaray.

Murat Papers, 31 AP 65

Dossier 5: Letter from Paul de Cassagnac.

Correspondence de la Division criminelle du Ministre de la Justice Sub-Series BB[18]

Cartons:

1679 -- *Diogène.* Cassagnac duel with Aurelien Scholl, Nov. 1863.

1743 -- Defamation suit brought against Cassagnac and Vermorel, Dec. 1866; hostilities between *Le Courrier français* and *Le Pays*, July 1867.

1769 -- Duel involving Cassagnac, 10 March 1868.

1771b - *L'Avenir d'Auch*: 1868-1870.

1784 -- Élections législatifs, 1869. Campaign of A. Granier de Cassagnac in Gers; continuation of papers on *L'Avenir* in 1771b.

Administration générale de la France Series F

Cartons:

F[lb] I 10/12 -- Personnel du ministère de l'intérieur, 1860-1866.

Contains material on the establishment of the Fifth Bureau,

Direction générale du personnel et du cabinet, where Paul de
Cassagnac worked from 1865 to 1867.

F^{1b}II Gers 9 -- Correspondence relative to the appointment of mayors
in Gers during the 1870s.

Gers 14 -- Couloumé, *idem.*, mayors of Couloumé.

Gers 19 -- Plaisance, *idem.*, mayors of Plaisance.

F^7 12428-30 -- "Agissements bonapartistes." Administrative and
espionage reports on the comings and goings of Prince Napoléon
from 1891 to 1891; on travelers to Chislehurst for the coming-of-
age ceremonies for the Prince Imperial in 1874; and on the
impact on public opinion of the deaths of Napoleon III (1873) and
the Prince Imperial (1879).

F^{18} 400 -- *Le Pays*. Includes materials 1848-1880. Of particular
interest are the reports and clippings for the years 1865-70 and
1876-77.

F^{18} 2495 -- Auch. Dossier on Mgr Gouzot, Bishop of Auch from
1887 to 1895.

ARCHIVES DE LA PRÉFECTURE DE POLICE (A.P.P.), PARIS

A scholar using these archives can do no better than to follow the counsel
of Léon Renault, Prefect of Police from 1871 to 1876: "These reports may be
helpful for research, but must never be considered sufficient evidence for
conviction." [Deposition of Renault before the parliamentary inquiry committee
on the Nièvre election, 1875. *Annales, A.N.*, vol. 37, p. 269.]

Besides police reports, these dossiers contain press clippings and occasional
pamphlets which even the most exhaustive researcher might otherwise miss.
They provide a mine of information, subject to cross-checking and verification.

The series B^A is by far the richest, but some useful materials can be located
in series E as well.

Cartons and/or dossiers consulted on Bonapartist and royalist activities:

B^A 62 -- Comités bonapartistes (1874-1889).

B^A 68 -- Anniversaires de la mort de Napoléon III.

B^A 404 and 405 -- "Menées légitimistes." The first file contains
materials from 1882-83; the latter file, 1884-88, is primarily on
the activities of the "Blancs d'Espagne" group from 1885 on, but
does contain some useful reports on the activities of the Comte de
Paris and his organization for 1884.

B^A 417 through 419 -- Famille impériale/affaires bonapartistes. The first file dates from 1869-72; the second contains only materials from 1873; and the third covers the period from 1874 to 1891.

B^A 581 and 589 (Gers) -- Élections législatives 1877.

B^A 611, and 613 through 616 -- Élections législatives 1885.

Cartons and/or dossiers consulted on individual persons (listed alphabetically):

B^A 864 and 865 -- Jules Amigues.

B^A 997 through 1001 -- Paul de Cassagnac (five large cartons).

B^A 909 -- Jean-Joseph Cornély.

B^A 1038 -- Henri Dichard.

B^A 909 -- General F.-C. du Barail. [Supplements in E/a 33 (15).]

B^A 1059 -- F. Dunal.

B^A 1094 -- Eugène Gibiat (owner of *Le Pays* and *Le Constitutionnel*).

B^A 1099 -- A. Granier de Cassagnac and Georges Granier de Cassagnac

B^A 1129 -- Eugène Jolibois.

B^A 908 -- Louis Lacave-Laplagne (senator from Gers).

B^A 1134 -- H.-A. Lacaze (*gérant* of *L'Autorité*, 1887-1899).

B^A 1197-1202 -- Prince Jérôme-Napoléon (Supplements in E/a 100).

B^A 1202 and 1203 -- Louis, Prince Imperial.

B^A 69 and 70; B^A 1634 -- Prince Victor-Napoléon.

B^A 1212 -- Duc de Padoue (Arrighi de Casanova).

B^A 1242 -- Jules Richard and Maurice Richard.

B^A 1255 -- Albert Rogat (journalist at *Le Pays* & *L'Autorité*).

B^A 1257 and 1258 -- Eugène Rouher.

ARCHIVES DÉPARTEMENTALES DU GERS (A.D. Gers), AUCH

When I first visited these archives in 1967, there was as yet no satisfactory set of printed guides and researchers were literally at the mercy of the archivists. Two guides to materials have since been published that can greatly expedite a researcher's work:

Archives départemental du Gers (Henri Polge, archiviste).
Guide des Archives du Gers. Auch, 1975.

Bibliothèque nationale. Département des Périodiques.
Bibliographie de la presse française politique et

d'information générale, 1865-1944. 32 - Gers, by Patrice
Caillot. Paris, 1975.

Cartons and dossiers consulted:

Famille Cassagnac

Five unnumbered dossiers on members of the family. These contain a
number of articles, pamphlets, etc., by and on Paul de Cassagnac and his father,
Bernard-Adolphe Granier de Cassagnac; prefectoral correspondence for 1868-69
concerning the distribution of judicial announcements (the State's means of
subsidizing the local newspaper of its choice); and correspondence concerning
Cassagnac's election to the *conseil-général* in 1869.

Comtes morales et politiques
Series M

Dossiers:
   1865 -- Cabinet. Correspondance. État d'esprit. Affaires
   confidentiels. 1869-1904.
   2237 -- Rapports hebdomadaires (commissaires de police) sur la
   situation politique, morale et économique, 1876-77.
   2278 -- Continues material in 2237.
   2230 -- Continues material in 2237 and 2278, for the years 1878 and
   1879.

Presse, imprimerie, librairie
Series T

Dossiers:
   109 -- Presse. Journaux distribués dans le Gers. Tableaux
   numériques, 1832-1878.
   148 -- Imprimerie et librairie. Dépôt légal -- Registres, 1835-78.
   Provides an index of the relative strength of political newspapers
   in Gers, especially during the 1870s.

BIBLIOTHEQUE NATIONALE (CABINET DES MANUSCRITS)

Here one finds only random, incidental letters from Paul de Cassagnac addressed to various political personalities. These are scattered through the *Nouvelles acquisitions françaises* (Nouv. acqu. fr.). None have made a significant contribution to this study.

As of 1970, I had consulted letters located in the following collections:

13580 -- Papers of Joseph Reinach.

22903 -- Collection of autographs.

24233 -- Papers of Louis Veuillot.

24264 -- Nadar collection of autographs.

25161 -- Papers of Edouard Lockroy, Victor Hugo

Since that time a few others have been identified.

2. Government Documents

France. *Almanach national. Annuaire officiel de la République Française.*
1873-1896.

――――. *Journal Officiel de la République Française. Débats parlementaires.*
Chambre des députés. 1876-1893.

――――. Assemblée Nationale. *Annales de l'Assemblée nationale.*
1871-1875. Vols. 1-45.

――――. Chambre des Députés. *Annales du Sénat et de la Chambre des*
députés. 1876-1880.

――――. Chambre des Députés. *Annales de la Chambre des députés. Débats*
parlementaires. 1881-1893.

――――. Corps Législatif. *Annales du Sénat et du Corps législatif.* 1868.

――――. Institut National de la Statistique et des Études Économiques.
Direction Régionale de Toulouse. *Évolution de la population totale*
légale des communes du département du Gers de 1876 à 1954.
Toulouse, 1960.

3. Almanacs, Handbooks, and Encyclopedias

Avenel, Henri. *Annuaire de la presse française.* Paris, 1886, 1890, 1892, and
1893.

Curinier, C.-E., ed. *Dictionnaire national des contemporains.* 5 vols. in 2.
Paris, 1899-1905.

Daniel, André (pseud. A. Lebon). *L'Année politique.* 1874-1893. Paris, 1875-
1894.

Dictionnaire de biographie française. 11 vols. Paris, 1933- (in progress).
In 1990, the most recent fascicule available is no. 104: Jacob-
Jauberthou.

Hoefer, J.-C.-F. *Nouvelle biographie universelle.* 46 vols. Paris, 1852-1877.

Hutton, Patrick H., ed. *Historical Dictionary of the Third French Republic,*
1870-1940. 2 vols. New York, 1986.

Jolly, Jean. *Dictionnaire des parlementaires français, 1889 à 1940.* 8 vols.
Paris, 1960-1977.

Larousse, P., ed. *Grand dictionnaire universel du XIXe siècle.* 15 vols. Paris,
1865-1876. 2 vols. supplement. Paris, 1878, 1890.

Marcheix, H.-P. *Bibliographie analytique des biographies des parlementaires*
français de 1871 à 1960. Paris, 1961.

Pierrard, P. *Dictionnaire de la IIIe République.* Paris, 1968.

Robert, A. and Cougny, G., eds. *Dictionnaire des parlementaires français, 1789-1889*. 5 vols. Paris, 1889-1891.

Vapereau, G., ed. *Dictionnaire des contemporains*. 5th ed. Paris, 1880, and 6th ed., Paris, 1893.

4. Newspapers

Paul de Cassagnac published an article daily during most of his political career. These articles appeared primarily in the following newspapers:

Le Pays, 1871-1885. Paris.
> From October 1871 until November 1885, Cassagnac edited this afternoon daily, which was considered to be the most "violent" of the independent Bonapartist publications.

Le Matin, 1884-1886. Paris. *Le Matin Français*, August-October 1884.
> "Grand journal d'opinion." Daily. Featured weekly columns by representatives of the four major parties during the 1880s -- opportunist republican (Emmanuel Arène); radical republican (Jules Vallès); royalist (Jean Cornély); and imperialist (Paul de Cassagnac). When Cassagnac left in early 1886 to found his own newspaper, he was replaced by Jules Delafosse.

L'Autorité, 1886-1904. Paris.
> Sub-titled: "Pour Dieu, pour la France!" This morning daily was Paul de Cassagnac's own newspaper. Following his death in 1904, publication was continued by his sons Paul-Julien and Guy until mid-1913.

Le Petit Caporal. Paris.
> Many of Cassagnac's articles were reprinted in this popular "imperialist" five-centime paper, which stimulated considerable competition from the Jeromists during the 1880s. After the Victorist schism in 1884, the supporters of Prince Victor were divided into "solutionist" and "anti-solutionist" factions, represented respectively by *Le Petit Caporal* and *Le Souverainété*.

5. Published Works of Paul de Cassagnac and other family members

The bulk of Paul de Cassagnac's writings was published in the daily press (see section 4, Newspapers, above) but he also published a number of popular pamphlets, the most important of which are listed below in order of their publication.

A Rabagas. Paris, 1872.
A 16-page pamphlet in which Cassagnac attacked Gambetta and the war "à outrance" waged by the Government of National Defense in 1870.

Empire et royauté. Paris, 1873.
A 40-page pamphlet written during late 1873, criticizing the royalist attempt to restore the Comte de Chambord. Cassagnac contrasted the "modern ideas" represented by the empire with the pre-revolutionary concern for "divine right" and "legitimacy" that prevailed in the royalist camp.

Le Mémorial de Chislehurst, 1808-1873. N.p., N.d.
An 8-page brochure that appears to be the introduction for a subsequent history of Napoleon III.

Histoire populaire abrégée de Napoléon III. Paris, 1874.
Best described as *petite histoire*, with a strong anti-Bourbon, anti-Orleanist bias.

Bataille électorale. La Revanche du scrutin. Histoire de nulle part et de partout. Paris, 1875.
A 64-page pamphlet. Electoral propaganda. Addressed to "the people." Paints a fictitious picture of an electoral gathering in the Midi, with a heroic imperialist candidate and his opponents -- a retrograde royalist, a free-thinking, materialistic Orleanist, and a scrofulous republican.

Two longer works, which can also be considered pamphlets, are:

Histoire populaire illustrée de l'Empereur Napoléon III. 2 vols. Paris, 1874.
Co-authored by Paul de Cassagnac and his father. Publication coincided with the coming-of-age of the Prince Imperial.

Histoire de la Troisième République. Paris, 1876.
Deals primarily with the period from August 1870 to May 1871. A breviary of the anti-republican arguments employed by the Bonapartists.

The accounts of Cassagnac's two major press trials are generally attributed to him:

Le Procès de Sedan. Paris, 1875.
This 64-page pamphlet, with a picture of Cassagnac on the cover, also appeared in a 128-page format entitled:
La Journée de Sedan devant la Cour d'Assises de la Seine -- Procès Paul de Cassagnac. Cour d'assises de la Seine. Audiences des 12, 13, et 15 Février 1875. Publié par Le Gaulois. Paris, 1875.

Le Procès de Belleville: 13 Décembre 1875. Discours de la Salle Graffard. Plaidoiries de MM. Paul de Cassagnac, Edmond Tarbé, Me Grandperret. Paris, 1875.

Cassagnac also produced almanacs containing reprints of articles from his newspapers:
L'Aigle, almanach illustré du suffrage universel. Paris, 1875-1878.
L'Aigle, almanach du "Petit Caporal." Paris, 1879 and 1880.
Almanach de l'Autorité. Paris, 1893, 1894, 1898, and 1902.
Aux Électeurs. 1902.

He wrote occasional prefaces for books by others:
Letter-preface to F. Daynaud, L'Appel au peuple. Auch, 1873.
Preface to Gaston Jollivet, Nos Petits grands hommes. Paris, 1884.
Preface (along with Arthur Ranc and Anatole de La Forge) to Jules Jacob, Le Jeu de l'épée. Paris, 1887.

Following his death in 1904, Cassagnac's widow and his two sons published an eight-volume anthology of his articles. These collected works include many, although not all, of his most important articles and a number of his major speeches.
Paul de Cassagnac: Oeuvres. Paris, 1905.
The first three volumes, "Principes, caractère, politique," contain most of the specifically political articles. Vol. IV is devoted to speeches. Vol. V, "Effigies républicaines," contains articles about various political personalities. Vol. VI contains articles on morals and religion. Vol. VII concerns socio-economic questions, and Vol. VIII, political-social questions. The bulk of the articles date from the 1890s.
Many of Cassagnac's speeches in the Chamber of Deputies and his articles have appeared as separate offprints. These are not listed here as I have relied on official accounts for the speeches and have, in all cases, referred to the original articles in the press.

Paul de Cassagnac took many of his historical arguments from the published histories written by his father, Bernard-Adolphe Granier de Cassagnac. These works are listed below in order of their publication.

Histoire des classes ouvrières et des classes bourgeoises. Paris, 1838.

Histoire des classes nobles et des classes annoblies. Paris, 1840.

Histoire des causes de la Révolution française. 3 vols. Paris, 1850.
This work was dedicated to Pope Pius IX.

Récit complet et authentique des événements de décembre 1851. Paris, 1851.
The authorized account of Louis-Napoleon's *coup d'état.*

Histoire du Directoire. 3 vols. New ed. Paris, 1863. Original ed., Brussels, 1851-52.

Histoire de la chute de Louis-Philippe, de la république de 1848 et du rétablissement de l'Empire. 2 vols. Paris, 1857.

Histoire des Girondins et des massacres de septembre. 2 vols. 2nd ed. Paris, 1860.

L'Empereur et la démocratie moderne. Paris, 1860.
An authorized explanation of the decree of 24 November 1860.

Other works by Granier de Cassagnac pertinent to this study are:

Voyage aux Antilles. Paris, 1842.

A chacun sa part dans nos désastres. Sedan, ses causes et ses suites. Paris, 1871.

Souvenirs du Second Empire. 3 vols. Paris, 1879-1882.

Paul de Cassagnac's son, Paul-Julien, who also wrote under the name of Paul de Cassagnac (thereby creating considerable confusion for unwary historians), published a book in 1910 that reflected many of his late father's ideas. In this work he offered a call for the organization of the Catholic opposition:

Pour la tradition: le Solutionnisme. Paris, 1910.

6. Biographies and Biographical Materials on Paul de Cassagnac

Prior to my own study, no full-length biography of Paul de Cassagnac had been attempted. Shorter works and important articles on which I have drawn for particulars include the following: for annotations on these works, see my dissertation, 1971 (below).

Alméras, H. d'. "Paul de Cassagnac." *Avant la gloire: leurs débuts.* Second series. Paris, 1903.

Audouard, Olympe. *Silhouettes Parisiens.* Paris, 1883.

Branicki, le comte. *En Souvenir de Paul de Cassagnac.* Paris, 1904.

Champsaur, Félicien, and Le Petit, Alfred. *Les Contemporains, journal hebdomadaire. No. 26 -- Paul de Cassagnac.* Paris, 1881.

"Chez M. de Cassagnac." Interview in *Le Matin,* 14 November 1899.

Croquez, Albert. *Paul de Cassagnac.* Paris, 1911.

Demesse, Henri. *Paul de Cassagnac.* Paris, 1879.

Drumont, Edouard. "Paul de Cassagnac." *La France contemporaine: album illustrée, biographique.* Vol. III. Paris, 1904. Unpaginated.

--------. Obituary tribute in *La Libre Parole,* 8 November 1904.

Duchaussoy, Roger. "Duels et duellistes du XIXe siècle: Les Cassagnac." *L'Escrime Française,* no. 159 (December 1961), 3-6; no. 160 (January 1962), 4-9.

"F. D." *Paul de Cassagnac.* Amiens, 1889.

"La Famille Cassagnac." *L'Autorité,* 18 February 1902.

Gallier, H. de. "Deux polémistes." *Le Carnet,* VI (1903), 107-16.

Gaubert, Ernest. Obituary for Paul de Cassagnac. *La Revue Universelle,* no. 123 (1 December 1904), 659-60.

Jollivet, Gaston. "Un Improvisateur," *L'Éclair,* 8 November 1904.

Laurent, Charles. "M. Paul de Cassagnac." *La France,* 2 April 1875.

--------. "Tartarin de Tarascon et de Paris." *La France,* 11 September 1877.

--------. "Les Croquemorts politiques." *La France,* 18 November 1877.

--------. "Adorable rondeur." *Paris,* 25 August 1886.

--------. "Impérialisme et bonapartisme." *Paris,* 6 November 1886.

--------. "Les Bimonarchistes." *Paris,* 11 September 1887.

--------. "Paul de Cassagnac." *Le Matin,* 6 November 1904.

Mirecourt, Eugène de. *Histoire contemporaine. Portraits et silhouettes au XIXe siècle. No. 93 -- Paul de Cassagnac.* Paris, 1870.

Mitchell, Robert. "Paul de Cassagnac -- mes souvenirs." *Le Gaulois,* 6 November 1904.

"Mme Renée" (pseud.of Caroline Rémy Guebhard, called Séverine). "Nos Députés -- M. de Cassagnac." *Le Gaulois*; reprinted in *L'Autorité*, 21 October 1888.

"Montjoyeux." Article on Cassagnac and his new bride. *Le Gaulois*, 14 November 1878.

Normand, F. "Les Cassagnac." *Les Contemporains*. No. 1092 (14 September 1913).

"Notice nécrologique." *Polybiblion*, 2nd series, LX (December 1904), 539-40.

Offen, Karen. "The Political Career of Paul de Cassagnac." Unpublished doctoral dissertation, Stanford University, 1971.

--------. "Paul de Cassagnac," in *Historical Dictionary of the Third French Republic*, ed. Patrick H. Hutton, 2 vols. (1986).

"Paul de Cassagnac." *Correspondance Nationale et les Nouvelles*. 9 November 1904.

Vauxcelles, L. and Pottier, P. *"L'Autorité."* In a series, "La Presse d'aujourd'hui." *Gil Blas*, 4 February 1904.

7. Primary Sources

[Multiple works by the same author are listed in their order of publication.]

Amigues, Jules. *Les Aveux d'un conspirateur bonapartiste: histoires d'hier, pour servir à l'histoire de demain.* Paris, 1874.

Andrieux, Louis. *Souvenirs d'un préfet de police.* 2 vols. Paris, 1885.

Audiffret-Pasquier, Duc de. *La Maison de France et l'Assemblée Nationale: Souvenirs, 1871-1873.* Paris, 1938.

Avenel, Henri. *Le Monde des journaux en 1895.* Paris, 1895.

--------. *Histoire de la presse française depuis 1789 jusqu'à nos jours.* Paris, 1900.

Barbey d'Aurevilly, Jules. *Journalistes et polémistes, chroniqueurs et pamphletaires.* Paris, 1895.

--------. *De l'histoire.* Paris, 1905.

Barbier, Emmanuel. *Histoire du catholicisme libéral et du catholicisme social en France du Concile du Vatican à l'avènement de S. S. Benoît XV (1870- 1914).* 6 vols. Bordeaux, 1924.

Bashkirtseff, Marie. *Journal de Marie Bashkirtseff.* 2 vols. Paris, 1887. Also in English as *Journal of Marie Bashkirtseff,* tr. A. D. Hall. Chicago, 1908.

--------. *Cahiers intimes inédits,* ed. Pierre Borel. Paris, 1925.

Baudrillart, Alfred. *Vie de Monseigneur d'Hulst.* 2 vols. Paris, 1912-1914.

Bavoux, Evariste. *Du Principe d'autorité et du parlementarisme.* Paris, 1869.

--------. *La France sous Napoléon III: L'Empire et le régime parlementaire.* Paris, 1870.

Benda, Julien. "L'Affaire Dreyfus et le principe d'autorité." *La Revue Blanche,* XX (1899), 190-206.

Benoist, Charles. "Le N'importequisme." *RDM* (15 December 1925), 801-18.

--------. *Souvenirs de Charles Benoist.* 3 vols. Paris, 1932-1934.

Bernanos, Georges. *La Grande peur des bien-pensants, Edouard Drumont.* Paris, 1931.

Bertaut, Jules. *Figures contemporains. Chroniqueuers et polémistes.* Paris, 1906.

Bodley, J. *France.* 2 vols. New ed. London, 1900.

Boinvilliers, Edouard. *Le Septennat.* Paris, 1874.

--------. *A Quoi servent les parlements, 1815, 1830, 1848, 1870.* Paris, 1883.

Bournand, François. *Les Juifs et nos contemporains (l'antisémitisme et la question juive).* Paris, 1899.

Breteuil, Marquis de. "Les Coulisses du Boulangisme." *RDM* (1 June 1969), 467-94, and (1 August 1969), 252-80.

--------. *La Haute société: journal secret 1886-1889.* Paris, 1979.

Broglie, Albert de. "Mémoires." Series III. *RDM,* (15 October 1929), 793-823; (1 November, 15 November, 1 December 1929), 130-61, 364-87, 559-95.

Castellane, Marquis de. *La Politique conservatrice: les cahiers conservatrices en 1889.* Paris, 1889.

Castille, Hippolyte. *Les Journaux et les journalistes sous le règne de Louis-Philippe.* Paris, 1858.

Chambord, Comte de; Paris, Comte de; Orléans, Duc d'. *La Monarchie française: Lettres et documents politiques (1844-1907).* Paris, 1907.

Champsaur, Félicien, and Le Petit, Alfred. *Les Contemporains, journal hebdomadaire: Jean Cornély.* Paris, 1881.

Cheyssac, L. de. *Le Ralliement.* Paris, 1906.

Cinglais, Pierre de. *Gustave Cunéo d'Ornano, 1845-1906.* Cognac, 1908.

Cohn, Adolphe. "Boulangism and the Republic." *Atlantic Monthly* (January 1891), 92-98.

"Un Conservateur." *Le Parti Bonapartiste et ses hommes.* Paris, 1875.

Constant, C. *Petit manuel des électeurs et des candidats.* Paris, 1889.

Cordier, P. *Boulangisme et bonapartisme, ou la réaction masquée.* Paris, 1889.

Corticchiato, Paul. *Les Corses et le parti bonapartiste à Marseille en 1870 et pendant les premières années de la République.* Marseille, 1921.

Coubertin, Pierre de. *L'Évolution française sous la IIIe République.* Paris, 1896.

Croissy, T. de. *Droits et devoirs des électeurs.* Paris, 1889.

Cunéo d'Ornano, Gustave. *Gambetta plébiscitaire.* Paris, 1895.

--------. *La République de Napoléon.* Paris, 1894.

Daudet, Léon. *Fantômes et vivants.* New ed. Paris, 1931.

--------. *Salons et journaux.* Paris, 1917.

--------. *Flammes,* Paris, 1930.

Daynaud, F. *L'Appel au peuple.* Auch, 1873.

Decaux, Alain. *La Castiglione.* Paris, 1959.

Delafosse, Jules.*Le Procès du 4 septembre. Le Crime de l'opposition. Qui a voulu la guerre? Sedan! La Justice de l'Assemblée. Pièces justificatives.* Paris, [1875].

--------. *A Travers la politique.* Paris, 1889.

--------. *Études et portraits.* Paris, 1894.

--------. *Figures contemporains.* Paris, 1899.

--------. "Le Bonapartisme." *Revue Hebdomadaire* (19 February 1910), 308-32.

--------. *Théorie de l'ordre.* Paris, 1901.

Despagnet, Franz. *La République et le Vatican, 1870-1906.* Paris, 1906.

Dichard, Henri. *Le Victorisme et le parti Bonapartiste.* Paris, 1885.

--------. *La Fin d'un prince.* Paris, 1886.

Donoso Cortés, Juan, Marquis de Valdegamas. *Oeuvres*, introduced by L. Veuillot. 3 vols. Lyon, 1876.

--------. *An Essay on Catholicism, Authority and Order Considered in their Fundamental Principles.* Tr. from the Spanish by M. V. Goddard. New ed. New York, 1925.

Dréolle, Ernest. *Napoléon IV. 1856-1873. Souvenir de Chislehurst.* Paris, 1873.

--------. *Guide de l'électeur bonapartiste.* Paris, 1875.

Dreux-Brézé, Marquis de. *Notes et souvenirs pour servir à l'histoire du parti royaliste, 1872-1883.* 4th ed. Paris, 1899.

Drumont, Edouard. *La Fin d'un monde.* Paris, 1889.

--------. *La Dernière bataille.* Paris, 1890.

--------. *Testament d'un antisémite.* Paris, 1891.

Ducamp, Maxime. *Souvenirs.* Vol. II. Paris, 1949.

Dugué de la Fauconnerie, Henri-Joseph. *Si l'Empire revient.* Paris, 1875.

--------. *Souvenirs d'un vieil homme.* Paris, 1912.

Dupanloup, Félix. *Avertissement à la jeunesse et aux pères de famille sur les attaques dirigées contre la religion par quelques écrivains de nos jours.* Paris, 1863.

--------. *L'Athéisme et le péril social.* Paris, 1866.

--------. *La Liberté de l'enseignement supérieur.* Paris, 1868.

--------. *Journal intime de Monseigneur Dupanloup; extraits recueillis et publiés par L. Branchereau.* Paris, 1902.

Éspinay de Bricort, Ch. d', ed. "Une Correspondance inédite. Le Prince Impérial et E. Lavisse." *RDM*, (1 April 1929), 555-91.

Falloux, Alfred, Comte de. *Mémoires d'un royaliste.* 3 vols. Paris, 1925-1926.

Faure-Biguet, Charles. *Paroles plébiscitaires, 1906-1913.* Paris, 1913.

Ferry, Jules. *Lettres de Jules Ferry, 1846-1893.* Paris, 1914.

"Fidus" (pseud. E. de Balleyguier, called Loudun). *Journal de Fidus sous la république opportuniste.* Paris, 1888.

--------. *Journal de dix ans.* 2 vols. Paris, 1886.

Filon, Augustin. *Le Prince Impérial. Souvenirs et documents (1856-1879).* Paris, 1912.

--------. *Souvenirs sur l'Impératrice Eugénie.* 13th ed. Paris, 1920.

Fleury, Émile-Félix, comte. *Souvenirs du général c^{te} Fleury.* 2 vols. Paris, 1897-1898.

Fleury, Maurice, comte. *Memoirs of the Empress Eugenie.* New York, 1920.

Fouquier, Armand. *Causes célèbres.* Vol. II. Paris, 1859.

Freycinet, Charles de. *Souvenirs 1878-1893*. 4th ed. Paris, 1913.

Friedrichs, Otto. *Le Journal de M. de Cassagnac et Louis XVII; réponse à un article paru dans* l'Autorité *du 26 janvier 1887*. Paris, 1887.

Gambetta, Leon. *Lettres de Gambetta* (ed. Daniel Halévy and Émile Pillias). Paris, 1938.

Gay, Ernest (pseud. of Ernest Garennes). *Dernière défaite*. Paris, 1891.

Girardeau, Fernand. *L'Empire*. Paris, 1884.

Guyot, Yves. "France and Boulangism." *Westminster Review* (June 1888), 748-64.

Hanotaux, Gabriel. *Histoire de la France contemporaine*. 4 vols. Paris, 1903-1908.

--------. *Mon temps*. Vols. I and II. Paris, 1933 ff.

Haussonville, Gabriel-Paul-Othenin de Cléron, Comte d'. "Le Comte de Paris -- Souvenirs personnels." *RDM* (1 September 1895), 5-38.

--------. "Le Seize Mai jugé par M. Hanotaux." *Le Gaulois*, 21 November and 6 December 1908.

--------. *Ombres françaises et visions anglaises*. Paris, 1914.

Hilbey, Constant. *Vénalité des journaux, révélations accompagnées de preuves*. Paris, 1845.

--------. *Plaidoyer de Constant Hilbey en réponse à l'assignation de M. Granier de Cassagnac*. Paris, 1845.

--------. *Réponse à tous mes critiques*. Paris, 1846.

--------. *Nouveau procès des quatre couverts et des six petites cuillères d'argent*. Paris, 1846.

Hoog, Georges. *Les Conservateurs et la IIIe République*. Paris, 1910.

Irisson d'Hérisson, Maurice, comte de. *Le Prince Impérial (Napoléon IV)*. Paris, 1890.

Keller, Émile. *L'Encyclique du 8 Décembre 1864 et les principes de 1789, ou l'eglise, l'état et la liberté*. 2nd ed. (Paris, 1866).

Labat, Emmanuel. *L'Ame paysanne; la terre, la race, l'école*. Paris, 1919.

La Chapelle, Comte de. *Les Représentants de l'Appel au peuple*. Paris, 1875.

Lachaud, Georges. *Les Bonapartistes et la république*. Paris, 1877.

--------. *Nos Politiciens: voyage au pays des blagueurs*. Paris, 1879.

--------. *Histoire d'un manifeste*. Paris, 1883.

Latour du Moulin, P.-C. *La France et le Septennat*. Paris, 1874.

Laudet, Fernand. *Soixante ans de souvenirs*. Paris, 1934.

Laugel, Auguste. "Mémoires de Laugel." *La Revue de Paris* (15 December 1925), 52-80.

--------. "Le Maréchal de Mac-Mahon et le 16 mai." *La Revue de Paris* (1 August 1926), 500-36.

Lavelaye, E. de. "La Démocratie et le régime parlementaire." *RDM* (15 December 1882), 824-50.

Lavergne, Bernard. *Les Deux présidences de Jules Grévy, 1879-1887: Mémoires de Bernard Lavergne*, notes et commentaires de J. Elleinstein. Paris, 1966.

Lenglè, Paul. *Le Neveu de Bonaparte: souvenir de nos campagnes politiques avec le prince Napoléon Bonaparte, 1879-1891.* Paris, 1893.

Leo XIII. *The Great Encyclical Letters of Leo XIII.* New York, 1903.

Le Page, Auguste. *Les Boutiques d'esprit.* Paris, 1879.

Lespes, Pascher. *Haiti devant la France. . . Réponse à Monsieur Paul de Cassagnac.* 2nd ed. Port-au-Prince, 1891.

Luçay, H., Comte de. Secrétariat Général des Droites de la Chambre. *Rapport sur les travaux du Comité d'études parlementaires.* 4 vols.

--------. *Répertoire contenant l'indication des brochures et tracts de propagande, des ouvrages à consulter et des sources de renseignements fournis par les documents parlementaires, à l'usage des candidats et des conférenciers.* Paris, 1889.

Mackau, A.-F.-A., Baron de. *"L'Union, prfface de la victoire." Discours prononcé . . . à la dernière réunion de l'Union des Droites (12 juillet 1889).* Paris, 1889.

Marcère, Émile de. *Histoire de la République, 1876-1879.* 2 vols. Paris, 1908-1910.

Martinet, André. *Le Prince Impérial, 1856-1879.* Paris, 1895.

--------. *Le Prince Victor-Napoléon.* Paris, 1895.

Maurras, Charles. "Le Duc Albert de Broglie, esquisse du libéralisme parlementaire." *La Revue hebdomadaire* (February 1901), 115-30.

--------. *Enquête sur la monarchie.* 3rd ed. Paris, 1909.

Maynard, Ulysse. *Monseigneur Dupanloup et M. Lagrange son historien.* 2nd ed. Paris, 1884.

Meaux, Marie, Vicomte de. *Souvenirs politiques, 1871-1877.* Paris, 1905.

Mels, A. *Wilhelmshoehe 1871: Souvenirs de la captivité de Napoléon III.* Paris, 1880.

Merson, Ernest. *Confessions d'un journaliste.* 2nd ed. Paris, 1890.

--------. *Confidences d'un journaliste.* Paris, 1891.

Meyer, Arthur. *Ce que je peux dire.* Paris, 1912.

--------. *Ce que mes yeux ont vu.* Paris, 1912.

Mitchell, Robert. "Souvenirs de captivité," *La Revue hebdomadaire* (8 May 1909), 217-34.

Mitchell, Robert, and Fleury, [Maurice], Comte. *Un Démi-siècle de mémoires.* Vol. I -- *Avant et pendant la guerre.* Paris, 1911.

Monti de Rézé, René-Marie-Joseph-Place de, comte de. *Souvenirs sur le comte de Chambord.* Paris, 1930.

Napoleon III. *Napoleonic Ideas* (ed. Brison D. Gooch). New York, 1967. Originally published in French 1839.

North Peat, Anthony B. *Gossip from Paris during the Second Empire; Correspondence (1864-1869) of Anthony B. North Peat*, ed. A. R. Waller. New York, 1903.

Ollivier, Émile. *Lettres d'exil, 1871-74*. Paris, 1921.

--------. *L'Empire libéral: études, récits, souvenirs*. Vol. 10 -- *L'agonie de l'Empire autoritaire*. Paris, 1905.

--------, and Carolyne de Sayn-Wittgenstein. *Correspondance, 1858-1887*, ed. Anne Troisier de Diaz. Paris, n.d.

Pascal, Ernest. *Discours politiques, 1878-1887*. Paris, 1889.

Perron, F. *Le Reveil de la France*. Paris, 1875.

Piou, Jacques. "Le Boulangisme." *La Revue de Paris* (15 March 1932), 301-20.

--------. *Le Comte Albert de Mun: sa vie publique*. Paris, 1919.

Raffalovitch, A. *"L'Abominable vénalité de la presse..."*. Paris, 1931.

Ranc, Arthur. *Souvenirs-Correspondance: 1831-1908*. Paris, 1913.

Rémusat, Charles de. *Mémoires de ma vie*. Vols. III and IV. Paris, 1960-1962.

Remy de Simony, H. *Le Parti conservateur et son avenir*. Lille, 1885.

Richard, Jules. *Le Bonapartisme sous la République*. 2nd ed. Paris, 1883.

Rogat, Albert. *Les Hommes du 4 septembre devant l'enquête parlementaire*. Paris, 1874.

Siegfried, André. "Une Crise ministérielle en 1887, d'après le journal de mon père [Jules Siegfried]," *Hommes et Mondes*, no. 45 (1950), 477-500.

Simon, Jules. *Le Soir de ma journée*. Paris, 1901.

Soderini, Eduardo. *Leo XIII, Italy and France*. Tr. from the Italian by Barbara B. Carter. London, 1935.

Teste, Louis. *Les Monarchistes sous la IIIe République*. Paris, 1891.

Texier, Edmond Auguste. *Critiques et récits littéraires*. Paris, 1853.

--------. *Le Journal et le journaliste*. Paris, 1868.

Thézan, A. de. *Réponse à la Revanche de M. P. de Cassagnac. La dynastie napoléonienne et la moralité de ses oeuvres*. Auch, 1875.

Thiers, Adolphe. *Thiers au pouvoir, 1871-73*. Paris, 1921.

Troplong, Raymond. *Du Principe d'autorité depuis 1789, suivi de nouvelles considérations sur le même sujet*. Paris, 1853.

Truman, Ben C. *The Field of Honor*. New York, 1884.

T'Serclaes de Woomersom, Charles. *Le Pape Léon XIII; sa vie, son action religieuse, politique et sociale*. 2 vols. Paris, Lille, 1894. In English as *The Life and Labors of Pope Leo XIII*, tr. by Maurice Francis Egan. Chicago, 1903.

Verly, Albert. *Le Général Boulanger et la conspiration monarchique*. Paris, 1893.

Veuillot, Eugène. *Louis Veuillot*. Vol. III -- *1855-1869*. Paris, 1904.

Villemessant, Jean-Hippolyte Cartier, dit de. *Mémoires d'un journaliste*. 6 vols. Paris, 1867-1878.

Vizetelly, Ernest ["Le petit homme rouge"]. *Court Life of the Second French Empire, 1852-1870*. New York, 1907.

--------. *Republican France, 1870-1912*. Boston, 1913.

Weiss, J.-J. *Combat constitutionnel (1868-1886)*. Paris, 1893.

"X" (Gabriel Terrail). *Les Coulisses du Boulangisme*. Paris, 1890.

Zola, Émile. "La Presse parisienne." *Études de Presse*, nouv. ser., VIII (1956), 261-78. Originally published in Russian in *Messager de l'Europe* in August 1877. Tr. from the Russian by A. Trifounovitch.

8. Secondary Works

Acomb, Evelyn M. *The French Laic Laws, 1879-1889.* New York, 1941.

Acomb, Evelyn M., and Brown, Marvin L., eds. *French Society and Culture since the Old Regime.* New York, 1966.

Adorno, T. W. et al. *The Authoritarian Personality.* New York, 1950.

Agulhon, Maurice. *Marianne into Battle: Republican Imagery and Symbolism in France, 1789-1880,* tr. Janet Lloyd. London and New York, 1981. Originally published in French, 1979.

--------. *Marianne au pouvoir. L'Imagerie et la symbolique républicaines de 1880 à 1914.* Paris, 1989.

Albert, Pierre. "Histoire de la presse politique nationale au début de la Troisième République, 1871-1879." Thèse d'état, University of Paris IV, 1977.

Alexander, V. Cleve. "Jules Lemaître and the Ligue de la Patrie Française," unpublished doctoral dissertation, Indiana University, Bloomington, 1975.

Anderson, Thomas. "Edouard Drumont and the Origins of Modern Anti-Semitism," *Catholic Historical Review,* LIII (1967), 28-42.

Atlas historique de la France contemporaine: 1800-1965. Paris, 1966.

Baqué, Z. "Les Origines vicoises de Lissagaray et sa parenté avec Granier de Cassagnac." *BSAG,* XLIX (1948), 126-31.

Bainville, Jacques. *The French Republic, 1870-1935.* Tr. from the French by Hamish Miles. London, 1940.

Barker, Nancy Nichols. *Distaff Diplomacy: The Empress Eugenie and the Foreign Policy of the Second Empire.* Austin, Texas, 1967.

Barral, Pierre. *Les Fondateurs de la Troisième République.* Paris, 1968.

Bayaud, Pierre. "Luttes électorales dans le Gers en 1876-79." *BSAG,* LX (1959), 347-58.

Beau de Loménie, Emmanuel. *La Restauration manquée: l'affaire du drapeau blanc.* Paris, 1932.

--------. *Les Responsabilités des dynasties bourgeoises.* 2 vols. Paris, 1943-1947.

--------. *Edouard Drumont, ou l'anticapitalisme nationale.* Paris, 1968.

Bédarida, François. "L'Armée et la république: les opinions politiques des officiers français en 1876-78." *Revue Historique,* CCXXXII (1964), 119-64.

Bellanger, Claude et al. *Histoire générale de la presse française.* Vol. III -- *De 1871 à 1940.* Paris, 1972.

Bellet, Roger. *Presse et journalisme sous le Second Empire.* Paris, 1967.

Bertocci, Philip A. *Jules Simon: Republican Anticlericalism and Cultural Politics in France, 1848-1886.* Columbia, Mo., 1978.

Bluche, Frédéric. *Le Bonapartisme: aux origines de la Droite autoritaire, 1800-1850.* Paris, 1980.

Bordès, Maurice. "Contribution à l'étude de la presse dans le département du Gers, sous la IIIe République." *Recueil des Actes du XIIe Congrés d'Études de la Fédération des Sociétés Académiques et Savantes Languedoc, Pyrénées, Gascogne.* Toulouse, 21-23 avril 1956. Albi, 1958. Pp. 114-23.

--------. "De la Gascogne à Paris: 'La Gazette' de Marie Poirée, militante républicaine des années 80." *BSAG,* LXVI (1965), 431ff.

--------. "La Presse gersoise et le ralliement." *Congrès de Rodez des Fédérations des Sociétés Savantes Languedoc-Méditerranéen et du Languedoc-Pyrénées. Juin 1958.* Rodez, 1958. Pp. 345-62.

--------. "Un Prefet de combat sous la IIIe République: Léonce Boudet (1887-1894)." *BSAG,* LX (1959), 373-84.

--------. "L'Évolution politique du Gers sous la IIIe République." *L'Information historique,* 23 (1961), 19-22.

Boussel, Patrice. *L'Affaire Dreyfus et la presse.* Paris, 1960.

Brogan, D. W. *The Development of Modern France (1870-1939).* New ed. London, 1963.

Brown, Marvin. *The Comte de Chambord.* Durham, N.C., 1967.

--------. "Catholic-Legitimist Militancy in the Early Years of the Third Republic," *Catholic Historical Review,* LX (1974), 223-54.

--------. *Louis Veuillot: French Ultramontane Catholic Journalist and Layman, 1813-1883.* Durham, N. C., 1978.

Brugmans, Henri. "Pourquoi le fascisme n'a-t-il pas 'pris' en France?" *Res Publica,* VII (1965), 77-85.

Bruneau, William Arthur. "An Apologia for Biography in French History," *Proceedings of the Western Society for French History, 1980,* VIII (1981), 568-76.

Brunet, Roger. *Les Campagnes toulousaines: étude géographique.* Toulouse, 1965.

Burnichon, Joseph. *La Compagnie de Jésus en France: histoire d'un siècle, 1814-1914.* Vol. IV. Paris, 1922.

Burns, Michael. *Rural Society and French Politics: Boulangism and the Dreyfus Affair.* Princeton, N. J., 1984.

Bury, J. P. T. *Gambetta and the Making of the Third Republic.* London, 1973.

--------. *Gambetta's Final Years: The Era of Difficulties, 1877-1882.* London, 1982.

--------, and Tombs, R. P. *Thiers, 1797-1877.* London, 1986.

Byrnes, Robert F. *Antisemitism in Modern France*. New Brunswick, N.J., 1950.

--------. "The French Publishing Industry and its Crisis in the 1890s." *Journal of Modern History*, XXIII (1951), 232-42.

Cadéot, Noël. "Un Journaliste républicain sous l'Empire: Lissagaray (1838-1901)." *BSAG*, XLVIII (1947), 285-306.

Cahuet, Albéric. *Moussia; ou la vie et la mort de Marie Bashkirtseff*. Paris, 1926.

Campbell, Peter. *French Electoral Systems and Elections since 1789*. 2nd ed. Hamden, Conn., 1965.

Campbell, Stuart L. *The Second Empire Revisited: A Study in French Historiography*. New Brunswick, N. J., 1978.

Capéran, L. *Histoire contemporaine de la laïcité française*. 3 vols. Paris, 1957-1961.

Capitan, Colette. *Charles Maurras et l'idéologie de l'Action française: étude sociologique d'une pensée de droite*. Paris, 1972.

Chapman, Guy. *The Dreyfus Case: A Reassessment*. London, 1955.

--------. *The Third Republic of France*. Vol. I. London, 1962.

Charnay, Jean-Paul. *Les Scrutins politiques en France de 1815 à 1962. Contestations et invalidations*. Paris, 1964.

Chastenet, Jacques. *Histoire de la Troisième République*. Vols. I-III. Paris, 1952-1955.

Christie, R. and Jahoda, M., eds. *Studies in the Scope and Method of "The Authoritarian Personality"*. Glencoe, Ill., 1954.

Collins, Irene. *The Government and the Newspaper Press in France: 1814-1881*. London, 1959.

Coppa, Frank J. *Cardinal Giacomo Antonelli and Papal Politics in European Affairs*. Albany, N.Y., 1990.

Corley, T. A. B. *Democratic Despot: A Life of Napoleon III*. New York, 1961.

Cosnier, Colette. *Marie Bashkirtseff: un portrait sans retouches*. Paris, 1985.

Cox, M. R. "The Liberal Legitimists and the Party of Order under the Second French Republic." *FHS*, V (1968), 446-64.

Curtis, Michael. *Three Against the Third Republic: Sorel, Barrès, and Maurras*. Princeton, N.J., 1959.

Dagnan, J. *Le Gers sous la Seconde République*. Vol. I -- *La réaction conservatrice*. Auch, 1928. Vol. II -- *Le Coup d'état et la répression dans le Gers*. Auch, 1929.

--------. "Le Gers sous le Second Empire." *La Révolution de 1848*, XXIX (1932-33), 51-61, 104-13, 161-78, 228-45; XXX (1933-34), 43-54, 192-99.

Dansette, Adrien. *L'Affaire Wilson et la chute du Président Grévy*. Paris, 1936.

--------. "Ernest Constans et le Boulangisme." *La Revue Universelle*, LXXI, no. 13 (1 October 1937), 14-32.

--------. *Le Boulangisme*. 9th ed. Paris, 1946.

--------. *Histoire religieuse de la France contemporaine*. New ed. Paris, 1965.

--------. "Le Rétablissement de l'Empire." *RDM* (15 September 1965), 168-86; and (1 October 1965), 334-52.

--------. *Du 2 décembre au 4 septembre: Le Second Empire*. Paris, 1972.

Débidour, Antonin. *L'Église catholique et l'état sous la Troisième République*. 2 vols. Paris, 1906-1909.

Dechamps, Jules-Albert. *Sur la légende de Napoléon*. Paris, 1931.

Denais, J. *Un Apôtre de la liberté: Jacques Piou, 1838-1932*. Paris, 1959.

Descotes, Maurice. *La Légende de Napoléon et les écrivains français du XIXe siècle*. Paris, 1967.

Desternes, Suzanne, and Chandet, Henriette. *Louis, Prince Impérial*. Paris, 1957.

Dogan, Mattei. "La Stabilité du personnel parlementaire sous la Troisième République." *Revue Française de Science Politique*, III (1953), 319-48.

Dominique, Pierre. *Les Polémistes français depuis 1789*. Paris, 1962.

Dormer Creston (pseud. Dorothy Julia Baynes). *Fountains of Youth: The Life of Marie Bashkirtseff*. London, 1936.

Doty, C. Stewart. "Parliamentary Boulangism after 1889." *Historian*, XXXII (1970), 250-69.

Droz, Jacques et al. *Restaurations et révolutions*. Paris, 1953.

Dunois, Amédée. "Notice sur Lissagaray." In H.-P.-O. Lissagaray, *Histoire de la Commune de 1870*. Paris, 1929. V-xxxvii.

Dupuy, Aimé. *1870-1871: La Guerre, la commune et la presse*. Paris, 1959.

Duroselle, Jean-Baptiste. *Clemenceau*. Paris, 1988.

Duvall, William Evan. "Bernard-Adolphe Granier de Cassagnac and Right-Wing Bonapartism under the Second Empire, 1860-1870." Unpublished doctoral dissertation, University of California at Santa Barbara, 1973.

--------. "René Rémond and the French Right, 1815-1870," *Proceedings of the Western Society for French History, 1977*, V (Santa Barbara, Calif., 1978), 283-91.

Duverger, Maurice et al. *L'Influence des systèmes électoraux sur la vie politique*. Paris, 1950.

Earle, E. M., ed. *Modern France: Problems of the IIIe and IVe Republics*. New ed. Princeton, N. J., 1964.

El Gammil, J. "Un Préralliement: Raoul-Duval et la droite républicaine, 1885-1887." *Revue d'histoire moderne et contemporaine*, XXIX (1982), 599-621.

Elwitt, Sanford. *The Making of the Third Republic: Class and Politics in France, 1868-1884*. Baton Rouge, La., 1975.

--------. *The Third Republic Defended: Bourgeois Reform in France, 1880-1914*. Baton Rouge, La., 1986.

English, Donald E. *Political Uses of Photography in the Third French Republic, 1871-1914*. Ann Arbor, Mich., 1984.

Englund, Steven. "The Origins of Oppositional Nationalism in France, 1881-1889." Unpublished Ph.D. dissertation, Princeton University, 1981.

Farmer, Paul. *France Reviews its Revolutionary Origins*. New York, 1963.

Fierain, Jacques. *Les Raffineries de sucre des ports en France, XIXe - début du XXe siècles*. New York, 1977.

Fisher, H. A. L. *Bonapartism*. Oxford, 1912.

Flory, Maurice. "L'Appel au peuple napoléonien," *Revue internationale d'histoire politique et constitutionnelle*, n.s. II (1952), 215-22.

Fox, Edward W. "An Estimate of the Character and Extent of Antiparliamentary Thought in France, 1887-1914." Unpublished doctoral dissertation, Harvard University, 1942.

--------. *History in Geographic Perspective: The Other France*. New York, 1971.

Fremantle, Anne, ed. *The Papal Encyclicals in their Historical Context*. Expanded ed. New York, 1963.

Fulton, L. B. "The Political Ascent of Ernest Constans: A Study in the Management of Republican Power," unpublished doctoral dissertation, University of Toronto, 1971.

--------. "Ernest Constans and the Presidency of the French Republic, 1889-1892," *Australian Journal of Politics and History*, XXX (1984), 31-45.

Furet, François, ed. *Jules Ferry, fondateur de la république*. Paris, 1985.

Gadille, Jacques. *La Pensée et l'action politiques des évêques français au début de la IIIe République, 1870-1883*. 2 vols. Paris, 1967.

Gaillard, Jean-Michel. *Jules Ferry*. Paris, 1989.

Galtier, F. *La Suppression de l'octroi*. Paris, 1901.

Gargan, Edward T., ed. *Leo XIII and the Modern World*. New York, 1961.

Garcon, Maurice. "Une Madone cosmopolite: Marie Bashkirtseff." *Les Annales*, nouvelle série, no. 39 (January 1954), 5-18.

--------. *Histoire de la justice sous la IIIe République*. 3 vols. Paris, 1957.

Gay, Peter. *Voltaire's Politics*. Princeton, N. J., 1959.

Geyl, Pieter. *Napoleon: For and Against*. New Haven, Conn., 1963.

Girard, Louis. *La Politique intérieure de la Troisième République, 1871-1914*. Vol. I. "Les cours de Sorbonne." Paris, n.d.

Girardet, Raoul. "Notes sur l'esprit d'un fascisme français, 1934-1939," *Revue française de science politique*, V (1955), 529-46.

--------. "Pour une introduction à l'histoire du nationalisme français." *Revue Française de Science Politique*, VIII (1958), 505-28.

--------. "Autour de l'idéologie nationaliste, perspectives de recherche," *Revue Française de Science Politique*, XV (1965), 423-45.

--------. *Le Nationalisme français*. Paris, 1966.

Goguel-Nyegaard, François. *La Politique des partis sous la IIIe République*. Paris, 1946.

--------. *Géographie des élections françaises de 1870 à 1951*. Paris, 1951.

--------. *Histoire des institutions politiques de la France de 1870 à 1940*. 3 vols. Paris, 1952. [Cours de droit, 1951-1952. Polycopie. Institut d'Études Politiques.]

--------, and Dupeux, Georges, eds. *Sociologie électorale*. Paris, 1951.

--------, and Grosser, Alfred. *La Politique en France*. Paris, 1964.

Goldstein, Robert J. *Censorship of Political Caricature in Nineteenth-Century France*. Kent, Ohio, 1989.

Golob, E. O. *The Méline Tariff: French Agriculture and Nationalist Economic Policy*. New York, 1944.

Gooch, Robert K. "The Antiparliamentary Movement in France." *American Political Science Review*, XXI (1927), 552-72.

--------. *The French Parliamentary Committee System*. New York, 1935.

Gouault, Jacques. *Comment la France est devenue républicaine*. Paris, 1954.

Graham, John T. *Donoso Cortés: Utopian Romanticist and Political Realist*. Columbia, Mo., 1974.

Griffiths, Richard M. *The Reactionary Revolution: The Catholic Revival in French Literature, 1890-1914*. London, 1966.

--------. "Anticapitalism and the French Extra-Parliamentary Right," *Journal of Contemporary History*, XIII (1978), 721-40.

Grubb, Charles Alan. "The Politics of Pessimism: A Political Biography of Duc Albert de Broglie during the Early Third Republic, 1871-1885." Unpublished doctoral dissertation, Columbia University, 1969.

--------. "Domestic Spying: The Case of the French Government and Royalists in the Early Third Republic," *Journal of Political Science*, III (1975), 11-20.

Guerard, Albert. *French Prophets of Yesterday: A Study of Religious Thought under the Second Empire*. New York, 1920.

--------. *Reflections on the Napoleonic Legend*. New York, 1924.

Guiral, Pierre. *Adolphe Thiers*. Paris, 1986.

Guilleminault, Gilbert, ed. *La Jeunesse de Marianne*. Paris, 1958.

Guillouet, Brigitte. *Le Royalisme de Barbey d'Aurevilly*. Maule, 1983.

Guiral, Pierre. "Le Libéralisme en France (1815-1870): Thèmes, succès, et lacunes." In *Tendances politiques dans la vie française depuis 1789*. Paris, 1960. Pp. 17-39.

Gurian, Waldemar. "Louis Veuillot." *Catholic Historical Review*, XXXVI (1951), 385-414.

Hale, R. W. *Democratic France: The Third Republic from Sedan to Vichy.* New York, 1941.

Halévy, Daniel. *La Fin des notables.* Paris, 1930.

--------. "Pour l'étude de la Troisième République." *RDM* (15 October 1936), 811-28.

--------. *La République des ducs.* Paris, 1937.

Hammer, Karl and Hartmann, Peter Claus, eds. *Le Bonapartisme/Der Bonapartismus: phénomène historique et mythe politique.* Munich, 1977.

Higgs, David. *Ultraroyalism in Toulouse: From its Origins to the Revolution of 1830.* Baltimore, Md., 1972.

Howard, Michael. *The Franco-Prussian War.* London, 1961.

Hutton, Patrick H. "Popular Boulangism and the Advent of Mass Politics in France," *Journal of Contemporary History*, XI (1976), 85-106.

--------. *The Cult of the Revolutionary Tradition: The Blanquistes in French Politics, 1864-1893.* Berkeley, Calif., 1981.

Irvine, William D. "French Royalists and Boulangism," *FHS*, XV (1988), 395-406.

--------. *The Boulanger Affair Reconsidered: Royalism, Boulangism, and the Origins of the Radical Right in France.* New York and Oxford, 1989.

Isser, Natalie. *The Second Empire and the Press: A Study of Government-Inspired Brochures on French Foreign Policy in their Propaganda Milieu.* The Hague, 1974.

Jaillet, Pierre. "Un Régime autoritaire en matière de presse: Rouher et la presse sous le Second Empire." *Études de Presse*, I (1946), 285-91.

Jones, Philippe. "La Presse satirique illustrée entre 1860 et 1890." *Études de Presse*, no. 14 (1956), 13-113.

Joughin, Jean T. *The Paris Commune in French Politics, 1871-1880.* 2 vols. Baltimore, Md., 1956.

Kayser, Jacques. "La Presse de province sous la Troisième République." *Revue Française de Science Politique*, V (1955), 547-71.

--------. "Le Radicalisme des radicaux." In *Tendances politiques dans la vie française depuis 1789.* Paris, 1960. Pp. 65-88.

--------. *Les Grandes batailles du radicalisme.* Paris, 1962.

Kendall, Willmore and Carey, George W. "Towards a Definition of Conservatism." *Journal of Politics*, XXVI (1964), 406-22.

Kleeblatt, Norman L., ed. *The Dreyfus Affair: Art, Truth & Justice.* Berkeley and Los Angeles, 1987.

Konvitz, Josef. "Biography: The Missing Form in French Historical Studies." *European Studies Review*, VI (1976), 9-20.

Kurtz, Harold. *The Empress Eugenie, 1826-1920.* Boston, 1964.

La Gorce, P. de. *Histoire du Second Empire.* Vol. V. 5th ed. Paris, 1903. Vol. VI. 4th ed. Paris, 1904.

Lagrange, l'abbé F. *Vie de Mgr Dupanloup, évêque d'Orléans.* 3 vols. Paris, 1883-1884.

Lajusan, A. "Les Origines de la Troisième République. Quelques éclaircissements (1871-1876)." *Revue d'Histoire Moderne,* V (1930), 419-38.

--------. "A. Thiers et la fondation de la République, 1871-1877." *Revue d'Histoire Moderne,* VII (1932), 451-83; VIII (1933), 36-52.

Larkin, Maurice J. M. "The Church and the French Concordat, 1891 to 1902." *English Historical Review,* LXXXI (1966), 717-39.

--------. *Church and State after the Dreyfus Affair: The Separation Issue in France.* London, 1974.

--------. "'La République en danger'? The Pretenders, the Army and Déroulède, 1898-1899," *English Historical Review,* C (1985), 85-105.

Latreille, André, and Rémond, René. *Histoire du catholicisme en France.* Vol. III - *La Période contemporaine.* 2nd ed. Paris, 1962.

Lebrun, Richard. *Throne and Altar: The Political and Religious Thought of Joseph de Maistre.* Ottawa, 1965.

Lecanuet, E. *L'Église de France sous la Troisième République.* Vol. II -- *Les premières années du pontificat de Léon XIII, 1878-1894.* Paris, 1910.

Legrand, Louis. *L'Influence du positivisme dans l'oeuvre scolaire de Jules Ferry.* Paris, 1961.

Letainturier-Fradin, Gabriel. *Le Duel à travers les ages.* Paris, 1892.

Levillain, Philippe. *Boulanger, fossoyeur de la monarchie.* Paris, 1982.

Lhomme, Jean. *La Grande bourgeoisie au pouvoir.* Paris, 1960.

Locke, Bobby R. "The Legitimists: A Study in Social Mentality. The Royalist Right in the French National Assembly of 1871." Unpublished doctoral dissertation, University of California at Los Angeles, 1965.

Locke, Robert R. *French Legitimists and the Politics of Moral Order in the Early Third Republic.* Princeton, N. J., 1974.

Magraw, Roger. *France 1815-1914.* London and New York, 1983.

Manévy, Raymond. *La Presse de la IIIe République.* Paris, 1955.

Martin, Benjamin F. *Count Albert de Mun, Paladin of the Third Republic.* Chapel Hill, N.C., 1978.

Mastron, J. "Les Verreries dans le Gers: la verrerie de Montpellier." *BSAG,* V (1904), 290-98.

Maurois, André. *Olympio: The Turbulent Life of Victor Hugo.* Tr. from the French by Gerard Hopkins. Pyramid ed. New York, 1968.

Mayer, Arno J. *Dynamics of Counterrevolution in Europe, 1870-1956: An Analytic Framework.* New York, 1971.

Mayer, Jacob Peter. *Political Thought in France from the Revolution to the Fifth Republic.* 3rd enlarged ed. London, 1961. [Reprint, New York, 1979].

Mayeur, Jean-Marie. *Les Débuts de la Troisième République.* Paris, 1973.

Mayeur, Jean-Marie, et al. *Cent ans d'esprit républicain.* Paris, 1964. [Vol. V of *Histoire du peuple français*, directed by L.-H. Parias]

Mayeur, Jean-Marie and Rebérioux, Madeleine. *The Third Republic from its Origins to the Great War, 1871-1914*, tr. from the French by J. R. Foster. New York and Cambridge, 1984.

Mazgaj, Paul. *The Action Française and Revolutionary Syndicalism.* Chapel Hill, N.C., 1979.

McKay, Donald. "The Third Republic in Retrospect." *Virginia Quarterly Review*, XXXIII (1957), 46-60.

McManners, John. *Church and State in France, 1870-1914.* London, 1972.

Ménager, Bernard. *Les Napoléon du peuple.* Paris, 1988.

Middleton, W. L. *The French Political System.* London, 1932.

Mitchell, Allan. *The German Influence in France after 1870: The Formation of the French Republic.* Chapel Hill, N.C., 1979.

Mohler, Armin. *Die Französische Rechte: von Kampf um Frankreichs Ideologienpanzer.* Munich, 1958.

Montclos, Xavier de. *Le Toast d'Alger: Documents 1890-1891.* Paris, 1966.

Morazé, C. et al. *Études de sociologie électorale.* Paris, 1947.

Morienval, Jean. *Les Créateurs de la grande presse en France.* Paris, 1934.

--------. *Sur l'histoire de la presse catholique en France. Rapport pour l'exposition retrospective de la presse catholique française au Vatican en 1936.* Paris, 1936.

Muret, Charlotte. *French Royalist Doctrines since the Revolution.* New York, 1933.

Néré, Jacques. "The French Republic." *The New Cambridge Modern History.* Vol. XI. London, 1962. Pp. 300-22.

--------. *Le Boulangisme et la presse.* Paris, 1964.

Nolte, Ernst. *Three Faces of Fascism: Action Française, Italian Fascism, National Socialism.* New York, 1966.

Nord, Philip G. *Paris Shopkeepers and the Politics of Resentment.* Princeton, N.J., 1986.

O'Boyle, Leonore. "The Image of the Journalist in France, Germany, and England, 1815-1848." *Comparative Studies in Society and History*, 10 (1967-68), 290-317.

Osgood, Samuel. "Charles Maurras et l'Action Française: État des travaux américains." *Revue Française de Science Politique*, VIII (1959), 143-47.

--------. *French Royalism under the Third and Fourth Republics*. The Hague, 1960.

--------. "The Third Republic in Historical Perspective." In Gerald N. Grob, ed., *Statesmen and Statecraft of the Modern West: Essays in Honor of Dwight E. Lee and H. Donaldson Jordan*. Barre, Mass., 1967.

Ozouf, Mona. *L'École, l'église et la République, 1871-1914*. Paris, 1963.

Palmade, Guy-P. "Évolution de l'opinion publique dans le département du Gers de 1848 à 1914." Unpublished *mémoire* submitted for the Diplôme d'Études Supérieures, Faculté des Lettres de Paris, 1949.

--------. "Le Département du Gers à la fin du Second Empire." Auch, 1961. Offprint from *BSAG*, LXII (1961), 73-95 and 177-99. Also published in *Bibliothèque de la Révolution de 1848*. Vol. XXI (1960), pp. 184-204.

--------. *Capitalisme et capitalistes français au XIXe siècle*. Paris, 1961.

Payne, Howard C. "Preparation of a Coup d'état: Administrative Centralization and Police Powers in France, 1849-1851." *Studies in Modern European History in Honor of Franklin Charles Palm*, ed. Frederick J. Cox et al. New York, 1956.

Phillips, C. S. *The Church in France, 1789-1907*. Vol. II -- *1848 to 1907*. London, 1936.

Pinkney, David H. "The Myth of the French Revolution of 1830," *A Festschrift for Frederick B. Artz*, ed. David H. Pinkney and Theodore Ropp. Durham, N.C., 1964.

Pisani-Ferry, Fresnette. *Le Coup d'état manqué du 16 mai 1877*. Paris, 1955.

--------. *Jules Ferry et le partage du monde*. Paris, 1962.

Plamenatz, J. P. *The Revolutionary Moment in France 1815-71*. New York, 1952.

Plessis, Alain. *The Rise and Fall of the Second Empire, 1852-1871*. Cambridge, 1985.

Polge, Henri. *Auch et la Gascogne*. Toulouse, 1958.

Ponteil, Félix. *Les Institutions de la France de 1814 à 1870*. Paris, 1966.

Power, Thomas F. Jr. *Jules Ferry and the Renaissance of French Imperialism*. New ed. New York, 1966.

Prélot, Marcel. "La Signification constitutionnelle du Second Empire," *Revue Française de Science Politique*, III (1953), 31-56.

--------. *Le Libéralisme catholique*. Paris, 1969.

Pressac, Pierre de. *Les Forces historiques de la France*. Paris, 1928.

Prost, Antoine, and Rosenzveig, Christian. "La Chambre des députés (1881-1885), analyse factorielle des scrutins." *Revue Française de Science Politique*, XXI (1971), 5-50.

Puy de Clinchamps, P. de. *Le Royalisme*. Paris, 1967.

Raoul-Duval, E. "Raoul-Duval." Preface to *Gustave Flaubert. Lettres inédites à Raoul-Duval*, ed. Georges Normandy. Paris, 1950.

Ratcliffe, Barrie. "The Decline of Biography in French Historiography: The Ambivalent Legacy of the 'Annales' Tradition," in *Proceedings of the Western Society for French History, 1980*, VIII (1981), 568-76.

Reardon, Bernard. *Liberalism and Tradition: Aspects of Catholic Thought in Nineteenth-Century France*. Cambridge, 1975.

Rebérioux, Madeleine. *La République radicale? (1899-1914)*. Paris, 1974.

Reclus, Maurice. *Le Seize mai*. Paris, 1932.

--------. *Émile de Girardin*. Paris, 1934.

Rémond, René. "Droites classiques et droite romantique," *Terre humaine* (June 1951), 60-69.

--------. "Y a-t-il un fascisme français?", *Terre humaine* (July-Aug. 1952), 37-47.

--------. *La Droite en France de 1815 à nos jours: continuité et diversité d'une tradition politique*. Paris, 1954.

--------. "L'Originalité du socialisme français." In *Tendances politiques de la vie française depuis 1789*. Paris, 1960. Pp. 41-64.

--------. *La Droite en France: de la première restauration à la Ve République*. 2nd ed. Paris, 1963. In English as *Right Wing in France: From 1815 to De Gaulle*, rev. ed., tr. by James M. Laux. Philadelphia, 1969.

--------, ed. *Pour une histoire politique*. Paris, 1988.

Renouvin, Pierre. "Research in Modern and Contemporary History: Present Trends in France." *Journal of Modern History*, XXXVIII (1966), 1-12.

Rioux, Jean-Pierre. *Nationalisme et conservatisme, la Ligue de la Patrie Française, 1899-1904*. Paris, 1977.

Roche, Alphonse V. *Les Idées traditionalistes en France de Rivarol à Charles Maurras*. Urbana, Ill., 1937.

Rogger, Hans, and Weber, Eugen, eds. *The European Right: A Historical Profile*. Berkeley, 1965.

Rollet, Henri. *Albert de Mun et le parti catholique*. Paris, 1947.

Rothney, John. *Bonapartism after Sedan*. Ithaca, 1969.

Rudelle, Odile. *La République absolue: Aux origines de l'instabilité constitutionnelle de la France républicaine, 1870-1889*. Paris, 1982.

Ruggiero, Guido de. *The History of European Liberalism*. Tr. from the Italian by R. G. Collingwood. Paperback ed. Boston, 1959.

Rutkoff, Peter M. "The *Ligue des Patriotes*: The Nature of the Radical Right and the Dreyfus Affair," *FHS*, VIII (1974), 585-603.

--------. "Rémond, Nationalism, and the Right," *Proceedings of the Western Society for French History, 1977*, V (Santa Barbara, Calif., 1978), 292-300.

--------. *Revanche and Revision: The Ligue des Patriotes and the Origins of the Radical Right in France, 1882-1900.* Athens, Ohio, 1981.

Schmandt, Raymond H. "The Life and Work of Leo XIII," in *Leo XIII and the Modern World*, ed. Edward T. Gargan. New York, 1961.

Schnerb, Robert. "Napoleon III and the Second French Empire." *Journal of Modern History*, VIII (1936), 338-55.

--------. *Rouher et le Second Empire.* Paris, 1949.

Schnir, R. "Une Épisode du ralliement: contribution à l'étude des rapports de l'église et de l'état sous la Troisième République." *Revue d'Histoire Moderne*, IX (1934), 193-226.

Scott, J. A. *Republican Ideas and the Liberal Tradition in France: 1870-1914.* New York, 1951.

Scoville, Warren C. *Capitalism and French Glassmaking, 1640-1789.* Berkeley, 1950.

Seager, Frederic H. *The Boulanger Affair: Political Crossroad of France, 1886-1889.* Ithaca, 1969.

Sedgwick, Alexander. *The Ralliement in French Politics, 1890-1898.* Cambridge, Mass., 1965.

Seignobos, Charles. *Le Déclin de l'Empire et l'établissement de la IIIe République.* Paris, 1921.

--------. *L'Évolution de la IIIe République, 1875-1914.* Paris, 1921.

Shapiro, David, ed. *The Right in France 1890-1919: Three Studies.* London, 1962.

Silvestre de Sacy, J. *Le Maréchal de Mac-Mahon.* Paris, 1960.

Smith, William. *Eugénie, impératrice et femme.* Paris, 1989.

Soltau, Roger. *French Parties and Politics: 1871-1921.* Oxford, 1930.

--------. *French Political Thought in the 19th Century.* New ed. New York, 1959.

Soucy, Robert. "The Nature of Fascism in France," *International Fascism, 1920-1945*, ed. Walter Laqueur and George L. Mosse. New York, 1966. Originally published as vol. 1, no. 1 of the *Journal of Contemporary History*.

--------. *Fascism in France: The Case of Maurice Barrès.* Berkeley and Los Angeles, 1972.

--------. *Fascist Intellectual, Drieu La Rochelle.* Berkeley and Los Angeles, 1979.

Soulier, Auguste. "La Troisième République entre dans l'histoire." *La Revue Internationale d'Histoire Politique et Constitutionnelle*, V (1955), 151-72.

Sourbadère, Gilbert. "Un Polémiste du XIXe siècle: Bernard-Adolphe Granier de Cassagnac." 2 vols. Mémoire de maîtrise, Université de Toulouse-Mirail, n.d. [1980s].

Spencer, Philip. *Politics of Belief in Nineteenth-Century France: Lacordaire, Michon, Veuillot.* London, 1954.

Spitzer, Alan. "The Good Napoleon III." *FHS*, II (1962), 308-323.

Stannard, Harold. *Gambetta and the Founding of the Third Republic.* London, 1921.

Sternhell, Zeev. "Paul Deroulède and the Origins of Modern French Nationalism," *Journal of Contemporary History*, VI (1971), 46-70.

--------. *Maurice Barrès et le nationalisme français.* Paris, 1972.

--------. *La Droite révolutionnaire, 1885-1914; les origines françaises du fascisme.* Paris, 1978.

--------. *Ni Droite ni Gauche. L'Idéologie fasciste en France.* Paris, 1983. In English as *Neither Right nor Left: Fascist Ideology in France*, tr. from the French by David Maisel. Berkeley and Los Angeles, 1986.

Sutton, Michael. *Nationalism, Positivism, and Catholicism: The Politics of Charles Maurras and French Catholics, 1890-1914.* New York, 1983.

Swart, K. W. *The Sense of Decadence in Nineteenth-Century France.* The Hague, 1964.

Tallez, P. "Adolphe Granier de Cassagnac et la Société d'Agriculture du Gers." *Revue de Gascogne*, nouv. ser. XXIX (1934), 123-33.

Talmon, J. L. *The Origins of Totalitarian Democracy.* London, 1952.

--------. *Political Messianism: The Romantic Phase.* London, 1960.

Terrien, Eugène. *Monseigneur Freppel, sa vie, ses ouvrages, ses oeuvres, son influence et son temps.* 2 vols. Paris, Angers, 1931-1932.

Thibaudet, A. *Les Idées politiques de la France.* Paris, 1932.

Thomson, David. *Democracy in France since 1870.* 4th ed., revised. New York, 1964.

Thuillier, André. "Aux Origines du 16 mai 1877: Mgr. de Ladoue et Lucien Gueneau." *Revue d'histoire de l'église de France*, LXI (1975), 37-59.

Thureau-Dangin, P. *Histoire de la Monarchie de Juillet.* Vol. VII. 2nd ed. Paris, 1892.

Tudesq, André-Jean. *Les Grands notables en France (1840-1849): Étude historique d'une psychologie sociale.* Paris, 1964.

Tulard, Jean. *Le Mythe de Napoléon.* Paris, 1971.

Valynseele, J. "Deux personalités protestantes sous la Troisième République: Edgar Raoul-Duval et Léon Say." *Bulletin de la Société de l'histoire du protestantisme français*, CXVII (1971), 214-29.

Viereck, Peter. *Conservatism from John Adams to Churchill.* Princeton, N. J., 1956.

Waldman, Martin R. "The Revolutionary as Criminal in 19th Century France: A Study of the Communards and Deportés." *Science and Society*, 37 (1973), 31-55.

Ward, James E. "The French Cardinals and Leo XIII's Ralliement Policy." *Church History*, XXXIII (1964), 60-73.

--------. "Cardinal Richard vs. Cardinal Lavigerie: Episcopal Resistance to the *Ralliement*." *Catholic Historical Review*, LIII (1967), 346-71.

Warner, Charles K. *The Winegrowers of France and the Government since 1875*. New York, 1960.

Watson, D. R. "The French Third Republic (Review Article)." *Historical Journal*, XXIII (1980), 481-87.

--------. *Georges Clemenceau: A Political Biography*. London, 1974.

Weber, Eugen. "New Wine in Old Bottles." *FHS*, I (1958), 200-24.

--------. *The Nationalist Revival in France, 1905-1914*. Berkeley, 1959.

--------. "The Right in France: A Working Hypothesis." *AHR*, LXV (1960), 554-68.

--------. *Action Française*. Stanford, 1962.

--------. "Nationalism, Socialism, and National-Socialism in France." *French Historical Studies*, II (1962), 273-307.

--------. *Varieties of Fascism*. Princeton, N.J., 1964.

--------. *Peasants into Frenchmen: The Modernization of Rural France, 1870-1914*. Stanford, Calif., 1976.

--------. "Ambiguous Victories," *Journal of Contemporary History*, XIII (1978), 819-27.

Weill, Georges. *Histoire du parti républicain en France, 1814-1870*. Paris, 1900.

Williams, Roger L. *Gaslight and Shadow: The World of Napoleon III, 1851-1870*. New York, 1957.

--------. *Henri Rochefort: Prince of the Gutter Press*. New York, 1966.

Wilson, Stephen. *Ideology and Experience: Antisemitism in France at the Time of the Dreyfus Affair*. East Brunswick, N. J., 1982.

Winnacker, R. A. "The Third French Republic, 1870-1914." *Journal of Modern History*, X (1938), 372-409.

Winock, Michel. *Edouard Drumont et c^{ie}: Antisémitisme et fascisme en France*. Paris, 1982.

--------. *La Fièvre hexagonale: les grandes crises politiques 1871-1968*. Paris, 1986.

--------. *Nationalisme, antisémitisme et fascisme en France*. Paris, 1990.

Woodall, John. "The *Ralliement*: Origins and Early History, 1876-1894." Unpublished doctoral dissertation, Columbia University, 1964.

Wormser, Georges. *Gambetta dans les tempêtes, 1870-1877*. Paris, 1964.

--------. *La République de Clemenceau*. Paris, 1961.

Wright, Gordon. "The Distribution of French Parties in 1865: An Official Survey." *Journal of Modern History*, XV (1943), 295-302.

--------. *France in Modern Times*. Chicago, 1960.

Yarrow, Philip J. *La Pensée politique et religieuse de Barbey d'Aurevilly*.
    Geneva, 1961.

Zeldin, Theodore. *The Political System of Napoleon III*. London, 1958.

--------. *Émile Ollivier and the Liberal Empire of Napoleon III*. Oxford, 1963.

--------. *France, 1848-1945*. 2 vols. Oxford, 1973-1977.

Zévaès, Alexandre. *L'Affaire Pierre Bonaparte*. Paris, 1929.

--------. *Henri Rochefort, le pamphlétaire*. Paris, 1946.

INDEX

This index has two parts. The first part covers proper names, terms, national governmental institutions and political groups, and most major events mentioned in the text; only biographical profiles from the notes are indexed here. The second part provides references to all periodicals mentioned in the text.

I